JUNGLE WARRIORS

'This is an aspect of military science that needs to be studied above all others in the Armed forces: the capacity to adapt oneself to the utterly unpredictable, the utterly unknown.'
—Michael Howard, Chesney Memorial Gold Medal Lecture, 30 October 1973

'Such conditions of rain, mud, rottenness, stench, gloom, and, above all, the feeling of being shut in by everlasting jungle and ever ascending mountains, are sufficient to fray the strongest nerves. But add to them the tension of the constant expectancy of death from behind the impenetrable green screen, and nerves must be of the strongest, and morale of the highest, to live down these conditions, accept them as a matter of course, and maintain a cheerful yet fighting spirit.'
—'Report on Operations 3 Aust Div in Salamaua Area 23 April to 25 August 1943'

JUNGLE WARRIORS

From Tobruk to Kokoda and beyond,
how the Australian Army became the
world's most deadly jungle fighting force

ADRIAN THRELFALL

First published in 2014

Copyright © Adrian Threlfall 2014

All rights reserved. No part of this book may be reproduced or transmitted in any form or by any means, electronic or mechanical, including photocopying, recording or by any information storage and retrieval system, without prior permission in writing from the publisher. The Australian *Copyright Act 1968* (the Act) allows a maximum of one chapter or 10 per cent of this book, whichever is the greater, to be photocopied by any educational institution for its educational purposes provided that the educational institution (or body that administers it) has given a remuneration notice to the Copyright Agency (Australia) under the Act.

Allen & Unwin
83 Alexander Street
Crows Nest NSW 2065
Australia
Phone: (61 2) 8425 0100
Email: info@allenandunwin.com
Web: www.allenandunwin.com

Cataloguing-in-Publication details are available
from the National Library of Australia
www.trove.nla.gov.au

ISBN 978 1 74237 220 4

Map by Janet Hunt
Set in 12/17 pt Minion Pro by Midland Typesetters, Australia
Printed and bound in Australia by Griffin Press

10 9 8 7 6 5 4 3 2 1

The paper in this book is FSC certified.
FSC promotes environmentally responsible,
socially beneficial and economically viable
management of the world's forests.

CONTENTS

MAP OF SOUTH WEST PACIFIC AREA		vi
LIST OF ABBREVIATIONS		vii
INTRODUCTION		1
CHAPTER 1	'No Military Knowledge of the Region': 1914–1941	5
CHAPTER 2	'Everything was so Different': The 8th Division in Malaya	23
CHAPTER 3	'Completely Devoid of Ideas': The 6th Division on Ceylon	56
CHAPTER 4	'Physical Fitness is Vital': Training in Australia, 1942	74
CHAPTER 5	'Jesus Christ! I Can't See Anything': Milne Bay and Kokoda	96
CHAPTER 6	'Deep in Unmapped Jungles': 21st Brigade on the Kokoda Track	116
CHAPTER 7	'The Worst Experience of the War': Kokoda to the Beachheads	133
CHAPTER 8	'Rain, Mud, Rottenness, Gloom': 17th Brigade's Wau–Salamaua Campaign	158
CHAPTER 9	'The Ideal Training Ground': Atherton Tableland 1943	179
CHAPTER 10	'No New Lessons of Importance': The Final Campaigns	209
CONCLUSION		231
ACKNOWLEDGEMENTS		235
NOTES		237
BIBLIOGRAPHY		279
INDEX		301

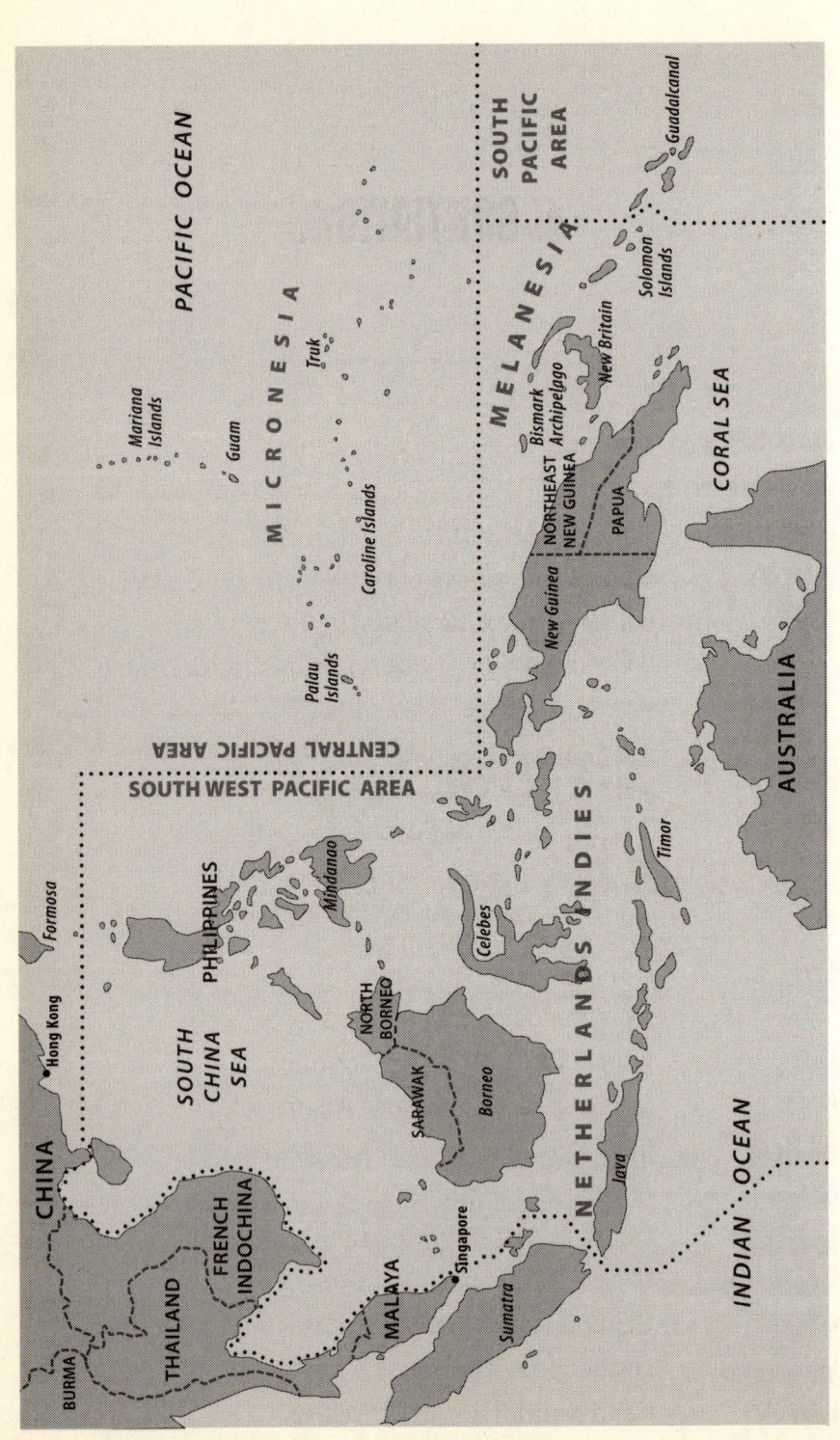

ABBREVIATIONS

AAWFA	Australians at War Film Archive
ABDACOM	American British Dutch Australian Command
AHQ	Army Headquarters
AIF	Australian Imperial Force
AMF	Australian Military Forces
ANGAU	Australian New Guinea Administrative Unit
Armd	Armoured
Arty	Artillery
ATM	*Army Training Memorandum*
AWM	Australian War Memorial
CGS	Chief of the General Staff
CO	Commanding Officer
Coy	Company
CRA	Commander Royal Artillery
DMT	Directorate of Military Training
DVA	Department of Veterans' Affairs
Fd Regt	Field Regiment
FSR	*Field Service Regulations*
GOC	General Officer Commanding
GSO1	General Staff Officer 1st Class
GSO2	General Staff Officer 2nd Class
HQ	Headquarters
KMSA	Keith Murdoch Sound Archive

LHQ	Land Headquarters
MG	machine gun
MMG	medium machine gun
MTP	*Military Training Pamphlet*
NAA	National Archives of Australia
NCO	non-commissioned officer
NGF	New Guinea Force
PT	physical training
RAA	Royal Australian Artillery
RAAF	Royal Australian Air Force
RAE	Royal Australian Engineers
RAF	Royal Air Force
RAN	Royal Australian Navy
Regt	Regiment
VC	Victoria Cross

INTRODUCTION

Over the course of the Second World War, the Australian Army underwent an extraordinary transformation. From a force that was ill equipped, poorly organised and with outdated doctrine and training methods in 1939, it had been completely remade by 1945. The first transition, needed to enable the 2nd Australian Imperial Force (AIF) to operate effectively in the North African and Mediterranean Theatres, was noteworthy but did not demand the swathe of adaptations and improvisations of the second. The entry of the Imperial Japanese Army into the war in December 1941 saw the Australian Army facing an unknown opponent in an unforeseen locale. It would also see a new term enter the military lexicon: 'jungle warfare'. This second transition, between 1942 and 1945, saw substantial modifications to weapons, uniforms, equipment and, most importantly, doctrine and training. Without these last two crucial elements, events in the South West Pacific Area would have unfolded very differently.

In March 1942, as the first AIF units returned from the Middle East, there was—notwithstanding the experiences of the 8th Division during the Malayan campaign—little understanding of the difficulties that lay ahead, nor how to overcome them.[1] An army that was equipped, trained and experienced in large-scale, multi-unit, open warfare had to rapidly reconfigure itself to meet the unexpected challenges posed by combat in the jungles, swamps and mountains of Papua, New Guinea, Bougainville and Borneo.[2] More often than not, this was achieved by soldiers at the front line who fought—and died—at Milne Bay, Kokoda, and the beachheads of Buna, Gona and Sanananda. The lessons of those first campaigns, although acquired at great cost, provided the basis for the training and doctrine that would, with slight modification and improvement, be applicable for the remainder of the war. Those lessons made the Australian Army by 1945 the preeminent jungle fighting force in the world.

In 1939 this was a world away. The first two and a half years of the Second World War saw Australian forces fighting in the deserts of North Africa as well as in Greece, Crete and Syria. The types of combat in these theatres and the training, doctrine, weapons and tactics employed there were familiar to the Australians. Exercises alongside British troops on the plains of southern England or in Palestine and the Egyptian desert would not have differed markedly from those the troops had undertaken in New South Wales or Victoria before they sailed.[3] Although there were many differences between the battles of the First World War and the Western Desert campaign of the Second World War, an infantryman who fought in both wars would have found many similarities, most notably in weapons, training, tactics and doctrine. The same cannot be said for those units thrust into battle in Malaya, Papua or the islands of the South West Pacific in 1942.

When the Pacific War broke out on 7 December 1941, the only Australian units that had received any jungle warfare training were two brigades of the 8th Division, which had, since mid-1941, been stationed in Malaya. As the division's commanding officer, General

Gordon Bennett, stated, 'a few minutes in the jungle was sufficient to convince me that we had to start afresh on our training'.[4] While the veracity of his account has caused heated discussion over the years, the conviction that the tropical environment required different training methods is indisputable.[5] Lieutenant-Colonel Phil Rhoden, later the commanding officer of the 2/14th Australian Infantry Battalion, which fought in the Syria campaign and on the Kokoda Track, discussed at some length the major differences between combat in the desert and the jungle, and how those differences made a commander's job immeasurably harder in the tropics than in other environments.[6] The Australian War Memorial historian Albert Palazzo agreed, arguing that 'combat in the South West Pacific Area was fundamentally different from that which the AIF had experienced in the Middle East'.[7] Many Australian units were thrust into battle with little or no comprehension of the vastly different challenges they would face.[8]

Arguably the greatest revolution the Australian Army has ever undergone occurred in the years between 1942 and 1945. Virtually overnight, the Australian Army had to reinvent itself to face the very different problems posed by combat in the tropical environment of New Guinea and the islands of the South West Pacific. This very rapid transition was felt at all levels, from the Chief of Staff to the lowliest private soldier. Military forces are traditionally resistant to change, but the Australian Army managed this turnaround in a remarkably short period of time. Historical examples abound of armies that were unable to successfully adapt to new and unforeseen forms of conflict, from Napoleon's army in Spain to the US Army in Vietnam.[9] How the Australian Army managed to succeed where others have failed thus holds valuable lessons.

The changes to which the Australian Army was forced to resort during the jungle campaigns epitomise an army adapting itself to the unknown. From platoon-level tactics to the employment of support weapons, and from infantry–tank cooperation to close air support in the jungle, the Australians had to develop a slew of new methods. In the three decades after the end of the Second World War, the army was involved in several operational deployments in tropical environments, notably during the Vietnam War. Its first confrontation with combat in jungles and rainforests sheds light on those later deployments. This book shows just how the Australian Army mastered that most difficult of combat arts: jungle warfare.

Chapter 1

'NO MILITARY KNOWLEDGE OF THE REGION': 1914-1941

On 11 September 1914, 25 naval troops from HMAS *Sydney* rowed ashore at Herbertshohe, south-east of the port of Rabaul, on the island of New Britain. Their mission was to seize the German wireless stations located nearby. So began the first Australian military operation of the First World War, and the first to involve jungle warfare. Although the military challenges those troops faced were trivial in comparison with those of 1942, the 'hopelessly inadequate' preparation of sections of the Australian Naval & Military Expeditionary Force (AN & MEF) would be mirrored in the early stages of the South West Pacific campaign of the Second World War.[1]

On 6 August 1914, two days after the outbreak of the First World War, the Secretary of State for the Colonies sent a telegram to the governor-general of Australia asking the Australian government to seize German territories in the south-west Pacific, particularly the wireless stations on New Britain, Nauru and the Caroline Islands.[2] Within days, a 'hastily kitted and rudimentarily trained' force sailed north from Sydney Harbour.[3] Stopping for several days at Palm

Island, north of Townsville, the force went ashore each day to train, and 'the lesson afterwards proved invaluable in the dense jungles of New Britain'.[4]

As they remained at Palm Island for less than a week, it is open to doubt just how well prepared the infantry could have become in such a short period. Ultimately, the minimal training did not prove costly, as most of the fighting was over in less than a day, with fewer than a dozen casualties.[5] However, in a sobering precursor to the experience of the first Citizen Military Forces (militia) battalions deployed to Port Moresby in 1941, the contingents were extremely poorly equipped, and one was said to be 'unfit for tropical campaigning'.[6] The AN & MEF, and their replacements, Tropical Force, would not see any further military action, but the enervating climate and tropical diseases, especially malaria, would cause dozens of deaths before the deployment ended in 1921.[7] These incidents, combined with Australian troops' experiences in Macedonia and Palestine during the First World War, showed just what damage malaria could do to a modern army.[8] The Australian historian Charles Bean recorded that 'for the [Australian] Light Horse, despite full measures against malaria, this was the hardest service of the war'.[9] More than twenty years later, when the 7th Division was deployed to Syria in June 1941, its rate of malarial infection increased dramatically. It was not until the pioneering work of the Australian Army Land HQ Medical Research Unit in 1943 that truly effective treatments became available.[10]

'The years that the locusts ate': The inter-war period

Like most nations engaged in the Great War, Australia spent much of the following two decades attempting to recover and rebuild and hoping that the 'war to end wars had been fought and won, and military affairs could safely be accorded a minor place in the nation's concerns'.[11] Defence spending was drastically cut, as were the sizes of all three services. After the deaths of 61,000 men, the turmoil of the conscription referenda, and the huge financial costs of the war, Australian governments saw few votes in defence issues. That remained the case for the next twenty years, with one government after another seeing no pressing need to attend to, or spend money on, the military.

For much of the interwar period, Australian defence policy continued along much the same lines as before the Great War, with the 'ultimate reliance on the British Navy'[12] and its huge base at Singapore. As the historian Peter Cochrane put it: 'After the immense cost of World War I, the Singapore strategy had great appeal to Australian governments keen to rein in defence expenditure. An imperial system of defence was cheaper and far more feasible than self-reliance.'[13]

The need for a 'Singapore strategy' to provide a bulwark against Asia can be explained only when we recognise which powers—and peoples—were believed to pose a threat to Australia. The 19th-century fear of the 'yellow peril', which can be traced to the gold-rush era, had never completely abated. During the gold rushes of the 1850s and 1860s many hundreds of thousands of people came to Australia seeking their fortunes, including approximately 50,000 Chinese. The predominantly white, Anglo-Saxon and Anglo-Celtic population witnessed this large multicultural influx with some trepidation. Rising social tensions culminated in major riots. Soon the governors of Victoria and New South Wales imposed restrictions on Chinese immigration and levied residency taxes on Chinese people living in those states.

Later in the century, the expansion of sugar-cane fields in Queensland witnessed more racial tensions as thousands of indentured labourers from various Pacific islands, known colloquially as kanakas, were brought to Australia. Trade unionists complained that these workers took jobs from white Australians, as they worked for much lower wages and accepted considerably poorer working conditions. In the late 1890s the urge to preserve Australia's 'Britishness' would culminate in the first piece of legislation passed by the fledgling Australian Parliament, the *Immigration Restriction Act 1901*, known ever after as the 'White Australia Policy'. While this targeted all non-European races, it was clearly intended to keep out Asians. This general fear of being swamped by the Asian hordes to Australia's north only increased with the Japanese victory in the Russo-Japanese War of 1904–05.[14]

The wartime treaty between Britain and Japan alleviated these fears somewhat, but when it terminated in 1920, fears of a powerful Japanese military increased.[15] Within eighteen months of the end of the Great War, George Pearce, the Minister for Defence, convened a meeting of the most senior Australian Army generals. Within weeks, this conference released a report emphatically stating that 'the Empire of Japan remains... in the immediate future, as the only potential and probable enemy'.[16] The government accepted this argument, and the recommendations of the report, but took little concrete action.

Two years later, the Imperial Conference of 1923 resolved to build a naval base at Singapore that would 'service the main British fleet, offering a deterrent to the Japanese such that they could not contemplate war'.[17] Soon 'the Singapore strategy had become an article of faith' and justification for Australia's continued minimal levels of defence expenditure.[18] With strong British Admiralty influence over the Australian Navy, combined with ongoing Australian reliance upon Britain for intelligence about the region and Japanese intentions in the Pacific, this inability to see beyond the Singapore strategy is perhaps understandable.[19]

This is not to suggest that acceptance of the policy was universal. Almost from the day it was instituted, Australian Army leaders raised doubts about several of its premises. In a highly prescient statement, in 1933 Lieutenant-Colonel Vernon Sturdee told senior officers that the Japanese were Australia's most likely threat, that in the event of war they would act quickly and would:

All be regulars, fully trained and equipped for the operations, and fanatics who like dying in battle, whilst our troops would consist mainly of civilians hastily thrown together on mobilisation with very little training, short of artillery and possibly of gun ammunition.[20]

Despite these criticisms, no alteration in Australian government thinking occurred. Finally, in 1937, at the last Imperial Conference before the Second World War, the British Chiefs of Staff admitted that the strength of any fleet sent to the Far East 'must be governed by consideration of our home requirements... [and that Britain] must keep sufficient strength in home waters to neutralise the German Fleet'.[21]

As a direct corollary of the fixation upon the Singapore strategy, and the commensurate lack of spending on the home forces, the outbreak of war in 1939 found the Australian Army less capable than in 1919.[22] From the large, well-trained and combat-experienced force of November 1918, only 1600 Permanent Army and 31,000 Citizen Forces personnel remained in 1922.[23] During the Depression these figures were reduced even further. After all, if the Singapore strategy was correct, there was no need for a large standing army to defend Australia from an invasion. A small army able to repel limited raids—not one capable of defeating an actual invasion force—would suffice.[24] Thus the army was forced to construct and man numerous coastal defensive positions instead of building up the mobile multi-divisional force that was its preferred option.

With these decisions, over the course of the 1920s the development of the army stagnated, notwithstanding its best efforts. In an attempt to improve the quality of training, in 1920 the army established a Central Training Depot at Liverpool.[25] Six months later it was closed because of budget cuts and would not reopen until 1939. Throughout the interwar period members of the Citizen Military Forces were required to attend only six to eight days continuous camp and a further six days at their home unit a year. This was clearly not sufficient to provide an adequately trained formation that could form the nucleus of an expanded force in the event of war. Training of officers was equally desultory, with year-long exchanges to the British or Indian Armies the only real opportunity to gain useful experience. In the early years of the Second World War, General Iven Mackay would say of the 1920s and '30s that officers had rarely had the opportunity to move a unit as large as a battalion, let alone a brigade.[26] The lack of funding also had negative consequences for army equipment and weaponry. As Ian Kuring stated: 'Australian infantrymen entered World War II looking as if they had just stepped out of World War I. Little had changed in their equipment, organisation, tactical thinking or training during the period 1919–1939.'[27]

These deficiencies had direct consequences once war broke out, and it would be fortuitous that it was a year before the Australian Army was called on to fight in the Western Desert.

'Little Australian interest in Papua and New Guinea': Japan and jungle warfare

A chronically under-resourced army, combined with a defence policy almost wholly reliant upon the supposed guarantee of protection afforded by Singapore and the Royal Navy, meant that the possibility of the army having to fight in the islands to the north of Australia was barely contemplated. But with Japan identified as the most likely threat to Australia, it is curious that more action did not occur. In fact, as the war historian Lionel Wigmore stated, by the 1930s, 'only cursory measures had been taken by the Army to gain knowledge of the Japanese language and to acquire first-hand experience of Japan and the Far East generally'.[28] One of the few measures undertaken by the army—approximately a month before the outbreak of war in Europe—was to request from the British War Office copies of the document 'Notes on the Japanese Army 1939'.[29] Three hundred of these were printed in early 1940, and the number was eventually increased to 2000. Based on observations of the 'Sino-Japanese hostilities', this large document was a revised version of the 'Handbook of the Japanese Army, 1928'—also supplied by the British. However, at the same time—mid-1939—the Australian delegation to the Wellington Defence Conference rejected the idea that 'raiding forces' in the islands east of New Guinea could pose a threat to trans-Tasman trade, let alone the Australian seaboard.[30] It would not be until after the fall of France and the Low Countries in June 1940 that Australian policies on the colonial possessions of those nations, as well as other south-west Pacific islands, became subjects for discussion. By that stage, of course, the bulk of the Australian Army was in the Middle East and Britain.

When Nazi Germany became the enemy in September 1939, it was assumed that Australian forces would fight alongside Britain in Europe and the Middle East, as they had in the First World War. Few people in the military or government felt the need to prepare for any other contingency. The little information that could have been gleaned from the AN & MEF experience of the First World War seems to have been long forgotten. According to the war historian Dudley McCarthy, 'there was little real . . . Australian interest in Papua and New Guinea before the [Second World] war . . . and virtually no military knowledge of the region'.[31] His fellow historian Wigmore concluded that 'in the field of tactics no effort appears to have been made to gain experience of and develop doctrines about the kind of tropical bush warfare that was likely to occur in conflict with Japan'.[32]

Although it is clear that little information was obtainable via traditional sources, several less regular avenues existed. One suggestion, that 'valuable experience might have been gained by attachment of officers to British garrisons in tropical Africa or Burma, by sending observers to China, or by exercises in suitable areas of Australia or New Guinea', was not acted upon by Australia.[33] Over the course of the 1920s and '30s, however, several British Army officers were despatched as observers for periods of up to a year with the Japanese Army. One Captain Kennedy, in particular, wrote insightful articles on the 'extraordinary powers of endurance ... intense patriotism' and fighting abilities of Japanese soldiers in their campaigns in China.[34]

When war broke out, the two most important tactical manuals available to the Australian Army were *Field Service Regulations* (1935) (*FSR*) and *Infantry Training (Training and War) 1937*.[35] Until the 1950s, most Australian Army doctrinal material was British, leavened with some Australian and US manuals. Although it has been argued that *FSR* and *Infantry Training* had 'stood the Army in good stead', it is beyond doubt that these manuals 'did not, in any manner, constitute a well established doctrinal base for conducting brigade and battalion operations'.[36] Nor were they of much use at the sub-unit level, as would be demonstrated when war broke out in the Pacific. As early as 1909, the inability of *FSR* to adequately address real-world scenarios had been identified; *FSR* 'stressed that the principles of war were unchanging and could be applied by trained officers and NCOs to all military situations'.[37,38] Although updated at regular intervals since it was first published after the Boer War, *FSR* in 1939 reflected two constants—the vast experience of the British Army in 'policing' the empire, and the mostly static warfare that characterised operations on the Western Front in 1914–18.

While these oversights with regard to conventional warfare were themselves major problems, the treatment of 'irregular' conflict in *FSR* was cursory at best. Only eight of its 256 pages were devoted to 'Special Types of Warfare'. The sub-section devoted to 'Forest and Bush Warfare' was only three pages long, and would prove of limited value to those wanting insights into operations in tropical or jungle terrain. It was also very general, noting that observation was difficult and that heavy rain and disease 'have often to be taken into account'.[39] The suggestion that in the event of combat with a 'savage enemy' troops should consult the Colonial Office pamphlet 'Notes on Training in Bush Warfare' and the appropriate section of *FSR* would have been of little help to those in Papua and New Guinea in 1942–43.[40] Although *Infantry Training* contained a seven-page chapter on 'Fighting in Close Country, Woods and Villages', it also reflected colonial military experiences over the previous 50 years. It did not envisage what combat between modern, professional armies in tropical battlefields would entail.

Several other brief Colonial Office pamphlets existed, but most were produced for units such as the Burma Military Police or the Royal West African Frontier Force.[41] This is not to suggest that no suitable manuals existed, for at least two recent publications were available. In 1937, the Dutch Army had published a 160-page manual, based on decades of policing and fighting insurgents and nationalist forces throughout the Dutch East Indies, that covered numerous aspects of operations in jungle terrain.[42] Although it was created to help the Dutch Army engage in operations short of war-fighting, it contained many sections relevant to the conditions the Australians would encounter: on ambush and patrol tactics in the jungle, river crossings and the movement of riverine forces, and the problems of logistics and medical services in the tropics. With 23rd Brigade, 8th Division, being deployed to Ambon and Timor in 1941 and serving alongside Dutch troops, the relevance of this manual is self-evident. Yet it was not until 1941 that Australia made an attempt to 'investigate coordination of defence with the Netherlands East Indies'.[43]

The other manual was also a recent creation. The United States Marine Corps *Small Wars Manual* was an extremely long and detailed work based on decades of experience in amphibious and anti-guerilla operations in the jungles of Central and South America.[44] Although neither it nor the Dutch manual envisaged the scale or severity of the combat that would take place in the South West Pacific Area, they both contained much information that could have assisted Australian forces fighting in the tropics after February 1941. Owing to the continuing reliance upon the Singapore strategy—and, after the outbreak of war, the demands of an active theatre in the Middle East—virtually no attempts appear to have been made to acquire information about the islands of the South West Pacific and the challenges an army would face there.

'We had axe handles for rifles': 1939–1941

The declaration of war on 3 September 1939 was met with a muted response, in contrast to the enthusiasm of 1914. Unsurprisingly, the Australian Army was largely unprepared for the outbreak of war, and 'Australia passed the first year of the Second World War in a state of uncertainty and, at times, confusion'.[45] While few military personnel would have agreed that an 'Australian [soldier] did not need to begin his military training until war began', that was effectively the situation that faced the Australian Army prior to the embarkation of the 6th Division for the Middle East in early 1940.[46] It had been hoped that at least 50 per cent of the volunteers for the 2nd AIF would be militia personnel, with a further 25 per cent having had previous service.[47] In reality the ratio was closer to 25 per cent militia, meaning that an unexpectedly large proportion had no previous service. With the Central Training Depot re-established only in 1939, many new units were unable to receive the benefit of a visit by the overstretched Australian Instructional Corps. This further limited the standard of training imparted to the new recruits.

One of the main difficulties in training and equipping the 2nd AIF—quite apart from shortages caused by longtime government parsimony—was the decision to form, train and equip the AIF and the militia at the same time. This need 'to maintain two armies . . . placed an enormous strain on the provision of equipment'.[48] Understandably, already-formed militia units were reluctant 'to release officers and NCOs, in view of their own training commitments'.[49] Also, as they had been ordered to train their own personnel they were loath to surrender the few rifles, machine guns and/or mortars they had to the newly created AIF units. William Booth, of the 2/3rd Battalion, stated that when he enlisted at Ingleburn, New South Wales, in September 1939 the recruits were issued with 'axe handles, wooden handles, for rifles'. His experience was by no means unique.[50] For 17th Brigade, training at Puckapunyal, Victoria, the situation was particularly dire: it would be October before they received their first issue of 1915-era .303 rifles. Most units' weapons, uniforms and equipment were of First World War vintage; some were of 1908 pattern.[51]

The shortages meant that when the first troopships sailed in late January 1940, the majority of 6th Division's soldiers were accustomed to 'route marches, squad drill, lectures, and fatigues' but had little idea of platoon tactics, let alone company or battalion manoeuvres.[52] Virtually no unit had seen the new Bren light machine gun, only some had handled its predecessor, the First World War–era Lewis, almost none had used a hand grenade, and most units had to pretend that tree limbs or stove pipes scrounged from the kitchen were mortar tubes and artillery pieces.[53] Nor were the engineers or artillery any better resourced than the infantry. The 2/8th Field Company, Royal Australian Engineers, had to improvise with picks and shovels as their only engineering equipment for several months, an ongoing handicap that would later lead one of their officers to state 'that the unit was fully equipped on the day the war ended' and never before that day.[54]

When the troops arrived in Palestine and Egypt, training and equipping began in earnest. Many officers and men were sent to specialist British Army schools to obtain the skills they had not had time to learn before departure from Australia. Over the course of 1940, the units of the 6th Division gradually received their required allotments of weapons, equipment and vehicles. For the 2/1st Battalion in Palestine, this did not happen until 3 May 1940, when they received Bren guns, Boyes anti-tank rifles and 2-inch mortars.[55] These were few in number and did not bring the unit up to full war establishment. As the first artillery regiment to arrive in the Middle East with the 6th Division, the 2/1st Field Regiment was relatively well equipped by May 1940. When its sister regiment, the 2/2nd Field Regiment, arrived later that month with no equipment at all, the disparity was 'fixed' by the simple expedient of an order to transfer half its guns, vehicles and equipment to the 2/2nd.[56] For many units, 'scrounging'—from allied units, from captured enemy troops, or from detritus on the battlefield—became the only way to ensure they could function adequately.[57] The story would be the same for the majority of the units of 6th, 7th and 9th Divisions when they arrived in the Middle East.

The fall of France in June 1940 had further wide-ranging repercussions, some of which also affected the Australians in the Middle East. When General Thomas Blamey arrived in Palestine on 20 June, he came 'not to the training area of a force intended for the Western Front, but to a theatre of operations in which [the] troops might be called on to go into action at short notice'.[58] Over the course of 1940, however, all units of the division were able to progress through company, battalion, brigade and divisional exercises.[59]

Combined with these various problems was the fact that none of the 6th, 7th or 9th Divisions was complete. Although better off than the 7th Division with its 'fluid composition', the 6th was nonetheless short of two artillery regiments, most of its engineers and pioneers and its machine-gun battalion.[60] By the time it went into battle in January 1941, the 6th Division was whole. The other divisions were not so fortunate, with 7th and 9th having battalions and brigades interchanged—the 7th not being complete until May 1941, a month before it went into action in Syria. For a period, some of the divisions' units would train in Britain while their sister battalions remained in Australia, with still others in Palestine.[61] Unsurprisingly, this disruption was not conducive to systematic training.

Late in 1940, the 6th Division was notified that it was to prepare for action and subsequently moved forward to positions near the

Libyan port of Bardia. In the weeks before the attack, all the battalions gained valuable experience in patrolling. One lesson that would be reinforced in the later jungle campaigns was the importance of training in terrain that was the same as, or at least very similar to, that over which actual fighting would occur. Unlike the 9th Division, which in a few months found itself besieged in Tobruk, the 6th was able to learn from and correct its mistakes before going into action. For the rest of the desert campaigns, the comment by Private Arch McLellan that 'we became expert nocturnal patrollers and learned to do the most extraordinary things silently, with only a compass and the desert stars' would have resonated with all who served in the theatre.[62] Reconnaissance and fighting patrols, mine-laying and lifting, resupply, medical evacuation, ablutions and improvements to defensive positions would all take place during darkness. Anything else was an invitation to almost instantaneous enemy fire. Once the Pacific War broke out and these units entered the jungle, near-complete changes to these procedures would be necessary. In the inky blackness of the triple-canopy jungles of the South West Pacific, the 2nd AIF would find that movement by night—especially by sizeable forces—was almost impossible. Many units in the Pacific enforced standing orders to shoot anything that moved above the level of a slit trench; even in one's own defensive area.

Before their first battle, at Bardia in January 1941, 6th Division identified a problem that would recur until the middle of 1943: specifically, the numbers of reinforcements who were arriving at units almost completely untrained. Some 'had not fired a service rifle and a majority had no training whatever on the Bren gun'.[63] Units dealt with this problem in two ways. They either distributed the reinforcements across platoons to be trained individually or they created a small training cadre—usually under an officer and a senior NCO—whose responsibility was to bring them up to an acceptable standard before they were allotted to a platoon. This unit-level and rather haphazard approach was clearly not adequate, and in late 1940 each brigade established a training battalion.[64] This eventually meant that all the Australian divisions in the Middle East received soldiers as ready for action as training could make them. Although the situation in the Middle East would improve over the course of 1941–42, it would recur during the Malayan campaign, and again in the early stages of the Papuan campaign. In contrast, the problems experienced by the returning AIF units in their initial jungle campaigns had more to do with 'well-trained troops suffering from ignorance of skills and tactics necessary in an environment that was new to them'.[65]

It would not be until the establishment of the Australian Recruit Training Centre at Cowra, New South Wales, in November 1943—and more importantly, at least with respect to jungle training, the Australian Training Centre (Jungle Warfare) at Canungra, Queensland, in December 1942—that the problem of inadequately trained reinforcements was overcome.[66] Before this, training was done on a state by state basis and varied greatly.

The longstanding issue of shortages of weapons and equipment continued to be a problem for the Australian Army, arguably until 1943. Many units of the 6th Division had little opportunity to fire their support weapons, with the artillery regiments especially restricted. In December 1940, 2/2nd Fd Regt 'fired its first and only live ammunition practice . . . during the whole of its stay in the Middle East before going into action'.[67] Two days before the Australian attack on the Italian fortress of Bardia, 'frontline infantrymen were still desperately looking for essentials such as sights and baseplates for their mortars [and] wirecutters'.[68]

Brigadier Stanley Savige, the 17 Bde commander, would later complain of these shortages, but the situation merely highlighted how prescient had been Lieutenant-Colonel Sturdee's summation of 1933.[69] The theatre-wide shortages of vehicles, weapons, equipment and ammunition often meant that units had to collect equipment as they went into action and relinquish it to new units as they were replaced.[70] A month after the siege of Tobruk began, for example, the commanding officer of the 2/28th Battalion gathered his men around him and 'threw a couple of grenades over the perimeter wire' to demonstrate what one looked like and the blast radius—none of the unit had seen one in training.[71] The ability—in fact, need—to 'learn on the job' and to improvise would become a trait of the Australian Army, never more so than when confronted with the challenges of jungle warfare in 1942–43.

Closely aligned to the issues of equipment, weaponry and the training of reinforcements was the question of doctrine. The British manuals *FSR* and *Infantry Training* were seen to provide all the solutions to tactical and doctrinal problems that an officer would confront in battle. The early—and apparently easy—defeats of Italian forces by both Australian and British formations seemed to support this contention. But once Rommel's vastly experienced Afrika Korps was despatched to stem the advance towards Tripoli in early 1941, the situation changed.[72]

Recourse to *FSR*, *Infantry Training* and other pre-war training manuals could provide only a modicum of assistance. It was only through the acquisition of combat experience that the best and most appropriate methods were arrived at—a similar scenario to the experience in Papua in 1942–43. Although they provided a basic starting place, the contemporary training manuals and doctrine were not especially useful in preparing the Australians for combat in the desert. This is despite the fact that the training areas in Australia did not differ as markedly from the desert as the Pacific jungles did. The main problem was that much of *FSR* drew upon the lessons of colonial warfare.[73] Information on the best way to counter the German employment of well-coordinated armoured vehicles, field artillery, mechanised infantry and tactical air support was nonexistent.

The most important deficiencies—for the Australian Army at least—in the current manuals related more to the infantry than to the other combat arms. The nature of the desert led to changes in pre-war infantry tactical formations to make them more suitable to the terrain.[74] The most obvious of these changes was an insistence on the wide dispersal of any formation during daylight hours. In the desert, as Owen Curtis of the 2/12th Battalion later observed, to concentrate men in a small area would have been suicidal, as a single shell or burst of machine-gun fire 'would have got the lot'.[75] The section, platoon and company formation diagrams in *Field Drill for Rifle Battalions* (1938) described how best to deploy 'into action from the march' but were not as important to units operating in the desert as the battle drills that would later be adopted in the jungle.[76] There, battle or contact drills would become crucial, because it was often unclear when or from what direction fire would come. All members of a unit had to respond instantly when they came under fire whatever the terrain, but unexpected contact was clearly more likely in thick jungle than in the flat expanses of North Africa, where carrying out surprise attacks was much more difficult.

In the desert, painstaking reconnaissance to determine the nature and depth of the enemy's defences was essential. Approaches and attacks were therefore more deliberate 'set piece' affairs, and 'manoeuvre, as opposed to mobility, was limited . . . by the good visibility'.[77] Australian infantry would thus find themselves modifying the formations depicted in *Field Drill for Rifle Battalions*. The most notable differences would be the wider dispersal and the change to a less cautious 'two up, one back' formation for sections or platoons. So when an infantry company attacked an enemy position in the desert, two of its three platoons would be to the fore, with only one platoon in reserve. This formation provided more firepower at the head of the force to compensate for the lack of cover. *Infantry Minor Tactics, 1941, Australia* would reflect these lessons, much to the detriment of the units in 1942, who would try to apply them to the markedly different terrain of Papua.[78]

Soon after meeting the Japanese in 1942, units would realise that a more cautious 'one up, two back' formation was best suited to the jungle, where contact often occurred unexpectedly and from the flanks or rear. After two and half years of service and combat in the Middle East, the men of the AIF had learned their lessons well. They knew the best ways to attack and defeat a German or Italian position, but they soon discovered that these tactics would be very costly in the jungle.[79] The lessons of the desert had to be unlearned or men would die. Of equal importance was that over the course of those years in North Africa and the Middle East: 'A subtle, but significant change in doctrine had occurred from infantry based tactics to motorised/mechanised infantry tactics [which] were to be entirely inappropriate to the coming battles in New Guinea.'[80]

Notwithstanding these doctrinal problems, over the course of 1941 and 1942 the AIF would build on its Middle East training and early combat experiences and become a well-trained and highly respected force. The experiences of the 7th Division, in particular, during the Syrian campaign would go some way towards preparing them for the challenges they would face in Papua. The mountainous terrain would make radio and wireless communication difficult and at times impossible.[81] Resupply by packhorse, precautions against malaria and the need to disperse sub-units on individual tasks foreshadowed similar issues in Papua and New Guinea.[82] Most importantly, perhaps, when the men of the 6th, 7th and 9th AIF Divisions met the Japanese in battle, it was as combat-hardened soldiers. As the historian Jeffrey Grey commented, the 'first two full years of the war were an important preparation for the great struggle in the Pacific which was to follow'.[83] The troops' doctrine and training would prove to be inappropriate to the terrain and the enemy they were to face, but most had been in uniform for over two years. They were experienced, extremely fit and determined to halt the Japanese advance. However, the first Australian units to face the Japanese onslaught were not these formations, but the 22nd and 27th Brigades of 8th Division stationed in Malaya.

Chapter 2

'EVERYTHING WAS SO DIFFERENT': THE 8TH DIVISION IN MALAYA

2 February 1941. As the train pulled in to Central Station in a cloud of steam and squealing of brakes, the loud and exuberant voices of its passengers, heads thrust from every available window, rang out. The 2/19th Australian Infantry Battalion, men from the Riverina and Monaro regions of southern New South Wales, had arrived in Sydney from their training areas outside Bathurst. Soon they and the rest of 22nd Brigade, 8th Division, would make their way to Circular Quay and board the magnificent British liner the *Queen Mary*. Slogans like 'Berlin or Bust' and 'Look out Adolf', written in chalk on the outside of the carriages, highlighted the fact that the troops had not been told their true destination.[1] It was only after their departure that they worked out where they were going. Singapore and Malaya, not Palestine and North Africa, would be their training area and, eventually, battleground. Although they had no way of knowing it, eleven months later, in January 1942, they would be the first Australians to see combat against the Japanese—and the first in the Second World War to experience jungle warfare.

Only two months earlier, on 7 December 1940, the men of the 22nd Brigade had been involved in a series of exercises in the rolling countryside around Bathurst. As 8th Division's commanding officer, Major-General Gordon Bennett, made clear, the division was to prepare for the type of conflict that the empire forces—shortly to include the 6th Australian Division—were involved in against the Italians in North Africa.[2] To this end, their training exercises in the latter half of 1940 closely resembled that of 11 November, which ordered that '8 Div is to advance against the Italian forces holding the Sidi Barrani area' near the Libya–Egypt border.[3] Further, the 2/18th Battalion felt that their training was to prepare them for 'open warfare, obviously relevant to the Middle East... and as a consequence great trench lines were dug'.[4]

The relevance and usefulness of training that involved digging large trench systems, even for the type of warfare the division was expecting to face in North Africa or the Middle East, suggests that some of its officers had tactical ideas that had altered little from the 1914–18 war. The historian Peter Henning observed that the officers of the 2/40th Battalion, which was captured on Timor in March 1942, 'were trained in the orthodoxies of World War One tactics' and adds that there was a pressing need in 1940–41 for 'in-service training for senior officers'.[5]

Soon after 22nd Brigade had departed Australia, most of the troops were informed by senior officers of their destination, but others found out by less conventional means. Nineteen-year-old Donald Wall, from Narrandera, southern New South Wales, was sailing on the *Queen Mary*. As it arrived in Fremantle, he went down into the hold with some other men 'and opened a case and the title [of the booklets inside] was Notes on Malaya'.[6] Even the men of 27th Brigade, who did not depart Australia until late July 1941, assumed that they were going to join their comrades in the Middle East. As Erwin Heckendorf, of the 2/30th Battalion, remembered, 'we were training to go to Europe. In fact our section was detailed to do a crash course in German, French and Italian.'[7] It was only after their convoy had left Melbourne in mid-July 1941 that they too realised their destination was Singapore.

Training in Australia at the individual, unit and brigade levels was premised upon the belief that the 8th Division would soon be joining their comrades in the Middle East. Unfortunately, the Australian Army's standard of training and equipment had not improved since the departure of the 6th Division for the Middle East. This was true for artillery and signals units, as well as for the infantry. If every man in a unit had a .303 rifle, that unit could consider itself fortunate.[8] Nevertheless, the men were confident that they would give a good account of themselves.

The last three months of 1940 saw the Australian government involved in occasionally heated discussions with the British government, particularly Prime Minister Winston Churchill, over the defence of Singapore and the broader region to Australia's north. At the Singapore Conference in late October 1940, it was determined that it should be possible for Australia to provide a brigade group by the end of December 1940. One outcome of these discussions was the despatch of the 22nd Brigade to Singapore.[9] That the Australian forces would be unfamiliar with and untrained for a tropical environment was not discussed. At this stage, it was generally believed that Malaya was not under threat of attack. The first mention of the forthcoming deployment appeared in the 8th Division General Staff Branch war diary on 31 January 1941, when Major Charles Kappe, 8th Division's GSO2, left for 'destination of "Elbow Force"'.[10] He was followed during the first week of February by the divisional commander, Major-General Bennett; the 22nd Brigade's commanding officer, Brigadier Harold B. Taylor; and his brigade major, Major C.B. Dawkins. The first deployment of Australian forces to a tropical environment since the First World War had begun.

Upon arrival in Malaya, Taylor and Dawkins spent about ten days visiting various British and Indian Army units and trying to ascertain what types and levels of jungle warfare training they were engaged in. Taylor's diary recorded that he 'saw a company of [2/1] Dogras training in jungle warfare. [They] do it according to green book tactical notes on Malay.'[11] Taylor said the majority of British units had not developed detailed training methods or a syllabus. This was because the vast majority of the British believed 'that the jungle was impassable for large bodies of troops'.[12]

Major Angus Rose, of the 2nd Argyll and Sutherland Highlanders, claimed that when his unit proposed to embark on jungle warfare training 'we received very little encouragement from Malaya Command and they assured us that if we were not drowned in the seasonal rains we would be decimated by malaria'. Later, Brigadier William St John Carpendale of the 28th Indian Brigade expressed surprise upon his arrival in Malaya in August 1941 that there was 'no jungle-training school for officers'.[13] Notwithstanding Malaya Command's lack of interest in the Highlanders' jungle warfare training ideas, by the time the 22nd Brigade arrived in late February 1941, the Argylls had conducted regular exercises in jungle and rubber plantations, and had laid the groundwork for a jungle training syllabus. Despite this, it was clear that their 'tactics and tng [training] had only gradually developed with experience and finally crystallised some few months before the war'.[14] From these inauspicious beginnings, the officers of the 22nd Brigade therefore had to create their own training programs once their units disembarked at Singapore on 18 February 1941.

Malaya, and to a greater extent New Guinea, Bougainville and the other islands of the South West Pacific, posed formidable challenges for any army. As experienced soldiers, Taylor and Dawkins knew that engagements in jungle or rubber plantations would take place at much closer range than on 'traditional' European or North African battlefields. Fields of fire were reduced to yards, or at times feet, from one's position, thus increasing the speed at which events unfolded. Ambush would be an ever-present danger: 'Tactical features [such as hills] lost their significance, roads and tracks were vital; static defence spelt defeat, and all round protection would be essential.'[15] Observation and fire support, by the unit's own weapons, such as mortars or medium machine guns (MMGs), and by field artillery or aircraft, was made considerably more difficult. Communications and control by higher authority were correspondingly harder in the jungle, when a general or brigadier could often not see any of the forces under his command and therefore had to rely upon unit and sub-unit commanders to carry out his orders and make their own judgements and decisions. According to Lionel Wigmore, 'as Taylor saw it, the section and platoon commanders would become all-important; if they lost, you had lost'.[16] Although Malaya generally had a good road network, once off the main highways transport would rapidly become bogged, meaning resupply would rely on manpower.

Despite the division's rushed departure, planning to overcome the problems associated with a tropical environment had begun. In particular, the dangers of disease, especially malaria, were recognised, and lectures and handouts on the subject were prominent on the voyage to Singapore.[17] Lectures given to 22nd Brigade officers on the voyage also included topics such as 'care and responsibility of arms and equipment with particular reference to climatic conditions'.[18] A lecture on 'outline of experiences in jungle warfare' was delivered by Major Charles Anderson, second-in-command of the 2/19th Battalion, who had served in the British East African jungle campaigns during the First World War. His knowledge was to prove of great value to his unit.[19]

The single most valuable source of information, however, was the booklet mentioned by Taylor and Wall, which troops had found in the hold of the *Queen Mary*. *Tactical Notes for Malaya 1940* was a 29-page British Army booklet, copies of which had been supplied to Australian Army Headquarters in 1940 and reprinted in bulk to be distributed to 22nd Brigade. It described 'local conditions in Malaya, the characteristics of the Japanese army and minor tactics in densely forested terrain'.[20] The detailed booklet, which included maps and illustrations, provided the first substantial source of training information for many of the Australians. While not as detailed as other intelligence information available to British and Australian High Commands, *Tactical Notes* was seen as very useful to the newly arrived units, as it synthesised information from many sources.

The booklet gave a much more realistic view of the capabilities of the Japanese military than prevailed in Malaya at that time.[21] It accurately discussed the country's terrain, how one should fight in it, the strengths and weaknesses of the Japanese military, and how to defeat them. Adequate preparations based upon the information contained in *Tactical Notes* would have gone a long way towards preventing the forthcoming disaster. Why the Japanese Army was still so underrated given works such as *Tactical Notes*, as well as the numerous reports, articles and intelligence summaries available to the Allies, can only be attributed to overconfidence or a sense of racial superiority.

A second training manual was also available to the Australians, but the extent of its use is difficult to determine.[22] *Military Training Pamphlet No. 9 (India), Extensive warfare—Notes on Forest Warfare* was 'produced by the Indian military authorities ... [and contained] guidance about forest fighting for its units being sent to Malaya'.[23] Like *Tactical Notes*, it was also reprinted at the behest of Army HQ Melbourne, and distributed down to divisional level. A secret training circular despatched by HQ 8th Division to all its units still in Australia made clear that both of these documents were sent to HQ 23rd and

27th Brigades.[24] However, *Notes on Forest Warfare* does not appear to have been sent to the battalions or regiments of 8th Division. This decision, while not critical, appears unfortunate, as *Notes on Forest Warfare* does include valuable information that could have been used as an adjunct to *Tactical Notes*. Nevertheless, the wide distribution of *Tactical Notes* demonstrates that the 22nd Brigade had in its possession, upon arrival, information 'containing the basic fundamentals of jungle warfare'.[25] The units were therefore able to expand upon existing knowledge, including advice from British Lieutenant-Colonel Ian Stewart of the 2nd Argylls and suggestions by Major Anderson of the 2/19th Battalion, and develop training ideas.

'Jungle Training is intense': 22nd Brigade in Malaya

Tactical Notes was included as the set text in the first training instruction issued by 22nd Brigade, and in 8th Division's first training instruction as well. Dated 20 February 1941, two days after the arrival of 22nd Brigade at Singapore, this ordered that '"Tactical notes for Malaya" . . . should be kept before all ranks at all times during their tng'.[26] It added that 'the problem is to apply the tng already undertaken by the Inf Brigade to the type of country . . . three types of country are . . . extensive rice fields, rubber plantations, jungle'. This was somewhat contradictory: the first sentence suggested that no great tactical changes would be necessary, yet the second listed three different types of terrain and foliage in which the Australians would have to operate, none of which had been experienced before.

The units spent the first few days acclimatising to the heat and humidity. Lectures continued, they settled into their new quarters, and mosquito nets were issued, along with the unanimously disliked 'Bombay Bloomers', an awkward cross between shorts and slacks.[27] Soon the Australians were ready to take their first steps into the jungle.

Only days after the 22nd Brigade made its first section and platoon marches in the new environment, both officers and men had noted how different it was from what they had become used to in Australia. Although Bennett's book on his division's time in Malaya has been criticised as self-serving, his views on the changes he believed would be necessary are worth noting:

> A few minutes in the jungle was sufficient to convince me that we had to start afresh on our training. Our textbooks, our tactical methods, our equipment, our clothing, had been designed for a European War. Recent desert fighting had modified methods to suit the desert. Jungle conditions were such that, while textbook principles were sound, the methods had to be varied fundamentally.[28]

Major Dawkins, of 22nd Brigade, after observing his troops' first faltering exercises in the jungle, concluded that training 'carried out in open Australian country ... would have been invaluable for desert fighting' but required major change for jungle conditions.[29] The troops themselves confirmed that adjusting to the new training environment was a challenge. Frank Colenso, of the 2/18th, remarked that 'jungle training is intense ... you couldn't credit that you could hide yourself two yards from somebody and they wouldn't be in the race to see you'.[30]

An especially vivid account of the challenges posed by operating in jungle terrain appeared in the second edition of the 2/19th Battalion's magazine, printed in April 1941:

> At first we were raw recruits again. We had to learn elementary lessons in a strange terrain and a strange climate. We had to adapt our [training] to new conditions. The Malayan jungle was a different proposition to the bleak, bare hills of Ingleburn and Bathurst. A 'nose for direction' was likely to get out of joint in the forests and their jigsaw puzzle of

narrow tracks. It was a hard school we learned in. We sweated and toiled and swore in the jungle and the hilly rubber country. Bivouacs meant sleeping under mosquito nets and wondering whether one would roll over into a King Cobra during the night. We dragged through steamy, stinky swamps and cursed as we got entangled in labyrinthine vines and creepers on rubber estates. Leeches, scorpions, snakes, mosquitoes—we suffered them all.[31]

These and many similar accounts show that the first Australian Army units in the Second World War faced with tropical conditions found them confronting and not a little unsettling, and that for many, simply 'apply[ing] the [training] already undertaken . . . to the [new] type of country', was not going to be easy.[32]

To overcome the troops' unease and, in some cases, fear of the new environment, Bennett's initial training instruction stated that 'the first essential is to train the troops to become jungle-minded'.[33] It listed three essentials for jungle warfare: 'offensive action wherever possible, the highest standard of section etc, training [and] maintenance of direction'. The latter two points became the early priority, and throughout the rest of the 8th Division's time in Malaya, at some stage during each week, units from section to battalion level practised keeping direction and manoeuvring in jungle and rubber-tree groves. The use of prismatic compasses took on central importance, as navigation and reconnaissance proved far more complicated than in the open Australian countryside where the units had initially trained.

Marching between distant but visible landmarks, standard practice in Australia, was virtually impossible in Malaya, as was navigating by orienting a map to the ground over which the troops moved. Inaccurate and sometimes nonexistent maps added to these problems.[34] The Australian artillery units, in particular, spent a considerable amount of time in survey work and the creation of gridded maps, so that when called upon they could deliver accurate barrages and defensive fire in support of the infantry battalions to which they were attached.[35] In a country where lack of observation of fall of shot was the norm rather than the exception, accurate maps became even more crucial. Often these were not available, and units had to make their own. A shortage of prismatic compasses and qualified survey teams added to the problem. The techniques of sound ranging—usually involving the use of three separate observers to judge where shells had landed by triangulation—did not become a standard procedure until later in the war.[36] Upon examining the gun positions chosen for his unit, Colonel Wright, commanding officer of the 2/15th Field Artillery Regiment, noted in his diary that 'this was certainly NOT artillery country. It was almost impossible to get observation posts.'[37] Eventually, of course, field artillery would be used to great effect by the Australian Army in New Guinea and the islands, but at this embryonic stage, most units were struggling to come to terms with the challenges posed by conditions in Malaya. Air cooperation to direct and adjust the fall of artillery fire was also in its infancy in this theatre, further adding to the difficulties all units faced.

The infantry units immediately set about tackling the new challenges, with the 2/20th Battalion issuing its first training syllabus only days after arrival in Malaya. It stated that the object of the syllabus was to 'train Secs [Sections] and Pls [Platoons] to move through semi close and close country . . . [further that] lectures will be given regarding types of country . . . [and] a high standard of snap shooting at short range is necessary [both] kneeling and standing'.[38] *Tactical Notes* would be the prescribed text and 'should be kept before all ranks during training'. The 2/18th Battalion syllabus for early March saw the unit moving beyond section and platoon exercises to 'coy [company] attack [and] defence in rubber'.[39] At the same time, the 2/19th Battalion stated that 'all officers to meet 2000hrs each day for discussion on training problems'. While the units had a basic set of ideas to use, incorporating their own experiences of operating in the new terrain was also crucial.⁴⁰ Brigadier Taylor spent considerable time visiting his battalions and overseeing their training in jungle conditions, but Bennett, as divisional commander, was occupied with other issues.⁴¹

Within a few weeks of beginning training, the Australians started to grow more accustomed to the new conditions. Some soldiers appear to have enjoyed the experience of 'being thrown straight into the jungle with water up to your knees, and not being able to see more than ten yards clearly, [it] was quite exciting actually. Everyone got stuck into it, we were doing things the British troops hadn't been doing.'⁴² For most, however, it was hard and unpleasant work. Colin Finkmeyer, a member of the 4th Anti-Tank Regiment, commented that 'we did a lot of jungle training . . . we did manoeuvres right through the jungle'.⁴³ As well as familiarising the 22nd Brigade with their new surroundings, this training highlighted some areas that would continue to cause problems for all Australian units operating in jungle environments, not only the 8th Division.

Communications were a particular problem, with the climate and terrain creating difficulties that would bedevil all units in the South West Pacific until the war ended. Closely aligned to the problems affecting communications—at all levels—was the impact this had on command and control. As Lieutenant-Colonel Ian Stewart wrote, 'control is decisive, and control depends on comms. Break control and an army will disintegrate. The jungle enormously increases the difficulties of control . . . for it prevents even visual means beyond the section'.⁴⁴ No units were able to avoid the communication difficulties imposed by the tropical climate of Malaya, but before the outbreak of war they were generally able to work around them. Motorcycle despatch riders and even, on occasion, the local telephone system became widely used.

The artillery units were the worst affected by these communication problems, finding that 'the heavily timbered, undulating country rendered the standard wireless telegraphy sets almost useless'.⁴⁵ Keith Pope, a signalman, recalled that 'you're [sic] wireless was absolutely useless inside a rubber plantation'. This meant that 'poor comms kept the guns out of touch with each other and with those directing them. It was a problem we never solved.'[46] Several of the fallback solutions—semaphore, Lucas lamps and heliographs—were rendered useless by the thick jungle vegetation or rubber trees, as they all required a clear line of sight to operate properly. As in all other theatres the Australians served in, the 'most dependable method was by field telephone and Sig cable'. The burden upon the various signals units was greatly increased by the many extra miles of cable they had to lay in order to connect units. Once battle was joined, signalmen regularly put their lives at risk when retrieving cable under heavy Japanese fire.[47]

The jungle also caused problems for communications by signal cable, not all of which were expected. Allan McNevin, of the 2/10th Field Artillery Regiment, had to regularly repair signal lines because local baboons had taken to swinging on them.[48] Understandably, dealing with baboons had not previously been an issue for Australian units. Nevertheless, on Borneo in 1945 other units would have to deal with the same problem. Unreliable communications meant a return to the oldest method of passing messages: runners, or, if units were lucky enough to have one, a motorcycle despatch rider. Both methods were vulnerable to ambush, especially in the close confines of the jungle.[49] Rain often left signal lines waterlogged. In an effort to overcome these problems, the 2/18th and 2/20th Battalions experimented with carrier pigeons.[50]

Another aspect of jungle warfare that all Australian units would encounter was the need to cross rivers and creeks—far more frequently than their training had envisaged, and thus often without help from engineers or pioneers.[51] The 22nd Brigade war diary noted that part of one coming week's training was in 'river crossings using improvised rafts'.[52] The 2/20th's diary listed the types of materials the battalion should use to make the rafts and prescribed a chapter from a training manual to further assist.[53] The 16th and 17th Brigades, which a year later would train for jungle warfare on Ceylon, do not appear to have had access to this training pamphlet or to have received any of the lessons learned by the units in Malaya. As a result, they were forced to make improvised rafts in their own river-crossing exercises. Such struggles to adapt would be repeated in later jungle campaigns, especially Papua and New Guinea.

The first two months after the arrival of the 22nd Brigade in Malaya saw a good deal of experimentation. Troops had begun using local knowledge—in May, a large party of 22nd Brigade troops took part in an elephant hunt.[54] As their familiarity with the countryside increased, more patrols without assistance occurred. The 2/19th appears to have devoted much consideration to the weight carried by its troops in the field, with the aim of reducing their loads to the bare essentials in the enervating climate. After three months of trials, 'each man was stripped to . . . 30 lbs per man', including his weapon and 40 rounds of ammunition.[55] That was half the weight infantrymen would carry in subsequent campaigns, including on the Kokoda Track, but in those battles resupply was generally far more difficult than in Malaya, so troops had to carry all they would need.[56] How much the 30-pound limit changed once battle began is not recorded. Although 40 rounds of ammunition does not appear much, a year later the 2/2nd Battalion marched to the front at Kokoda carrying only 50 rounds per man.[57] Other units took 150 rounds.

The many patrols undertaken by the Australians provided valuable learning experience. Those that lasted several days, in particular, forced troops to adjust to jungle conditions more fully than did day patrols.[58] These exercises were seen as vital to familiarising troops with operating in jungle and rubber vegetation, and, as an AIF Malaya Memorandum put it, '*fighting in the jungle* is far less important than *moving in the jungle*'.[59] By July, most units of the 22nd Brigade believed they were mastering jungle operations. Many worked with the

Sakai—the indigenous Malays, who lived in the jungles.[60] The 2/20th Battalion noted that 'the men [are] finding night work in rubber and light jungle not too difficult'.[61] Soldiers operating in the South West Pacific Area had to be fitter than did their counterparts in the Middle East or Europe. To this end, long route marches were still a favourite training tool.

Despite their progress with training, some soldiers thought even greater changes, especially in equipment, were needed. The author of the 2/20th Battalion history observed that 'much of our equipment was considered unsuitable for local conditions... the helmet was noisy, any twig hitting it could be heard for some distance, rifle was designed for open warfare [and] our clothing was brown-coloured for the desert'.[62] In subsequent jungle campaigns, many units discarded their steel helmets, finding them too hot and awkward. All Australian troops would eventually wear jungle-green uniforms, and many would carry shorter and lighter weapons, namely sub-machine guns, which proved extremely valuable in close-quarters combat in the jungle.[63] At this early stage, however, only small changes to accepted practices appear to have occurred; there were few or no real changes to set war establishments. Thompson sub-machine guns were not issued because of any recognised benefit of sub-machine guns in jungle warfare: Australian units in the Middle East were also beginning to receive them at the same time.[64]

One training innovation, which has been used by Australian infantry units ever since, was repeated firearms practice at close range, from 'unorthodox' stances and at fleeting targets. The drills were designed to inculcate rapid or, if possible, automatic reactions when the enemy was sighted. Soon after the troops arrived in Malaya, training in 'snap shooting' proved that 'much more of this is necessary before the men are sufficiently efficient to give a good account of themselves in jungle fighting', with troops averaging only a 50 per cent hit rate.[65] The 16th and 17th Brigades would 'learn' the same lessons and 'invent' the same close-quarters combat drills on Ceylon a year later, highlighting that the transmission of knowledge from Malaya was erratic and partial.

The only plausible explanation for the failure to pass on such important information to other units is that at the time—April 1941—the Australians in the Mediterranean theatre were fighting for their lives in very different terrain and against a very different enemy from the one that the 8th Division would meet in Malaya seven months later. The commander of the 2nd AIF, General Thomas Blamey, was attempting to extricate the 6th Division from the disastrous Greek campaign. In late April, about half of the division was evacuated to Crete, where it fought a ferocious battle against invading German paratroopers. Understandably no one in the Middle East theatre, or back in Australia, was overly worried about 'lessons learned' material coming from units training in the backwater of Malaya.

As the months went on, the training undertaken by 22nd Brigade increased in complexity and scale, and involved exercises with British and Indian units, cooperation with other arms and services, and numerous exchanges of personnel between units.[66] The cooperative efforts had a practical as well as social purpose, aiming to increase the knowledge base of the units involved as well as breaking down divisions between the various national forces. Many of these exercises were designed to test the ability of the units to break camp, board motor transport, move a certain distance rapidly, then debus and be ready for action.[67] In late July 1941, the 27th Brigade was despatched to Malaya to join the 22nd while the majority of the 23rd Brigade continued its training in Australia.

For the other two infantry brigades of 8th Division, the 23rd and 27th, the period since the departure of the 22nd to Malaya in February had been one of contrasting fortunes. The 27th Brigade, with its three infantry battalions spread widely over the eastern seaboard, had continued standard infantry training.[68] By late May 1941 it was clear that the brigade had been notified of its subsequent move to Malaya, with training instructions stating that movement 'in the steepest and thickest country available' was essential.[69] By June 1941, these instructions had been received by the battalions under command, who began to implement them. The 2/29th Battalion undertook an exercise in late June whose object was to 'exercise a Battalion in movement and fighting in close country'.[70] The various war diaries of the 27th Brigade do not specifically mention information being transmitted from the units already stationed in Malaya, but once they knew of their forthcoming deployment, those units would have tried to get as much information as possible before their departure. At the very least, both of the brigades still in Australia had been sent copies of *Tactical Notes on Malaya*.[71] On 15 August the brigade disembarked in Singapore. It would have about three months to acclimatise and adjust to the new theatre. Fortunately, the collected training experience of the 22nd Brigade would provide it with a valuable resource to draw upon.

'Doomed Battalions': The 23rd Brigade

1941 was a much more disjointed year for the 23rd Brigade and would eventually see its three battalions widely dispersed as fortress defence units on various islands to the north of Australia. Before their departure at different stages during 1941, these units had received training that can at best be described as erratic. The 2/21st (Vic) and 2/40th (Tas) Battalions spent much of the year based in various locations in the Northern Territory, generally near Darwin, preparing to defend the region. The 2/22nd (Vic) had, by late-April, arrived at its new defensive location, Rabaul, the main town and harbour on the island of New Britain. The war diaries of the 2/21st and 2/40th make clear that no coherent and sustained training program was possible owing to the constant calls upon them to provide guard picquets, road-making and other work details.⁷² What training they did manage was a combination of 'recapitulation of elementary [training]', interspersed with company and battalion exercises involving working with other arms and services to defend Darwin and surrounding areas.⁷³

By April 1941, the unit commanders had been told they would soon be deployed to the north of Australia. In May the 23rd Brigade commander, Brigadier E.F. Lind, and the commanding officer of the 2/21st Battalion, Lieutenant-Colonel Leonard Roach, made a reconnaissance to Ambon and Timor. The state of the defences at the two locations, and the proposed tasks of the two battalions that were to be deployed, led both officers to raise objections with Army Headquarters in Melbourne.⁷⁴ They were concerned about the size of the forces available to them to carry out the tasks allotted, the shortfall in weaponry and equipment, the nature of cooperation with Dutch allies, and the level of air and naval support they could expect from Australia.⁷⁵ Eventually, despite the great reservations of their commanding officers, both battalions would be deployed as planned: the 2/21st to Ambon and the 2/40th to Timor.

Despite the higher-level disputes over the role of these units, the training undertaken prior to departure shifted in emphasis, clearly to better prepare them for the challenges ahead. A training instruction in late May 1941, which discussed improvised methods of 'tank hunting and destruction', had as one of its two reference materials a booklet entitled 'Japanese Army—Notes'.⁷⁶ Three months later, a memo from the 2/21st Battalion to HQ 23rd Brigade stated that 'a syllabus is also being worked up for a special course in Jungle fighting, Traps and Ambushes and Patrols'.⁷⁷ As the year progressed, the unit focused more of its attention upon training for jungle warfare and, to an extent, incorporating the lessons of jungle training.

A training exercise in early November, though centred on stopping an invasion of northern Australia, at the tactical level offered practice in jungle war-fighting.⁷⁸ In late November, further training based upon jungle warfare learning occurred, with the troops completing small-arms courses involving close-quarters combat drills.[79] These exercises closely resembled the types of training that the 22nd Brigade had developed over the previous nine months in Malaya. Documents showing the transmission of lessons from Malaya to Australia are scarce.[80] The historian Joan Beaumont rightly notes that the 'unsuitable nature of the terrain around Darwin for jungle training meant that training was not directly relevant to the situation that eventually confronted the battalion on Ambon'. But it is clear that, to the best of its ability, the unit was attempting to prepare itself for the task ahead[81]—though, as Private Benjamin Amor of the 2/21st noted, the troops themselves realised that the terrain was not 'jungle in the true sense of the word'.[82]

In late December the commanding officer of the battalion, however, made it abundantly clear to the Australian Army that with the means at its disposal, his unit would be unable to hold Ambon for any significant period.[83] That the battalion would be quickly overrun by the Japanese in early 1942 was ultimately not the fault of any deficiencies in its training, or the unsuitability of its Australian locale for teaching jungle warfare tactics. Gull Force was doomed from the outset because of the massive superiority in numbers and materiel of the Japanese.[84] Any lessons that the embattled men of the 2/21st Battalion learnt from their time on Ambon were lost with them and therefore could not supplement the tentatively growing body of Australian knowledge on jungle warfare.

The 2/40th Battalion followed a similar trajectory in its training to that of the 2/21st, and in early 1942 it would come to a similar end, overrun by numerically superior Japanese forces on Timor. Before that the unit was attempting, as best it could, to complete the required training, despite constant interruptions for work parties and sentry picquets. By July a shift in emphasis had occurred. The stated object of a training exercise undertaken in late July was to 'exercise Battalion in movement in close country'. In August similar exercises would take place. Mention of 'lecturette [sic] by OC as for Jungle Warfare' in early September suggests that the unit was about to alter the focus of its training. When the first-aid cadre received a series of lectures on 'aspects of diseases in the tropics', no further confirmation would have been needed.[85] As the time for their deployment to Timor drew nearer, more time became available for training.

The situation upon their arrival in Timor was similar to that confronted by Gull Force on Ambon. The battalion was expected to fight from half-completed fixed defences with inadequate resources and widely separated responsibilities. The little jungle warfare training they had undertaken was undermined by the inability of the Australian Army to supply them with enough appropriate clothing, equipment and weaponry. During his visit to the island in October 1941, the battalion commander, Lieutenant-Colonel Geoffrey Youl, had identified the need for the Australians to have uniforms specifically camouflaged for jungle warfare. His practical solution 'that Dutch uniforms be supplied . . . The green of the Dutch uniform is suited to the country and very hard to see even at a short distance' was not taken up.[86] Youl also recommended that the Australian troops be issued with 'breeches and puttees', which offered greater leg protection—they were being scratched and infected by the jungle foliage—than did the shorts on issue, but this too appears to have been ignored. Even in the longer term, neither of these recommendations was implemented, and the Australian soldiers on Timor and Ambon met the Japanese in the same uniforms as their comrades fighting the Germans and Italians in North Africa.

More disturbing is the fact that nearly ten months before the Australian Army confronted the Japanese in New Guinea's Owen Stanley ranges, one of the most basic requirements for operating in the jungle—appropriately camouflaged uniforms—was identified but not acted upon. It may be understandable that the period between

October 1941, when Youl made his recommendations, and February 1942, when the units on Ambon and Timor were overrun, was simply too brief for the changes to be implemented. This, however, does not withstand scrutiny with regard to the Kokoda Track battles nearly six months later. That the 39th Militia Battalion, and then the 21st Brigade of the 7th Division, in July and August 1942 had to face the Japanese in uniforms appropriate for the desert is an indictment of the higher echelons of the Australian Army. This example demonstrates that bringing about change in an organisation such as an army can be extremely difficult and take an inordinate amount of time, even when it is patently necessary.[87] But the inability to adapt to the changed circumstances of jungle warfare would cost many Australian soldiers their lives before the introduction of jungle-green uniforms in late 1942. Even worse, as late as August 1943, some 9th Division units had to dye their own uniforms green while in Milne Bay, Papua, on the way to the amphibious landings around Lae.[88] The only other explanation for this glacial pace of change is that Army Headquarters did not believe there was anything markedly different about operating in tropical jungle. It would take the Papuan campaigns to decisively alter this perception.

The final battalion of the 23rd Brigade, the 2/22nd, had departed for Rabaul, New Britain, in March and April 1941. Its officers used the time on board ship to give the troops information about their destination.[89] Soon after they arrived, modifications were made to webbing, haversacks and other means of carrying ammunition, and recommendations were sought from the companies. Although it was based in a very different location from its sister battalions, the 2/21st and 2/40th, the 2/22nd at Rabaul faced similar problems. Foremost was the time and effort needed to construct beach and aerodrome defences, and gun emplacements.[90] Aligned with this issue was the fact that, as with the forces that would eventually be sent to Timor and Ambon, those at Rabaul were preparing to defend fixed positions in a township and harbour location. Since Rabaul's large enclosed harbour was the most important strategic feature of New Britain, this is perhaps understandable. As a consequence, reconnaissance or training exercises in the jungle-clad terrain outside of Rabaul do not appear to have been a priority. Fred Kollmorgen, of the 2/22nd, recalled that while 'a certain amount of training was done out in those areas by just the companies . . . there wasn't much more, at that stage, there wasn't much more training one could do'.[91]

In late June 1941, the battalion issued its first training information bulletin. This document discussed numerous experiments carried out by the companies, the majority of them involving improvisation and adaptation of equipment and weaponry already under issue.[92] The first page discussed ways 'to determine the best dress for troops moving in the jungle' and what tactics to employ in jungle warfare. The problems identified and the conclusions reached closely resemble those arrived at by the 22nd Brigade units in Malaya—yet the 2/22nd's war diary makes no mention of *Tactical Notes for Malaya*, suggesting that it had to come up with its own training ideas based upon experimentation.

September and October saw the extent and variety of training increase as the unit attempted to gain a greater understanding of the nature and problems of combat in a jungle environment. On 4 September, the 2/22nd conducted 'section trng [training] in the attack in jungle country—ambush and counter ambush', and on 8 September the diary recorded that 'conduct of patrols constitutes major portion of company trng'.[93] Several later entries, however, call into question just how well the companies were adjusting to working in the jungle. Persistent problems centred around the overall standard of infantry training and the unfamiliarity of the environment. The standard was gradually being improved with regular courses, although the continuing requirement for construction of defensive works would remain an issue. But familiarising the troops with operating in the jungle would prove more difficult and time-consuming.

Two reports by observers of exercises during this period illuminate several failings identified by the units training in Malaya. In thick jungle, men tended either to move in single file and bunch up, presenting an easy target for ambushers, or to become separated from one another, meaning that all control and cohesion were lost.[94] Scouting and observation were poor, with patrols stumbling into staged ambushes. As in Malaya, the 2/22nd set up special assault courses to speed the men's responses to sudden and unexpected engagements. Rapid fire from the hip at 'moving targets' was one of the set drills. Major Leggatt, in an instruction to all junior commanders, urged 'SPEED in all your operations'.

Instant, instinctive responses to unexpected and close-range challenges would be crucial to this new form of combat. Developing them required frequent and vigorous training in situations as realistic as possible. As Lieutenant-General Sydney Rowell would later put it, 'the only way to train for jungle operations is to train in actual jungle'.[95] And, as a 27th Brigade training instruction would argue, thick jungle foliage 'would necessitate more responsibility falling on junior leaders'.[96] This would require both high levels of confidence in those junior commanders by their superiors, and high levels of training for the section and platoon leaders. As the training in Malaya had identified, jungle warfare would be a devolved and small-unit warfare. Crucial decisions would be made by corporals, sergeants and lieutenants. Those decisions would have to be made instantly without recourse to superior officers, who would generally be unable to see the situation on the ground for themselves. The very nature of the jungle would stymie communications, lessening the ability of more senior officers to respond to problems and increasing the importance of junior NCOs and officers out of proportion to their rank.

Ultimately, however, the 2/22nd would be unable to put its jungle training into practice. It would defend Rabaul from its fixed defences in the harbour area and the aerodrome. Along with its two sister battalions, it would be rapidly overrun in early 1942. It is thus difficult to judge the usefulness of the war diary entries and training reports compiled by the 2/22nd during its time on New Britain. The rapidity with which it and the other battalions were overrun caused great consternation and embarrassment to Army Headquarters and the CGS, which had inadequately prepared, supplied and supported them. Whether this reaction had any bearing upon the subsequent apparent lack of interest in any lessons they might have learned from the defeat is hard to determine. Even if no useful tactical lessons were identified, at the very least Youl's suggestions about adopting green-camouflaged uniforms should have been acted upon. In this way something of value might have been retrieved from a very dark hour in Australian military history.

'Confidence was unbounded': Final training for 8th Division

Before those units fell in January and February 1942, however, the two brigades of 8th Division now in Malaya would become, in mid-January, the first Australian troops to meet the Japanese. The 27th Brigade underwent training soon after the 22nd, and benefited from the lessons it had learned. As with that of the 22nd, its training in the initial stages was 'directed towards accustoming all ranks to the climate and to new tactical considerations'.[97] To this end the troops, for the first two weeks after arrival, undertook individual, section and platoon-level exercises such as route marching, compass work and stalking. The importance of *Tactical Notes* to this and much subsequent training is clear. The system of movement in jungle, according to Training Instruction No. 14, was 'clearly set out in "Tactical Notes on [sic] Malaya, 1940" Chap II, para 4. This system will be closely followed and impressed upon troops as normal.'[98] *Tactical Notes* stated that in moving through jungle, 'single file is the only possible formation', and that 'movements must be on compass bearing and by fixed distances'.[99] There followed a description of the type and size of formation to be used, and a guide to how such formations should operate. The fact that the 27th Brigade was following exactly the method laid down in *Tactical Notes* suggests that the 22nd had made no fundamental alterations during its time in Malaya.

Like the men of the 22nd Brigade, the newly arrived troops at first found the climate and terrain confronting and had difficulty in adjusting to the humidity in particular.[100] For other members of the 2/30th Battalion the strange noises at night caused much angst.[101] Like the 22nd Brigade, this unit would take time and considerable repetition and reinforcement of lessons to gain confidence in the unfamiliar territory. Every subsequent unit that served in the South West Pacific Area would face similar adjustment problems. For the men who had served in other theatres, adjusting to the strange and at times eerie jungle was often as difficult as confronting an alien and fanatical enemy.

Another problem that would adversely affect the Australian Army's performance against the Japanese was equipment. Many of the units despatched to the Middle East in late 1940 and early 1941 departed well below their war establishment, and the 27th's strength had not improved by the time it arrived in Malaya. This shortage of manpower affected most units, from infantry to signals and artillery.[102] In mid to late December 1941, after the Japanese attacks, Bren light machine guns and Thompson sub-machine guns were still being issued to infantry units. That these standard infantry weapons, vital in any form of warfare, but none more so than jungle warfare, could arrive so late is difficult to understand.[103] For some artillery units in Malaya things were no better than for the infantry: the 4th Anti-Tank Regiment, for example, was equipped with Italian weapons captured in the Western Desert of North Africa by the Australian 6th Division and shipped to Malaya.[104] It was late December before the 2/15th Field Regiment received the last of its new 25-pounder artillery pieces. The only test firing and calibration possible occurred well after the Japanese invasion.[105] These problems hampered the preparations of the Australian Army at a time when those units were desperately trying to overcome the myriad of issues that the new environment posed.

Soon after their arrival in Malaya, the brigade commander and battalion commanding officers went on a reconnaissance and information-gathering tour of the Kluang and Mersing areas, where they would be stationed if war broke out.[106] They also discussed the terrain and training ideas and problems with their counterparts in the 22nd Brigade. Despite this, war diary entries show that the newly arrived units relied on three main sources of training information: *Tactical Notes*, the various *Small Arms Training (SAT)* manuals, and the ubiquitous *Infantry Training* manual.[107] Combined with the regularly issued brigade training instructions, these were the sources from which all training exercises appear to have been drawn. The 27th introduced no substantially different or new techniques. Instead, they followed the ideas and programs already being used by the 22nd Brigade, as Brigade Commander Brigadier Maxwell confirmed.[108]

In the time available to them before the Japanese attacks, the 27th Brigade, like the 22nd, soon moved onto larger-scale exercises. With each passing day, the men felt they were becoming more competent and accustomed to operating in rubber plantations and jungle.[109] By 7 December, all the Australian units appear to have been confident in their own ability to match and overcome the Japanese.[110] Some tactical problems, however, had still not been solved. An entry in the 2/18th Battalion war diary in mid-November, after that unit had been in Malaya for nine months, indicates that the problems of defence in jungle terrain had not been adequately dealt with.[111] In thick jungle, it was all too easy for men to infiltrate between battalions and even between company and platoon defensive positions. There were also persistent communications problems and trouble with mines failing to detonate because of a waterlogging issue that would be identified only after the fighting had begun.[112] Foreshadowing the problems that would cause great suffering in the Kokoda and Beachheads campaigns, the 27th Brigade would attempt to address 'evacuation of wounded in both jungle and rubber'.[113]

The issue of how confident the Australians should have been in their ability to match the Japanese is a complex one. The Australian Army had trained hard in Malaya. It had undertaken more rigorous experiments and training exercises in jungle and rubber conditions than any other troops, with the possible exception of the Argylls, who had been stationed there for more than two years. It was believed that 'Japanese troops have had little experience in bush fighting, and in this particular our troops in Malaya should have a distinct advantage over them.'[114] After the fall of Singapore and the subsequent defeats of other Allied nations in South-East Asia, however, it was widely stated that the Japanese were highly trained in jungle warfare tactics.[115] More recently, several authors have disputed this claim, including the historian Bryan Perrett, who concludes that 'they had less practical experience of the jungle than their opponents, a fact which caused them such concern that in January 1941 they established a special unit in Formosa to study the problem'.[116] Clearly, for the most part the Japanese were not the jungle warfare experts they were later made out to be.[117] None of the fighting they had been involved in during the preceding years had taken place in tropical or jungle-clad regions. The Australians thus had some grounds for believing that they were better trained than the Japanese, at least in jungle conditions.

The reasons for the defeat lay elsewhere, and in fact were summed up comprehensively in *Tactical Notes* before the conflict began. Under 'enemy characteristics', the booklet stated that the Japanese soldier had a

> [h]igh standard of armament and technical training, great physical endurance, few bodily requirements, compared with British troops,

ruthlessness. He does not surrender, or take prisoners; a genius for imitation [and] a very high standard, and ample experience of landing operations.[118]

Added to this remarkably accurate summation should have been the fact that virtually every Japanese unit that took part in the Malayan campaign had previous combat experience; many units had fought for four years, some for even longer.[119] This was, of course, well known to the Australian troops at the time, but it was frequently contradicted by army lecturers who discussed the inferiority of the Japanese.[120]

This underestimation of the enemy could be attributed to the fact that the Japanese had not defeated a fully equipped modern army since 1905. The Western powers did not rate the Chinese military very highly, so the fact that they remained undefeated by the Japanese after several years of war convinced the British, among others, that the latter were not a force any European army need fear. That the Japanese troops were combat-hardened veterans while the Allied troops were not does not seem to have been taken into account.

In their defensive positions in Johore, southern Malaya, the Australians watched with increasing unease the rapid Japanese advance down the peninsula. For many units the outbreak of hostilities at least resulted in the long-awaited arrival of weapons and ammunition, though even these increases did not bring them all up to full war establishment.[121] From 7 December until mid-January, the Australians tried to obtain as much information as possible on the tactics of the Japanese: 'Officers who had been in the north lectured on Japanese methods and gave advice on probable counter-measures to be taken', not all of which was useful.[122] On 15 December the Australians got the first concrete information on enemy tactics—in a widely distributed report that continued the previous trend of downplaying Japanese weapons, equipment and methods.[123] It is difficult to see how calling the latter 'gangster tactics' would have helped the Australians very much.

Soon afterwards, Major C.B. Dawkins, GSO2 of 8th Division, returned from an inspection tour of the front line. He had been attempting to obtain first-hand information on the fighting, as the Australians had yet to see combat. On 20 December, all Australian units received a three-page message from 8th Division Headquarters. The following day this message was typed up and, according to the author of the 2/19th Battalion diary, 'promulgated to all officers and NCOs'.[124] Bennett obviously felt it had great value, as he included a copy of it in a letter to General Vernon Sturdee in Australia. Sturdee forwarded it to the Directorate of Military Training (DMT) 'to prepare notes so that the locals may get some inside information on Japanese tactics'.[125] The gradual creation of a body of information on the Japanese and jungle warfare was continuing.

The main points of the message were that the Japanese travelled quickly and were lightly armed, that they outflanked and infiltrated through static or linear defences, and that they cut units off by severing their lines of communication, inducing panic and precipitating retreat.[126] A reduction in the war establishment of heavy weapons, equipment and transport was recommended to help Australian troops move through the jungle more rapidly. The message reiterated the well-worn points about Japanese weapons and ammunition being less effective than the British and Australian ordnance. Suggested countermeasures were for units to practise all-round defence and patrol aggressively from their positions.[127] The Australian units were, however, already employing very similar training methods and felt confident in their ability to apply them in combat.[128]

Major Dawkins soon began making visits to various 8th Division units and expanding upon the information he had listed in the messages of 20 December.[129] At approximately the same time, Bennett sent a letter to the Australian forces containing similar information to that supplied by Dawkins.[130] The officers were clearly trying to ensure that when the Australians did enter combat, their knowledge of the enemy would be as up to date as possible. On 11 January 1942, the 2/29th Battalion destroyed all the bicycles in the Segamat area after receiving information from Brigade HQ that this was one of the main Japanese forms of transport.

For the Japanese, the bicycle was a simple substitution for the horses they had frequently used in China.[131] It was not a secret weapon; it was a means to an end—rapid movement. Malaya's excellent primary road network made bicycles a viable way to move large numbers of troops rapidly and cheaply. Their use was a necessity brought about by the chronic Japanese shortage of motor transport combined with a belief—from their exercises and training on Taiwan—that horses would be unsuited to the Malayan climate and landscape.

Determining how much information from Malaya was making its way to Australia at this stage is relatively easy. Most units sent copies of their war diaries for December 1941 back to Australia as standard practice, although some were more diligent about this than others. All the collected training information and knowledge of Japanese weapons and tactics gained since the deployment began in February should therefore have been available to units in Australia. However, once battle was joined and the situation became increasingly confused, this system was not followed as rigorously as before. Consequently, many lessons learned during this period could not benefit the forces in Australia, putting a premium on the information later supplied by escapees from Singapore, including Lieutenant-General Bennett.

Meanwhile, the 8th Division in Malaya was involved in a particularly bloody four weeks of fighting as Allied forces retreated down the peninsula. Several local engagements checked the Japanese momentum, but not decisively enough to halt it, either before or after the Australians joined the battle. The 2/30th Battalion was the first Australian unit to meet the enemy, when it ambushed and killed several hundred Japanese troops at Gemas on 14 January 1942.[132]

Unfortunately the outcome was not as decisive as it could have been, as communications to the supporting artillery unit failed after the lines were cut by infiltrating patrols.[133] Frederick 'Black Jack' Galleghan, commander of the 2/30th Battalion, therefore 'hesitated to unleash the artillery' and a barrage was not called down to complete the Japanese force's destruction.[134] As training had demonstrated, all forms of communication were unpredictable in jungle and tropical conditions, but even more so during battle.

The following day Brigadier Maxwell, commander of the 27th Brigade, and members of his staff discussed the lessons of the action. They came up with nine separate points, dealing with the weapons and tactics of the Japanese as well as the Australian responses. These overturned several stereotypes about the ability of the Japanese, but they also highlighted the positives of the Australian troops' performance. Maxwell carried the report to 8th Division Headquarters and briefed Bennett on the findings. Within days, Maxwell would be imparting the information to units that had yet to see combat.[135] At this stage, the process of knowledge acquisition and exchange was clearly still functioning. As the retreat gathered pace, however, the system gradually broke down.

Soon the other Australian units were also embroiled in the fighting. The Victorian 2/29th and later the NSW 2/19th Battalions conducted an extraordinary fighting withdrawal along the road from Bakri to Parit Sulong between 20 and 22 January, opposed by a greatly superior Japanese force.[136] Assailed by tanks, aircraft and artillery, the soldiers experienced combat of a ferocity unparalleled in the Malayan campaign. Of almost 1800 men, fewer than 500 survived. Days after the battle of Muar-Bakri, Major Anderson, the commanding officer of the 2/19th, reported to Bennett that the Australians had performed very capably and 'showed complete moral ascendancy of the enemy'.[137] On 24 January he spoke with Bennett, who asked him 'what lessons he had learnt during the last seven days'. Two of these were that there should be a reduction in motor transport and an increase in the number of riflemen per battalion. One of the most important of his observations, and one that would be confirmed in later jungle campaigns, was 'that the establishments of Battalions were short of bodies—riflemen for use in bush warfare or jungle fighting'.[138] This belief that jungle warfare required more men in the rifle companies, less transport and fewer supporting troops later helped lead to a change in the makeup of jungle divisions.[139] From 1943 on, under the Jungle Division War Establishment, Australian infantry units would lose their transport, anti-aircraft and Bren-gun carrier platoons, freeing their members to serve as riflemen. For now, however, no major changes occurred.

While Anderson and others were drawing valuable conclusions from the fighting taking place, Bennett had not completely grasped the lessons of the Malayan campaign. According to Bennett's biographer A.B. Lodge, Anderson said he had 'never really understood jungle warfare. In my contacts with Gordon Bennett I formed the impression that... he may have been influenced by WWI experience'.[140] Although Bennett had seen much combat as the commanding officer of an infantry battalion at Gallipoli, and later as a brigade commander on the Western Front, most of this experience was in the largely static conditions of the Great War and it is debatable whether this was really useful in the rapidly changing Malayan campaign.

It is not surprising that Bennett would liken enemy tactics in this new war to those he had observed two decades earlier. In his letter to Sturdee, Bennett argued that the Japanese approach was 'exactly the same as that used by the AIF against the Germans in 1918', in that small infiltrating parties crossed the front line and threatened rear areas, causing their opponent to withdraw to prevent large numbers of units from being left isolated.[141] The Japanese tactics in Malaya, however, more closely resembled German blitzkrieg tactics in the Second World War.[142] Strong conventional forces using major roads and spearheaded by tanks moved as rapidly as possible with overwhelming close air support. When held up, they sent troops to outflank and cut the British lines of communication, thereby precipitating withdrawal and allowing their own main combat forces to continue advancing down the roads. The speed with which events unfolded and the ferocity with which the Japanese fought shocked the Allied forces, but their tactics were not new or revolutionary. Nor was the correct response to them: counterattacks and all-round defence.[143]

By the time the last of the British and Australian forces had retreated over the causeway onto Singapore Island, the battle for Malaya was lost. Even though it was too late to change the outcome, the Australian soldiers now knew that the Japanese were not the invincible jungle warfare experts that their rapid advance seemed to suggest.[144] But this information does not appear to have filtered back to Australia, so many continued to view the enemy troops as 'supermen'.[145] For the Australians the final two weeks of the campaign highlighted the risks of asking largely untrained soldiers to fight an experienced and aggressive enemy.[146] After their experiences in North Africa, it is almost beyond comprehension that practically untrained recruits would be flung into battle days after their arrival. The several thousand Australian reinforcements who arrived in Singapore in the last few weeks did not make a noticeable difference to the defence, and the units to which they were sent were forced to give them as much basic training as time and circumstances allowed.[147] Many had never fired a rifle and most knew nothing of bayonet drill. There was, of course, no way to give them adequate jungle warfare training. That this lesson would have to be learned all over again in New Guinea calls into question the judgement of the higher echelons of the Australian Army.[148] On 15 February 1942, Singapore fell, and with it most of the Australian officers and NCOs who might have assisted in creating the basis for an Australian jungle warfare training syllabus.

The few men who managed to escape—including, most controversially, General Bennett, the 8th Division commander—worked over the next three months to collate a series of documents that they hoped would assist in the fight against the Japanese. Unfortunately, the bitter divisions within the higher echelons of the Australian Army, exacerbated by Bennett's escape and by the fact that his 'lessons learned' material was most applicable to combat in Malaya, meant that little of value was salvaged from the Malayan campaign to help prepare forces in Papua and New Guinea. Jungle warfare was to prove a difficult concept to grasp, and the Australians would have to endure the protracted campaigns of Milne Bay, Kokoda and the beachheads before truly valuable information was collected and training programs could be developed. These would eventually lead to the establishment of the Jungle Warfare Training Centre at Canungra, in south-east Queensland, and see Australian troops become the acknowledged experts in jungle warfare. The first of the Middle East veterans to begin to prepare for combat in the tropics were the soldiers of 16th and 17th Brigade of 6th Division, who would spend the next four months on the Indian Ocean island of Ceylon.

Chapter 3

'COMPLETELY DEVOID OF IDEAS': THE 6TH DIVISION ON CEYLON

On 2 March 1942, John Curtin, the Australian prime minister, informed Sir Winston Churchill, the British prime minister, that despite the growing threat to Australia, his government would detach two of the three brigades of 6th Division to bolster the defence of Ceylon.[1] The previous three weeks had been devastating ones for Australia and her allies. On 15 February, Singapore had fallen. Four days later, Darwin was bombed. The war was no longer 'over there', it was on Australian soil. In the Philippines, General Douglas MacArthur's forces were desperately holding out on the Bataan Peninsula and the island of Corregidor. The day before Curtin's telegram, resistance in the Dutch East Indies had effectively ended as ABDACOM (American-British-Dutch-Australian Command) had been dissolved. The loss of the cruiser HMAS *Perth* and hundreds of men in the Battle of the Sunda Strait on 1 March was another grievous blow. It is against this backdrop that the decision to send 16th and 17th Brigades to Ceylon must be understood.

During the same period, a plethora of cables and telegrams flew backwards and forwards between London, Canberra, and Washington, DC, interspersed with communiqués from the various theatres of operation in the Middle East and Far East. As the Japanese forces continued their apparently inexorable advance south, the Australian government and people became increasingly worried. The most experienced Australian forces—the 6th, 7th and 9th Divisions of the 2nd AIF—were stationed in the Middle East, preparing to go back into the line against Rommel's Afrika Korps. Curtin and his ministers wanted them home to defend Australia. But Churchill and US President Franklin Roosevelt had other ideas. While they sympathised with Curtin's viewpoint, for them the bigger picture was what the Americans referred to as the CBI: the China, Burma and India theatre.

An at times acrimonious three-way exchange—during which Churchill and Roosevelt had tried to convince Curtin to allow the 7th Division to be diverted to Burma on 18 and 19 February—had ended with Curtin insisting that the convoy continue its journey to Australia. As the strategic situation in the region continued to deteriorate and Ceylon came under greater threat, Curtin extended his olive-branch offer of troops for the island's defence. Churchill gratefully accepted, and soon afterwards the 16th and 17th Brigades, en route home from the Middle East, docked at Colombo, Ceylon. For the next four months, most of 6th Division awaited the Japanese invasion—and took the opportunity offered by the unexpected deployment to train in tropical conditions.

Four months earlier, the entry of Japan into the Second World War, on 7 December 1941, had caused little interruption to the daily routines of 6th Division as it trained in Syria. Any suggestion that the men would soon be preparing to defend the island of Ceylon from Japanese invasion would have been dismissed as not worth thinking about. But from their first tentative steps into the jungle, they were improvising and learning constantly. Mistakes were made, and their initial encounters with the Japanese in New Guinea showed that more learning was needed. But the time on Ceylon was not wasted. By July, the two brigades were better prepared for the challenges of jungle warfare than any other units in the Australian Army.

Back in December 1941, however, jungle warfare—as far as the 6th Division was concerned—was very much a topic of speculation. At the Divisional Conference on 13 December, the main topic under discussion was the battle plan of the division if it should be attacked in defensive positions in the mountains of Syria.[2] Two weeks later, the first hint that the division was about to move came at a meeting called to discuss the relief of the 16th and 17th Brigades.[3] Some men of the 6th Division would come to look back fondly on Syria and its precipitous mountains. As John Armstrong, of the 2/3rd Battalion, recalled: 'I thought half the mountains in the world were in Syria and the Lebanon, and the other half in Greece; but in the light of our later experiences in New Guinea, these mountains fade into mere molehills.'[4] During the final weeks of their deployment in the mountains of Syria, both the 16th and 17th Brigades engaged in training exercises involving the use of mules as pack animals.[5] For some men of the 17th, this experience would prove valuable a year later when they used mules as part of Kanga Force in the mountainous jungles around Wau, in north-eastern New Guinea. Training continued during the early weeks of 1942, but with the fall of Singapore on 15 February and the loss of the Australian 8th Division, among other units, a change of plans soon occurred.

The men of 6th Division would spend the rest of their war in another theatre. The 2/7th Infantry Battalion passed a frustrating month doing 'route marching, company drill and organised sports' before the commanding officer addressed a full-unit parade.

Lieutenant-Colonel Henry Guinn told his men that warfare against the Japanese would be completely different from the combat they had previously experienced: 'they would have to begin learning all over again'.[6] Several days later, 16th and 17th Brigades boarded transport ships of the *Stepsister* convoy and sailed east towards Australia.[7] Their comrades in 6th Division's 19th Brigade did reach home, and would spend more than a year training and preparing to defend Darwin.

While little information had been received from Army Headquarters in Australia regarding the problems of jungle warfare, the units themselves began addressing the problems during the two-week voyage to Ceylon. The 17th Brigade held daily discussions on the various problems the unit would face when it next went into action. These continued throughout the brigades' stay on Ceylon. The larger question of whether major tactical or doctrinal changes actually needed to occur in order for the Australians to succeed in jungle warfare was deemed irrelevant by commanders.[8] But the shock of the new, and of the defeat in Malaya, had convinced most Australian soldiers that dramatic change was required to defeat the Japanese. Although the historian John Moremon has argued 'that the principles of war were not altered' by jungle warfare, the men themselves found great differences between what they had previously experienced and what they now had to confront.[9]

Within days of their arrival at Colombo, on the west coast of Ceylon, the Australian units began sending out patrols into the jungle and rubber plantations surrounding their base areas. These helped them gain a clearer picture of their designated defensive areas in the event of a Japanese invasion and, more importantly, become acclimatised to operating in this new environment. On 26 March, senior officers of 16th Brigade reconnoitred the local terrain and concluded that 'we are confronted with something entirely different, both as regards country over which we will operate and the methods to be employed'.[10]

Several problems, however, were to hamper the rapid transition to a systematic jungle warfare training program. All units had to juggle the conflicting demands of training and defensive works. The 2/2nd Battalion HQ, for example, 'laid down a work and training policy ... designed to give Coys equal time for tactical training and digging of the perimeter of the camp'.[11] However, with the threat of a Japanese invasion imminent and the need to construct defences critical, little attention was paid to jungle warfare training.

On Easter Sunday, 5 April, the Japanese attacked. Bombs rained down on Colombo and Zero fighters from the same aircraft-carrier force that had attacked Pearl Harbor and Darwin strafed targets across the island. The Australian soldiers manned their defences, preparing to repel the Japanese invasion force that was expected to follow. It did not appear, but four days later the Japanese planes returned with a vengeance. Trincomalee Harbour was hit, as were the massive fuel tanks nearby; more than 700 people died. Warned of the arrival of the Japanese force, the aircraft carrier HMS *Hermes* and her escort HMAS *Vampire* left harbour in hopes of evading the attackers. Japanese dive bombers soon turned *Hermes* into a smouldering wreck. As she disappeared beneath the waves of the Indian Ocean, they turned their attention to *Vampire*. Soon she broke in two and followed her charge to the ocean floor. Although the commander of the British Eastern Fleet, Admiral James Somerville, was able to preserve his two other carriers from the enemy, it was clear that the Japanese now controlled the region's seas. The 16th and 17th Australian Infantry Brigades therefore remained in a state of high readiness.

There was little time to devote to training. The 16th Brigade war diary noted that 'progress has been very good and the programme of work [on the defences at Katukurunda aerodrome] will be finished by Wednesday, when training on forest warfare will be commenced by 2/1st Bn'.[12] The other issue outside the control of the units was the climate. After 'half a winter spent in the mountains of Syria, [17th] Brigade personnel were finding it difficult to become accustomed to the humid heat of the island'.[13] And about two weeks after their arrival in Ceylon, B Company of the 2/7th Battalion recorded: 'more training still required mainly due to strangeness to [sic] close country'.[14]

As the 8th Division troops had gradually grown accustomed to Malaya's humidity, so would their comrades in the 6th Division adjust to the climates of Ceylon and the South West Pacific islands. Lew Manning, who fought with 9th Division in North Africa and later in New Guinea and Borneo, might have been speaking for almost any Australian soldier who fought in the two theatres when he recalled: 'I didn't like the jungle. Lots of our men are country blokes used to open spaces. If you had to be at war the desert was a good place to fight in, no civilians, you felt at home. More like Australia. It was the unknown and unseen in the jungle.'[15]

To overcome the 'unknown and unseen', the initial jungle warfare training on Ceylon combined individual unit experimentation with exercises adapted from a small number of training handbooks supplied by Land Headquarters, Melbourne, and the DMT. These included the 200-plus–page *Infantry Minor Tactics*, which appeared to cover virtually all an officer should know, from proper leadership to the correct methods of dealing with gas attacks.[16]

Unfortunately, as Major Angus Rose, a British officer serving with the Argyll and Sutherland Highlanders in Malaya, recalled, many of the manuals were: 'Pompous, heavy, often platitudinous and otherwise equivocal . . . if anybody had the perseverance and determination to read them (which was no mean feat), they could interpret them in any way they liked.'[17]

Australian training manuals, being based almost entirely upon their British counterparts, suffered from the same problems. Worse still, any officer wanting advice on operating in tropical jungle or mountainous terrain could study a combined total of eight pages on

'Forest and Jungle Warfare' and 'Mountain Warfare' at the back of the booklet. It is therefore not surprising that, at least initially, the majority of Allied units struggled to come to terms with a form of warfare they had never trained for. But such information as was available would prove invaluable for the two brigades as they tried to develop an understanding of combat in the jungle.

On 28 March, three days after the 16th Brigade arrived in Ceylon, it held a commanding officers' conference at which training was discussed. Included under the heading 'training' were dot points such as 'fieldcraft and bush warfare' and 'night training'. More important was the statement: 'basis of training to be pamphlets recently issued on Tactical methods of Japanese'.[18] The following day, a training instruction from the adjutant of the 2/2nd Battalion stated that the

> Greatest attention must be paid to 'MTP [Military Training Pamphlet] 9 Précis' and 'Tactical Methods of Japanese Operations'. These pamphlets must be made the basis of training with comd's thoughts directed to movement along lines of enemy methods, and measures to counter enemy methods.[19]

These two handbooks—the second of which was a set text for officers at the 17th Brigade Jungle Warfare School at Akuressa—were the basis for most of the training undertaken by the two brigades on Ceylon.[20]

Before the Jungle Warfare School was established, in early May, units had to devise their own training programs, using the training manuals as guidance. Most moved as quickly as possible to begin acclimatising their men to the new conditions. Four days after its arrival on Ceylon, the 2/2nd Battalion recorded that:

> Training for the first week will concentrate on individual and section tng [training] in moving and campaigning in wooded and jungle country; commencing with simple movements of secs [sections] and

pls [platoons] through rubber plantations, and working up to two-sided exercises by day and night.[21]

The war diary of the 2/7th Battalion noted on 1 April that 'this morning all Coys [Companies] marched out from their alarm areas and practised movement through the jungle and maintenance of direction under these new conditions'.[22] The first month of their stay on Ceylon also saw much experimentation and improvisation as individual units tried to come to terms with the new country.

These efforts centred around applying the supposedly crucial lessons of Malaya to the current situation, and overcoming the problems posed by Ceylon's tropical climate. Ken Brougham, a member of the 2/6th Battalion, wrote home that 'life goes on just the same with plenty to learn in this new type of country and many lessons... from Malaya'.[23] Whether 8th Division CO Bennett's information was valuable is largely immaterial; during the first six months of 1942, the lessons of Malaya were virtually the only ones available to Allied forces.

An eight-page document entitled 'Notes on fighting in Malaya'[24] was sent out on 26 March 1942 by the Director of Military Training to every base and training establishment under the control of the Australian Army. After discussing 'Japanese tactics—Equipment and Armament', it suggested counters to these tactics and listed the lessons from the Malayan campaign that should be learned for future reference.[25] That much of this document was based on discussions with the British officer Lieutenant-Colonel Ian Stewart, and not Major-General Bennett, was also largely irrelevant to those desperately trying to come to terms with a new kind of theatre and new ways of fighting.

For the Australians in Ceylon the above handbook, combined with two other texts, *MTP 9 Précis* and Lieutenant-Colonel Francis G. Brink's *Tactical Methods*, would be the foundation of their jungle warfare training program. *MTP 9 Précis*, or, to give it its full title,

Military Training Pamphlet No. 9 (India), had been printed for the British Army in 1940 and provided instruction in 'forest warfare'.[26] Although the Australians on Ceylon lacked the more comprehensive jungle warfare training establishments and syllabuses that were available in 1943–45, they did have access to a greater range of information than was available to the units of the 8th Division in Malaya.

The most detailed handbook the Australians on Ceylon had on Japanese tactics and operations in the jungle came from a more unusual source. Lieutenant-Colonel Brink had been a US military observer in Singapore and an old hand in the Far East, deeply involved in the creation of, among other organisations, ABDACOM.[27] After witnessing the Malayan campaign and being evacuated before the fall of Singapore, he prepared a 23-page handbook on the Japanese Army's tactics, weapons and equipment.[28] The work was initially distributed by the British, rapidly acquired by the Australian Army, and reprinted with additional information from Malaya. The original British edition stated that the work is 'worthy of careful study by everyone who may have to train troops to fight the Japanese'.[29] The edition that was distributed to Ceylon goes further than this and includes the statement by the CGS, Lieutenant-General Vernon Sturdee, that 'this pamphlet will be studied by all Commanders of the Australian Army and by such other Officers as are responsible for its training'.[30] As the commanders' conference on 28 March stated, this pamphlet was to be the 'basis of training'.[31]

In the end, however, there was no substitute for the units getting out into the paddy fields, rubber plantations and tropical jungle and seeing for themselves what worked and what did not. The men's willingness to experiment in the new terrain was critical. A week after their arrival, the 2/7th Battalion recorded that a 'camouflage school conducted by Lieut Rooke commenced this morning. One man per section per rifle coy will attend and receive instruction in tropical camouflage.'[32] While this occurred, the remainder of the men 'of the rifle coys have begun practising the art of climbing palm trees, the object of which is for observation purposes. Each man takes up with him his rifle and pair of binoculars.'[33] The difficulties of observation and spotting in dense jungle that the Australian units had experienced in Malaya were also an issue on Ceylon.

Two ideas about jungle warfare figure prominently in war diaries and unit histories. One was based on the supposed lessons of Malaya, the other on the terrain of Ceylon. The first—using bicycles for transport—was short-lived and did not reappear after the Australians left Ceylon. The second, improvising ways to cross rivers, would recur in every campaign they would be involved in for the rest of the war. The brief flirtation with incorporating bicycles into combat units highlights the need to evaluate and reflect before adopting new practices, and the fact that in times of uncertainty, rapid judgements can impede learning. Presumably, if more time had been available for a calm study of the lessons of the defeat in Malaya, it would have become clear that the country's first-class road network had played a large part in the ability of the Japanese to move rapidly down the peninsula, whether on bicycles, motor vehicles or tanks. Their use of bicycles in Malaya was not applicable to other jungle campaigns. But some Allied officers, desperate to draw lessons from the harrowing defeat, seized on any new phenomenon that might help explain how things had gone wrong so fast.

Until the Japanese were observed using them in Malaya, it is doubtful that anybody in the Australian Army had contemplated using bicycles except for transport around base camps. Within two weeks of their arrival in Ceylon, however, units began receiving bicycles, and not just for use in rear areas. After the 2/1st was issued with five bicycles per company, its war diarist noted that 'these will greatly assist the mobility and efficiency of recce parties and runners'.[34] Although he appeared unperturbed by the new equipment, others did not face the changes with such equanimity. On 16 April, the 2/2nd Battalion

[r]eceived an issue of 30 odd bicycles, which were allotted to A Coy to form a bicycle Pl[atoon]. There being no pamphlet on the formation or the probable role of such a pl[atoon], it was devolved on A Coy Comdr's shoulders to work out a drill for their employment and work out a tactical role.[35]

But soldiers are soldiers and orders must be followed, and it is clear that both brigades pressed ahead with attempts to use bicycles for a variety of tasks, from transporting Boyes anti-tank rifles and mortars to serving as adjuncts to Field Ambulance units.[36] By the end of April the 16th Brigade's experiments with bicycles were advanced enough for it to include in a report to Canberra a section on methods of employing them in combat, though 'this unit's tng [training] on bicycles is still very much experimental'.[37] The ultimate value of such experiments can be inferred from the fact that in the 48-page document covering all aspects of the 16th Brigade's stay in Ceylon, bicycles are mentioned only in passing.

One reason for the concentration upon Malaya is that it was virtually the only source of information. In addition, 'visiting officers who had escaped from Singapore and Burma told us that the Japs had made extensive use of bicycles, so some were obtained for each coy'.[38] The immediate adoption of such ideas from the Malayan campaign demonstrates a failure to grasp its particularities or properly evaluate the ideas' applicability to other campaigns. That much of Malaya was covered in jungle, and that future fighting would also largely take place in tropical conditions, were regarded as justification enough. That such conflation of locales and campaigns could prove problematic is underscored in the 17th Brigade's war diary, which argued that to appoint an officer who had fought in Malaya, Burma or the Philippines would be unwise because 'most officers who had served out in these three campaigns would have a twisted vision of the happenings and be unable to correlate the various events in their true perspective'.[39] Clearly, many senior officers did not share that judgement, so much time was wasted on largely pointless experimentation, both in Ceylon and in Australia.

Further experiments (before the establishment of the 17th Brigade Jungle Warfare Training School in early May) focused on the best ways to modify current weapons systems and operational procedures to cope with the changed environment. They ranged from using bullocks as transport animals to using Universal (so-called Bren gun) Carriers in the jungle.[40] The problems of using carriers in jungle were highlighted at a conference of 17th Brigade officers, which was able to come up with very few ideas.[41] As Captain Bennett, of 2/5th Battalion, later recorded, 'everywhere we went we got bogged or bellied on the logs and stumps' in the jungle and paddy fields. Although he thought 'carriers had their uses if they were closely supported by the infantry', he was appalled to learn that his carriers had been used as tanks at Buna, New Guinea, in December 1942.[42]

A report by the 2/1st Battalion on training exercises involving attacks by infantry upon Universal Carriers and other vehicles in jungle terrain stated that 'one man using his head should be able to account for a section of carriers'.[43] These reports were apparently not heeded, with the result that unnecessary casualties were sustained at Buna. Further experiments included constructing wire-mesh screens to protect the open-topped carriers from hand grenades; these 'proved very strong when being driven through tree foliage'.[44] Like bicycles, such screens do not appear to have been used in action, presumably because after the disastrous attack during the New Guinea Beachhead campaign it was realised that carriers—with or without grenade screens—were not suitable for jungle warfare.

Not all the improvisation and experimentation carried out during the early weeks on Ceylon was wasted. The 2/2nd Battalion built 'improvised floats for the ferrying of gear across streams and rivers.

It was found that an excellent light float could be made from the issue ground sheet.'⁴⁵ Other units also developed various methods of crossing rivers, and the 2/7th Battalion history records that 'these experiments . . . were to be proved in New Guinea'.⁴⁶ The 16th Brigade was also working on river-crossing ideas, especially for heavier weapons such as mortars.⁴⁷ Later training in Australia before its final jungle campaign in 1944–45 would see the division revisit and recapitulate these experiments.

Arguably the most useful training the two brigades did on Ceylon, at least for the infantry units, involved patrolling, contact and ambush drills, and firing practice on miniature ranges. All of these were, of course, standard infantry training practices, but the very different terrain ahead meant they could not be tackled in the same way as at Puckapunyal training camp in Victoria, or in Egypt. Patrolling and dominating no man's land had long been considered crucial in the Australian Army. *Army Training Memorandum No. 11* (June 1942) (*ATM No. 11*) argued that its importance was, in fact, increased with the advent of jungle warfare.⁴⁸ Throughout their time in Ceylon, all units devoted as much time as possible to ensuring that their troops developed confidence in operating in jungle terrain. As the 16th Brigade stated, 'training in close country, movement and fighting have been the main objectives and troops have entered into this training with great interest'.⁴⁹

Despite the often inappropriate training material, some valuable lessons were being learned. A 16th Brigade training report sent to Australia stated that 'in close country and semi-jungle fighting, it is apparent that the fight will be even more a section or group fight. It is suggested therefore, that even more time should be devoted to Sec[tion] tng.'⁵⁰ This lesson would be reinforced continuously in New Guinea, Papua and the islands. Command and control in jungle warfare devolved onto small groups of men and required a high degree of training in contact and ambush drills. The phrase 'one-man front' would be applicable to many of the jungle campaigns the Australians would face over the next three years.[51]

Not formally passed back to Australia was a lesson that eventually became an accepted practice of jungle warfare. This was the need for an increased number of automatic weapons for front-line units that would be involved in close-quarters fighting in the jungle. A sentence crossed out of the 16th Brigade report's first draft notes that 'the following are recommended to increase the firepower ... of the section and group. More automatic weapons, up to even two or three T.S.M.Gs [Thompson Sub-Machine Guns] per section ... for very close country only.'[52] A hand-written note in the margin reads: 'GOC [General Officer Commanding, AIF Ceylon] not in favour'. No reason is given. Still, upon their return to Australia, many of the infantry units tried to follow the example of the 2/1st Battalion and their commanding officer, who 'arranged an exchange with the 2/1st Field Regiment of 43 rifles for 43 Tommy guns. This nearly doubled the firepower of the rifle companies for close in fighting in the jungle.'[53] In September 1942, the higher authorities must have reconsidered their stance, and the number of automatic weapons provided to infantry units in the tropics was increased. Valuable lessons had been learned in Ceylon. Unfortunately, however, there was a delay in grasping them—and in listening to the men who would actually be required to engage in jungle warfare at the unit and sub-unit levels.

To increase realism in training and highlight the need for rapid reactions in close country, several units constructed modified firing ranges near their bases. The 2/7th Battalion noted that 'more movable targets are now under construction for training the Bn to deal with moving targets and Jungle Warfare',[54] while the 2/1st Battalion recorded that:

> [a] 25 yd miniature range was built ... with practice ammo in excellent supply, the troops had more firing of their weapons and practice in tests

of elementary training than the battalion had ever found possible previously. This training proved its worth six months later. [On the Kokoda Track] The Bren gunners excelled at firing from the hip and Tommy gunners also became very proficient.[55]

This training was not the norm, however. The 2/2nd Battalion war diarist noted that 'unorthodox shooting was also carried out, i.e. from the hip, with both rifle and Bren gun'.[56] The standard prone, kneeling, and standing firing positions took too long to adopt in close country. These 'unorthodox' drills would prove valuable in Papua and New Guinea.

Among other adaptations made by the troops on Ceylon was the use of carrier pigeons, which the 16th Brigade presumably adopted in response to problems with its radio and wireless telegraphy sets. Although the unit would not need pigeons in their operations in the South West Pacific islands, other units did use them.[57] Most found that the heat, humidity and thick jungle made radio and wireless communications more unpredictable than in other theatres.

The 2/1st Field Ambulance, attached to the 16th Brigade, also changed its operating procedures in response to the jungle environment. It noted that 'from a tactical point of view, most time was devoted to developing mobile sections' to help expedite the evacuation of casualties.[58] The answer to difficult terrain was to develop more flexible or 'elastic' formations and procedures. One reason the Field Ambulance changed its methods was the recognition that the difficulties of transportation were likely to increase. On Ceylon, the engineers constructed bridges and repaired roads, which left very little time for training exercises in jungle terrain.[59]

Apart from a bland observation that 'the task of the artillery was naturally a restricted one owing to the nature of the country', the 2/1st Australian Field Regiment seems not to have made many changes in training; it spent much of its time on Ceylon digging defensive positions.⁶⁰ As its guns and equipment did not arrive when the men did, perhaps this is understandable. When the unit was eventually able to carry out training, the focus in the relatively short time available was upon overcoming the difficulties of movement in a tropical environment. At the same time, the lack of coordination between the various units' training programs caused the 17th Brigade's commanding officer, Brigadier Moten, to instigate changes.

In an attempt to collate and standardise units' experiments during their first five weeks in Ceylon, two training schools were established. The more important was the 17th Brigade's Jungle Warfare School under the 'auspices of the Brigade Tactical School at Akuressa'.⁶¹ At the same time, a weapons training school was formed at Bussa⁶² to provide NCOs with 'weapon training, unarmed combat, drill, and ... a study of elementary Japanese tactics, as they appeared to be from reports based on operations in Malaya and the N.E.I'. Once the Brigade Tactical School was fully operational, the Weapon Training School would cease to teach the theory of jungle warfare and concentrate on weapons and unarmed-combat training. On the other hand, the Brigade Tactical School was for officer training, and proposed to 'cover tactical training, jungle warfare, and platoon and section leading'. Initially it appeared that the school would only provide instruction in section and platoon training, but its purview later expanded.

A four-page document released on 1 May 1942 noted that the Brigade Tactical School aimed 'to form a common basis throughout the Bde, on which to instruct troops in jungle tactics'.⁶³ This was believed to be necessary as 'recent coy exercises had shown coys enthusiastic but lacking in appreciation of the basic problems involved in jungle warfare'. Two different 'schools' or courses would run at the centre: a junior and senior tactical school. The object of the junior school was 'to set a common standard for sec[tion] and Pl[atoon] tng in jungle warfare'. While the junior officers of the Brigade were attending the three-day course at the School, all tactical training at their parent battalions ceased. The paper also noted that 'when sufficient officers have attended Schools, unit Tactical Training to recommence, with units concentrating solely on section and Pl[atoon] training'. The seven-day course at the Senior Tactical School was to 'teach Senior Officers Coy and Bn and [attached] arms tactics in jungle warfare and beach defence' and also to highlight administrative duties.

Officers who had completed the Tactical School course applied those lessons to future training within their units.[64] Soon, all junior officers of the rifle companies had passed through the three-day course, and on 30 May the junior wing of the Jungle Warfare School closed.[65] As the levels of knowledge and expertise increased, so did the size and scope of the training exercises in which the two brigades participated. This training was put to the test in a brigade exercise carried out in late May, in which the Australians were routed by their Indian opponents.[66] A 2/5th Battalion officer who acted as an observer at this exercise recalled that the Australians had 'been taught a sound lesson about the potential for rapid movement over difficult country, even at night under appalling conditions . . . Later in New Guinea this lesson was well and truly rammed home by the Japanese.'[67]

As a main focus of jungle warfare training was the art of moving rapidly through jungle, the debacle came as a shock to the Australian units. Commenting on the 'defeat' of 17th Brigade in a similar exercise, in early June, Lieutenant-Colonel Cremor, the chief instructor at the Brigade Tactical School, identified problems with leadership, control, initiative and inter-arms cooperation.[68] Interestingly, 'the Senior Offrs and a few Junior Offrs seemed surprised to imagine that anyone could regard them and their [troops] as not being 100 per cent efficient'.[69] These difficulties suggest that, despite Jungle Warfare School training, even combat-experienced units were finding it difficult to adjust to the new challenges posed by fighting in the jungle.

In spite of the continuing problems highlighted in exercises, and the fact that the lessons learned were primarily taken from the Malayan campaign and therefore largely irrelevant to the forthcoming battles, war diaries and personal accounts make clear that the four months spent on Ceylon were valuable to the Australians.[70] George Tarlington, who served with the 16th Brigade on Ceylon and New Guinea, believed that the training they received 'was to stand them in good stead in the New Guinea jungles later on in the year'.[71]

From the first hesitant experiments by individual units of the 16th and 17th Brigades in late March, through to the brigade-level exercises in June, much had been accomplished. Mistakes had been made and irrelevant tactics and methods practised, but in a country where the enemy was not able to punish those mistakes on the battlefield. The two brigades had had time to train and experiment in an environment that shared the heat, humidity, torrential rain and jungle of New Guinea. They had also passed on valuable information to headquarters in Australia for use by units that had not been able to train in a tropical environment. The 16th Brigade, soon to see action on the Kokoda Track, would later record the benefits of their time on Ceylon,[72] while the 17th Brigade would put their training to the test in January 1943 when they joined Kanga Force holding back the Japanese at Wau.

Chapter 4

'PHYSICAL FITNESS IS VITAL': TRAINING IN AUSTRALIA, 1942

The five months between the return of the first AIF units from the Middle East in March 1942 and their initial despatch to Papua in August 1942 were arguably the most critical in Australian history. Ultimately, strategic events outside Australian control—namely the Battles of the Coral Sea and Midway in May and June 1942—would determine the fate of the nation. While these momentous battles were taking place, however, the Australian military was working frantically to prepare defences to meet the expected Japanese invasion, leaving little time or resources for jungle warfare training or doctrine development.

The time spent on troopships returning to Australia was not free of work. For the NCOs and other ranks, cramped conditions restricted training largely to PT, games and small-arms drills,[1] but their officers did actively discuss problems such as the use of artillery in the jungle, the evacuation of casualties, and the occupation of defensive positions at night.[2] At this stage the units appear to have developed solutions based upon assumptions of what jungle warfare would entail, but the officers' suggestions, particularly with regard to the necessity of decentralisation of artillery units, were prescient.[3] A feature of the jungle campaigns would be the use of artillery sub-units, frequently four-gun troops, and at times single guns. This was not standard operating procedure and required improvisation by the units concerned.

In some respects, events on the voyage home were more frustrating than helpful. On the day of departure from the Middle East, the commanders of the 21st Brigade were handed secret documents and maps pertaining to their presumed next area of operations, Java.[4] More than three weeks later, the closest they had come to Java was when two recently evacuated RAF officers briefed the Brigade Commander and CRA on 'Japanese tactics and the general situation [in Java]'.[5] To the frustration of the brigadier, instead of joining Colonel Blackburn and his forces on Java, the 21st Brigade would arrive in Australia with the rest of the division in early March. After examining the available training materials, a member of the 2/10th Battalion stated that 'there was little indeed about jungle fighting in any of the text-books, and that little was quite indefinite', suggesting that the return to Australia was a blessing in disguise.[6]

About a week before the convoy arrived in Australia, Headquarters 7th Division released a four-page training memorandum based on the lessons of Brigadier Stewart, the commander of the Argyll and Sutherland Highlanders. Titled 'Warfare in Thick Country', it directed officers to use 'Operations in Malaya: Dec 41–Feb 42', which had been issued by I Australian Corps on 17 February.[7] Although Stewart's main recommendation, that training in the jungle was the only way to properly prepare for jungle warfare, was retained, the memo was more relevant for countering a Japanese invasion of northern Australia than for combat in Papua or New Guinea. Given the high likelihood of Japanese attack at the time, this is not surprising, but it meant that much of the training 6th and 7th Divisions received before going to Papua was not directly relevant to their forthcoming battles.

The objectives of all the training instructions and memoranda issued at this time were very clear: achievement of 'the highest possible standard of PHYSICAL FITNESS' and development of 'A REAL HATRED OF THE JAP'.[8] To this end the bane of every infantryman, the route march, would form a major component of training.[9] Some believed that the rudimentary river-crossing exercises at Sandy Creek in South Australia were the beginning of lessons for the tropics.[10] The majority of training, however, was firmly focused upon physical hardening and strengthening, combined with exercises designed to help the troops combat a Japanese invasion, using the lessons of the Malayan campaign.[11]

This concentration on the supposed lessons of Malaya meant the units that would soon be fighting the Japanese on the Kokoda Track and at Milne Bay were diligently working to perfect tactics that would be of little use to them.[12] Although the training the units received later, in Queensland, did include basic jungle warfare tactics, an inordinate amount of time continued to be devoted to irrelevant ideas.

Although the entire army was preparing to repel a Japanese invasion, there were differences among units in training ideas and emphasis. A central reason for this was that, 'before the establishment of... Canungra, each brigade and division was responsible for training its soldiers in operational procedures'.[13] I Corps issued directives and training memoranda to 7th Division Headquarters, which transmitted them to units under its command. Implementation, however, was left to individual battalions and regiments, which tended to leave company and platoon commanders considerable latitude in deciding what training areas to stress. This led to a lack of standardisation of techniques and training within the army.[14] What each unit learned also depended to some extent on the officers appointed as trainers.

During training in April, for example, the 2/14th 'Company Exercise' had as its stated objective to 'Exercise all ranks in fighting in close country (special thought to be given to lessons brought out in Jungle Fighting)'.[15] Only days before this, a 2/16th Battalion training instruction stipulated that 'while jungle warfare is to be studied and discussed it is not to form part of this [training] period'.[16] As both units were training in the rolling farmland of the Echunga region south-east of Adelaide, it could be argued that the 2/16th was the more realistic, delaying jungle warfare training until it found itself in terrain that more closely resembled jungle. Soon after these exercises, the 7th Division spent several weeks training in northern New South Wales.

This training period, focused on countering a Japanese invasion of Australia, prioritised the lessons of Malaya, but it was still referred to as 'jungle warfare' and 'jungle [training]'.[17] After experiencing the conditions of Milne Bay, Buna and Sanananda, however, no member of the 2/12th Battalion would ever again mistake the terrain of northern New South Wales for jungle. Bill Spencer, of the 2/9th, recalled that after his unit's sister battalion moved to Queensland for training in the Jimna Ranges, it 'commenced what the army thought was jungle training. Both they and we were in for a huge shock.'[18]

The 2/27th Battalion war diary for much of late April and early May recorded training exercises with artillery units, Bren-gun carriers and motor transport on a reduced scale.[19] Aside from preparing the men for combat in Australia that never eventuated, these exercises highlighted the poor transmission of intelligence from Papua to Australia. Why no one appeared to have obtained information on terrain and weather conditions in the Owen Stanley Ranges or at Milne Bay is hard to understand. Yet doing so would have prevented numerous problems and several wasteful incidents. The 2/12th, for example, arrived at Milne Bay with Bren-gun carriers and trucks, wasted an entire day trying to use them, then put them in storage for the remainder of the campaign.[20] If the suggestion that vehicles operating in jungle should be equipped with 'skid [snow] chains' had been acted upon when it was first brought up in June, some of these problems might have been alleviated.[21] The inability of commanders in Australia to educate themselves on the terrain and conditions in Papua and New Guinea would cause countless more problems in the coming months.

'Long, hard route marches': The 7th Division moves to Queensland

Before this could become an issue, however, the 7th Division continued its gradual move north, crossing the border to training areas near Yandina, Kilcoy and Caloundra in southern Queensland. Training in a region with 'real' jungle appeared to be the next step in the evolution of an Australian jungle warfare doctrine. But despite the best intentions of unit commanders to devote as much time as possible to training in jungle conditions, factors outside their control continued to foil them. As the 16th and 17th Brigades were finding at the same time on Ceylon, the pressing need for defensive and engineering works continuously disrupted training programs.[22] As the 2/27th Battalion history put it: 'unfortunately much valuable training time was lost by the battalion being required to supply working parties on road-making tasks in the Blackall Ranges'.[23] Why the most experienced, well-trained and combat-hardened soldiers in Australia were being used as labourers calls into question the judgement of military authorities. Another distraction was the requirement that units provide companies on a rotational basis for 'coast-watching' duties.[24] To some extent this was of value to the unit—rather than just the authorities who ordered it—as the men in the listening positions were able to practise stalking and moving across jungle-clad coastal terrain. Coast-watching duties were deemed critical at the time because of invasion fears, but those were ended by the events of May and June 1942.

* * *

The Japanese had had one success after another. Unbeknown to Tokyo, however, US intelligence had a priceless advantage—Magic. By early May 1942, this cryptanalysis project allowed the Americans to read approximately 85 per cent of Imperial Japanese Navy (IJN) coded messages, known as JN-25.[25] As a result, Allied commanders knew in advance about Operation MO, the Japanese plan to invade and capture Port Moresby, Papua, and the island of Tulagi, in the Solomons, as a prelude to seizing Guadalcanal. While the arguments about Japanese intentions with regard to an invasion of Australia continue to rage, this series of actions, if successful, would have effectively cut northern Australia off from the US mainland and prevented Darwin—and indeed much of northern Australia—from being used as a base for attacks on Japanese-occupied territories in the South West Pacific.

As soon as Admiral Chester Nimitz, the Hawaii-based commander in chief of the US Pacific Fleet, learned of the Japanese intentions, he ordered Allied naval forces to the Coral Sea to intercept the invasion force. Apart from a handful of Australian soldiers of the 2/1st Independent Company and four PBY Catalina flying boats of No. 11 RAAF Squadron, Tulagi was undefended. Once the size of the invasion force became clear, the Australians evacuated,[26] so on the evening of 3 May the Japanese landed unopposed and immediately began constructing a seaplane base. Carrier-borne aircraft from the USS *Yorktown*, which was sailing south of Guadalcanal, launched air raids on this force but were unable to repel it. The Japanese, now aware that American carriers were in the vicinity, sailed into the Coral Sea in an attempt to sink them and, of course, to cover the Port Moresby invasion force.

The Battle of the Coral Sea, on 6–8 May, was the first naval battle in history in which the vessels of both sides could not see nor fire on each other. The Japanese scored a tactical victory, losing only one light carrier, the *Shoho*, sunk and a fleet carrier, the *Shokaku*, seriously damaged. The Americans lost one of their few large fleet carriers when the

USS *Lexington* had to be scuttled after taking multiple torpedo and bomb hits. The US destroyer *Sims* and fleet tanker *Neosho* were also lost, and the *Yorktown* was seriously damaged, requiring urgent repairs before she could take part in the Battle of Midway a month later.[27] Strategically, however, the battle was an Allied triumph, as it was the first time in World War II that a Japanese amphibious invasion fleet had failed to achieve its objective. Fearing further losses and worried that more American forces were in the area, Japanese Admiral Shigeyoshi Inoue ordered his remaining vessels to return to their bases at Rabaul, on New Britain, and Truk, in the Caroline Islands. In early June the Japanese carrier fleet would be devastated during the Battle of Midway, losing four of its fleet carriers and, just as importantly, hundreds of carrier aircraft and their crews. While these events were occurring, Australian commanders were understandably more concerned about preparing for an invasion than about ensuring that 7th Division received satisfactory training for planned future operations in New Guinea.

By early June, however, all the 7th Division units had moved to Queensland and were devoting as much time as possible to training. The issue of General Bennett's *ATM No. 10* in June, and of 'First Army Training Instruction No. 3: Jungle Warfare' in late May, set the basis for future training.[28] Some units had also received US Army Colonel Francis Brink's *Tactical Methods*, but they appear to have been in the minority.[29] The various *Army Training* memoranda, particularly Bennett's, were more widely used. The unit history of the 2/14th Battalion notes that the Bennett document was 'studied exhaustively', while the 2/27th explained that:[30]

> A careful study had been made by all ranks of all available information on the fighting in Malaya. A training pamphlet based on the experiences

of the 8th Division had been studied and practised and a most useful and instructive report of the operations of a battalion of the Argyll and Sutherland Highlanders in Malaya had also been available.[31]

Large-scale exercises throughout June and July continued to focus on perfecting the lessons of Malaya: 'protection [of motor transport convoys] on the move', 'defence by mobile [columns]' and the destruction of 'rd-blocking parties which may have infiltrated to our rear'.[32] As Lieutenant-General Rowell would later write, 'the training was solid and realistic for our task of operating in relatively open country ... what was lacking, of course, was work in the jungle conditions that were to follow'.[33] This startling admission again calls into question the competence of the Australian Army High Command: clearly, the only way to prepare to fight in jungle conditions is to train in the jungle.

Even in the far from jungle-clad Blackall Mountains, the areas around Hazeldean and Jimna, and near Coolum and Noosa on the coast, some useful drills and practices were developed. As with the two 6th Division brigades on Ceylon, during mid-May the 2/14th and 2/27th Battalions were training their soldiers in firing the 'Bren and [Thompson sub-machine gun] from hip', with the 2/27th describing it as 'jungle snapshooting'.[34] For most units, however, this was the exception, and most firing-range practices were at the prescribed distances of 100 to 400 yards. Standard small-arms drills from the relevant *Military Training* pamphlets and the *Infantry Training* manual of 1937 dominated training courses throughout this period.[35] This suggests that many commanders thought soldiers battle-hardened from the Mediterranean theatre would not need to modify their training very much to defeat the Japanese in New Guinea.[36] Nevertheless, some were concerned about the lack of specific jungle knowledge. In late May 1942, for example, I Corps sent a signal 'asking 7 Aust Div to forward views and suggestions for modified war [equipment] tables etc suitable for tropical warfare'.[37]

Like their counterparts on Ceylon, the units in southern Queensland also devised their own experiments to solve the potential problems of jungle warfare. The 25th Brigade memo 'Experiments in Jungle Warfare' addressed such topics as uniforms, gaiters, horses and the attachment of Bren guns to trees.[38] At least one of its battalions, the 2/25th, appointed an officer as 'OC Jungle Warfare Experiments'.[39] During patrol exercises in the forests and swamps of the region, officers and NCOs evaluated the type and amount of equipment and ammunition carried by the men, and the most appropriate rations.[40] Several patrol reports stated that the standard rations of bully beef and biscuits should be replaced, or at least augmented, by rice, which was lighter to carry and provided more energy.[41] These reports were then collated and forwarded to brigade and division headquarters, though the rice idea was not taken up. Both the 18th and 21st Brigades would carry the same rations in Papua as they had in Syria. When the 25th Brigade joined its sister units in Papua in late September 1942, its quartermaster, Captain Ernest Owens, noted that 'it is considered that the addition of rice to the [troops'] ration would be an excellent idea'.[42] It was to no avail. Once again, the refusal by higher command to act on the suggestions of the men on the ground would cause unnecessary problems when combat was joined.

The southern Queensland patrols were regarded as among the most important training conducted during this period because of the insights they offered into problems the men were likely to face in Papua. The unit histories almost uniformly agree with the statement by the historian of the 2/10th Battalion that 'here [Kilcoy and environs] it was possible at last to commence some true jungle training; training that was to prove invaluable within a matter of weeks'.[43] Not all the men agreed, however. Lindsay Mason, of the 2/14th, was convinced that the training he received in Australia was 'Alright for the desert. Alright for Syria . . . but definitely not on the Owen Stanley Ranges.'[44]

Others were even more adamant that training in southern Queensland was not an adequate substitute for the real thing. As Bill Spencer would later write:

> Queensland could not prepare us for the ravages of malaria, hookworm and scrub typhus; it could not prepare us for the humid, clinging heat and torrential tropical downpours; it could not teach us that our equipment and weapons (so applicable in the desert) were heavy and energy-sapping in the jungle ... I don't think it dawned on us that we had been fighting a European-style war, with European-style equipment and tactics against European foes, and that we were about to embark on an Asian war, where the conditions, weapons and tactics and the enemy were unique.[45]

If the men were not convinced that the training they were undertaking was of much value, their officers were very concerned that they 'weren't being given the chance to adjust to real jungle conditions in New Guinea'.[46]

After a large-scale jungle warfare training exercise in late June, a scathing report by the 21st Brigade major highlighted problems with everything from the employment of artillery and cavalry units to communications, command and control, and tactical appreciation and leadership.[47] Some of these related to the Malayan-style combat envisaged by Bennett's *ATM No. 10*: fighting a motorised infantry column along a road surrounded by thick forest. Others, however, would continue to be issues throughout the Australian Army's service in the South West Pacific. The most important of these revolved around command, control and communications.[48]

Radio communications, particularly with the army-issue 108 set, were a regular problem.[49] In Papua it would only become worse when torrential rain was added to thick jungle and mountainous terrain. As the 108 set had been identified as a problem in the mountains of

Syria, during the 7th Division's campaign a year earlier, it is surprising that no suitable replacement had been found.[50] At least one unit became so frustrated with the standard of wireless equipment issued to it that 'commercial wireless sets [were] purchased from Battalion welfare funds [and] issued to companies'.[51] The 108 Mk II was an improvement on the Mk I, but was still not adequate for the conditions in Papua. The normal fallback options, such as signal flags or heliograph, which had been viable in Syria, would be of little use in the jungle, where line of sight was almost impossible to achieve. US-manufactured 'walkie-talkies' would eventually help alleviate the communications problems, but they were not issued until the 7th and 9th Division campaigns of 1943–44.

Just as important were the problems related to tactical control and the employment of the various supporting arms. None of these would be adequately solved before the troops left for New Guinea, and all would have ramifications during the forthcoming campaigns. As the brigade major's report put it: 'the problem of control proved to be one that caused considerable worry from the CO down to the [second in command] . . . This subject of control in close country is one that will have to be tackled much further.'[52] Company commanders became frustrated with the difficulty of observing and therefore directing their platoons during the exercise, and platoon commanders experienced similar problems with regard to their sections.

The report did suggest one change in the way units were led in the field, arguing that 'a [company commander] cannot control his [company] from the rear and must be well up fwd the whole time.'[53] The 25th Brigade—using information supplied by the 18th Brigade after their operations at Milne Bay—drew up a series of diagrams of formations that placed the company and battalion commanders much further forward than had been the case in the desert.[54] This was not a new approach but a reversion to pre-war tactical doctrine. In another reversion to pre-war tactics, the 25th Brigade suggested a change to patrol formations 'for movement in close country when contact with the enemy is likely'.[55] The new formation, which placed one section forward and kept two in the rear, otherwise known as 'one up, two back', was a logical adaptation to terrain where contact could occur at any time, and from any direction.[56] It allowed a commander to manoeuvre the bulk of his forces to support the section—or platoon—that had initiated contact, and allowed for more covering fire if a withdrawal was necessary.

For many members of the 2nd AIF who had served in the Middle East, however, these changes required an adjustment to tactics they had become accustomed to using in combat. While a minority of the 2nd AIF had pre-war militia experience, even those who did were unlikely to have adequate knowledge of different patrol or assault formations and the conditions or terrain in which they should be applied. Still, some units had begun to adapt to the new problems posed by jungle conditions, as a 25th Brigade training instruction from 22 June 1942 makes clear. Among the points highlighted were that 'the CO must be well fwd to control the movement of fwd [companies]' and that 'action by [troops] when the enemy is contacted in close country must be immediate—it will all be close quarter work—shooting from the hip—bayonet'.[57] As discussed in Chapter 2, this second lesson had been identified by Lieutenant-Colonel Stewart before the outbreak of the Pacific War and would eventually lead to 'battle drills'—automatic manoeuvres enacted upon contact by infantry units.[58] The Australians training in Malaya and on Ceylon had also identified the need to react instantaneously at the extremely close ranges found in the jungle.

On three separate occasions, over the course of eighteen months, units independently developed training and weapons drills specific to jungle warfare conditions. Yet this information was clearly not transmitted between divisions, nor more broadly across the army. In 1941, for example, the first time the 22nd Brigade of 8th Division developed close-quarter combat drills, the details—included in the copies of unit war diaries sent to LHQ in Melbourne before 7 December 1941—should have been collected by a central training agency. If this had happened, a training syllabus and list of lessons learned would have been available to the 6th Division on Ceylon and the 7th Division in Queensland as soon as they began their jungle warfare training, saving much time and effort. The devolution of training responsibility to divisions and down to unit level worked against the creation of a collective body of knowledge related to training matters, whether jungle warfare or otherwise. The wealth of reports that appeared in early 1943, after the first Papuan campaigns, would give greater impetus to efforts by the DMT to standardise jungle warfare training methods across the Australian Army.

'A new type of warfare': Can artillery be employed in the jungle?

The role and employment of the supporting arms in jungle warfare conditions also raised concerns. Using artillery, traditionally the most important means of supporting the infantry, proved extremely challenging. That the use of field artillery in the jungle would be problematic appears to have been decided before the 21st Brigade's late-June exercise began. One of the questions in the 'General Notes' issued before the exercise asks 'can the unit comd use his fd arty?'[59] The results of the exercise presumably supported these doubts. As the 21st Brigade major stated with reference to the artillery, 'tasks were few and of very doubtful value. Considering the results achieved against the amount of protection the guns needed, Arty were a doubtful asset.'[60] Beliefs such as this almost certainly contributed to the view that artillery was too difficult to use in jungle warfare. A few months later, the terrain of the Owen Stanley Range would appear to confirm this belief. As a consequence, only single guns or, at times, four-gun troops were used in the fighting at Milne Bay and the beachheads. While it is correct that logistical problems in transporting and supplying the guns in forward areas would provide great challenges, the parsimonious use of artillery during these battles made the tasks of the infantry more difficult—and costly—than would otherwise have been the case.

Whether or not similar views to that of the 21st Brigade major were to blame, the artillery units training in Australia were largely overlooked when preparations began for the move to Papua.[61] Several artillery regiments, in the course of their training exercises in southern Queensland, had begun to realise that they would need to operate very differently from the way they had done in the Middle East. After an exercise with a militia infantry battalion in late June, the 2/4th Field Regiment recorded that the 'danger of infiltration was forcibly demonstrated. Also difficulty of fighting guns in close country because of no observation.'[62] Perhaps as a result of such reports, senior commanders appear to have concluded that deploying artillery in a tropical environment was too difficult.

Many artillery regiments were deployed as fortress or static coastal defence units in southern Queensland in mid to late 1942, and some remained in defensive positions in Queensland for many months or even years.[63] While serving in these areas in 1942–43, unit members were able to participate in rudimentary jungle warfare training exercises.[64] One artillery regiment officer recalled that 'we used to think it was jungle training but ... it was just a joke compared to what we really found when we went to New Guinea'.[65] (It should be noted that before the New Guinea operations of 1943–44 and the 1945 Bougainville and Borneo operations, all units undertook far more extensive jungle warfare training than before the 1942 Papua campaigns.) As with the infantry units, the equipment issued to artillery regiments changed little: 'We still used our desert clothes,'[66] for example. It was not until they arrived in Papua that the transition to jungle-green uniforms and webbing occurred.

The second problem identified in the 21st Brigade's training-exercise report concerned the cavalry units and more particularly the use of Bren-gun carriers by any unit, cavalry or infantry. The cavalry's role as the 'eyes and ears' of the infantry battalions was greatly hindered by the thickly forested terrain. The report noted that 'it became very evident early in the exercise that cav were at a considerable disadvantage in the type of country encountered' and most were quickly knocked out by infantry or anti-tank guns.[67] This finding supports the conclusion reached by the 6th Division units training at the same time on Ceylon. A 25th Brigade Training Instruction issued only a week before the report stated that 'in close country the advisability of using carriers is doubtful. They are noisy, easily stalked and destroyed.'[68] There was little room for conjecture; all experiments had shown that Bren-gun carriers used in thickly forested or jungle terrain could not survive.[69] The carriers were designed to bear weapons and ammunition in support of infantry attacks over open countryside, where their chief assets were their speed and manoeuvrability.[70] Both these attributes were negated in the jungle. The carriers were not designed as substitutes for tanks or even armoured cars, as they were inadequately armoured for that task. Their eventual use, and the subsequent slaughter of their crews at Buna in December 1942, demonstrates a callous disregard for those crews and a distinct failure to digest lessons clearly brought out in training and highlighted on numerous occasions by the units who would have to carry out orders against their better judgement.

The director of the exercise concluded that engineers were 'essential and they must be well up' near the head of the column so that any demolition or construction work could be done rapidly.[71] Although this is arguably true of any operation over any ground, in no terrain would it become more important than in the jungles and tropical rainforests of the South West Pacific. The frequency with which rivers and streams had to be forded and Japanese booby-traps and bunkers

Men of 6th Division training in the deserts of North Africa in 1940. The widely dispersed formations are a precaution against attack, but these tactics would need to change completely in the jungle. (AWM 003397)

The 6th Division charging through the ruins of the Italian fortress town of Bardia, 3 January 1941. The light uniforms blend perfectly with a Mediterranean environment. (AWM 006083)

Troops of 2/21st Battalion training at Darley Camp, Bacchus Marsh, Victoria. Their uniforms, webbing and equipment are little changed from those used in the Great War. (AWM 009133)

Malaya, May 1941. Men of 22nd Brigade, 8th Division, training in thick jungle. They are wearing the same uniforms as their comrades in the Middle East. (AWM 007179)

Well-camouflaged Japanese troops fording a stream during the Malayan campaign, January 1942. The contrast with the Australian troops is obvious. (AWM 127898)

Despatch riders from an 8th Division signals unit crossing a river in Malaya. Operations in the tropics made life immeasurably more difficult for all units. (AWM 011269)

Milne Bay, October 1942. The desert uniforms and the lack of anti-malarial precautions used by Australian troops is evident in this photograph. (AWM 013335)

For the men of 18th Brigade, 7th Division, the terrain around Milne Bay was completely different to that of their last campaign, the defence of Tobruk in North Africa. (AWM 013317)

For pioneers and engineers, bridge building was a regular feature of the jungle campaigns, often under appalling conditions. (AWM 013598)

Approaching Buna in late 1942, Australian troops cross one of the many improvised bridges constructed by the engineers. (AWM 013756)

Wounded members of 39th Battalion marching south towards base hospitals near Port Moresby. It was a long and arduous trip for the fit and healthy but an incredible test of endurance for the wounded. (AWM 026320)

Japanese Type 95 HA-GO light tanks, bogged at Milne Bay. Although this was an inauspicious beginning, tanks would prove invaluable in all the later Australian jungle campaigns. (AWM 026632)

Australian soldiers cutting down trees to enable a 25-pounder field gun to be manhandled forward to Imita Ridge, where it will fire on the Japanese. (AWM P02424.004)

The number of men and amount of effort required to move one 25-pounder was enormous. It is scenes such as this that saw some in higher authority question the usefulness of artillery in the jungle. (AWM 026851)

Stuart M3 light tanks firing on well-concealed Japanese bunkers while infantrymen of 2/12th Battalion, 7th Division, mop up the Japanese survivors. (AWM 014005)

In November 1942, Australian soldiers drag themselves through the thick mud of the Kokoda Track as they near Buna. A Japanese bicycle lies discarded in the foreground. (AWM 013620)

blown up made engineers indispensable. The close cooperation of infantry, tanks, engineers and artillery that became a feature of the later campaigns arguably had its genesis in exercises such as this.

The majority of engineer field companies were unable to devote enough time to training in jungle conditions, as they were required for road and bridge-building tasks throughout southern Queensland during this period.[72] The 2/6th Field Company, Royal Australian Engineers, which would in September become the first engineer unit working on the Kokoda Track, spent May, June and July on road works, with occasional breaks for anti-invasion exercises—none of which were useful preparation for New Guinea.[73] The engineers were at least trying to obtain information on the Japanese and the possible role of engineers in jungle operations. After receiving yet another report on engineers in the Middle East, the unit plaintively stated that 'any information regarding the operation of 8 Div Engrs in Malaya would be welcomed'.[74]

The lack of any useful information based on the experiences of engineers and pioneers in the Malayan campaign, almost six months after it ended, again suggests that the military was struggling to come to terms with a new paradigm. As General Bennett's 49-page report only devoted a page and a half to engineer issues, and as the January and February 1942 unit war diaries were lost during the retreat to Singapore, perhaps it is not surprising that little information was forthcoming.[75] The 2/4th Field Company, soon to be toiling in the horrendous conditions at Milne Bay, like the 2/6th Field Company, spent the months before it deployed on tasks that provided little useful preparation for the challenges ahead.[76] Despite this lack of direction from above, the units themselves were trying to predict the challenges of a tropical environment. The 18th Brigade, in a prescient report, stated that 'in jungle warfare the necessity of members of [the pioneer platoon] being detailed to [forward companies] during any advance cannot be over stressed'.[77]

Although by mid-1942 some units believed their training was serving as more realistic preparation for Papua and New Guinea, the content of their training programs suggests otherwise. It seems that the Australian government, along with General MacArthur and the CGS, were unwilling to commit too many forces to Papua until after the clear defeat of the Japanese fleet at Midway on 6 June 1942.[78] As a consequence, the Australian I Corps and 7th Division were unable to concentrate wholly on jungle warfare training. Instead, they continued with exercises in mobile defence, movement with reduced—but still some—transport, and hardening up in the forests of southern Queensland.

The Australian Army was clearly preparing for the sort of war it had already experienced and therefore knew how to fight. As the US General John Galvin argued, 'we tend to invent for ourselves a comfortable vision of war, a theatre with battlefields we know, conflict that fits our understanding of strategy and tactics, a combat environment that is consistent and predictable, fightable with the resources we have'.[79] It would take the vicious battles at Milne Bay and Kokoda to jolt the Australian Army out of that familiar vision of the conflict ahead.

Nevertheless, attempts at increasing the training and experience of all units throughout Australia continued. Detachments of militia personnel were fostered in to regular units, and training cadres were posted temporarily to other militia units. The 2/14th Battalion recorded that nearly 60 members of the 24th Battalion trained with the unit for the majority of July.[80] These attempts to improve the standard of the militia also saw many AIF officers and NCOs transferred to new units. But although such measures were necessary to improve the standard, experience and training of the militia, they would have a detrimental effect upon the units, which lost many experienced soldiers.[81] Brigadier Ken Eather, commanding officer of the 25th Infantry Brigade, 'became deeply worried that the numbers were too great and that the fighting capacity of his command was being markedly reduced'.[82] At a time when the AIF was grappling with the new paradigm of jungle warfare, it is arguable that the policy should have been delayed until the immediate threat to Australia had been removed.

In the weeks before the 18th and 21st Brigades left for Papua, a more systematised approach to jungle warfare training was being inaugurated. This would arrive too late for the majority of the 7th Division and was most likely directed at the commanders of militia and US units. After viewing a III Corps exercise in Western Australia in mid-July that was 'apparently aimed at teaching Japanese tactics and methods', General Blamey secured the services of the organising officer, Lieutenant-Colonel John Wolfenden.[83] He was to 'pass on these lessons and teach those methods to formations in First and Second Armies'.[84] However, Wolfenden had no experience of jungle warfare, and according to the 2/6th Field Regiment, his 'remarks were based upon notes supplied by Gen Gordon Bennett'.[85] These notes included Bennett's report on the Malayan campaign and his *ATM No. 10*. Once again the Australian Army would be practising the lessons of Malaya.

In late August, the 25th Brigade conducted an exercise in the countryside near Caboolture, Queensland, which was viewed by over 300 officers. The demonstrations included 'mobile defence' and 'advance against minor opposition'.[86] The report stated that the viewing difficulties created by the 'thickly timbered' terrain were overcome and 'the exercises successfully carried out'.[87] The exercise may have been successful from Wolfenden's perspective, in that it demonstrated how to counter the types of tactics the Japanese had used on the roads of Malaya. However, in no way was it useful in terms of preparing the observers and participants for combat in the swamps and mountains of Papua and New Guinea.[88] Despite Wolfenden and his team's lack of jungle warfare experience, a month later he would lecture the recently returned 17th Brigade 'on infantry tactics in jungle country'.[89]

For those units of the 7th Division soon to embark for Papua, the last few weeks of training were spent much as the previous months had been. Battalion exercises—based upon *ATM Nos 9* and *10*—with supporting arms continued, as did patrolling and close-quarters combat drills on the range.[90] A standard feature of the war in the Middle East, patrolling at night—at which the Australians were particularly adept—was conducted regularly.[91] At least one night a week, and often several, was devoted to all-night exercises. Once the 7th Division engaged the Japanese in Papua, however, it was quickly discovered that movement at night was far more difficult than in the desert. Most units banned movement both inside and outside their perimeters after dark, and night patrols were rarely conducted. As George Connor, a member of 2/33rd Battalion, stated: 'you couldn't see anywhere... and they could have crept up on you anywhere. So we put in a rule at night—anybody that walked got shot... you never got up, because we didn't know if the Japs came in.'[92] A higher standard of intelligence work and some simple local knowledge would have allowed the army to better align its training with the conditions in which they were soon to operate. Learning on the job is expected in many fields, but for an army it comes at a very high price, usually paid with men's lives.

Information on experiments conducted by the units continued to be forwarded to 7th Division HQ and onwards to Corps and Army HQ, to no apparent effect. The 2/10th Battalion reported that 'training during the month was carried out in jungle country, and naturally this played havoc with the troops [Khaki Drill] trousers, shirts and shorts'.[93] Within days of their arrival at Milne Bay, the harsh conditions and torrential rain had accelerated the deterioration of their sun-bleached desert uniforms. The need for uniforms made of stronger material or an increase in the issue to each soldier was clear. The statement above by the 2/10th Battalion's quartermaster suggests that this information should have been known before deployment. That it was not underscores the army's lack of understanding of the problems its units would face in jungle warfare.

Discussions on 'whether gaiters are considered essential' in jungle conditions further highlighted the command's lack of knowledge of the new battle area.[94] A week later, a letter from the 18th Brigade to 7th Division stated that gaiters were essential and that 'the ordinary issue type US Army Legging is the type required'.[95] In a handwritten comment in the margin, the brigade commander, Brigadier George Wootten, noted that 'the cloth SD uniform tears too easily and will not stand up to the wear and tear of bush fighting'.[96] Clearly, the men who would bear the brunt of the jungle conditions had begun to identify problem areas, but higher command and the administration were still unable to provide tactical or equipment solutions. The 18th Brigade would find soon after their arrival in Papua that much of their equipment was 'quite inadequate in the boggy swamps and swollen creeks of Milne Bay'.[97]

About half of 21st Brigade would receive US-issue gaiters before marching forward to Kokoda,[98] but they would still be wearing their pale khaki shirts and shorts, wholly inappropriate to the dark-green jungles of Papua. It was almost a year since Lieutenant-Colonel Geoffrey Youl, commander of the 2/40th Battalion on Timor, had recommended that units serving in the jungle adopt camouflage uniforms. The 7th Division Headquarters clearly agreed with this view. One of its final reports, containing information based on experiments by 25th Brigade, noted that 'it is strongly recommended that where [troops] are liable to operate in jungle country, clothing be dyed a green colour (similar to that used by Dutch troops)'.[99] One who did not believe in the need for such uniforms was the commander in chief of the Australian Army, General Thomas Blamey. Asked by war correspondent Chester Wilmot, in a stormy press conference in September 1942, if camouflaged uniforms were necessary, Blamey said 'khaki had been designed in India as the ideal camouflage for the jungle; and that he had no evidence that this jungle was different from that in India'.[100] The units therefore deployed in the same uniforms they had worn at Tobruk and in Syria.

In the days before their departure, the 18th and 21st Brigades continued training and made preparations to sail. Amendments to the units' war establishment continued until the day they embarked. On 30 August the 2/25th Battalion received an issue of 42 Thompson sub-machine guns, doubling the number previously held.[101] At the same time the infantry battalions of the recently returned 16th Brigade, 6th Division, were also being issued with a further 42 Thompson sub-machine guns.[102] This suggests that at least one of the lessons of jungle training evident in both southern Queensland and Ceylon—that in close-quarters combat a higher ratio of automatic weapons was essential—had been accepted by Army Headquarters. Although this marginal increase in automatic weapons would not have a marked effect during these campaigns, by the following year the number of automatic weapons issued to front-line units would increase substantially.

Only days before they boarded ship, the 2/14th Battalion received *ATM No. 11*, which listed more lessons of Malaya; it was to be 'thoroughly read by all [officers] and principles applied to future [training]'.[103] The fifteen-page appendix, 'Operations in Malaya Dec 41–Feb 42', was a reprise of Bennett's and Stewart's reports.[104] The fixation on Malaya showed no signs of abating. Yet most members of the 7th Division appear to have believed that their training would prepare them well for the coming fight. The statement by the 2/16th Battalion's historian that 'the men were certainly tough and in some measure prepared, but later actual jungle fighting exposed weaknesses in equipment in supply and in methods' was closer to the truth.[105]

In the six months since their return from the Middle East, the AIF soldiers had done very little useful training. Fitness and hardening-up exercises, combined with anti-invasion exercises, had dominated.

As a result, they were physically fit but still poorly prepared for the challenges of Kokoda, Milne Bay and the beachheads.[106] The men had studied and practised the lessons of those who had fought in Malaya, the Philippines and the Netherlands East Indies. They had pored over the training manuals of Bennett, Stewart and Brink, and conducted numerous exercises based upon those works. They had made experiments in terrain that they believed was similar to that in Papua and New Guinea. But the commanding officers had not had sufficient time to devote to training in between the obligatory road-making parties and coast-watching duties.

Responsibility for the troops' poor preparedness must be borne by Land Headquarters in Melbourne and New Guinea Force Headquarters in Port Moresby. From March to July 1942, no member of the 7th Division had the opportunity to see first-hand the conditions the division would soon face. As a result, it had no well-grounded understanding of what jungle warfare in Papua would entail. Even the suggestions made by many units, concerning changes in equipment, uniforms, weapons, rations and doctrine, had not been implemented. The overriding belief, from high command to sub-unit level, was that significant changes were unnecessary. Within days of arriving in Papua, the 18th and 21st Brigades would alter this presumption and the development of an Australian jungle warfare doctrine would begin in earnest.

Chapter 5

'JESUS CHRIST! I CAN'T SEE ANYTHING': MILNE BAY AND KOKODA

In early August 1942, two of the campaigns that would decide the war in the Pacific began. One would be an American affair, while the other would involve predominantly Australian forces. Both would last for six months, and their outcome would be victory for the Allies—a victory that made the eventual defeat of Japan a certainty. The Guadalcanal and Kokoda campaigns call up images of troops slogging through knee-deep mud amid swarms of malarial mosquitoes; of clinging, stinking jungle; of enervating heat and tropical rashes; of a deadly enemy lurking unseen; and of waves of Japanese soldiers charging headlong at Allied positions. In August 1942, 'jungle warfare' was a concept that Australian and American soldiers had yet to come to terms with; by February 1943, the Diggers, in particular, were well on their way to mastering it. When the two major units that fought these campaigns, the 7th Australian Division and the US 1st Marine Division, next went into action, in September and December 1943 respectively, they were supremely well-trained and battle-hardened formations, skilled in the arts of jungle warfare.

In August 1942, however, all that was in the future. On 7 August, the 1st Marine Division began landing on the islands of Guadalcanal, Tulagi and Florida, in the eastern Solomon Islands. Having been spread around the Pacific to such locations as Pearl Harbor, British Samoa, New Caledonia and New Zealand, the Marines had had no opportunity to train as a division or prepare to meet the new challenges posed by jungle warfare. In late July they departed New Zealand for the Solomons. While a handful of the division were old 'China hands', the vast majority had never seen combat.[1] The initiation for those who landed on Tulagi and Florida would be shocking and brutal, with the Japanese troops on those islands fighting to the death. The Australians of 7th Division at least had the advantage of combat experience in the Syrian campaign. The bulk of the Marines, 11,000 men, had a considerably easier time on Guadalcanal—at least initially. At sea, the Battle of Savo Island (8–9 August) was a disaster for the Allies, and on land the Japanese soon recovered their composure and rapidly despatched a force from Rabaul, on New Britain, to retake Guadalcanal. Once these forces had landed on Guadalcanal in mid-August, the now outnumbered Marines had a real fight on their hands. At the same time, less than 1000 kilometres to the west, Australian forces were also preparing to fight the Japanese for the first time.

On 12 August 1942, the troopships carrying the 18th and 21st Australian Infantry Brigades to Milne Bay and Port Moresby arrived at their respective docks.[2] After months spent training and manning defences in Australia, many of the troops were looking forward to meeting—and defeating—the much-vaunted Japanese. The historian of the South Australian 2/27th Battalion would later write that his unit was 'at full strength, fit and ready for action. It felt confident of its ability to fight in jungle country, and to master a new type of warfare'; while Queenslander Ronald Hansen, of the 2/9th Battalion, recalled that his comrades 'thought they'd [the Japanese] be a pushover'.[3]

While they were extremely fit, well trained and battle-hardened, however, the Australians had little real understanding of the challenges, or the enemy, that lay ahead. Lessons that could and should have been learned beforehand would have to be assimilated and applied in battle. Units would be thrown hurriedly into combat as soon as they arrived in theatre, with little time for acclimatisation or reconnaissance. Until the retreat to Imita Ridge, the Japanese would hold the tactical initiative, with the Australians reacting awkwardly to both their enemy and the terrain.[4] Modification to infantry tactics that had brought success in the Middle East was imperative, yet it was slow to occur. Hundreds of unnecessary casualties were the predictable result. Nevertheless, the six months of merciless fighting that followed ultimately laid the groundwork for the first realistic jungle warfare training manuals and would see the establishment of the LHQ Training Centre (Jungle Warfare), Canungra.

'Tyros in jungle fighting': Port Moresby, August 1942

For the men of the 21st Brigade's 2/14th and 2/16th Battalions, disembarking at Port Moresby, none of this could be foreseen. The disorganisation that had characterised the earlier arrival of each of the three militia battalions of the 30th Brigade stationed in Port Moresby had improved in the months since.[5] What had not improved was the lack of information available to the commanders of the 21st Brigade about the terrain over which the Japanese were advancing, in particular the Kokoda Track. This was despite the fact that LHQ in Melbourne had up-to-date information collected by militia units already in Port Moresby.[6] Further, as historian Hank Nelson put it, the 'Kokoda Track—for 40 years a mail run—was one of the best known tracks in Papua'.[7] Numerous government officials, postal workers, officers of the Australian New Guinea Administrative Unit (ANGAU), expatriate planters, and the natives themselves could have provided detailed information about the conditions on the Track. The failure to provide the units on the ground with all the available information was yet another symptom of the Australian military's struggle to grapple with new circumstances in an unfamiliar environment.

The 21st Brigade's Brigadier Arnold Potts insisted on moving his units to Itiki, several kilometres inland and at a higher elevation than the town, to reduce the risk of malaria. The brigade had also been issued with quinine tablets as a precaution against malaria problems at Port Moresby. While this suggests that the military had learned from the disastrous delay in issuing quinine to the militia units—the 30th Brigade at Port Moresby and the 7th Brigade at Milne Bay— the move to Itiki rendered it largely superfluous. As Regimental Medical Office Henry Steward would later write, 'the space they [the quinine tablets] occupied in my pack could have at least been shared by sulphaguanidine [a treatment for intestinal infections], salt and vitamin B tablets'.[8] At Milne Bay and the beachheads—all heavily malarious areas—the troops had little or no protection against the disease.

With the air supply of military forces in its infancy, the main focus of the 21st Brigade was on what they could and could not carry. The three days at Itiki were therefore spent in 'urgent preparation for battle'. The 2/14th war diary noted that 'each Coy was asked to supply one man fully [equipped] to demonstrate what they considered to be the best and most comfortable method of carrying'.[9] Eventually the entire 21st Brigade would adopt the design of the 2/16th Battalion, but at this stage each battalion arrived at a solution independently. Two of the first items to be left behind—owing, it was argued, to their weight and the difficulty of resupply—were the support weapons the battalions would desperately require once the fighting began: 3-inch mortars and Vickers MMGs.[10]

While there is some virtue in the argument that these weapons were too heavy and awkward to be of use in jungle warfare, it is clear that traditional tactical thinking played a major part in the decision to leave them at Port Moresby. After a reconnaissance flight over the Kokoda area in late July 1942, Captain M.L. Bidstrup, of the 39th Militia Battalion, discovered that higher authority had preconceived ideas of jungle terrain. As Bidstrup was about to march over the track to rejoin his unit on 29 July, he was approached by New Guinea Force Commander General Basil Morris, who asked about the flight. When Bidstrup said he believed mortars could be used, Morris yelled, 'Rot, boy! Bloody rot! The mortars would burst in the tree tops!'[11] This view clearly filtered through to the 21st Brigade when it arrived less than two weeks later. Robert Iskov, a mortarman serving with the 2/14th Battalion, recalled being told that the 'mortars would not be of much use because of the terrain and the fact that you wouldn't get many opportunities for fire because of the overhead cover'.[12]

On the day the exchange between Morris and Bidstrup took place, the Japanese were bombarding the 39th Battalion's positions at Kokoda with mountain guns and mortars.[13] Clearly no one had told the Japanese that heavy support weapons could not be used in jungle warfare. Whether this information had been relayed to New Guinea Force Headquarters in Port Moresby is unclear, but the 39th Battalion war diary for the period repeatedly lists the types of weapons the Japanese were using. This means that New Guinea Force HQ *should* have had this information available to pass on to the 21st Brigade two weeks later when it was preparing to advance in support of the 39th. If Colonel Potts had known that the Japanese were using mortars, heavy machine guns and mountain guns, it is inconceivable that he would have left Port Moresby without a reasonable proportion of his own support weapons. Further, the fact that the Japanese had successfully used mortars and heavy machine guns eight months earlier in the jungles of Malaya, the Netherlands East Indies and the Philippines does not appear to have been taken into consideration by planners before the Kokoda operations. Nor does there appear to have been an understanding that Japanese doctrine stressed the need for a preponderance of mortars so that they 'could dominate the battlefield during close-quarters fighting between infantry units'.[14]

As well as mortars and small artillery pieces, the Japanese also used their large numbers of heavy and medium machine guns to keep the militiamen pinned down in their defensive positions, so that an assaulting force could advance with less opposition. Clearly, the Japanese did not believe these weapons were impossible to deploy in the jungle.[15] Militating against their employment by the Australians—either the militia or later the AIF—was the longstanding view that machine guns, and to an extent mortars, needed a clear field of fire so the fall of shot could be observed and fire adjusted onto the targets.[16] The lack of this in thick jungle seemed to support the idea that these weapons would be of little value in Papua and New Guinea.

With both 3-inch mortars and MMGs having been used by the 21st Brigade in Syria where line of sight was rarely a problem, it is understandable that these units did not argue vigorously for their retention once they saw the thickness of the jungle they were soon to enter. However, what the Japanese realised—and some Australian commanders clearly did not—was that 'suppressive area fire' could be just as effective as pinpoint direct fire on a distant position.[17] The sheer weight of fire that MMGs such as the Vickers or the Japanese Juki or Woodpecker could lay down on an enemy position was arguably more devastating in close-quarters jungle combat, where it was difficult to identify exactly where that fire was coming from or to respond adequately. The weight of these weapons—more than 30 kilograms each—also appears to have persuaded some commanders that it would be too difficult to move them forward. Eventually, however, the value of MMGs would be recognised and jungle warfare training manuals would state that 'in tropical warfare, the medium machine gun can be used to full advantage in supporting the infantry with a concentrated volume of sustained accurate fire'.[18]

For the time being the 21st Brigade had to make do with the weapons it was felt the men could comfortably carry. The order to leave support weapons behind was a response not to the enemy but to the perceived difficulties of the terrain. It would take until at least the advance north along the Kokoda Track for the Australian Army to replace this instinctive or 'reactive' response to jungle warfare with an 'adaptive' response.[19] This reluctance to change quickly would have a detrimental impact throughout the campaign. The decision to dispense with the majority of support weapons also illuminates an ongoing problem with the army and its attitude to jungle warfare—inconsistency. On the one hand LHQ, and many officers, argued that few changes were needed to operate successfully in the tropics.[20] This view is reflected in the minimal changes that occurred during and after the 7th Division's three-month training period in Queensland. On the other hand, dramatic and telling changes occurred immediately before combat, in this case because of the belief that support weapons would be either too difficult to transport or of little value in combat.

The difficulties of transportation and a lack of native carriers made it a priority to reduce the weight the units would be carrying; this played some part in the decision to leave most support weapons behind. Despite these reductions, long before the AIF battalions joined combat with the Japanese, the punishing loads they were forced to carry had begun to take their toll. Charles Sims recalled 'everyone having to cart seven days' rations on them plus all the ammunition . . . it was a total weight of well over sixty to sixty-five pounds per man and in that sort of terrain that's a killer'.[21]

The mountainous terrain and hot, humid climate of the South West Pacific would force major logistical changes on the Australian

Army at the strategic, operational and tactical levels. The extraordinary difficulty of supplying ammunition, food and medicine to the men on the front lines was in marked contrast to the experiences of the 2nd AIF in the Middle East and Mediterranean, where movement was relatively straightforward as long as transport was available. With the destruction of many transport planes at Port Moresby's Seven Mile Drome between April and September 1942, and the high rate of wastage of those supplies that were air dropped at various points along the Track, the issue of supply would become one of the most important to all commanders throughout the campaign.[22] To an extent, the only supplies the men could rely on were those they carried to the battlefield on their backs. They were thus weighed down far more heavily in the Pacific campaigns than they had been in the more mechanised battlefields of the Middle East. The excessive weight, combined with the torturous terrain, would soon see men on the Kokoda Track discarding equipment as they began to climb.[23]

Preparations continued and last-minute supplies were issued. Several hundred pairs of American-style knee-length gaiters were issued to the 2/16th and 2/27th battalions, providing greater protection from mud and leeches to about half the total force.[24] Route marches through the surrounding jungle were conducted to give the troops some sense of the terrain in which they would soon be operating. An ANGAU officer 'demonstrated the more common native plant foods and methods of cooking them'.[25] Experimentation continued even as the units marched up the Track. For example, it was soon determined that a long walking staff was necessary for support on the slippery slopes. Even today this is one item that all who attempt the Kokoda Track climb should carry. One adaptation that would become imperative in all later jungle campaigns had not occurred at this stage. As Thompson noted, 'up in New Guinea, we didn't have any tools to dig trenches and we had to dig them with bayonets and steel helmets. That's not easy.'[26] A report written at the end of the

Kokoda and Beachheads campaigns would state that 'some kind of light digging tool is essential where time counts' and that scrounged American and Japanese tools were carried.[27]

While the men were preparing themselves, their commanders were also struggling desperately to come to terms with the new operational theatre as well as the environment. One of the greatest concerns was the lack of maps: the first survey staff officer was appointed to New Guinea Force HQ just days before the 21st Brigade arrived.[28] A week after their arrival in Port Moresby, 7th Division HQ noted despairingly that 'owing to acute shortage of maps of New Guinea, it was found impossible to issue units of 7 Aust Div with even one complete set'. On 16 August an ANGAU officer who had recently returned from Kokoda briefed 21st Brigade officers on the terrain in the area, but 'otherwise our knowledge was limited to [information] gleaned from the study of a single air photo and a track report map graph which subsequently proved extremely inaccurate'.[29] With the Pacific War more than eight months old, and General Basil Morris having been based in Port Moresby for more than six months, the inability to supply newly arrived troops with maps is inexplicable.

The lack of preparation for the conditions at hand extended to all aspects. At Itiki, bayonets were sharpened and weapons stripped and cleaned, bootmakers were found to nail strips of leather to the soles of boots to increase grip in the muddy conditions, while loads were lightened by cutting many items in half, including blankets, mess tins and even toothbrushes.[30] In several cases, though, these reductions in weight were only temporary. While watching the 2/14th Battalion preparations, the Australian war correspondent Osmar White noticed a 'corporal pleading for two more Mills grenades and one tin less bully beef. "All the chaps feel the way I do sir," he said earnestly.' White noticed 'that their packs weighed 65 pounds . . . that they were half naked when they should have been covered; that their uniforms were the colour of desert dust and not the colour of green jungle; that their webbing shone white from long bleaching in the desert suns'.[31]

This was not the first time White had commented about the inappropriateness of the Australian khaki uniforms for jungle conditions. While they had been with the 2/5th Independent Company and the New Guinea Volunteer Rifles operating from Wau in July 1942, both White and cameraman Damien Parer had 'observed Kanga Force dyeing their uniforms in coffee grounds to darken them'. This was only a temporary solution, however, as the coffee grounds accelerated the uniforms' disintegration. A Kanga Force report, written at the time of White and Parer's visit, unequivocally argued for changes to the standard issue Australian Army uniform because it 'is too easily seen against the dark green jungle background [and] it is recommended that in future units destined for jungle warfare be issued initially with dark green clothing'.[32]

Although White and Major Norman Fleay—Kanga Force commander—had clearly identified the problem, no official changes had occurred by the time 21st Brigade was deployed. In the days before they set off up the Golden Staircase, the men made vain last-minute attempts to dye their khaki uniforms dark green, using a plant extract and dyes from Australia.[33] Several weeks earlier, at Milne Bay, the militia units had also experimented with dyes in an effort to produce effective camouflage. They were similarly unsuccessful. Worse, the dyes greatly exacerbated skin complaints, and soon as many as eight men out of ten in the 61st Battalion had severe dermatitis or eczema, which was already a problem in tropical climates.[34]

It would be late August before the first supplies of roughly dyed green uniforms were issued to some men of the 2/14th Battalion.[35] The majority of the 21st Brigade, like the 18th Brigade at Milne Bay, 'went into that action with desert clothing on' and would not be issued with properly camouflaged uniforms until after they were withdrawn from combat in September and October.[36] Soon the dangers of non-camouflaged uniforms in the jungle would become starkly evident, but unfortunately it would take the deaths of many men to bring about official change—change that had been clearly identified as necessary more than twelve months earlier, in Malaya and Timor. This episode showed once again the intransigence and unwillingness of the army to adapt to new circumstances. The units on the ground— not higher authority—would provide the impetus for change at the tactical level. This would be as true of the operations at Milne Bay as it was at Kokoda.

'A malarial pest-hole': The 18th Brigade at Milne Bay

Between 12 and 17 August, the 18th Brigade disembarked at Gili Gili wharf, Milne Bay. Unlike the 21st Brigade, they would not have to face the back-breaking struggle up the mountain ranges towards Kokoda. The torrential rain, calf-deep mud and waves of malaria-carrying mosquitoes, however, made Milne Bay if anything more unpleasant. Having fought at Tobruk alongside the 9th Division, they were now in a vastly different theatre of operations. The new arrivals—in an echo of the 21st Brigade's experiences at Port Moresby—discovered that the army 'Knew absolutely nothing about that end of New Guinea . . . So I sent out patrols [as] there were no maps, just what we learned ourselves.' Nor was the 18th Brigade any better prepared than the 21st in terms of uniforms and equipment.[37] With regard to protection against malaria—in one of the most malarious regions in Papua—they were ironically worse off, as were the militia and US Army Engineer units working to construct the runways. Some advice on the surrounding topography was forthcoming from members of the 7th Brigade, who had been stationed at Milne Bay for about a month.[38]

These preliminary reconnaissances confirmed the men's initial impressions from the boats. Here the terrain and climate would be far worse enemies than the Japanese. All who served at Milne Bay would agree with Queenslander Desmond Rickards, who recorded that 'There is no doubt about it ... with malaria, typhus, bombs, mosquitoes, rain, scorpions, leeches, multitudes of insects, rats and falling coconuts ... this place is on its own.'[39] When they were not constructing their primitive camp areas, assisting the engineers with road and bridge works, or unloading ships at the wharf, the newly arrived AIF battalions were patrolling in an attempt to fill in the gaps in their largely blank maps.[40] Within two weeks they were in action in 'conditions [that] were so different to what we'd been used to'.[41] As each unit went into action, its men were forced to learn quickly. Many were killed or wounded before they were able to do so.

Visibility was minimal. Many veterans of Tobruk would have echoed the reaction of an 18th Brigade intelligence man on first sighting the jungles surrounding the bay: '"Jesus Christ! I can't see anything." We were used to long views in the desert. I was conscious of this bloody jungle that closed in all around you and sort of enveloped you.'[42] In combat, this reaction was, if anything, magnified. Owen Curtis 'couldn't get used to not seeing who was shooting at you ... you'd be within six or eight feet of a person ... and you couldn't see whose [sic] shooting at you in the thick scrub'.[43]

The fact that 'you didn't see the Japs' before they opened fire[44] made the rate of advance 'painfully slow', as it was 'necessary to thoroughly comb the thick jungle on both sides of the track'.[45] The reasons for this were twofold: the Japanese placed snipers in the coconut palms—and sometimes at their bases—and they often shammed death and shot passing Australians in the back.[46] When the 2/9th replaced the 2/12th, 'they warned us to watch the trees and be careful'.[47] Soon a technique was developed to deal with the treetop snipers. As a 2/9th Battalion corporal explained, when the Japanese created their firing positions, 'the fronds cut ... often fell to the base of the palm and were easily seen'.[48] At this telltale sign, shots would be fired into the crown of each tree to bring the snipers crashing to the ground.

Lessons were clearly being recorded and passed on almost instantly, through both informal and formal channels. On the day the 2/12th first engaged the Japanese, 'we were given the orders to make sure that we weren't to pass any Jap on the ground without making sure he was dead'. Initially this measure was taken because the Japanese were simulating death, and the order was clearly 'repugnant to the men'.[49] Once AIF troops discovered the mutilated bodies of Papuan civilians and militia members, fury overcame self-preservation.[50] Knowledge of the Japanese barbarity, combined with the 'severe psychological by-products of close-fighting jungle warfare', arguably led to a situation in which no quarter was asked nor given.[51]

As nightfall approached, the battalions initially adopted their standard defensive positions, setting up listening posts a certain distance from the perimeter to warn the main body of approaching enemy. In the desert and other theatres, this tactic almost invariably worked. Here, however, a 2/12th listening post less than 80 metres from the unit's perimeter was overrun and the soldiers manning it killed. As Howell said, 'we were still [mentally] back in the desert. We put blokes out in the front of us, just out in the jungle the other side of the road as a listening post for Japs ... The Japs got them.'[52] The 18th Brigade after-action report would reiterate the dangers of listening posts; its suggestion 'that Listening Posts should not be left outside perimeter camps' indicated that lessons learned in action were rapidly being incorporated into training notes.[53]

Soon, units setting up defensive positions at night began to 'completely fell all trees etc., in an area big enough for us to lie within touching distance of each other'.[54] If Japanese tried to approach, they would not have the benefit of thick foliage to shield their movements. While clearing the jungle around their position was a commonsense measure, both it and the placement of listening posts inside camp perimeters were definite alterations to accepted practice in desert campaigns. Another significant difference between the two theatres was the vastly reduced size of those night defensive positions. As Curtis stated, to 'concentrate a lot of men in one little concentrated area . . . it would be absolutely fatal in open [desert] warfare to have done that'.[55] With visibility greatly reduced, it was now imperative that defensive positions be reduced in size both to prevent enemy infiltration and allow a commander to keep all his men under observation.

At times during the Milne Bay operations, some of the AIF soldiers began to realise that the jungle could be an ally. A lookout of the 2/12th Battalion, which had taken up a night defensive position, noticed a large formation of Japanese approaching. The Australians waited quietly as the Japanese began to ford a river, then opened fire from cover, cutting them to pieces.[56] Some members of militia units, whose views had not been influenced by combat in North Africa, arrived at a similar understanding. Captain Mal Just, of 25th Battalion, said he preferred 'the jungle as a battle ground as it is much more personal and by honing your own and [your] soldier[s]' skills, you meet the enemy on your own terms and are not subject to long distance and unseen attack'.[57] To most of the 18th Brigade, however, the jungle was a dark, forbidding place that hid unseen numbers of Japanese who could open fire at point-blank range at any moment. Much more familiarity with the conditions would be necessary before they were comfortable with their new surroundings.

Experience continued to accumulate, but in combat the price was paid in men's lives. A major difference in jungle warfare was the severity of wounds and the ratio of killed to wounded. As Allan Walker noted in the medical volume of the *Official History of Australia in the War of 1939–1945*, 'enemy bombs and machine-guns at close range produced the most serious injury'.[58] The 2/12th Battalion at Milne Bay lost 39 killed and 44 wounded. On the Kokoda Trail, the 16th Brigade would calculate that one man was killed for every two wounded.[59] In 'normal' combat operations, one man might be killed for every three or four wounded.⁶⁰ In ambushes and firefights where the protagonists were only yards—and at times feet—apart, the severity of gunshot wounds in particular was drastically increased.

The difficulty of evacuating the wounded to a Regimental Aid Post and thence to an Advanced Dressing Station was also far greater. With few roads, field ambulance units were forced to rely heavily on stretcher-bearers.⁶¹ Carrying the wounded in this way naturally took longer in the jungle, partly explaining the higher mortality rate. The multitude of infectious disease agents in Papua and New Guinea also exacerbated the death rate, as men who were weakened by their wounds had little natural defence against dysentery, malaria or scrub typhus. In combat it was virtually impossible to use mosquito nets—if the men had them—and almost every soldier became infected. Reports compiled after the Beachhead battles conceded that 'the campaign presented many medical problems which had not been visualised nor experienced' and therefore 'solutions were improvised'.⁶² Once these reports' recommendations were implemented, the survival rate of front-line troops improved.⁶³

As the AIF battalions advanced along the narrow coastal strip, bounded by the sea to the south and the mountains to the north, the Japanese tactics continued to cause consternation. Fire lanes that were almost impossible to see had been cut diagonally into the jungle at ankle height, leading off the track. As the 2/12th Battalion's commanding officer recorded, 'ambush parties of 3 to 14, were located in small lanes cut in the jungle at right angles to the road, from where they engaged our [troops] from under cover'.⁶⁴ It took experience to identify these fire lanes. At the start of the battle, the 18th Brigade lacked such experience. By mid-December, however, when it was transported to Buna, its men had imbibed the lessons of Milne Bay and trained newcomers to recognise the telltale signs of Japanese forces.⁶⁵ Although no large-scale resistance such as at the beachheads was encountered at Milne Bay, tree snipers and fire lanes kept the

Australians constantly on edge, never knowing when or from what direction shots would ring out. With the critical support of the Kittyhawk fighters of Nos 75 and 76 RAAF Squadrons, Japanese resistance was soon crushed, and on the night of 6 September 1942 the survivors were evacuated. The previously all-conquering Imperial Japanese Army had suffered its first defeat on land.

In October 1942, after the attack on Japanese positions on Goodenough Island, Colonel Arthur Arnold of the 2/12th reported that the terrain made it virtually impossible to see the enemy; as a result, the Australian attack had faltered.[66] During the Milne Bay fighting, the use of support weapons, either the units' own mortars or the 2/5th Field Regiment's battery of 25-pounders, was therefore difficult. The combination of action occurring at extremely close range—meaning that mortar or artillery fire would endanger friendly as well as enemy forces—and the inability to observe and accurately direct that supporting fire posed previously unknown problems. As Edmond Jones of the 2/9th Battalion recalled, 'it was all right in the desert firing mortars and so on because you had a target to fire at'.[67] The thick jungle and torrential rain meant it was 'necessary to modify normal air and [artillery] methods for support of the [infantry] in the jungle'.[68] For most of this battle—as in the Kokoda campaign and the Beachhead battles to follow—the units on the ground were forced by trial and error to develop solutions to the new problems of jungle warfare.

'Difficulty of ranging in jungle country': The challenges of employing artillery

The effective use of artillery in the jungle was a vexed issue. An advance party of the 2/3rd Australian Field Regiment returned to Queensland from Milne Bay on 1 August 1942, but their report on the difficulties of establishing observation posts and gun positions appeared to confirm the belief that artillery was of dubious worth in tropical jungle.[69] Despite this—and apparently confirming that the army was responding erratically to the rapid approach of the Japanese and the problems posed by tropical terrain—9th Battery of the 2/5th Australian Field Regiment was deployed ten days later to Milne Bay: 'Much of its equipment had been designed for almost any sort of warfare other than that in the jungle.'[70] Within two weeks it would be in action in support of the 7th and 18th Brigades. At the same time, the 13th and 14th Field Artillery Regiments were stationed at Port Moresby, tasked with repelling attacks from the sea or land.[71] In mid-September, the 14th Field Regiment would be the only artillery unit to fire in support of Australian operations on the Kokoda Track.

The 2/5th Field Artillery Regiment was the first AIF artillery unit to see action in Papua. The horrendous waterlogged conditions made the selection of suitable gun sites extremely difficult and the supply of ammunition to those positions an exhausting process.[72] Anti-malarial measures were still inadequate and the 2/5th, like all units at Milne Bay, suffered more casualties from malaria than from enemy action.[73] Although unable to provide much support during the initial Japanese attacks, in which two of their forward observation officers were killed, once the Australians regained the initiative they supported the advance.[74] Improvisation by the forward observation officers became the norm both at the gun positions and in the field.

As the 2/5th Field Regiment's historian recorded, 'the new techniques of ranging by sound of burst and by splinter effect were now being evolved the hard way'. This tactic involved the forward observation officer calling for artillery fire—often as close as 30 to 50 yards from his position—and determining, from the subsequent explosions and sound of shell splinters whistling over his head, what adjustments he needed to make. These were then radioed back to the guns.[75] In thick jungle where visibility was at a minimum, and with wholly inadequate maps, such hazardous tactics became commonplace. On several occasions, a forward observation officer and his signalman were forced to move so close to enemy troops that they could hear their voices. As they were often on the foreshore, the officer would call for an artillery round to be fired into the sea—so it could be easily seen, unlike rounds that fell in the jungle—and use the subsequent explosion to adjust the artillery fire onto the unseen Japanese.[76]

Soon the Japanese retreat gathered pace, until the artillery could not be moved fast enough to support the advancing 18th Brigade's infantry units. With the daily torrential rain having turned the roads into quagmires and the Japanese having retreated beyond the range of the 25-pounders, more improvisation became necessary. A nearby anti-aircraft unit provided a solution. With the effective range of its 3.7-inch at least 7000 yards greater than that of the 25-pounders, it was decided to employ them in the field artillery role. The anti-aircraft shells initially failed to explode, but when fuses from 25-pounders were inserted they functioned effectively.[77]

The new conditions saw other previously unheard-of improvisations become almost routine. In at least one instance artillery fire was called down by an observation post officer standing neck deep in the sea so he could observe the fall of shot 19,000 yards along the coast.[78] While using anti-aircraft guns as field artillery never became standard practice, sound ranging certainly did. For the rest of the South West Pacific campaigns, Australian artillery units would employ these tactics, as observation of fire was rarely possible.[79] Each unit appears to have had to learn these lessons independently, some during combat, others later in training. This again highlights the irregular transmission of learning within and between units. Why this should be so is difficult to understand, as both during and after the early Papuan campaigns, numerous reports on the employment of artillery were produced, and all discussed methods of ranging artillery fire onto targets in jungle.[80] In fact, less than a week after the

18th Brigade's operations at Milne Bay, a report based on their experiences was distributed. Included were several paragraphs on the use of artillery.[81]

At the same time as the 2/5th Field Regiment was being forced to rapidly come to terms with operating in the new conditions, several artillery units were training and waiting to be deployed from Port Moresby. As noted, the first of these to see action was the 14th Field Regiment, which manhandled a single gun with extreme difficulty forward of Owers' Corner.[82] After the men had practised dismantling the gun and carrying it forward in sections, it took them a week to move it 3 kilometres and into a position from which fire could be brought to bear on the Japanese. The fact that it took more than 100 men of four different units to accomplish this task using block and tackle cast doubts about the suitability of artillery in this terrain into stark relief.[83] In his report on the operation, however, the battery commander was more confident that lessons learned would be valuable for future units.[84] Within weeks of its return to Port Moresby, the unit, in conjunction with the two AIF Field Artillery regiments that had recently arrived, had developed a rapid drill for breaking the gun into its constituent parts and using a handcart to transport them over jungle terrain.[85] The drill would prove useful, but the handcarts would never see action.

After the Japanese had retreated out of the range of the solitary 25-pounder forward of Owers' Corner, the artillery units 'languished' in Port Moresby for two months. Their men were, however, experimenting with dismantling the guns and preparing them for air transportation. These trials gathered momentum after a request for information was received from the CRA RAA 7th Division.[86] Inexplicably, apparently no one in authority in the Australian Army had grasped that the only way to transport heavy equipment in Papua and New Guinea was by air. Mining operations did this routinely, so the requisite experience was available if the Australian military had thought to look for it.[87] Nevertheless, within days both the 2/1st and 2/6th Field Regiments had provided the requested information to headquarters. They continued to experiment with ways to make guns easier to move in the jungle, including by welding aircraft wheels to the trail. On 1 November the four guns of 'E' Troop, 2/1st Field Regiment, were modified in this way.[88] While it would be a year before those experiments came to fruition, authorities in Australia had also identified the difficulties of moving artillery pieces in Papua and New Guinea, and development of a 'short' or lightened 25-pounder began in September 1942.

The fighting over 'the Track' would be an infantryman's war, supported by a handful of combat engineers and the crucial signalmen. Only four days after arriving in Port Moresby, the Victorian 2/14th Battalion of the 21st Brigade set off north along the Kokoda Track. Within days they would meet a far more deadly and ferocious enemy than the Vichy French forces they had fought in Syria more than a year before. They would be on the back foot from the outset, wearing uniforms that stood out almost white against the dark-green jungle, outgunned, outnumbered, and with virtually no time to reconnoitre or prepare to engage the Japanese on ground of their choosing. But they, and their comrades of the Western Australian 2/16th and South Australian 2/27th Battalions, would conduct a gallant fighting withdrawal that, combined with Japanese supply problems, brought that vaunted army to a standstill and then forced it back to the beachheads, where it would eventually be annihilated.

Chapter 6

'DEEP IN UNMAPPED JUNGLES': 21ST BRIGADE ON THE KOKODA TRACK

Late August 1942 therefore saw the infantry at Port Moresby and Milne Bay preparing to engage the Japanese while the artillery struggled to prove the doubters wrong. The experience of the few gun crews used at Milne Bay and later the beachheads would prove crucial in jungle warfare, though tactics and methods still needed refinement. The use of field engineers, meanwhile, appears to have been an afterthought, as the first of them did not arrive in Port Moresby until September and October. Those that were deployed were generally engaged on similar tasks to the militia battalions: road-making and constructing defensive positions and gun emplacements around Port Moresby and Milne Bay.[1]

With the incessant torrential rain at Milne Bay turning roads into rivers and the great shortage of four-wheel-drive vehicles, as many personnel as possible were employed on road-building. This prevented engineers from working with the forward infantry units. The need to unload ships would divert further men from assisting the infantry in their pursuit of the retreating Japanese. The infantry battalions were thus forced to rely heavily upon their overstretched pioneer platoons. It is clear that Blamey and MacArthur, back in Australia, failed to appreciate the challenges posed by climate and terrain when they sent increasingly exasperated telegrams to their commanders in Papua demanding swifter action.[2]

The most urgent task of the 7th Division Field Companies was described as 'the maintenance and improvement of the road through Rouna to Koitaki and Itiki, where carriers picked up their loads for transport... to Myola and thence to Isurava'.[3] This was easier said than done. The rain turned the precipitous track to slush and soaked men to the skin as they hacked steps into the hillsides.[4] Once the advance from Imita Ridge began in September, the engineers and pioneers faced the same problem as all other units: rationalising equipment loads so the momentum of the advance could be maintained. As the slow advance northwards gathered pace in September, the engineers with the leading infantry units realised that a bare minimum of tools was all that could be carried in the mountains.[5] Ultimately, they concluded, the 'use of local resources and improvisation is of paramount importance'.[6] Before the engineer and pioneer units had begun large-scale attempts to make the Kokoda Track less treacherous underfoot, the infantrymen of 21st Brigade marched off from Owers' Corner towards Uberi and on towards Kokoda.

'An infantryman's calvary': The 21st Brigade on the Kokoda Track

On 16 August 1942, the 2/14th Battalion (21st Brigade) was the first AIF unit to set off on the heartbreaking slog over the Kokoda Track. The men were fortunate in the first few days, as the rains held off. Nevertheless, the physical strain of climbing up and down steep slopes took its toll. As Bob Thompson recalled, 'you go up hills and you go down hills and you're crying your heart out by the time you get to the top of a hill'.[7] Things only got worse: as they gained elevation, the rain began—and did not seem to stop for the rest of the campaign.

For the men of the 2/14th, who like the rest of the 21st Brigade had seen action in the mountains of Syria and felt themselves to some extent prepared, the Kokoda Track would be a daunting challenge. The experience of the 2/16th—which was a day behind the 2/14th—was similar. 'When the Battalion reached the staging camp at Uberi, the men were ready to drop into any shelter that promised rest.'[8] With only a half blanket and a gas cape each to keep off the rain, all had a miserable night's sleep.

With little inkling of what lay ahead, the troops tried to gather as much information as possible en route. On 19 August, on the track to Menari, 'several walking wounded from 39 Bn came in and were questioned as to their experiences . . . they did not seem unduly impressed either by the Japs or the track'.[9] Evidently, many of the 21st Brigade believed they would prove a match for the Japanese. A week later, having had virtually no chance to survey the battlefield, the 2/14th were fighting alongside the 39th Battalion at Isurava in a desperate effort to hold back waves of attacking Japanese.[10] All commanders regard reconnaissance—particularly to determine the number and disposition of the enemy—as crucial; in unfamiliar terrain, being able to select the battlefield is even more important. However, at least one officer who fought throughout the campaign has argued that 'patrolling had been ineffective' because the Australians 'found the environment strange and threatening'.[11]

The combat that the brigades of the 7th Division had participated in—whether in Syria or at Tobruk—had generally been preceded by painstaking, detailed reconnaissance by section- or platoon-sized patrols, usually at night. This was necessary to determine the size and location of enemy forces and minefields, and the best path to take when an attack was planned.[12] Obtaining as much information as possible prior to attacking was also crucial if the fire support plan was to be successful. In the desert, with few places for either defenders or attackers to conceal themselves, it was quickly realised that 'showing one's head invited enemy mortar, artillery, machine-gun and sniper fire'.[13] Many units in the Mediterranean theatre—both Allied and Axis—consequently became almost nocturnal. As an officer of the 2/31st Battalion would later recount, 'in open warfare we had used the darkness to organise the firing positions, get out the wounded, bring in food and ammunition. We had to learn again.'[14] The AIF was thus accustomed to performing most tasks during the hours of darkness, including resupply and reconnaissance. In tropical jungle, it quickly found that 'it was quite impossible [to] do patrols at night'.

It also had to rethink how to 'fight campaigns in this sort of country'.[15] This was because the Australians had also become used to moving in open and widely dispersed formations: in the desert, these reduced individual soldiers' risk of being killed or wounded by that accurate artillery or machine-gun fire. By contrast, in the jungle a dispersed formation would quickly become separated and disjointed. Difficult as they found it at first, the men of the AIF would have to learn to move and fight close together.[16]

Also hindering adaptation to the new environment was the fact that the men's training manuals still reflected the experience of Syria and North Africa. The relevant chapter of *Infantry Minor Tactics* contained three formation diagrams, including one that depicted a 'platoon moving in very thick country' (visibility 10 yards).[17] The formation depicted had two of the platoons' three sections forward and the third behind, with the platoon commander moving with that withdrawn section. This formation was far more suited to open country, where the bulk of the unit's firepower was to the front to 'compensate for the absence of cover'.[18] In thick jungle, it was safer for a unit to move in single file with one section—or platoon—up ahead and two behind. This meant that in case of sudden contact, the commander could manoeuvre the bulk of his formation to whichever flank required the firepower. It would also prevent the bulk of the formation from being cut down in the event that they came under unexpected frontal fire.

Infantry Minor Tactics, however, argued that '*it is considered nevertheless that these three* [formations] *will fulfil all the section's requirements in modern battle*'.[19] This statement was inaccurate: none of the formations outlined was suitable for jungle warfare. New, or at the very least modified, section and platoon formations proved necessary in Papua and New Guinea. In fact, pre-war infantry tactical doctrine was more similar to that eventually adopted in Papua and New Guinea than it was to the doctrine used in the Middle East.[20] Pre-war doctrine, however, had changed in response to the demands of training and fighting in a very different theatre. This, at least initially, caused unnecessary casualties. When men of the 2/31st Battalion charged a Japanese position, they were quickly 'swallowed by the jungle', preventing their comrades from supporting them 'with effective aimed fire'.[21] Going into action in September, one can only assume that the lack of time for the survivors of the 21st Brigade to pass on information to their fellow 7th Division comrades of 25th Brigade explains why they should make the same mistakes as those who had gone before them.

Before they could successfully adapt their tactics to a new environment and a new enemy, many of the troops had to overcome their fear of the jungle. An officer of the 2/16th Battalion, from outback Western Australia, recalled that 'the jungle oppressed with its brooding malevolent silence . . . death struck without warning from an unseen source [and] the almost incessant rain and the pervading clinging, dragging mud brought on a feeling of helplessness'.[22]

When the 25th Brigade was thrust into action in late September, its troops had a very similar reaction.[23] Some were 'too frightened to venture into the jungle at night even for the relief of discomfort caused by nature'.[24] While marching up the Kokoda Track with 21st Brigade, war correspondent Osmar White commented that 'the bulk of them were troops trained for desert warfare... they were far more afraid of the country than the Japanese... a formally trained soldier thought of them [the hills of Papua] as deadly enemies eternally ready to baffle and trap him'.[25]

White's fellow Australian war correspondent Chester Wilmot reported his observations to Rowell and Major-General Arthur 'Tubby' Allen on his return to Port Moresby. He agreed that 'the AIF were novices at jungle warfare... and it is no wonder that they were driven back'.[26] Wilmot has been accused of laying all the shortcomings he discerned in Australian preparations at Blamey's door, but in the case of this lack of adequate jungle acclimatisation, he clearly had a point. If the recently returned AIF troops had been able to practise jungle patrolling and ambush techniques before deployment instead of labouring on road works in New South Wales, hundreds of casualties could have been avoided.[27] Within days the lack of preparation began to take its toll as the 21st Brigade's three battalions were successively fed into the bloody battles at Isurava and Brigade Hill.

Only days before they met the Japanese at Isurava, the 2/14th Battalion's intelligence party stopped at Eora Creek, 'where the IO had interview with Capt Stevenson 39 Battalion (Ex-2/14th) and learned something of Japanese war tactics'.[28] On the same day, Captain Bert Kienzle of the ANGAU passed on to the battalion as much information as he could on the terrain around Kokoda and of the recent fighting between the 39th Battalion and the advancing enemy. A 30th Brigade sand-table model of the Myola–Kokoda region provided additional information to the 2/14th Battalion companies as they marched towards Kokoda.[29]

As they gradually became accustomed to the jungle, the men of the 21st Brigade were slowly learning lessons. To make movement at night easier, some 2/14th Battalion troops picked up bark with phosphorus on it that glowed. Pieces of the bark were attached to the rear of each man's waistband, enabling those behind to see the faint glow as they stumbled forward in the pitch-black night.[30] On 26 August, near Isurava, the advancing Japanese attacked the remnants of the 39th and, for the first time, the 2/14th. From now on the AIF troops would be learning 'under the worst possible scenario—in combat against the Japanese'.[31]

With the Australian forces outnumbered, the 2/14th Battalion were rushed into action as soon as they arrived, generally by companies. Lessons were learned and then lost as men were killed or wounded as fast as they joined the desperate defence. The members of the 2/14th Intelligence Section moved rapidly around the battlefield, constantly updating the 'battle map' at battalion HQ.[32] In less hectic circumstances they would have been able to collect valuable information that would eventually have been passed to brigade or division command to build up a more complete picture of Japanese methods and tactics. In the maelstrom of Isurava they were only able to pass on information about numbers of wounded and killed and ammunition states, and desperate requests for assistance from units threatened with annihilation.

The differences between combat in the jungle and in the Middle East were profound. As the 18th Brigade at Milne Bay had discovered, foremost among them were the problems of visibility and observation. With their well-camouflaged uniforms and helmets, the Japanese were extremely difficult to see. Weeks earlier, a member of the 39th Battalion had noticed a 'bush' carefully moving down a track towards his unit. Soon another 'bush' also moved. The mobile shrubs were two Japanese soldiers in camouflaged uniforms with leaves and branches attached to their equipment.[33] Osmar White wrote: 'I must have heard the remark "You can't see the little bastards!" hundreds of times in the course of a day.'[34]

AIF members, 'with their badge of [Middle East] service, white hat band, white belt and white gaiters' were easily seen.[35] Even the faces of the Australians showed up stark white in the dim half-light of the jungle. As Lindsay Mason noted, 'After one day everyone knew it was best to rub mud on your face to get rid of that white glaring target.'[36] Less than a month later, the suggestion that 'green nets or veils should be worn to cover the face and the hands stained to match the woodwork of the rifle' would appear in training notes in Australia.[37] Although these particular camouflage ideas were rarely adopted in the field, ideas from the front line were clearly beginning to filter rearwards.

Another key lesson from these early experiences was that actions in the jungle unfolded faster and at much shorter range than in the desert. Small-arms practice ranges that required a soldier to make 'quick and accurate use of weapons when confronted with unexpected situations... observation [and] silent movement in jungle' would soon become standard in all training establishments.[38] Headquarters Second Army, for example, proposed in December 1942 'to construct rifle ranges in selected close and rugged country for the purpose of training troops in jungle warfare'. The various unconnected and disparate attempts to communicate such lessons—first by the 8th Division in Malaya, and later the 6th Division in Ceylon—eventually culminated in the exhaustively detailed and physically demanding ranges and assault courses at the Jungle Warfare Training Centre, Canungra. That hundreds of combat deaths occurred before these innovations were adopted is an indictment of the Australian Army's ability to heed and assimilate the advice of deployed units.

Although the outnumbered 21st Brigade, along with the 39th and 53rd Battalions, were in great danger of being overrun by the advancing Japanese in August and early September, it is arguable that more challenging tactical problems were posed once the Australians went onto the offensive. These would, to an extent, be exacerbated by the prior Middle Eastern experience of the 7th Division and—when they arrived in October—the 16th Brigade of the 6th Division. During the tactical withdrawal from Kokoda to Imita Ridge, the Australians, though constantly threatened with encirclement, were at least fighting battles of a kind they recognised against an enemy that could be engaged with conventional tactics.[39] Although at times the men in each defensive position seemed to be 'engrossed in their own little world, and... not know what the rest of the section was doing, let alone the platoon, company or battalion', these battles were basically standard defensive infantry actions.[40] The fact that 'each section post had to be a veritable fort in the line of posts forming the battalion perimeter' was not unique—the 18th Brigade and the 9th Division would have argued that it was also true of their defence of the Red Line at Tobruk.[41]

What was different in the jungle was the poor visibility, which made it harder for the commander to identify the main thrust of an enemy attack—or identify enemy positions during an Australian attack—and then to direct and control his unit in response to that threat: 'Control and communication were difficult unless [you] were right behind the leading company... but so fierce was the enemy's fire and so dense was the jungle that [you] could not gain an accurate picture of the battle.'[42] With battalion and company commanders regularly unable to see what all their men were facing, responsibility thus devolved to a lower level than had been the case in North Africa or the Middle East. As the historian Peter Charlton notes, this meant that jungle combat was 'a war for and of the junior leaders'.[43] The 2/2nd Battalion report of the first Papuan campaigns observed that 'the impetus of an attack depends almost entirely on the Sec Leader who must use far more initiative and accept far more responsibility than in open country warfare'.[44] This idea later appeared in training manuals and syllabuses that emphasised the importance of individual and section training.[45]

Jungle conditions also called for considerably smaller battalion and company defensive positions than had been normal in the Middle East—as the 18th Brigade had discovered at Milne Bay.

The 25th and 16th Brigades would learn the same lessons on the Kokoda Track. Eventually these lessons would be passed on to others back in Australia. A 30-page report by two company commanders of the New South Wales 2/2nd Battalion, for example, was widely distributed.[46] Information and suggestions from it would also appear in *6 Aust Div Training Instruction No. 11 Jungle Warfare*, published in June 1943.

While the lack of entrenching tools forced the Australians to dig in with helmets, bayonets and hands, once in their defensive positions they were able to slaughter the tactically naïve Japanese—provided they had enough men and ammunition. The 21st Brigade intelligence officer noted on 13 September that 'the Jap has little initiative or subtlety. He is content to batter his way through by superior numbers, and hits every head he sees.'[47] Neither Japanese jungle warfare training nor tactics were the main reason the Australians were forced to retreat to Imita Ridge; the sheer weight of Japanese numbers, paucity of supplies and lack of tactical air support played telling roles. Admittedly, the ferocity and drive of the Japanese, who advanced at all costs and refused to allow the Australians to regain their footing once they were off balance, was also an important factor.[48] While being forced back, however, the 7th Division began to realise, as the 8th had done in Malaya, that the Japanese were not supermen; after that, 'confidence in their individual superiority over the Japanese' grew.[49] The 2/14th noted that 'the enemy was adopting his usual tactics, pressure on the front coupled with an outflanking movement'. As the withdrawal continued, 'heavy casualties were inflicted on the eager and impetuous enemy as he pushed up the single track trying to regain contact with our troops'.[50]

A week before the Victorians of 39th and 2/14th Battalions launched their desperate effort to hold back the Japanese assaults on Isurava, the 1st Marine Division was experiencing similar tactics on Guadalcanal. From midnight on 21 August, Colonel Kiyonao Ichiki, commander of the 28th Infantry Regiment, ordered his troops to attack US Marine Corps positions on Alligator Creek. What would become known as the Battle of Tenaru would see Ichiki's unit annihilated as its members charged headlong at two battalions of the 1st Marine Regiment, which mowed the attackers down with machine-gun, mortar and artillery fire.[51] The tactical lessons drawn from this battle were arguably less important than its psychological impact. The Americans learned, as the Australians were in the process of learning, that the Japanese could be defeated.[52] However, the lesson that should have been learned—that frontal attacks in jungle conditions invariably resulted in mass casualties to the attacking force as they ran into well-concealed enemy defences—does not appear to have sunk in.[53] For the 21st Brigade and those who followed them, the challenges of 'observation of the enemy and mutual support' differed drastically from those of the desert war.[54]

'Making slow progress': Ioribaiwa to the beachheads

Before the long and arduous advance over the Kokoda Track occurred, the first lessons of the campaign were beginning to filter back to New Guinea Force HQ in Port Moresby and thence to LHQ in Melbourne. Even as the 21st Brigade desperately defended Mission Ridge and Brigade Hill in early September, notes on tactics were being collected. A number came from an unusual source: the journalist Chester Wilmot. Lieutenant-General Rowell, who had been appointed to replace Morris at New Guinea Force HQ in mid-August, 'arranged for a party comprising White, Wilmot and Parer to go forward to Myola to get and give a first-hand picture of what was happening'.[55]

The six-page report that Wilmot provided for Rowell in late September would eventually see wide distribution. First, however, a temporary return to the issuing of irrelevant and outdated training information would occur. On 5 September, the day after Wilmot's meeting with Rowell and Allen in Port Moresby, 7th Australian Division re-issued 'Warfare in Thick Country' to all units under its command, AIF and militia.[56] Why this report, based almost solely upon Malayan experience, should have been re-released at the exact moment the Australian forces were fighting in terrain markedly different from that of Malaya is difficult to comprehend. The only explanation appears to be that since no new training notes or memoranda had yet emerged from the current battles, the Australian Army was resorting to any notes it had on hand. That would soon change.

As a journalist for the ABC and BBC, Chester Wilmot had written numerous despatches, and from early August to mid-September 1942 more than a dozen of these were broadcast. These were increasingly scathing about the Australian Army's lack of preparedness for jungle warfare, and increasingly critical of the AIF command, especially General Blamey.[57] On 12 September, a compilation of these despatches was 'issued for information and guidance in training, and for distribution down to units'.[58] Its subtitle, 'Training Instruction No. 4, 2nd Aust Army', and the fact that it was issued to all units under that army's command, reflected the importance that Allen, the 7th Division commander, and Rowell, the corps commander, attached to Wilmot's conclusions. How widely the training instruction was circulated, however, is difficult to determine. When Blamey learned of the author's identity he ordered that the copies be returned.[59] It is not known how many of the units had time to copy and distribute them before the recall.

After the publication of 'Training Instruction No. 4', a regular series of after-action reports began to be distributed. Two weeks later, Wilmot compiled a more comprehensive document that Allen and Rowell also issued. *Observations on the New Guinea Campaign*, again sharply critical of Blamey, cost Wilmot his journalist's accreditation, but it was widely distributed throughout Australia.[60] As Wilmot's second report was being issued, LHQ published its first *Training Notes* on jungle warfare based on the experiences of Kokoda and Milne Bay. It was followed two weeks later by a second training note. The list of recipients encompassed every headquarters, unit and training establishment in Australia. The cover note made it clear that the army was still hesitant to have established doctrine altered to meet the new situation. Clearly, however, the new conditions of combat had persuaded some commanders that additional guidance and instruction were needed.[61] The first attempts at developing training ideas based upon combat experience in jungle terrain had begun. After the 21st Brigade was withdrawn from the front line, this process would gather momentum.

Beginning in mid-September, the remnants of the Brigade were pulled back to Port Moresby as the 25th and, soon after, the 16th Brigades arrived to relieve them. By 25 September, the three battalions of the 21st Brigade were in camp at Koitaki. Little time was available for rest and recuperation, however, with training detachments being sent to militia, AIF and US Army units within days.[62] The 2/1st recalled that 'they gave valuable talks on Jap tactics and what kind of country we could expect'.[63] Unfortunately, the situation on the Kokoda Track cut short this period of training and acclimatisation, as it had for the 21st Brigade in August.

A day after they had arrived at Port Moresby, the 16th was ordered forward. Its men were slightly more fortunate than the troops of the 25th Brigade, who, arriving before the 21st was withdrawn, did not have the benefit of the lectures the 16th received. Both brigades were in turn more fortunate than the 21st, as they were at least 'issued with greens and Yankee gaiters . . . [the 25th being the] First Bde to make use of Green KDs [Khaki Drill uniforms]'.[64] Because of the urgent need to get more troops up the Track, men 'stripped naked, moved over to a Sawyer (stove) issue point, dumped one's own khakis, picked up equivalent sizes, wet or dry, and put them on'.[65] Even though

General Blamey remained unconvinced of the need for jungle-green uniforms, HQ 7th Division had ordered that all uniforms be dyed before the 25th and subsequent brigades went into action. The 16th Brigade would record that their newly camouflaged uniforms and helmets 'looked very effective and blended in well with the surrounding country'.[66] Some units acquired green paint, which they used to camouflage their rifles and Bren guns.[67]

Other changes were in progress. The 2/33rd Battalion took one Vickers MMG, unlike the 21st Brigade a month earlier. When the 16th Brigade arrived two weeks later, the support-weapon situation had changed again, and the 2/1st Battalion took both a Vickers and a 3-inch mortar.[68] Reports written at this time by the survivors of the 21st Brigade argued for an 'increased use of long range close support weapons—3-in. Mtr and Vickers', reflecting the view that leaving them behind in August had been a mistake.[69] It is unlikely, however, that 16th or 25th Brigade commanders received these recommendations before their departure for the front line. The reasons for the decision to take the support weapons are therefore unclear, but it can probably be attributed to discussions between respective units. Rather than being ordered from above, most such changes came about when front-line troops passed on their experience to those who followed.

Soon the 25th and then the 16th Brigades would face the same problems as the 21st Brigade and the militia units before them. Although slightly better forewarned, they too would have to learn most of their initial lessons in jungle warfare tactics in combat, and suffer accordingly.[70] At least some of these problems could have been avoided if the 25th's Brigadier Eather had taken the opportunity to talk to Brigadier Potts 'when the two passed on the track'.[71] By this omission he thereby deprived his brigade of answers to some of those problems. One other valuable source of information also appears to have been under-utilised. The comprehensively detailed and astute 'Report on Operations—21 Aust Inf Bde Owen Stanley

Campaign', written by Potts and his brigade staff upon their return to Port Moresby, was sent to New Guinea Force HQ but promptly returned for corrections—that were unspecified.[72]

The 21st Brigade polished the report and then forwarded it to Advanced LHQ in Brisbane, but once again 'it was sent back with orders to condense its contents and emphasis'. This incident underscores Peter Brune's observation that there is 'no evidence that the Australian Army sought out or learnt more than a thread of information from Rowell, Allen or Potts'.[73] It is plausible that they—like Bennett after Malaya—were so tainted in the eyes of their superiors, especially Blamey, that anything they had to pass on was seen as equally tainted. Whatever the real reason, the delay is an indictment on those commanders back in Australia who refused to heed the valuable lessons and knowledge that officers such as Rowell, Allen and Potts could have passed on. Lives were lost unnecessarily because of this recalcitrance.

As the Japanese retreated, one traditional military theory came into sharper relief: the idea that an attacker had to have a 'superiority of 2 or 3 to 1 over well prepared defenders to have any chance of success. The attacker would also sustain two or three times the casualties of the defenders.'[74] In the jungle, this maxim was if anything even more apposite. The issue had not often confronted the 21st Brigade, which had been able to mow down attackers who often could not see the Australian defensive positions. The situation was now reversed, with the attacking Australians cut down by unseen Japanese guns.[75] Worse, not only did the jungle make it more difficult to see the enemy and therefore harder to provide suppressive covering fire during an attack, once your own men disappeared into the undergrowth during an attack, command and control virtually disappeared also. When the 16th Brigade joined the 25th, the 2/1st Battalion would plaintively state that 'we could not see the Jap positions so could only support the 2/2nd Battalion attack with mortar and [light machine-gun] fire.

This called for great care, for, although the enemy were only 40 to 60 yds in front of our positions, we could not see them nor . . . the 2/2nd Battalion.'[76]

Although his criticism is restrained, the official historian Dudley McCarthy is one of the few who have questioned whether the tactics employed by the 16th and 25th Brigades in their advance were appropriate. They had behaved 'with courage and energy, as witness their frontal attack over the bridges [at Eora Creek] . . . But it seems possible now that . . . there was more courage and energy than skill.'[77] This lack of skill can be directly attributed to largely incorrect training locations, inadequate time for acclimatisation and, most importantly, inappropriate doctrine. With supporting weapons cut to a minimum, visibility measured in yards instead of miles, and enemy troops prepared to die at their posts, standard tactics of charging an enemy position under well-aimed covering fire were almost suicidal. Reconnaissance patrols to identify Japanese machine-gun positions and 'feel' for gaps in fixed defences, flanking movements that would be hidden behind the jungle screen, and a more painstaking build-up were all necessary for success—and would have lessened casualties. The belief that little real change was required to succeed in thick jungle was being proven wrong.[78]

The need for shorter—and therefore more manoeuvrable—weapons became apparent. Colin McRostie of 2/16th Battalion was not alone in arguing that the issue .303 Lee-Enfield rifle was 'too tangly in the jungle'.[79] A report written after the Beachheads campaign reiterated this point. It would, however, be more than two years before the British Army issued a modified—lightened and shortened—Lee-Enfield for jungle warfare.[80]

Although the Australians in the jungle were often prevented from seeing their enemy, with experience they were able to smell them.[81] In the jungle, cigarette smoke was a telltale giveaway. Eventually the lesson of using all the senses, including the olfactory—like those of tree snipers, fire lanes and enemy soldiers hiding among the dead—would find their way into the syllabus at Canungra.[82]

Before then the 16th and 25th Brigade would come to the realisation—as had the 21st and 18th before them—that neither their previous combat experience nor their training in Australia had adequately prepared them for the Japanese and the jungle. Lieutenant-Colonel Alfred Buttrose, commanding officer of the 2/33rd Battalion, made the scathing observation that 'this Bn has been called upon to carry out action against the enemy over mountainous country for which we had not anticipated and had therefore not trained. From pamphlets and officers in Australia we had been badly instructed and misguided.'[83] Adequate preliminary reconnaissance of the Kokoda Track and Milne Bay areas, during the months before the Japanese landed in July and August, would have enabled units to modify uniforms, equipment, weapons, and—more importantly—tactics and training methods before they were flung ill-prepared into combat.

While some argued that there was no time available to make these preparations, it is now clear that the several months between the return of 7th Division to Australia in March 1942 and its move to Papua in August were very poorly used. The wrong units—namely 30th Brigade—were sent to Port Moresby, where they were used to unload ships and build roads instead of engaging in reconnaissance and infantry training. By September 1942, the first lessons from the fighting at Milne Bay and in the Kokoda campaign were starting to be imparted to troops in Australia. But one more campaign would have to be fought before new training methods were developed that would set the Australian Army on the path to jungle warfare supremacy.

Chapter 7

'THE WORST EXPERIENCE OF THE WAR': KOKODA TO THE BEACHHEADS

By mid-September 1942, the Japanese had advanced as far south towards Port Moresby as they would get—Imita Ridge. Here their forward units cheered as they looked down upon the lights of Port Moresby less than 25 miles away.[1] However, like the Australians earlier in the battle, whose supply lines were gravely overextended by the time they reached Kokoda, the Japanese now found themselves too far from their own supply bases at the northern beachheads. Exhausted and emaciated from weeks of combat on a handful of rice each a day, the Japanese soldiers were now faced with fresh Australian units who had arrived to bolster the sorely pressed 21st Brigade. General Tomitaro Horii ordered his men to dig in and wait. News from another theatre would soon have a major impact on the course of the Kokoda campaign. As the US official history of the Papuan campaign argued, 'success on New Guinea was directly related to success on Guadalcanal'. With the Japanese offensive against the US Marines on Guadalcanal driven back, 'on 18 September General Horii received orders to withdraw to Buna for a possible reinforcement of the Imperial Japanese Army forces on Guadalcanal'.[2]

Although the Australians holding out on Imita Ridge did not know it, the decision by the Japanese High Command meant that their opponents would be moving in only one direction from now on—north to the beaches of Buna, Gona and Sanananda. But this did not mean the Australian advance would be easy. As the Japanese had demonstrated throughout the war, they did not give up ground they had taken without a bitter struggle. The long, arduous push north up the Kokoda Track would cost many more Australian lives as they assimilated the lessons of jungle warfare and gradually applied them in combat.

'Linesmen wallowing in mud': Signals

One of the most important tasks in war is maintaining communication. In the jungles and swamps of the South West Pacific, this was immeasurably more difficult. According to Max Dimmack, 'conditions could hardly have been worse for the installation and maintenance of all kinds of communications'.[3] Commanding officers—at all levels—were faced with the problem of issuing orders to units they could not see, even though they may have been only 100 metres away. While the mountainous terrain of Syria had posed problems for all involved and 'for the signallers the campaign had been a nightmare', those difficulties paled into insignificance on the Kokoda Track and at Milne Bay.[4]

Although the great distances in the desert war, and even the Greek campaign, had made the laying and collecting of signal cable a formidable task, signals equipment there had generally been carried in a vehicle.[5] The lack of roads on most South West Pacific islands made this impossible. High temperatures, rainfall and humidity rapidly deteriorated cables and delicate electrical and wireless equipment. At the same time, because the terrain prevented the use of vehicles, 'excessive handling' of that equipment caused daily maintenance problems. In addition, the mountains, frequent rain and towering jungle canopy severely limited wireless and radio reception, forcing the increased use of cable, despatch runners and carrier pigeons.[6]

Later in the war, technological advances increased the effectiveness of signal and wireless communication. However, older methods continued to be used until the cessation of hostilities. Signalmen on the Kokoda Track struggled in horrendous conditions to keep the lines operating. With cables and lines repeatedly cut or damaged by enemy fire, fallen trees, flash floods, vehicles, or the tramping boots of exhausted infantrymen, repair parties were constantly required to slog up and down miles of mud-choked jungle tracks searching for the break.[7] These parties 'must always be prepared to take immediate action', as Japanese line-cutting parties would often be waiting to ambush the repair men.[8] Although they appeared an anachronism on the modern battlefield, carrier pigeons regularly accompanied patrols and forward troops. On New Britain, in particular, militia units found that carrier pigeons were the only effective means of communication with battalion headquarters.[9]

Another standard option for commanders unable to communicate by wireless or radio was the despatch rider. During the Wau–Salamaua campaign, 'any means had to be employed [including] pedestrian despatch riders, native policemen, motor cycles, jeeps, transport or fighter planes and barges ... one brigade was served by outrigger canoe'.[10] At unit and sub-unit level, the use of section, platoon and company runners, especially during an engagement, was an established tactic. In jungle warfare, the refrain 'communication possible between [companies] only by runners' became commonplace.[11] Often targeted by the enemy, runners were in regular danger in all theatres. In jungle warfare, however, the role was frequently a death sentence. In July 1942, Captain Bidstrup of the 39th Battalion was forced to withdraw as the Japanese advanced. He sent a runner to advise outlying platoons of his decision, but the man disappeared.

A second runner was sent, 'but he too disappeared in the intervening sixty yds of jungle'.[12] No trace of either man was ever found.

The AIF would experience the same problems, with many runners vanishing never to be seen again and others found dead and horribly mutilated days or even weeks later.[13] Although it became less prevalent, the disappearance of runners, even over short distances, would continue until the end of the war. The lack of visibility and the need to relay their messages quickly made runners' task immeasurably more dangerous in jungle warfare.

What these various methods all had in common was the time they took to convey messages, whether from a platoon in action to company headquarters only 200 metres away, or from a unit back to brigade or divisional headquarters. Control was thus reduced, since by the time a despatch arrived—if it arrived at all—and a reply was delivered, the situation had almost always altered. As Lieutenant-Colonel Stewart stated during the Malayan campaign, 'control depends on comms . . . break control and an army will disintegrate'.[14] With the problems in communications in the tropics thus identified, tentative solutions began to appear. Organisations such as the Commonwealth Scientific Industrial and Research body devoted much time and effort to developing moisture-proof equipment, which came into operation in 1944. Committees were set up to examine waterproofing of all stores, including communications.[15] These developments, combined with the introduction of more lightweight and portable US equipment such as walkie-talkies, eventually made communication in jungle warfare significantly easier. To an extent, the 'introduction of radio communications to company and platoon levels' did 'increase the tempo of operations' in later campaigns. For most units, though, the most reliable means of communication were still line and cable.[16]

Before these changes could occur, the men at the front line were learning as they went, and passing on their knowledge. The monthly

Army Training Memoranda contained regularly updated sections on various aspects of signals work.[17] These were generally extracts from after-action reports, and even at times from letters sent home to Australia, demonstrating the desperate search for any information that could shed light on operating in jungle conditions. The introduction of the *Signal Officer-in-Chief's Training Memoranda* in mid-1942 represented the first concrete attempt to transmit signals and communications lessons from New Guinea throughout the Australian Army. These three- to five-page training memoranda were issued every few weeks between August and December 1942. Subsequent issues appeared monthly. They were generally based on information 'obtained from a report by Signal units in New Guinea', and it was ordered that they 'will be studied by all officers'. A later issue stated that 'operations in Jungle country provide many difficulties which have not been encountered previously' and that training would need to reflect this.[18]

These memoranda underscored the growing realisation that maintaining communications in the jungle required a higher degree of preparation and training, a greater ability to improvise and, once it was available, a higher standard of equipment than had been necessary in either the Middle East or early New Guinea campaigns. After the Papuan campaign came to an end in late January 1943, training was modified to incorporate its lessons. In May 1943, for example, a 'jungle-line construction' school was established by New Guinea Force HQ.[19]

Reports written immediately after the campaign ended, in January 1943, discuss the need for more signals personnel, primarily owing to the increased requirement for line-laying between units and sub-units.[20] With radio communication almost impossible on the Kokoda Track, signalmen at division, brigade and battalion level were overworked trying to lay telephone cable that should have been a corps responsibility. But more signalmen would not have addressed the fact that during combat 'the only method for a battalion commander to keep proper control was for a line to be laid behind each [company] as it advanced'. The introduction of walkie-talkies for the 1943–44 campaigns would go some way to alleviating this problem.

The other major change was in the method of transporting heavy signals equipment. In the desert, vehicles were the obvious method. In the tropics, their use was generally impossible. A report released in late 1942 concluded that 'in all probability the only means of transporting signal eqpt over the country will be by native carriers'.[21] From this period onwards, vast numbers of carriers were employed to move units' wireless, batteries, generator and fuel, often at the expense of other tasks.[22] The availability or lack of carriers did not directly affect tactical developments, especially at the unit level. What it did influence was the speed with which units could move. Thus, while combat at the sub-unit level often took place more rapidly—with section or platoon contact and ambushes occurring with no warning—action at unit level tended to be slower, as information took longer to move between sections and platoons, and thence rearwards to their companies and battalions.

'Soldiering in the tropics': Australia—United States learning

Australian troops in Papua and New Guinea and Americans in the Solomons were understandably focused on their own respective zones of responsibility. This, of course, detracted from the creation of a common body of jungle warfare lessons that might have led to a coherent and universally applicable doctrine and training system. Nevertheless, at the same time as the 21st Brigade was fighting desperately at Brigade Hill, a handful of training pamphlets and manuals was appearing. They drew upon a wider range of sources than those written immediately after the falls of Malaya and the Philippines, which had concentrated solely upon the supposed lessons of those campaigns. The first of these new manuals, *Soldiering in the Tropics*, provided the individual soldier with information on the nature and conditions of the jungle.[23] This manual was written between 1935 and 1940 and based upon US experience in Venezuela and Panama. After the addition of information from the Malayan, Philippine and Dutch East Indies campaigns, the 36-page pocket-sized pamphlet was issued to all Australian and US servicemen in the South West Pacific.[24] Although it is arguable that a manual primarily based on service in Central America would be only marginally useful in the Pacific islands, August 1942 was such a critical stage of the Pacific War, for the Australians at Milne Bay and on the Kokoda Track, and for the US Marines on Guadalcanal, that it is understandable that any sources of advice on adapting to 'jungle warfare' would have been gratefully adopted.

In September 1942 the manual was modified again to include early lessons of New Guinea operations and brief discussions of Japanese weapons and tactics.[25] Its publication and wide distribution demonstrate that the Australian Army had come to the realisation that adaptation to jungle conditions was a prerequisite for defeating the Japanese. In early 1943, Major-General Allen, in a talk to officers in his new command in the Northern Territory, highly recommended that they use it.[26] Within months the US Army requested 20,000 copies of *Soldiering in the Tropics* for its Officers Candidate Schools and for 'troops in forward areas'.[27] Along with the first tentative training exercises carried out by Lieutenant-Colonel Wolfenden of the LHQ Training Team in the same month—and attended by US officers—the publication and dissemination of this training manual marked the beginning of Australian–US collaboration on jungle warfare training.

Throughout the second half of 1942, the exchange of information between the allies continued. In early September a report on Japanese tactics from US Intelligence sources was distributed throughout the Australian Army. Two months later, the US Marine Corps forwarded a bulletin on Japanese jungle tactics to LHQ. It too was issued across the entire Australian Army. Gradually, a mass of detailed information on Japanese methods and practices was accumulated.[28] Knowing and understanding the Japanese was important, but equally if not more so was 'for [troops] to experience living in the jungle in the later stages [of training] so that they will become used to it and not be afraid of it'.[29] Despite its lack of understanding of the difficulties faced by the soldiers at Milne Bay and on the Kokoda Track, LHQ was coming to the realisation of the vital importance of comprehensive jungle warfare training. This realisation led, in late November 1942, to the establishment of a specialised centre for training in jungle warfare.

Training in tropical and jungle warfare—Canungra

By September 1942, the necessity for systematic training in realistic jungle conditions was clearly recognised. Brigadier Potts's voluminous report on the 21st Brigade's Kokoda campaign stated that '[troops] must be trained in similar country and the faster and more individual tactics'.[30] On 20 September Lieutenant-General Rowell argued in a letter to LHQ that it was 'essential that troops get into actual jungle and learn to master its difficulties of tactics, movement and control'. Less than two weeks later, Rowell would expand on this point, stating that 'the only way to train for jungle operations is to train in actual jungle'.[31]

With the move of Advanced LHQ from Melbourne to Brisbane in August 1942, the first steps towards addressing Rowell's concern were undertaken. The appointment of Brigadier R. Irving—recently returned from the Middle East—as Director of Military Training LHQ hastened this change.[32] Irving's most important task was to oversee the centralisation of the training of Australian Military Forces (AMF) under a single command. With units being raised, trained and stationed in their home state, this was a logical system. For the foreseeable future, however, since all troops would serve in the tropics they would need to be trained in similar locales. As there was no suitable jungle warfare training area, the first step was to determine an appropriate location and develop a training centre.[33] In late October, the first official notification of the establishment of a jungle training centre appeared.[34]

As if to confirm that centralisation of training—especially for jungle conditions—was overdue, in September the New South Wales Line of Communication Area began setting up its own jungle warfare training centre. This was because Brigadier Maurice Keatinge, Commandant of Training Depots for New South Wales, believed that all reinforcements must arrive at their units with jungle warfare knowledge if they were to be useful to those units.[35] The fear that some units would be assigned tasks they were not adequately trained to accomplish had been realised during the Kokoda campaign as well as the Beachhead battles. Even the official report admitted that 'in the latter half of 1942 many formations that had had no previous battle experience were being ordered to New Guinea for immediate operations'.[36] As we have seen, throwing unprepared men into combat caused catastrophic losses.

It was therefore understandable that different formations would attempt to address the issue, especially as they failed to see appropriate action being undertaken by LHQ. By October, a 'Jungle Warfare Tng Depot' was under construction at Lowanna, near Coffs Harbour, on the northern New South Wales coast. By mid-November, when Canungra had been inaugurated, Lowanna was ready to receive troops. By late November more than 1000 troops were training at the camp.[37] In an attempt to prevent further instances of decentralisation, the CGS, Lieutenant-General Vernon Sturdee, ordered HQ First Australian Army 'based at Toowoomba [to] conduct a reconnaissance of suitable sites for a jungle warfare centre'.[38] Fairly soon after this, Lowanna was closed.

Although the final decision on the centre's location was still pending, it had been decided that the nucleus of its instructional staff would come from the Guerrilla Warfare School, at Foster, Victoria. This school had been established in February 1941 to train the AIF independent companies, which had been modelled on British commando units.[39] Although the rugged terrain of Wilson's Promontory helped create extremely fit soldiers, it did not adequately replicate the jungles—or climate—of Papua and New Guinea. When the final decision on a location was made, the Guerrilla Warfare School was relocated to Canungra 'to set up a Reinforcement Training Centre and also move the training of independent rifle company troops to the same area'.[40]

On 3 November 1942 the CGS issued instructions formally establishing a jungle warfare training centre.[41] The centre would consist of the LHQ Tactical School, the Reinforcement Training Centre (Jungle Warfare), and an Independent Company Training Centre. Owing to lack of appropriate buildings at Canungra, the LHQ Tactical School—for unit (lieutenant-colonels) and sub-unit (majors/captains) commanders—was moved to Beenleigh.[42] Canungra would therefore concentrate upon individual, section and platoon-level training. The extra 28 days' training a soldier received at Canungra would equip him to 'apply the principles of warfare in jungle fighting'.[43]

By early December the first draft of personnel arrived for training, direct from Australian Infantry Training Battalions (AITB). Reports on the first few months' arrivals were uniformly negative, stating that 'the vast majority appear unfit for [jungle warfare], bad feet, poorly trained, little knowledge of weapons [and] unfit'.[44] The rapid expansion of the army to cope with the situation in Papua, and the very high casualty rates during campaigns in tropical theatres, led to inadequate vetting of personnel forwarded from the AITB. By March 1943, the reports were much more positive. Originally intended to accommodate 1000 to 1500 trainee soldiers, Canungra in October 1943 had more than 6000 under training.[45]

Beyond the initial problems with the recruit pool, the biggest issues faced by its first chief instructor, Lieutenant-Colonel A.B.

'Bandy' MacDonald, were a lack of instructors with experience in jungle warfare and no applicable training manuals or doctrine around which to construct a training syllabus.[46] When MacDonald requested 32 more instructors from DMT, he received sixteen. All were from militia battalions and none had combat experience, in Papua or anywhere else. Over the next few months small numbers of instructors continued to arrive. None could be classified as completely suitable: some were too old, some had been medically downgraded, and others were listed as Services No Longer Required (SNLR). Those few who had experience of the fighting at Kokoda or Milne Bay were often recovering from wounds or recurrent bouts of malaria, or desperately attempting to return to their own units—again, not the most suitable instructors. As with the recruits, it would take until mid-1943 for Canungra to build a pool of instructors who were fully professional and experienced in jungle combat.

The paucity of appropriate training manuals was not adequately resolved until the publication of *Military Training Pamphlet Operations (Australia) No. 23 XX Jungle Warfare* and its 45-page supplement, intended for platoon and section leaders, in May 1943. As 'no war diary was maintained in the Directorate of Military Training until May 1943' it is impossible to accurately determine which training materials the instructors used.[47] With refreshing honesty, the DMT *Account of Activities* admitted that 'there was very little as a guide to initiate the syllabus for this type of training except [for] FSR Vol II'.[48] However, as noted in Chapter 1, neither *Field Service Regulations, Vol. II, Operations*, nor *Infantry Minor Tactics* provided much assistance to those seeking guidance on jungle warfare training or tactics. Consequently, the emphasis until mid-1943 revolved around developing maximal physical fitness, skill in infantry small arms, and discipline—with a newly added focus on movement and self-reliance in the jungle. In May 1943 General Blamey would note that it was crucial to have instructors who had seen combat in New Guinea.[49]

The majority of units sent to the Middle East had been judged underprepared. To overcome this deficiency, 'an AIF Reinforcement Depot' had been established. Reinforcements were trained by their parent training unit before being allotted to their unit. Canungra provided a similar role in training individual soldiers and sub-units before they were posted to their unit. For complete units and formations that were 'listed for movement to New Guinea' but had received no jungle warfare training, another solution was necessary.[50] Both Major-General Berryman and, only weeks later, Lieutenant-General Boase reached a similar conclusion.[51] Boase proposed that a First Australian Army training team be established; it would be attached to 'each formation of First Aust Army in turn, with the object of carrying out [battalion group] exercises in the nearest jungle country'. Obviously agreeing with Boase, within days LHQ announced that 'approval has been given for the raising of two LHQ Trg Teams'.[52] Their role would be to 'formulate and expound the tactical doctrine for jungle and mountain fighting'. At the time this training instruction was being circulated, the men who would command these teams—one Australian and one American—had already been despatched to New Guinea.

While not actually going into action, the training teams visited units recently withdrawn from combat and interviewed battalion and company commanders on their experiences. It was hoped to gain information on solutions to the problems of operating in the tropics, as well as countermeasures to Japanese tactics. Upon their return to Australia, the training teams would visit all units earmarked for service in New Guinea, conduct seminars and briefings for all unit officers, 'assist commanders in the preparation of exercises... and assist commanders in the capacity of directors during tactical exercises'.[53] To disseminate more widely the information the training teams had gathered in Papua and New Guinea, training notes were distributed throughout the army. The first of these appeared in

November, and by December they contained relatively detailed information with traces and diagrams of contact and battle drills that all units were ordered to practice.[54] Units then conducted training exercises based on these notes and produced further notes of their own. Suggestions found in both the 21st and 18th Brigade reports on operations are included in these notes. By early 1943, lessons from the training exercises conducted by the LHQ Training Teams were appearing in a more formalised context, namely the widely distributed *Army Training Memorandum*.[55]

Meanwhile, officers who had recently seen combat in Papua were seconded to LHQ to provide up-to-date assistance to the training teams.[56] While the emphasis was clearly upon infantry units and their training, eventually the training teams, and Canungra itself, would also encompass 'other arms and services'.[57] At this time it was perfectly understandable that the focus should be on the infantry, which did the vast majority of jungle fighting.[58] It would take longer for LHQ to grasp that artillery, engineers, signals and even medical units would also need to prepare and train differently for operations in the tropics. However, by the end of 1942 several measures had been undertaken that would see all units far better equipped to meet and overcome the challenges there.

While the mostly Australian forces were encircling the Japanese on the northern beachheads of Papua, the US forces on and around the island of Guadalcanal were gradually wearing down the Japanese forces there. Beginning in late October, and lasting for almost three weeks, the Battle of Henderson Field was the last major land offensive by the Japanese Imperial Army in the Solomons. Like many of the earlier battles, it was a disaster for the Japanese, who sustained about 3000 casualties, most killed in action, compared with only 80 for the Americans. Two days later, however, the Battle of Santa Cruz

Islands gained the Japanese a tactical victory, with the US Navy forced to retire after the aircraft carrier *Hornet* was sunk and the *Enterprise* badly damaged.[59] This was arguably a Pyrrhic victory, however: the loss of many experienced carrier aircrews in this battle, combined with the cumulative losses since the Battle of Midway in June, meant the Imperial Japanese Navy Air Service was now at breaking point. The ongoing need to resupply its forces on Guadalcanal, and the risks entailed in doing so, saw the Japanese Navy resort to the use of submarines. This method could clearly not provide enough supplies, however, and a decision on future operations was necessary.

Just as General Horii had been ordered to halt the advance on Port Moresby in mid-September because of the need to reinforce the battles in the Solomon Islands, so any further Japanese assaults on the US forces on Guadalcanal were now suspended by Lieutenant General Hitoshi Imamura, commander of the Eighth Area Army—which was divided between the Solomons and New Guinea—as posing the greater threat to his forces.[60] So while the exchange of information on jungle warfare between Australia and the US was still at the embryonic stage, the actions of the two forces in New Guinea and the Solomons were intimately connected.

'Up to my chest in water': The Battle of the Beachheads

As costly as the Kokoda and Milne Bay campaigns had been, the battles of attrition at Gona, Buna and Sanananda would see an even greater loss of life. The establishment of Canungra, the LHQ training teams and the rewritten training manuals had not yet borne fruit. The majority of the AIF soldiers who, along with the 30th Militia Brigade, would eventually capture the three strongly held Japanese positions were training and recuperating at Port Moresby and Milne Bay (the 21st and 18th Brigades) or still in action on the Kokoda Track, in the case of the 16th and 25th Brigades. The expansion of jungle warfare knowledge beyond these brigades continued with the arrival of the 17th Brigade at Milne Bay in October.[61]

After their enforced garrison duties on Ceylon and short training period in Australia, the 17th Brigade, like the other AIF units before them, were looking forward to meeting the Japanese in combat. While encamped at Greta, New South Wales, the brigade had conducted exercises in 'aggressively countering Japanese enveloping movements', with Lieutenant-Colonel Wolfenden acting as an expert jungle warfare adviser.[62] A report written three months later by the 17th Brigade commander stated that 'I expressed complete disagreement with the lessons being taught' during these exercises.[63] As the lessons that Wolfenden was imparting were based largely upon reports from Malaya, it is not surprising that the units who participated in them—the 17th and, earlier, the 25th Brigades—would question their value. Preparations continued, and days before they sailed for Papua, 'all khaki summer dress was tied in rough bundles and dyed green. The result wasn't a bad camouflage effect.'[64] The need for appropriately camouflaged clothing had obviously registered in Australia, but the ability to supply it was still lacking.

Information exchange was also occurring: a copy of the 7th and 18th Brigades' reports on their battles at Milne Bay was used while the 17th Brigade was still in camp at Greta.[65] On the voyage from Brisbane to Milne Bay, intelligence officers gave a series of lectures on the region and the Japanese Army.[66] Soon after arrival, the men commenced jungle training with a lecture by the commanding officer of the 2/9th Battalion 'on tactics used by the Japanese at Milne Bay'.[67] On the same day, the battalions of the 17th began patrolling to gain experience in jungle conditions as well as to kill or capture Japanese stragglers left behind after the defeat of their invasion force in September. The 17th also found that anti-malarial measures were given greater priority because of the experience of the units who preceded them to Milne Bay.

Also on 22 October, the 17th's commander, Brigadier Murray Moten, ordered the creation of a jungle training school similar to the one the brigade had established on Ceylon. The training syllabus would be focused upon movement and survival in the jungle rather than specific jungle warfare tactics. As the 17th Brigade war diary stated, 'the students [will] learn all about bush plants, native foods, the skinning of bush pigs and other useful accomplishments'.[68] While this particular school ran for only five weeks, other schools—for weapons training, infantry section leading and guerrilla warfare—continued throughout the deployment.[69] The Pack Transport training course would also prove valuable once the brigade arrived at Wau. Before engineers arrived to improve the tracks around Wau, horse and mule teams would carry forward supplies in the Crystal Creek and Black Cat areas.[70] The terrain of Papua, New Guinea and the Pacific islands would continue to demand improvisation and non-traditional solutions.

For approximately three months the 17th Brigade was based at Milne Bay, augmenting the defence force there and becoming more experienced in jungle movement and manoeuvre—when they were not required for road building. During its deployment the brigade was able to send a proportion of its officers to the 'NG Force [training] centre jungle fighting course', thus increasing the brigade's overall level of jungle warfare knowledge.[71] The time at Milne Bay enabled them to acclimatise to jungle conditions. According to one unit historian, the time at Milne Bay afforded an 'invaluable three months' preparation', as 'the jungle was there, the climate was authentic and the meaning of malaria precautions was hammered home'.[72] In fact, the jungle was mostly found in the mountains inland from Milne Bay; the coastal strip was dominated by coconut plantations, creeks and abundant secondary regrowth. The highlands of Wau–Salamaua, to which the brigade would eventually be deployed in late January 1943, more closely resembled the ranges around the Kokoda Track.

First, however, came the slow and bloody battles to destroy the Japanese defences at the beachheads. As mentioned earlier, few of the new jungle warfare training ideas and manuals being introduced at this time in Australia played any significant part in defeating the Japanese at Gona, Buna and Sanananda. As it was, most of the AIF units involved in those battles had previous jungle warfare experience, either on the Kokoda Track or at Milne Bay. But as Lieutenant-Colonel Geoff Cooper, commanding officer of the South Australian 2/27th Battalion, argued, this would be of little use because of the haste with which the operation was ordered by higher authority and the lack of support provided. In the end it is impossible to disagree with Cooper that 'Gona was a bloody massacre'.[73]

Even if the Australians had been allowed more time, the nature of the terrain and the Japanese defences would still have ensured that these battles resembled those of the First World War. Preparations for the attacks on the beachheads resemble the inadequate planning for the Kokoda and Milne Bay actions, with grossly inadequate maps, unreliable aerial photographs and little knowledge of the Japanese defences.[74] Poor intelligence on enemy numbers, insufficient time for careful reconnaissance, a debilitated attacking force, appalling terrain and weather, and a lack of support weapons saw the battles descend into costly massacres. Individual groups of Australians struggled through swamps and mud towards expertly sited and camouflaged defences, to be met by 'a wave of small-arms fire', adding to the impression that the Western Front was being revisited.[75]

The problems of transport and logistics meant that the attacking forces had entirely too little support, either air- or ground-based. Tactical air support in jungle conditions was in its infancy, and Allied aircraft occasionally strafed and bombed their own troops.[76] Air support doctrine had hardly changed except to incorporate information from desert operations, so major modification was needed to make it effective in the tropics.[77]

Artillery units were also struggling to come to terms with the new operational environment. Too few artillery pieces and rounds were available to support attacks on the Japanese positions. In one attack on Gona by the 2/14th Battalion, 'only forty rounds could be spared'.[78] Suffice it to say that the Australians and Americans were forced to fight on terms and in conditions that greatly aided the tenacious Japanese defenders, who had nowhere to escape to and were therefore forced to fight to the death—something they had proven in earlier battles they were perfectly willing to do.[79] In terrain similar to Milne Bay, but if anything more waterlogged, the Japanese had prepared their defences on the only elevated—and therefore relatively dry—ground available, around which the tropical vegetation had rapidly regrown, hiding them from ground and aerial observation. From these positions they cut the attacking Allied forces down repeatedly.

Gona was captured only after commanders at the front were allowed to adequately reconnoitre before they attacked and to destroy bunkers using delayed-action shells. Even then, the 39th Battalion found that their own support weapons, 3-inch mortars, sank in the mud while firing on Gona.[80] The debates over the tactical and operational decisions, the higher-level discussions between Blamey and Australian I Corps commander General Edmund Herring and their front-line commanders, as well as between MacArthur and General Robert Eichelberger and their unit commanders, and the impact these had upon the fighting, have been dealt with elsewhere.[81] Suffice it to say that few high-level commanders came out of the Beachheads campaign with increased standing.

Commanders at all levels discovered that the difficulty of movement and lack of visibility once off the few tracks severely constrained their options for manoeuvre.[82] In country where it could take an hour to move 100 yards, one of the advantages of modern warfare, speed—as experienced by both the 6th and 7th Divisions in their North Africa and Middle East campaigns—disappeared in the glutinous knee-deep mud, malarial swamps and tangled wait-a-while bushes. In short, inadequate and inaccurate intelligence, combined with a lack of patience by superior officers, forced those on the ground to commit men to battle without proper preparation. As in any battle fought under such conditions, lives were lost unnecessarily. Thankfully, the hard lessons that most Australian units had learned at Milne Bay and on the Kokoda Track could be applied to the fighting at Buna and Sanananda.[83] One change that the 18th Brigade had managed to make in preparation for their next experience of jungle warfare was to dye many of their uniforms and all of their webbing equipment jungle green before they left Milne Bay.[84]

Before the 18th Brigade launched their assaults through Duropa Plantation, near the village and mission station of Buna, and across the landing field dubbed the Old Strip, Vickers MMGs raked the tops of the coconut palms, searching out snipers. For the men of the 2/9th, 'the lessons of Milne Bay had taught that no enemy could be left alive behind the line of advance'.[85] Every Japanese soldier in every bunker and slit trench would have to be killed before the assault moved forward. For most of the militia units, however, the beachhead battles were a harsh initiation, and one they were ill prepared for. As Oscar Isaachsen, commander of 36th Battalion, suggested, 'the whole trouble with the militia units was they'd had no proper training' for war, in the jungle or anywhere else.[86] Unsurprisingly, reports written by their commanders after the battle stated that 'results can NOT be achieved and greater casualties must result if untrained troops are sent into battle'.[87]

With stalemate around the Huggins Road Block position south of Sanananda, and US forces making little headway in their attacks on the Japanese defences around Buna, it was decided to employ the 18th Brigade to break the deadlock. Two weeks earlier, a doomed attack by five Bren-gun carriers had resulted in the vehicles' destruction and the deaths of most of their crews in under an hour. As we have seen, this outcome had been predicted by all those who had used the carriers in jungle training, both on Ceylon and in southern Queensland. Designed as light, fast reconnaissance vehicles in open terrain, they were forced to operate at Buna with negligible visibility owing to the tall kunai grass, and had bellied on coconut stumps and then been shot to pieces. A 17th Brigade report written after the action made it scathingly clear that 'once again it was proved that Bren carriers are not tanks'.[88]

As was the case at Gona, 'almost nothing was known about the enemy defences' in the Duropa Plantation, through which the 2/9th Battalion advanced on 18 December.[89] Having arrived in the battle area the day before, the battalion had inadequate time for reconnaissance and planning. The subsequent slaughter of large numbers of attackers once again highlighted the consequences of insufficient time for planning as well as very poor intelligence, especially with regard to the numbers of Japanese defenders.[90] It also highlighted the 'failure of the higher commanders to appreciate the conditions in the forward areas'.[91] The relatively short distances on a map belied the difficulties of moving across such appalling terrain. For this new attack, it was decided to use tanks to support the infantry assault. Preparations were inadequate. The decision to use tanks, although correct, was ill thought-out. It resulted in rushed preparation, was undertaken with unsuitable equipment, and involved units with no previous training or experience in infantry–tank operations.

The original, and more suitable, choice of tanks for the attack, made in September 1942, had been the General Grants of 2/5th Australian Armoured Regiment. However, these M3 medium tanks weighed 28 tonnes, and there were no vessels that could transport and offload such heavy tanks in Papua.[92] It was therefore decided to despatch the 2/6th Regiment with their 13-tonne Stuart M3 light tanks.[93] Although these could be transported, they were not appropriate for the task they would be ordered to perform. As Trooper John

Wilson later recalled, the Stuart 'tanks were designed for fast running in open country, mainly for reconnaissance'.[94] When the tanks were forced to slow to walking pace, their engines overheated.[95] Their wireless communications system, also designed for open warfare, did not function properly in the jungle. After the Beachheads campaign, the 2/6th Armoured Regiment wrote that 'the strength of these tanks lies in speed and manoeuvrability... furthermore, visibility... is almost nil'.[96] Despite these drawbacks, the tank crews and the infantrymen attempted to make the most of a poor situation. The night before the attack at Gona, a tank commander and the commander of the infantry platoon to which he was attached made a careful reconnaissance of the Japanese defences.[97]

On the following morning, therefore, the tank was able to outflank and then enfilade the Japanese bunkers, killing many of their occupants with few casualties to the infantry. Further inland, among the coconut palms and the kunai, which hid the bunkers, the tanks were not as fortunate. Bill Spencer recalled the early stages of the attack 'as the tanks moved forward into a barbarous inferno ahead of the walking-paced infantry [who walked into] a wall of small arms lead'.[98] Having had very little time the day before to discuss tactics for communication, the infantrymen fired Very lights at the targets or bashed on the hull of a tank until a crew member stuck his head out and they could tell him what they wanted the tank to do.[99] In this manner the Japanese bunkers were painstakingly cleared, even as the 2/9th was slowly depleted. As with the earlier battles, the first tank–infantry engagement in jungle conditions cost far too many lives. This was directly attributed to the 'shortness of the time available for training tank crews and infantry together'.[100]

Before the next major attack, this time by the 2/10th Battalion on 24 December, HQ Buna Force distributed intelligence acquired over the preceding days. It included diagrams of various bunkers similar to those the 2/9th had overcome during their advance on Cape Endaiadere, just beyond Buna's Old Strip.[101] Despite this assistance, the 2/10th's attack was a disaster, with its tank support destroyed by Japanese anti-aircraft guns—used in an anti-tank role—as they crossed the Old Strip. The virtually unsupported infantrymen were then cut to pieces as they advanced over open ground.[102] Days later, another attack by the 2/10th failed. Lack of time for reconnaissance and inadequate infantry–tank training were again responsible.

On New Year's Day, the climactic assault by the 2/12th Battalion would see the experience of its sister battalions over the previous two weeks put into effect. Reports written after the campaign by personnel of the 2/6th Armoured Regiment included many suggestions for future operations. Foremost among these were a need for better information exchange and closer liaison between the infantry and armoured units.[103] Some of these changes were implemented for the 2/12th Battalion's attack. A better-coordinated and larger volume of air, artillery, mortar and MMG support also contributed greatly to the success of the attack.[104] The recent invention—two days before the assault—of a 'blast bomb', an M36 hand grenade attached to a 5-pound charge of ammonal, also played a crucial part.[105] The tanks carried a good supply of these, which they passed out to the infantrymen to hurl into Japanese bunkers.[106] The subsequent massive explosions destroyed the bunkers and killed all of their occupants. Dozens of such bombs were used.[107] Bandoliers of ammunition were also hung on the rear of the tanks so the infantrymen could simply reach up and resupply without the need to return to their forming-up positions. Within days, the Japanese resistance in the Buna area had been broken. The grim slogging match in the Killerton Track–Sanananda area would, however, continue for nearly a month.

Conditions there were, if anything, worse than at Gona or Buna. Chaplain Frank Hartley recalled that as he moved through the jungle towards the Huggins Road Block, the swamp was 'up to my arm pits ... At every bend there would meet the eye green and rotting corpses. The stench was sickening.'[108] Poorly trained militia units and debilitated AIF battalions eventually overcame the last vestiges of the Japanese defences in the beachheads area. In terrain where vehicles could not be used except on the handful of tracks, the infantry, supported when possible by artillery and aircraft, eradicated the remaining Japanese positions. Those Australians who survived would recall the fighting for Sanananda as the most ghastly of their wartime experiences.[109]

After the 18th Brigade's failed attack on 12 January 1943, General George Vasey would argue that they were 'repeating the costly mistakes of 1915–17' in ordering men to attack bunkers and pillboxes, with little more than small arms.[110] As the historian Peter Brune has shown, those directing the operations at Gona and Sanananda—including Vasey himself—made such mistakes continually.[111] That they did so is evidence of a failure by higher command to address the challenges posed by jungle warfare. The historian Lex McAulay's observation that 'no serious thought had been given to fighting in the Owen Stanley Ranges' applies equally well to the Milne Bay and Beachheads campaigns.[112] That lack of forethought meant the troops at the front had to adapt and improvise solutions to survive.

It is arguable that some of the lessons of Gona, Buna and Sanananda were not directly related to the terrain or the weather. Accurate intelligence, adequate time for thorough reconnaissance, appropriate levels of artillery and tactical air support, and training in infantry–tank warfare tactics would have shortened the Beachheads campaign. Nevertheless, even if all these problems had been identified and addressed beforehand, geography and climate would still have posed formidable challenges. It is clear that the vast majority of men who had served with distinction in those earlier campaigns found tropical jungle a fearsome new environment—initially, at least. The stygian daytime gloom and pitch-black nights; the ever-present threat of ambush and the need for constant watchfulness; the sense of being walled in, of always being soaking wet and dirty, and of having no safe rear area to return to—all these things combined to make jungle warfare an intensely unpleasant experience. The fact that most heavy weapons—especially artillery—could not be transported over the Kokoda Track and around the beachheads, the difficulty of getting vehicles through the thick vegetation, the constant rain and the severely restricted visibility all forced the Australians to adopt tactics different from those that had served them in the Middle East. Until they did so, they struggled to defeat the Japanese.[113]

The six months of combat that culminated in victory at the beachheads confirmed that in future all Australian troops would need to train in jungle conditions. As the battles progressed and more units gained experience in jungle warfare, the body of knowledge was gradually increased. With many units having to fight within days of arriving in theatre, such experience and knowledge, however, often came at a very high cost. The large numbers of casualties that occurred as successive battalions attacked dug-in Japanese defences during the Kokoda and beachhead battles—using the same tactics that had become standard in the Middle East and North Africa—demonstrated tactical naïvety and inflexibility.

While the claim that the front-line troops made 'quick and thorough adaptation to the demands of tropical and bush warfare' is not completely inaccurate, the price paid was unnecessarily high.[114] Opportunities to better prepare the brigades of 6th and 7th Divisions were spurned by keeping them for too long in Australia. They should have been training in Papua before being rushed into battle in late August. The argument that Australia was under threat of invasion and needed to retain these units at home does not withstand detailed scrutiny. The 14th and 30th Brigades were deployed to Papua when the threat to Australia was even greater and eventually flung into battle virtually untrained.[115] It would have made more sense to hold them in Australia until they had attained a satisfactory skill level, and to have despatched 21st and 18th Brigades to Papua considerably earlier.[116] In this way the combat-hardened AIF units would have gained experience fighting in the jungle, and the militia troops would have been brought up to a more adequate standard. That the latter were forced to fight completely unprepared after months spent as labourers and navvies is an indictment of LHQ and the officers who ordered their deployment.

Nevertheless, before the final defeat of the Japanese in late January 1943, measures had been put in place that would eventually see all future Australian troops far better prepared than the 21st and 18th Brigades were in August 1942. The establishment of Canungra, the creation of jungle warfare training manuals, and the dissemination of lessons by LHQ Training Teams throughout formations in Australia would ensure fewer unnecessary deaths. The training undertaken by the 6th, 7th and 9th Divisions on the Atherton Tableland between March and September 1943 was largely based upon the lessons of the first Papuan campaigns. Its usefulness was put to the test when the bulk of the AIF next saw action, in the Huon Peninsula and Ramu–Markham campaigns between September 1943 and February 1944.

Chapter 8

'RAIN, MUD, ROTTENNESS, GLOOM': 17TH BRIGADE'S WAU-SALAMAUA CAMPAIGN

In the ongoing evolution of an Australian jungle warfare doctrine, 1943 was the seminal year. It would witness marked improvements in the standards of training and preparation for jungle warfare, as the lessons of Kokoda, Milne Bay and the beachheads permeated the army. This occurred primarily through the Australian Training Centre (Jungle Warfare) Canungra, the publications of the DMT, and the Advanced Land Headquarters Training Teams. As the plethora of after-action reports from the first Papuan campaigns were trawled through and the most important lessons extracted, more appropriate training techniques and doctrine began to emerge. By the second half of 1943, the Australian Army was turning out soldiers who, having trained at Canungra under a more appropriate syllabus, were immeasurably better prepared for the challenges of jungle warfare than had been those rushed into battle in Malaya and Papua in 1942.

The urgent need to prevent the Japanese from overrunning New Guinea and Papua, and even Australia, subsided after the dark days of 1942. The subsequent lull in operations, which saw the majority of 6th, 7th and 9th Divisions training on the Atherton Tableland until September 1943, allowed for calmer reflection than had been possible before. It also enabled the battle-weary units of 6th and 7th Divisions to absorb the lessons of their first jungle campaign before passing them on to others. The focus of learning, adaptation and transition would then move upwards, to command level.

The training period in mid-1943 set the course for Australian jungle warfare operations for the rest of the war. The AIF's learning throughout this period was based largely on exchange of information between units—both formal and informal. The majority dealt with the tactical level: immediate-action and contact drills; how to deploy sections and platoons in the jungle; how to site company defensive positions; which weapons and equipment were useful and which were not; and how to respond to Japanese infiltration and encirclement tactics. As new protocols and skills were practised on jungle assault ranges and during exercises, they were recorded before making their way up to DMT and LHQ.

What was missing until late 1943, however, was an understanding of the modifications to doctrine that needed to occur at the brigade level and above. As Lieutenant-General John Coates has argued, there existed no 'overarching doctrine' for operations in jungle and tropical theatres, as the army was still in 'the trial and error stage of training and doctrine' development.[1] The vast number of reports that had been created during the first Papuan campaign were still being digested, and the DMT was desperately endeavouring to supply useful manuals to all those formations that had not yet served in a tropical theatre.[2] By late 1943, training manuals would for the first time provide relevant information, enabling units to provide more focused training. It was not until the second major training period on the Atherton Tableland in 1944–45, however, that integration of the previous years of experience resulted in the publication of more comprehensive training materials and better integration and understanding between the combat arms. In 1943 each of those arms was focused upon its 'own' jungle warfare problems, to the detriment of the bigger picture—all-arms combined operations.³

'Introduction to jungle training': 9th Division learns of its new role

To continue tracing the evolution of Australian jungle warfare learning it is, however, necessary to go back several months, and to a very different theatre—North Africa. By 4 November 1942, the involvement of the 9th Australian Division in the pivotal Battle of El Alamein was at an end. In the twelve days since the battle had commenced, on the night of 23–24 October, the 9th Division had fought magnificently and suffered a disproportionate number of casualties. For the next two months it rested, integrated reinforcements and continued to train in preparation for its next role.⁴ Although the division was on the other side of the world, this did not mean that it was uninformed about events in the South West Pacific. From early 1942 it had been receiving reports on the Japanese, their tactics and their methods.⁵ Regular intelligence summaries based on those reports and on lectures given by 'officers with first-hand knowledge of the Japanese' were compiled and distributed down to brigade level.⁶

In the first week of December 1942, the 9th Division commander, General Leslie Morshead, cabled General Blamey: 'Having regard to our future employment is there any particular form of training you wish us specially to practice?'⁷ The oft-quoted reply: 'One: combined [amphibious] training and opposed landings. Two: jungle warfare.' The rest of Blamey's response indicated that even at this stage of the war, the belief was still prevalent that it was possible to train for jungle warfare when not in the jungle. The general noted that although it was not as 'close as desirable for purpose there is considerable amount of rough scrub country near Beit Jibrin'.⁸ In an attempt to undertake the requested training, all three brigades of 9th Division 'carried out "enclosed country" exercises' during January 1943.⁹

One advantage 9th Division had over both 6th and 7th Divisions in 1942 was the number and variety of training manuals and 'lessons learned' documents available to assist with the preparation of those exercises. These included the full 'Notes on Ops in Malaya' discussed in Chapter 2, based upon interviews conducted by Major-General Allen and Brigadier Berryman the day after the fall of Singapore, and 'Notes on Ops at Milne Bay', compiled from 7th and 18th Brigades' after-action reports.[10] Also included was *MTP No. 9 (India)—Notes on Forest Warfare*, which had been supplied to 8th Division in Malaya and to 6th Division on Ceylon. Enough copies of these reports were supplied to the brigades to enable them to prepare training exercises for both platoons and companies. As each brigade had been allotted only three days for training, however, it is open to question how much information was actually imparted before they boarded their respective troopships on 25 January.

The usefulness of this training period—even with more suitable training materials—is difficult to determine, with judgements ranging widely. The 2/13th Battalion stated that the 'exercises gave valuable [training] in [movement] over mountainous country and some interesting lessons were learned'.[11] The 2/23rd stated that 'a final trg exercise was carried out . . . giving us our first taste of what to expect in jungle warfare. Perhaps the Hebron area was not really jungle, but it served the purpose.'[12] The most equivocal, and arguably most realistic, appraisal appeared in the 24th Brigade's war diary. It argued that 'the site was timbered with olive trees but was not a suitable one to present a realistic demonstration of jungle fighting'.[13] Possibly of more benefit were the lectures presented by Major H.T. Allan of 20th Brigade, who had worked in the Wau–Salamaua area before the war.

In the few weeks before they left the Middle East, 9th Division also attempted to address the other part of General Blamey's instruction:

combined operations and opposed landings. To this end, personnel from each of the brigades—generally the brigade commander, his brigade major and staff captain, as well as a selection of officers from each battalion—were sent to Kabrit in Egypt, to the British-run Bitter Lakes Amphibious Training School.[14] As there was time for only a few officers to attend Bitter Lakes, it is again open to question how useful the training was. Unlike 6th and 7th Division units before them, however, 9th Division would have time once in Queensland to adequately prepare for both jungle warfare and amphibious operations.

Training continued on the month-long voyage home, but owing to limitations of space this was restricted to physical training and daily lectures. The aforementioned Major Allan presented many of these lectures to 20th Brigade personnel.[15] The officers of 2/13 Battalion were divided into 'syndicates' and then had to present lectures to the rest of the unit. As the war diary noted, these subjects 'deal with Japanese Army and Tactics, and lessons learnt from Pacific operations'.[16] For units on other ships, lectures along similar lines were also the order of the day. By late February the 9th Division had arrived in Australia.

After a period of leave, the division would concentrate on the Atherton Tableland in April. First, there was at least one repeat of the 7th Division's experiences of the previous year. The 2/28th Battalion, a Western Australian unit, received its first training instruction for jungle warfare as it was re-forming in Perth. The troops attempted to put this into practice, as the 2/14th had tried to do in the Echunga region of South Australia a year earlier, but like the 2/14th, they had to admit that 'the local terrain does not lend itself particularly to this type of warfare'.[17]

As the 9th Division was steaming towards Australia, the 17th Brigade was fighting desperately to prevent the Japanese from capturing Wau aerodrome. The lessons its men fed back to the mainland over the following eight months contributed to the growing body of Australian jungle warfare knowledge. Most importantly, the lessons from 17th Brigade, and later 3rd Division, were incorporated by the GOC, Lieutenant-General Savige, into his manual, *Tactical Doctrine for Jungle Warfare*, prescribed for all II Corps troops.[18]

'The heart of the jungle-covered ranges': 17th Brigade at Wau–Salamaua

During the last three months of 1942, 17th Brigade used its time at Milne Bay to gain valuable experience in jungle conditions, although much of that time 'was spent making roads and unloading ships'.[19] Another problem was the ongoing lack of effective disease-control measures, which meant that many hundreds of soldiers contracted malaria and therefore went into battle already debilitated. The 2/6th Battalion, for example, was 300 men short of its full war establishment.[20] Last-minute preparations in Port Moresby before the flight to Wau included the issuing of green face veils to all 2/7th Battalion personnel,[21] but this attempt at camouflaging white faces that stood out like beacons in the jungle shadows went no further. Upon arrival at Wau elements of all battalions found themselves in action, some within minutes of deplaning.[22] Soon after the brigade's arrival, three of the most common problems of jungle warfare made their presence felt—lack of visibility, difficulty of command and communication, and the necessity for the wide dispersal of a commander's forces, whether companies, platoons or sections.

The 8th Division in Malaya and the 7th Division during the first Papuan campaign had identified these problems. But despite their training and preparations, the lack of any overarching doctrine meant that each individual unit had to overcome the challanges anew. While the solutions they arrived at generally coalesced, at this stage of the war DMT and LHQ were unable to provide satisfactory guidance and training materials. Units were therefore forced to learn lessons that others had learned before them. Being in combat and isolated at Wau, 17th Brigade clearly could not wait for more comprehensive tactical or doctrinal instructions to arrive from Australia. The situation demanded that it—like 7th Division on the Kokoda Track and at Milne Bay—learn by trial and error. As with 7th Division, this method of learning while in action led to unnecessary deaths, although not in the same numbers as on the Track or at the beachheads.

Between 28 January and 6 February, the brigade was involved in several major engagements, eventually resulting in the defeat of the Japanese forces attempting to capture Wau aerodrome. From the outset, the nature of the terrain and climate in the Wau–Salamaua campaign dictated both the scale and the pace of operations, arguably to a greater extent than at Milne Bay or the beachheads. The razorback ridges along which most of the fighting took place made logistics a greater problem than at either Milne Bay or the beachheads. All men, weapons, rations and equipment had to be airlifted into Wau, or airdropped at various Australian camps, such as the Summit, Skindewai and Ballams. Low cloud and violent tropical downpours severely constrained these resupply flights. Even the initial actions around Wau aerodrome, between sizeable forces with artillery and tactical air support and—at least for the Australians—short lines of communication, were marked by the confused and fragmented nature of the fighting. On the day they landed, individual platoons and sections of 2/7th Battalion were sent in different directions to try and identify the main thrust of the Japanese advance.[23] With little knowledge of the surrounding area and inadequate maps, they—and their sister battalions—became involved in a series of actions with a virtually unseen enemy that could appear from any direction.

The 17th Brigade war diary for 1 February highlights the difficulty of commanding and coordinating units in mountainous jungle terrain. Multiple reports from the battalions indicated that the enemy was sited on the brigade's flanks, to its rear, and even between companies and platoons.[24] As 7th Division had found on the Kokoda Track, in jungle warfare, all-round defence and self-sufficiency down to the smallest sub-unit, the rifle section, were critical. Command was difficult, with a battalion commander as likely to come under attack at battalion headquarters as was the lead section of his advancing company several hundred yards away. Providing supporting fire, a straightforward matter in the North African and Mediterranean theatres, was immeasurably more challenging in this terrain. As the 2/7th Battalion discovered, 'owing to the dense jungle and the deep re-entrant C Coy were unable to give fire support to A Coy'.[25] With visibility often restricted to feet or yards, platoons and companies were rarely able to see one another, let alone the enemy that their neighbouring unit was engaging. For the individual soldier the difference between the North African and Wau campaigns was as much psychological as it was physical: 'it was all little skirmishes all the time. There was no front line ... You could guard this track. But they could still infiltrate and be going down along the rivers or through the scrub and around you.'[26] The need to operate in sections or three-man patrols, out of contact with company or battalion headquarters for days at a time, and with little or no fire support—these were some of the new demands of jungle warfare.

After the defeat of the initial attacks, 17th Brigade settled into a long period that one battalion history has called the 'weary months'.[27] Slowly and painstakingly, 17th Brigade and the independent companies forced the Japanese back over the ranges north towards Salamaua. As the 2/5th Battalion's historian would recall: 'gone were the days of battalion attacks or the advance of large bodies of troops ... [rather] it was usually a war between small bodies of men up and down tracks and across razor-back ridges'.[28] The harsh climate and mountainous terrain, the equal of the Kokoda Track, made it a miserable campaign for all involved:

Such conditions of rain, mud, rottenness, gloom, and, above all, the feeling of being shut in by the everlasting jungle and ever-ascending mountains, are sufficient to fray the strongest of nerves. Add to them the tension of the constant expectancy of death from behind the impenetrable screen of green, and nerves must be of the strongest, and morale of the highest, to live down these conditions.[29]

The appalling conditions and disease meant that platoons and companies—which should have had 130 men—were often down to 40.[30] Even for those who did not have malaria, the conditions were extremely trying. General Savige later noted that in the Wau–Salamaua campaign 'man management [was crucial]. The men were wet all the time. They tended to become depressed and depression led to actual illness.'[31] Man management and logistics were the crucial roles of commanding officers in jungle warfare.[32]

As commanders had discovered on the Kokoda Track, with visibility frequently measured in feet or yards, once they had deployed their forces they could do little more than wait for reports to come in. When they eventually did, commanders would attempt to build from those scraps of information a picture of the battle and respond accordingly. It may have become a cliché, but there is some truth in the statement that 'battles in the South Pacific were run by captains, lieutenants, or sergeants'.[33] A company or battalion commander was more likely to be ensuring that his platoons and sections in combat were kept supplied with ammunition and that casualties were evacuated and any reserves deployed than he was to be making tactical changes. For much of the Wau–Salamaua campaign the role of a commander as a man manager was central. The competing demands of infantry patrol work, the evacuation of casualties, the construction and repair of tracks and footbridges, and the resupply of forward units all required his attention.

Often these demands could not be resolved to the satisfaction of all concerned. As the 2/5th Battalion noted, 'the evacuation of wounded presents a serious problem—200 natives required to evacuate 8 casualties to Skindewai thus disrupting [forward] supplies'.[34] With tracks following the narrow and precipitous ridgelines, it was often impossible to have two units moving forward and back at the same time. Thus the evacuation of casualties at times prevented adequate supplies being moved forward for an attack. The deep mud churned up by thousands of feet exacerbated this problem.[35] Although every movement was of necessity measured in hours, not miles, these unavoidable delays repeated—albeit on a reduced scale—the disagreements seen in the Kokoda campaign. The 2/5th recorded that owing to the terrain and distances, several days elapsed before their patrols could report their findings to brigade headquarters, thus undermining 'the Force Commander's desire for quick results ... the rift between BHQ back in Wau and the command up at the sharp end of the battle was becoming obvious'.[36]

Nonetheless, unlike at Kokoda, various senior officers moved forward from Wau to see for themselves the difficulties under which their men were operating. Brigadier Moten mentioned in passing that the terrain was 'not normal country for infantry'.[37] As all who had served in a similar environment had been forced to admit, he observed that 'the Wau–Salamaua area has proved equally difficult for both own [troops] and enemy ... the task of Kanga Force has been dictated by supply problems'.[38] This realisation came more quickly to those who had to face the challenges on a daily basis than to those, such as Lieutenant-General Edmund Herring, commander of I Corps, who were watching the—as far as they were concerned—overly slow progress across their maps at New Guinea Force and LHQ.[39]

Gradually, the soldiers grew accustomed to the conditions and adept at operating in them. As the 2/7th Battalion war diary noted, the men usually spent several weeks in the front line followed by several weeks assisting the engineers on track repair and construction, shorter periods of infantry training while in camp at Wau, and several days carrying supplies forward to augment the native carrier lines.[40] Another crucial engineering task, and one that would become a feature of all subsequent jungle campaigning, 'was the laying of booby traps round the positions of defending infantry with the object of discouraging Japanese penetration'.[41] Soon the engineers were demonstrating to the infantry units how to set and camouflage their grenades and tripwires and, equally important, how to deactivate them the next morning if the enemy had not tripped them.[42] A large section on booby-traps appeared in *MTP No. 23—Jungle Warfare*, published by DMT and LHQ in mid-1943.

With the numerous engineering tasks beyond the capabilities of the 2/8th Field Company, the pioneer platoons of each of the battalions of 17th Brigade were 'made available' to that unit.[43] Even this measure would not be enough, and, as had happened several times before, notably at Milne Bay and on Ceylon, the rifle companies of each battalion were required to work as labourers on a regular basis. As the units were rotated back to Wau, they found themselves subject to the same modifications to war establishment that most of the infantry divisions in Australia were undergoing.[44]

Throughout 17th Brigade's deployment, the diversion of infantry personnel to assist with engineering tasks became standard. In fact, as one of the unit's reports stated, in the type of terrain faced by the brigade 'the work of an [infantry battalion] can be estimated as being 60 per cent construction and 40 per cent operations'.[45] One company from each of the three infantry battalions would be engaged in track work on a rotational basis. In New Guinea, however, the weather regularly forced unforeseen changes to daily routines. In late March, seventeen separate mudslides blocked the track to Edie Creek. The 2/7th Battalion had to supply nearly 100 men to work for several days on repairs.[46] This diversion of infantry—and at times artillery personnel—to perform road and track work, or to carry supplies to front-line positions, was later repeated during the 7th Division's Ramu–Markham campaign and the 9th Division's Lae–Finschhafen campaign. Powell's statement with regard to natives on construction duties on the Wau–Bulldog road, that 'there was never enough native labour', was also applicable to the movement of supplies and the evacuation of casualties.[47] The appalling terrain—which was almost completely inaccessible to vehicles—and the vast distances proved to 17th Brigade, as it had to those who had fought in the first Papuan campaign, that fighting in mountainous jungle was more arduous and demanding than in any other landcape it had encountered. It was in an attempt to relieve some of that burden that two different solutions—one ancient and one modern—were introduced or expanded.

'Moving the guns wasn't easy': The problems of the supporting arms

The first solution, pack animals, had been operating in the Crystal Creek–Wau–Black Cat Mine area from October 1942, but as the roads around Wau were gradually improved it was felt they were no longer needed.[48] With the arrival of 17th Brigade, however, the 17th Brigade Pack Transport Unit was reinstituted and provided valuable service for several more months. As the animals churned up the tracks with their hooves and required much fodder, however, Jeeps, native carriers and airdropping gradually replaced them.[49] Supply by air to dropping grounds and thence by foot to various company and platoon positions became the norm in this campaign. In some especially inaccessible locations, however, the loss rate from airdropping was so prohibitively high—between 50 and 95 per cent—that alternative methods had to be tried.[50] When they became more freely available, parachutes proved successful and recovery rates improved dramatically. Messages from brigade headquarters were also dropped to forward units in an attempt to speed up the transmission of orders.[51] The use of aircraft to augment the limited artillery support available also went through a series of experiments and changes.

Tactical air support had already been used in jungle conditions, most notably during the first Papuan campaigns, although with limited success.[52] As a consequence of the problems experienced in those campaigns, changes were instigated to help improve coordination between the army and air force.[53] One of the first of these involved the appointment of Air Force Staff Officers 'to headquarters of Army formations in order that Direct Air Support and Army Co-Operation generally should be implemented to the fullest possible extent'.[54] Over the course of 1943, improvements would continue to be made to close air support doctrine and procedures. The 7th Division's Ramu–Markham campaign, and in particular the assault on Shaggy Ridge, would see considerably better air support than had been evident previously. For the Wau–Salamaua campaign, however, weather and the commensurate target identification problems would reduce the effectiveness of air power.

Once Kanga Force had pushed the Japanese beyond the effective range of the 25-pounders of 2/1st Field Regiment, firing from Wau, the only artillery support was the mountain guns of 1st Mountain Battery. In addition, the US 5th Air Force, including the Australian No. 22 Squadron, provided ground attack aircraft.[55] As the air force official historian noted, however, 'the value of these activities was limited by the difficulty of seeing the enemy from the air'.[56] This caused repeated problems, the most frequent being that the attacking aircraft found it extremely difficult to hit the targets the army believed it had identified. The difficulty of accurately identifying targets also, on occasion, led to friendly casualties.[57] These resulted not only from inaccurate bombing but also from the exigencies of the terrain. Close air-support doctrine required that Australian troops 'should not be closer than 500 yds to the bombline', which was sensible in 'normal' terrain.[58]

Before an attack in thick jungle country, the forward observation officer and the attacking infantry frequently approached as close as possible to the Japanese positions. This meant that as soon as the supporting fire—whether mortar, artillery or tactical air—lifted, they could charge the remaining distance before the surviving Japanese had come to their senses and returned to their bunkers or gun positions. To wait 500 yards from a defended Japanese position—a reasonable distance in the North African or Mediterranean theatres—and then to attack would have been suicidal. Five hundred yards over jungle-clad razorback ridges could take several hours to traverse.[59] The Australians 'gradually learning that only direct hits by supporting aircraft and artillery would be of much value', the necessity to 'hug' the target area before an attack was self-evident, if highly dangerous.[60] As a consequence of the difficulties of employing air support, the battalions preferred to rely upon artillery. For the artillery units, however, operating in the Wau–Salamaua area was arguably more challenging than the earlier jungle campaigns. Lack of observation of fall of shot, communications between the gun positions and the forward observation officer or observation post officer, difficulties of crest clearance and supply of ammunition were again constant challenges. Equally challenging was the continued lack of reliable maps.

In a sign that the lessons of the first jungle campaigns were beginning to be addressed, an artillery survey team was despatched in late February to begin work.[61] For the remainder of the campaign the teams struggled through the immensely difficult terrain, often being forced to employ methods that appeared in no training manual. The most rudimentary was 'compass and shouting'.[62] Andy Blackburn, one of the unit members, recalled that he would walk some distance behind a companion who 'would call out every so often. I would take a compass bearing in the direction from where his voice appeared to come thus recording the general trend of the route.'[63] The survey units gradually created an accurate survey of the area. This enabled the artillery units to deliver targeted fire without the need to make multiple ranging shots or endanger Allied forces. The fact that accurate maps had not been provided during the previous twelve months when Kanga Force had been operating in the area suggests that there were still problems at higher command levels in addressing the needs of those on the ground.[64]

Exacerbating these issues was the near-impossible task of moving artillery pieces up and down the towering mountain ranges as the infantry advanced. Following the large-scale battles of late January and early February, when the 25-pounders of 2/1st Field Regiment were brought into action an hour after they were unloaded from DC3 transport aircraft at Wau airstrip, it became evident that it would be impossible to move the guns further forward.[65] Still, in the time they were in action they contributed greatly to the defence of Wau. Of equal importance was the continuing accumulation of information on the employment of artillery in a tropical environment. After discussions with the air liaison officer and RAAF Wirraway pilots, a greatly simplified 'method of engaging targets with air co-op [was] evolved by Capt Wise and instructions issued to both troops'.[66] When the 1st Australian Mountain Battery arrived in late February, these lessons were passed on and used to good effect throughout its deployment.

The continuing necessity for improvisation became evident to the battery within days of its arrival on 21 February. With the assistance of a party from 2/1st Field Regiment, the artillerymen were able to move their guns from Wau to Kaisenik on trolleys. As these became bogged in the mud, the 'gunners very quickly adopted the native carrier method of carrying heavy loads—tie the load to poles and carry it on the shoulders'.[67] Occasionally they were able to use the horses and mules of the Pack Transport Unit, but for the most part shouldering the loads became the normal—if exhausting—method of moving the guns from one position to another. Almost as difficult was resupply of ammunition. A 17th Brigade report stated that to move a single round of artillery ammunition from the airstrip at Wau forward to the gun positions at Guadagasal took the equivalent of one carrier's labour for a week.[68] This problem would not be solved during the campaign. Equally important, and similarly challenging, was the question of communications, both for the artillery and the infantry they were supporting.

Inadequate signal equipment continued to bedevil the units operating from Wau. Some members of the 1st Mountain Battery were more fortunate in this regard, as they had borrowed American assault line and power phones while at Buna.[69] They were in the minority, however, and, as in the earlier campaigns, 'line communication [has] proved beyond doubt the safest method'.[70] As 7th Division signallers had found in 1942, 'cable laying is extremely difficult and arduous in jungle areas', and when combined with the ever-present threat of Japanese ambush, it was an unenviable task.[71] Even when the cable could be laid forward, there was no guarantee that amid the tangled jungle and razorback ridges 'a suitable [observation post] to control [the] mortars' could be found.[72] In similar circumstances to Milne Bay and the beachheads, for a forward observation officer to be certain that artillery or mortars would hit the target, he had to move dangerously close—within 50 yards—of the enemy. At times 'sound ranging', which had first been used in those earlier campaigns, was necessary. In at least one instance the only solution was for the officer to crawl as far forward as possible and range the guns on his own position.[73] By this process of experimentation and recording what worked and what did not, a successful operating method was developed.

The urgent need to increase the pool of knowledge on jungle warfare meant that throughout its deployment in the Wau–Salamaua area, 17th Brigade was collecting information both on Japanese weapons and tactics and on the best ways to improve its own. Orders regularly appeared from Brigade HQ in which company commands 'were asked for a report on their views on JAP TACTICS, [equipment], method used and lessons learned from Wau operations also any deficiencies in our [equipment]'.[74] As with the Kokoda campaign and Brigadier Potts' voluminous report, the most detailed report from 17th Brigade appeared after it had returned to Australia.[75] Nevertheless, a regular series of reports and documents containing suggestions for improvements to methods, tactics, training and equipment appeared throughout its deployment.[76] In order to better evaluate and incorporate these reports into subsequent training, changes were occurring in the DMT and LHQ.

By the middle of 1943, 17th Brigade was nearing the end of its deployment. While serving in the Wau–Salamaua area, it had also contributed to the dissemination of jungle warfare learning by fostering in units of 15th and later 29th Brigades.[77] Throughout July and August this involvement increased as the 17th prepared to hand over responsibility completely and return to Australia. But the collection of information on the enemy and operations in jungle terrain continued. The Japanese lack of tactical innovation was noted in the expanded 17th Brigade Group report.[78] Whether or not 'early victories [had] lent a certain complacency' and left the Japanese seeing little need to refine or improve their tactics is open to debate.[79] What appears beyond question, however, is that the Allies' early defeats forced them—the Australian Army included—to examine how and why they had occurred. Part of this learning process was the in-depth study of operations in the tropics.

In late August and September, 17th Brigade arrived in Australia, where, after a period of leave, they re-formed and began training for their next campaign. The lessons of January to August were not forgotten, however: Staff School courses run for units and formations of 3rd Division in late 1943 to mid-1944 were drawn from that period.[80] General Savige's instruction manual, *Tactical and Administrative Doctrine for Jungle Warfare*, which was issued to all units in II Corps serving under his command on Bougainville, was also largely based on the experiences of the Wau–Salamaua campaign.[81]

For 17th Brigade, the most important lesson of its operational experience in the Wau–Salamaua area—the centrality of effective patrolling—merely reinforced the lessons of the first Papuan campaign. As the report stated, 'patrolling, particularly aggressive patrolling, is the key to successful jungle fighting', and 'a high standard of training is required for patrolling the jungle'.[82] While this statement would not have been revelatory to any of the AIF divisions—for whom patrolling to obtain information on the enemy and the terrain had been standard operating procedure in North Africa, Greece, Crete and Syria—lack of reliable maps and the inability of aerial photos to provide adequate detail in a sea of green foliage meant that in jungle terrain, the importance of patrolling and reconnaissance could not be stressed too highly. Thorough jungle warfare training—for all members of the combat arms—and aggressive patrolling would be cornerstones of Australian operational effectiveness in the jungles of the South West Pacific Area.

'Training in battle conditions': LHQ, Canungra and Beenleigh

With 17th Brigade the only AIF infantry brigade in action between February and August 1943, a steady stream of visitors from Australia arrived to gather first-hand information on jungle and mountain warfare. Some of the more important, at least with regard to the future development of jungle warfare training and doctrine in Australia, were Lieutenant-Colonel McDonald and several teams of instructors from Canungra. As noted in Chapter 7, the standard of instruction—and therefore of trainees—at Canungra in the early stages was not satisfactory. With the return to Australia of jungle warfare–experienced officers and NCOs in early 1943, this gradually began to improve, although it was difficult to keep up with the rapid expansion in the size of Canungra. In late 1943 there were 1300 men in training; this increased to 3320 in April 1943 and was over 6000 by early 1944.[83]

In order to maximise the distribution of jungle warfare information, LHQ decided that the next most useful course of action was to provide a detailed outline of the syllabus from Canungra so that all units and formations in Australia could benefit. The March 1943 issue of the *Army Training Memorandum* therefore contained four pages outlining the type of training that occurred at Canungra, as well as a simplified breakdown of the training syllabus.[84] The necessity of increasing the number of units who had a basic understanding of the methods and tactics to be employed in jungle warfare appears to have outweighed the fact that many units would not be able to replicate jungle conditions in their current training locations. To improve the quality and wider applicability of the information distributed by Advanced LHQ and DMT via the *Army Training Memorandum*, 'observers were appointed who were able to send back reports for inclusion in [*ATM*]'.[85] In late 1943 an 'Operational Report Section' at LHQ was formed whose task was 'the collection and collation of reports on operations to ensure that the lessons learned [were] made available' to all commanders.[86] Although it had not reached its apogee, the ability of the army to provide considerably improved doctrinal and training material than even a year earlier was noticeable. These developments would also have an effect at Canungra and at Beenleigh—the LHQ Tactical School.

By March 1943, some of the first trainees to pass through Canungra had been assigned to units overseas, while others were sent to bolster the depleted 7th Division units on the Tableland. One reinforcement who joined the 2/6th Battalion at Wau commented that 'his ... [training] at Canungra proved invaluable. The country there was identical to that round Mubo. The patrol tactics were the same.'[87] With positive feedback on Canungra graduates from the commanding officer of an independent company in the Wau–Mubo area, Lieutenant-Colonel McDonald took the opportunity to examine for himself the terrain and tactics that he and his staff were attempting to replicate in Queensland. In mid-March he arrived at Wau, where he viewed the independent companies and examined the 17th Brigade Training School which Brigadier Moten had established.[88] In April, Major T.T. Lunn—the commanding officer of the Advanced Reinforcement Training Centre (Jungle Warfare) at Canungra, led an observer tour of New Guinea, visiting several battlefields and the New Guinea Force Training Centre.[89] On this occasion he was unable to visit Wau, but in mid-1943 he returned to do so. In May another group of instructors from Canungra flew to Wau and spent two weeks visiting the units in action in the area. As the tour leader later recorded, 'it was found that only after a visit to the [companies] in contact with the enemy, were the real problems of Jungle Warfare fully appreciated'.[90] Upon their return to Canungra, the instructors were able to incorporate the ideas and problems they had observed in action into the syllabus and create more realistic training scenarios. As a consequence of these improvements in instruction, units receiving recruits were able to state that they had a 'high degree of physical fitness and weapon efficiency' and that their jungle skills were very good.[91]

With the increasing number of units and formations that the training teams were required to visit, LHQ too was keen to keep its personnel up to date. To this end, in April four members of the training team were sent as observers to Wau.[92] The commander of the LHQ Training Teams, Lieutenant-Colonel Wolfenden, and his instructors also regularly visited Canungra, Advanced LHQ and DMT to collect 'up to date' material.[93] They were then attached—usually for a period of two to four weeks—to formations or commands and ran jungle warfare training exercises. The secondment of officers who had seen action in the first Papuan campaigns added to the authenticity of their lectures and training, as the 19th Brigade in the Northern Territory would attest.[94] In this manner, the dissemination of current techniques and tactics was able to occur on a broader basis. In a further measure to ensure that the training teams were providing realistic information to all units, Wolfenden was sent to Wau in June. He spent a month seconded as second in command of 2/6th Battalion, gaining much practical experience of jungle conditions.[95]

The training of higher-level officers—clearly the most important level in attaining operational success—was improved in early 1943 with the establishment of the LHQ Tactical School at Beenleigh, Queensland.[96] As DMT recorded, the school was to 'teach the tactical doctrine of fighting and teach the art of command'.[97] It had been intended that the school's commandant would also supervise training at Canungra. With the massive and extremely rapid expansion of Canungra, this was deemed impossible. Once all the AIF divisions had returned to Australia, and it was clear that all future operations would be in the South West Pacific Area, training at Beenleigh changed to 'examine and determine the differences of method which were necessary for fighting in tropical country'.[98]

Close liaison between Canungra and Beenleigh would continue for the duration of the Second World War, ensuring a uniformity of instruction and a timely integration of new jungle warfare techniques and tactics into training syllabuses. As at Canungra, officers experienced in jungle warfare were seconded to Beenleigh on a regular basis to assist with training and to ensure that instruction was up to date and reflected the reality of combat in Papua and New Guinea.[99] Officers of both the junior and senior wings of the Tactical School regularly visited Canungra during their six-week course, enabling them to improve their tactical knowledge.[100] The effect of these improvements was soon felt throughout the Australian Army.

Chapter 9

'THE IDEAL TRAINING GROUND': ATHERTON TABLELAND, 1943

In early 1943, the epicentre of the changes occurring in the Australian Army had moved north. While the establishment of the Jungle Warfare Centre at Canungra and the creation of LHQ Training Teams was occurring, other changes were also underway, all of which would make the Australian Army the most formidable jungle warfare force in the world. In Queensland a series of conferences were underway. The outcomes of these conferences and of the vast number of after-action reports generated by the first Papuan campaigns changed the shape of the Australian Army for the remainder of the war. Jungle Infantry Divisions, the Owen Gun, 'short' 25-pounder artillery pieces, jungle-green uniforms, 'stalker' ranges and tropical disease-control measures: all would enter the vernacular of the Australian soldier. The '39ers', those men who had enlisted in 1939, would not have recognised the army of 1945. But the men who served in Malaya, Borneo and Vietnam in the 1950s, '60s and '70s would have had less difficulty. The developments that the Australian Army experienced during the final two years of the Second World War foreshadowed the 'low-intensity' guerrilla conflicts of the Cold War, arguably setting in place the way in which the army would operate until 1975.

'A state of utter disrepair': 16th Brigade and 7th Division on the Atherton Tableland

While these discussions were occurring, the battle-weary soldiers of 7th Division and 16th Brigade (6th Division) were completing their leave before re-forming on the Atherton Tableland in March. As they returned, 2/14th Battalion was not alone in noting that 'the large incidence of malaria is seriously hampering the re-organization and training of the battalion'.[1] Relapses saw thousands of men who had served in the first Papuan campaign admitted to hospital over the course of 1943, many of them on multiple occasions. The problem of illness aside, as soon as the men marched into their camps in the area around Ravenshoe, Wondecla and Herberton, training began. All units appeared to follow the format recorded by 2/16th Battalion: route marches, weapons training, drill and PT.[2] The high level of fitness required to survive the rigours of jungle warfare—demonstrated beyond doubt during Kokoda—was acknowledged in the first 'Training Instruction' issued by 16th Brigade upon arrival at Ravenshoe.[3]

Simultaneously, the controversy surrounding the selection of a single sub-machine gun for the Australian Army to employ in jungle warfare continued. In late October 1942, both 16th and 21st Brigades had provided positive reports on the new Owen gun, specifically referring to its weight, the weight of its ammunition, and the fact that it was very reliable in jungle conditions.[4] They both suggested that it replace the American Thompson sub-machine gun then in use. The main reasons were that the Tommy gun was heavier, as was its ammunition, and needed to be kept scrupulously clean if it was to work properly, which was virtually impossible in the muddy tropics. In January 1943 the 2/10th Battalion would record that 'the OWEN gun was stated by the [troops] to be the better and Bde [was] advised accordingly'.[5] This was not, however, the end of the matter, as many in higher authority in the military and in procurement had decided that the Austen gun should be adopted instead of the Owen.[6] Eventually both would be produced in large numbers, although the vast majority of AIF infantry units preferred and used the Owen. These high-level discussions would, for the most part, not affect the soldiers on the front line. Clearly, however, the Australian Army was beginning to realise that the new combat environment required not only modified doctrine and training methods but different weapons and equipment from those used in the North Africa and Mediterranean campaigns.

As more men returned from leave, the length and complexity of training exercises increased. The training syllabus of the 2/16th Battalion was created after careful examination of battalion and brigade reports from the Kokoda and Beachheads campaigns.[7] While the units were taking these initial steps, planners at brigade level and above were trying to prepare a single, unified training program. The ultimate aim was to arrive at that 'overarching doctrine' that had previous been noticeably absent from Australian jungle warfare learning.

To this end, a series of conferences was attended by Australian II Corps as well as 6th and 7th Division officers. There were two main items under discussion, both of which would affect the manner in which the AIF trained and fought for the remainder of the war. The first of these conferences concerned the organisation and structure of the army and would not involve great input from the units themselves. High-level discussions had already seen the relevant decisions made. On 13 February 1943, LHQ notified all formations and units under command that three types of divisions would now exist: armoured, standard infantry and jungle infantry.[8] The first formations to undertake the changes would be 5th, 6th, 7th and 11th Divisions. When 9th Division arrived home, it would also become a 'jungle infantry division'.⁹ Only those divisions would require changes to their war establishment. The CGS, General John Northcott, said the new organisation would ensure that 'all units, sub-units, transport and equipment which are not essential for general operations in jungle conditions have been eliminated from the Div organization'.¹⁰

For the combat arms, the biggest practical changes would occur in the infantry battalions and their primary supporting arm, the artillery. Two of the platoons in the Headquarters Company of an infantry battalion, 2nd (anti-aircraft) and 4th (carrier), were no longer required. A Divisional Carrier Company would be created and carriers allocated as needed. An MMG platoon would be created for each battalion, equipped with four Vickers MMGs, and the mortar platoon's armament would be increased from four to eight 3-inch mortars. This was an attempt to increase the self-sufficiency and firepower of the infantry battalions. These changes would mean a reduction in personnel from the standard war establishment of 910 to approximately 800. Although this was not mentioned in the LHQ document, 2/14th Battalion recorded that the strength of its Pioneer Platoon doubled.¹¹ The comments by Captain Frank Sublet in December 1942 that 'it is pointless training personnel as Carrier-drivers, vehicle drivers, AALMG [Anti-Aircraft Light Machine Gun]', and that 'the people who count are the rifle men' had come to fruition.¹² In jungle warfare every member of a battalion would go into battle expecting to fight as an infantryman. There were no 'rear areas', as attack could come at any time and from any direction.

More importantly, these changes were an attempt to solve two problems with one measure. In the first Papuan campaign, the mountainous tropical terrain had proven a great impediment to the movement of transport and thus reduced the amount of support available to the infantry units. Infantry battalions had reduced their own support weapons—and paid the price when opposed by Japanese units that had a preponderance of light and medium machine guns and the ubiquitous mountain guns.

Never again, it was hoped, would there be a repetition of the situation at Alola on the Kokoda Track, where the Australians could see Japanese soldiers in the distance but had no weapons capable of hitting them. In fact, by mid-1943, the firepower of an Australian infantry division was vastly greater than in previous years. While the number of rifles in a jungle infantry division remained roughly the same—11,000—the increase in the number of automatic weapons and mortars was very substantial. In early 1942 a division employed fewer than 400 sub-machine guns; by 1943 a 'jungle division' had 2200.[13] Even when ambushed, an Australian unit could therefore call on far greater firepower than its Japanese opponent, and as technology improved, reductions in weight would allow even greater firepower to be carried by the same number of troops.[14] This overwhelming superiority was later commented upon by a Japanese officer, who recalled that 'we could not do much against their firepower'.[15] Although not as well resourced as the US Army, the Australian Army began to place greater reliance upon firepower to save lives. The final campaigns of 1945 would see the natural culmination of this trend.

For the artillery, the primary changes would be in the number of regiments assigned to each division, the introduction of the 'short' 25-pounder, and a vast reduction in divisional motor-transport establishments. Field regiments would be reduced from three to one per division.[16] Initially these changes appeared logical. As the historian Albert Palazzo has argued, 'fewer vehicles also meant [fewer] maintenance personnel and reduced the amount of supplies the division needed'.[17] The fact that the changes may have been too drastic would become evident when the 7th Division began to pursue the retreating Japanese across the plains of the Markham and Ramu valleys from September 1943 onwards. In some quarters, however, disquiet over the reduction in transport for infantry formations was raised before combat. One of the first of those to signal his doubts would be General George Vasey, commander of the 7th Division, who pointed out several problems to LHQ.[18] For example, the introduction of the two-wheeled metal handcarts officially termed 'Carts Hand Jungle Special' would not adequately compensate for the removal of much of a unit's own transport.

These carts were first noticed being used by the Japanese during the Kokoda campaign and appeared an effective solution to the problem of transport and movement of a battalion's support weapons, ammunition and supplies.[19] The infantry battalions of 7th and 9th Divisions would train with these carts before their deployment to New Guinea, but on the relatively dry tracks and roads of Australia, not on the tortuous mud-choked tracks they would face once in action. Although reports written after the Beachheads campaign had suggested that the carts would not prove useful in difficult terrain,[20] they were issued and deployed with 7th and 9th Divisions. Soon after their initial use in September–October 1943, they would be discarded by most units. A December 1943 report commented that the handcarts 'are not liked as they are hard to push and jeeps can be used almost anywhere jungle handcarts can'.[21] Although a few battalions commented favourably on them, the majority disliked them, and they would not be used during the final campaigns.

The second conference was more directly related to tactics and training, although by the time the resulting manuals had been distributed en masse, 7th and 9th Divisions had begun deploying to New Guinea. During the second week of February, 21st Brigade 'discussed the agenda paper of a conference to be held at HQ 7 Aust Div on 19 Feb on the subject of Jungle Warfare'. Representatives of all battalions and brigades in the division were ordered to attend. Over the next five days various topics were discussed. The first was the compilation and eventual publication of a jungle warfare training pamphlet. The next day saw discussion of the reorganisation required to bring the division into line with the newly proposed war establishment changes for 'jungle infantry divisions' as well as an examination of the 'equipment and training of the Div' for jungle warfare.[22] On 22 February, 'Direct Air Support' and the possibilities of its replacing artillery support in jungle conditions were considered.[23] The final day of discussions concerned the '7 Aust Div pl and sec comds handbook', eventually published as *Supplement to Military Training Pamphlet (Australia) No. 23 Jungle Warfare—Notes for Platoon and Section Leaders*. The conference decided that an outline of the pamphlet would be given to the brigades, which would then forward their suggestions on its content to 7th Division HQ.[24] Although those at the 7th Division conference could not know it at the time, decisions made at a higher level would eventually determine the content of those manuals.

The issues under discussion at this conference had their genesis at Advanced LHQ in Brisbane. As Advanced LHQ stated, 'many reports have been coming in from NEW GUINEA and the information has been collated ... and in due course will come out as complete publications or in the form of articles for inclusion in ATMs'.[25] A draft version of a training pamphlet to be called 'Jungle Warfare' was foremost among these.[26] Advance copies of this pamphlet were sent to all formations and commands in Australia on 2 March 1943 with a covering note stating that 'contents will be studied and applied to training where applicable'.[27] Before full distribution could occur, however, unfavourable reaction to the contents would be received at Advanced LHQ. Both General Vasey and General Allan Boase criticised numerous aspects of the pamphlet.[28] The statement by Boase that 'the publication gives evidence of being hastily prepared and inadequately edited' is hard to refute. The pamphlet was an amalgam of numerous reports dating from at least December 1941 through to the close of the Beachheads campaign. There also appears to have been some confusion about the intended purpose of the pamphlet. Vasey noted that although the first section stated that it was written 'primarily for the company and the battalion commander', it covered topics that are usually the responsibility of a divisional or corps commander, as well as section and individual training.[29]

Another criticism was that the pamphlet covered ground that had already been better dealt with by such manuals as *Infantry Training*, *Infantry Minor Tactics* and the two volumes of *Field Service Regulations*. What it should have done was to better enunciate 'those matters which are peculiar to jungle warfare'.[30] The hasty preparation that led to these problems was, of course, directly attributable to the urgent need for direction on training and doctrine. All units and formations in Australia wanted to know how they should prepare their soldiers for combat in the South West Pacific Area. To meet this demand, LHQ and DMT moved precipitously. The criticisms would eventually see the pamphlet re-issued in altered form, though not before several pages taken directly from the provisional copy appeared in *ATM No. 21*, in March 1943.[31]

To more clearly demarcate topics that concerned company and battalion commanders from those that were the purview of platoon and section commanders, the pamphlet was divided into two parts. The preface still stated that 'this pamphlet endeavours to collect all the available information which has been gained from the experience of fighting ... in Malaya, Philippines, New Guinea and the Solomons'.[32] Although improved, particularly with the addition of information from the recently completed Papua operations, the pamphlet still dealt in generalities, resembling a volume of *FSR*.

Of particular interest to those at the 7th Division conference was the discussion of jungle warfare training at the unit and sub-unit levels. The last day of the conference saw those present 'discuss and adopt [the] final draft of Pamphlet on Jungle Warfare, and methods of training for jungle warfare'.[33] The need for more relevant training manuals based upon recent experiences was highlighted by a

25th Brigade exercise in March. The training pamphlets officers were advised to review before the exercise included *Infantry Minor Tactics*, Bennett's *ATM No. 10* and Colonel Brink's *Tactical Methods*.[34] While *Infantry Minor Tactics* contained much useful information for the infantry officer, its benefits, and those of the other two pamphlets, were restricted to more open theatres of warfare, or to countries like Malaya or Ceylon with a developed road network. Provisional copies of *MTP No. 23 Jungle Warfare—Notes for Platoon and Section Leaders* were distributed to units in May. However, as noted, the final version of this 44-page pamphlet came too late to be used by 7th or 9th Divisions in this training period. It would provide the basis of individual, section and platoon tactics and training throughout the Australian Army until superseded in late 1944.[35]

The 'Jungle Soldier's Handbook', as *MTP No. 23* was called in its Introduction, was 'to be read with the existing textbooks and NOT to replace them'.[36] In an unambiguous response to what General Vasey described as 'too much Hoodoo' around the concept of 'jungle warfare', LHQ was insistent that 'the principles laid down in our existing army publications... all apply in jungle warfare'.[37] Nevertheless, the manual admitted that those principles and practices would need to be adjusted to meet the 'points and considerations peculiar to jungle operations'. To that end it defined the nature of 'tropical' and 'jungle' country, then moved on to 'Japanese characteristics' and the importance of hygiene before examining training.[38] As an adjunct to this manual, in early June LHQ distributed the 70-page handbook *Friendly Fruits and Vegetables*.[39] It contained descriptions and photos of many wild foods found in the tropics in the hope that troops in the jungle would use them to supplement their diet and, if they became lost, to survive.

MTP No. 23 progressed through chapters on individual, section and platoon training and tactics before finishing with a chapter on patrolling, which included diagrams of section and platoon formations for various patrols in jungle, and of ways to set booby-traps. The patrol diagrams differed markedly from those in *Infantry Minor Tactics*. Rather than having two sections forward and one behind, the platoon commander moving with the rear section, the new formation was for a two- or three-man scout group to be forward, followed by the section commander with the light machine-gun group, and then the rest of the section in file behind. This was clearly based upon combat experience of the first Papuan campaign.[40] In fact, the division of a section into 'scout', 'Bren' and 'support' groups appeared for the first time in *MTP No. 23* and would continue to form the basis of jungle patrols for the remainder of the war.

Another change that appeared at this time was also clearly based upon the experiences of that campaign. According to Laffin, the 25th Brigade commander, Brigadier Eather, 'made it clear in training that as soon as contact with the enemy was made, the platoons were to be committed, without reserve'.[41] Although the 25th Brigade war diary is not quite as emphatic, it emphasised that reserves should be committed 'without undue delay [to deny the enemy] the chance of regaining the initiative'.[42] While this appears to directly contradict the modified patrol formation that appeared in *MTP No. 23*, it actually complemented it. Prior to contact, a section or platoon would adopt the more cautious—and more appropriate—'one up, two back' jungle formation, but once contact had occurred the section, platoon or even company commander should not order his troops to go to ground and consolidate their position. Their preponderance in automatic weapons should be utilised and the Japanese position rapidly attacked. During the Kokoda campaign in particular, it had become accepted that the best way to overcome Japanese resistance was to attack as soon as a position was identified. Waiting for orders or support only gave the enemy time to reinforce the position, so that when the Australians did finally attack they suffered greater casualties than they would have if they had assaulted the Japanese position immediately. When the updated *Tropical Warfare* manuals were published in late 1944 and early 1945, these tactics were described and it was made clear that they were to be adopted.[43]

As Warrant Officer Ian Kuring has noted, the 1943 training period therefore saw the introduction of several new or refined tactical techniques to enable the Australian Army to operate more effectively in jungle warfare, including section and platoon immediate-action and contact drills—most of them devised to deal with Japanese tactics identified in the earlier campaigns.[44] Although it had taken time— and many casualties—more appropriate jungle warfare doctrine and training was now appearing. As the historian Tim Moreman has observed, 'a highly effective standardised tactical doctrine for jungle warfare was developed and pass[ed] on throughout the Australian Army' during 1943.[45] Modification would continue to occur until the end of the Pacific War, but to a large extent, the changes necessary to enable the Australian Army to successfully operate in jungle and tropical terrain had begun to be standardised. Although Coates's overarching doctrine was not yet a reality, it was moving steadily closer.

The contemporaneous debate over whether or not the Australian Army needed to make some of the changes contained in *MTP No. 23* is largely a matter of perspective and empathy. To the front-line soldiers in Papua who had fought in North Africa, there were marked differences between the two theatres. They had lost comrades at Milne Bay, Eora Creek and Gona, some of whom would have survived if jungle warfare–appropriate training systems and doctrine had been in place. For these soldiers, the need for change and adaptation was self-evident. Commanders such as Vasey and Boase, however, with their broad knowledge of military principles and doctrine as well as greater experience of warfare, saw many of the changes as unnecessary.[46] For them, the reduction in the number of artillery regiments and transport under the new 'jungle infantry division' establishment, as well as the views expressed in *MTP No. 23*, were hasty overreactions to a string of defeats. The ambivalence over the necessity for systemic change is reflected in the comments by Vasey quoted above. It is also noticeable in the lack of clarity identified by Boase and Vasey in the DMT's draft version of *MTP No. 23*. Ultimately, however, these higher-level discussions were beyond the purview of those who would be most affected by the changes, the combat troops. They simply hoped that the changes to training, weapons and equipment that occurred over the course of 1943 would allow them to operate in the jungle more effectively and defeat the Japanese.

A more immediate outcome of the conferences mentioned above was a concerted attempt to create a more unified training program across all AIF units training on the Atherton Tableland.[47] To this end, beginning in late March, 6th Division began issuing instructions on jungle warfare training. The first was similar to those being issued by 7th Division and stated that 'training for Jungle Warfare is additional to, and does NOT replace, the normal training'.[48] Three weeks later, however, 6th Division altered its stance and admitted that the 'special features of Jungle Warfare ... necessitate certain special training'.[49] Moreover, it stated that 'training in jungle warfare can only be effectively carried out in the jungle'. Included in the training instruction were orders for all units to begin construction of 'jungle stalker ranges'. The instruction made it clear that 'ALL arms and services' under command would commence this type of training. These training instructions would culminate in *6 Aust Div Training Instruction No. 11 Jungle Warfare*, which was issued in July 1943.[50]

This highly detailed training manual followed the same format as *MTP No. 23* and, as the front cover stated, was 'issued provisionally within the Division in amplification of *MTP (Australia) No 23*'. The chapter headings were virtually the same as those of *MTP No. 23*, but each chapter was longer and contained more diagrams of patrol formations and defensive and ambush positions. Elements of this manual were drawn from the suggestions put forward by two company commanders from the NSW 2/2nd Battalion who had fought on the Kokoda Track. In particular, the platoon diagrams and suggestions regarding the training of reinforcements in jungle warfare were revised versions of those that appeared in rough draft in the notes of Captains Donald Fairbrother and Ian Ferguson.[51] The purpose of the 6th Division manual was clearly set out from its beginning: it consolidated 'the experiences and opinions of Officers, NCOs and men who fought the Japanese in New Guinea . . . which will help us in our future encounters with the enemy'.[52]

The instruction made clear that this training manual would be 'adopted by all units of 6 Aust Div as standard'.[53] Elements of this training instruction were incorporated into General Savige's *Tactical and Administrative Doctrine for Jungle Warfare*, which, as mentioned earlier, was issued to Australian II Corps in 1945. Both *MTP No. 23* and *Training Instruction No. 11* were used by 6th Australian Division in its training until they were superseded by the *Tropical Warfare* training manuals issued in late 1944 and early 1945. Although it may appear that the publication of two manuals approximately a month apart demonstrates that the army was still searching for a uniform approach to jungle warfare training, the contrary is actually true. The great similarities between these manuals highlight the fact that an almost universally applicable training and doctrinal system for jungle operations was now in place. All units that had seen combat against the Japanese had taken remarkably similar lessons from those experiences and distilled them into very similar training manuals. This would allow DMT to disseminate more accurate training ideas to those units that had not yet fought in the South West Pacific Area.

Due to the many problems discussed earlier, jungle warfare training could not begin in earnest for 6th or 7th Divisions until late March. When it did, the familiar pattern of individual, section and platoon training followed, with the emphasis on hardening, 'bushcraft'—including 'living in bush or jungle'—and 'health'.⁵⁴ The 16th Brigade adopted a similar format, with the inclusion of assault and obstacle courses.⁵⁵ Another major change to the first jungle campaigns was the time devoted to education on tropical diseases. Troops had the importance of anti-malarial and anti–scrub typhus procedures drummed into them, with some units believing they spent as much time on those aspects of jungle warfare as on tactics.⁵⁶ That the two were seen as equally important is underscored by the comment of Colonel Frank Kingsley-Norris, 7th Division's assistant director of medical services, that when the division returned to Australia in early February, 95 per cent of the men had been hospitalised because of disease.⁵⁷

As the health, fitness and skill level of the troops improved, training methods evolved to sustain that improvement. Initially, this involved units following the suggestions in *ATM No. 21* of March 1943.⁵⁸ Soon more complex methods were developed. The construction of jungle assault or 'stalker' courses was one of the most useful. The 2/2nd Battalion created three of them, one each for a man using a rifle, a small machine gun or Bren gun. The comment that the jungle assault course consisted of 'ingenious devices [which] were arranged to give the firer the impression of being in typical enemy infested jungle country' applied equally to courses built by other AIF infantry units on the Tableland.⁵⁹ Between 200 and 400 yards long, they required a soldier to move along a jungle track and 'kill' a series of targets and life-size dummies operated by pulley systems.⁶⁰ Some needed to be engaged with small-arms fire, others with bayonet or grenade.⁶¹ The aim was to develop the soldiers' powers of observation and, most importantly, increase their reaction time. Men who missed the silhouettes or who took too long were told they had been killed and had to repeat the course until their accuracy and speed reached acceptable levels.⁶² With jungle terrain meaning that contact frequently occurred at point-blank range, and with no time to take a carefully aimed shot with a rifle brought up to the shoulder, such firing ranges were crucial in improving the chances of survival for Australian soldiers in jungle warfare. The Western Australian 2/16th Battalion's ranges involved 'firing from hip' at a distance of 30 yards.[63]

By early May, all units had constructed similar ranges. Most were based upon their experiences during the Kokoda or Beachheads campaigns, while others were collaborative and arrived at after consultation and exchange of ideas between battalions.[64] The earliest such ranges appear to have been constructed in January 1943, after visits by Australian personnel to the US 41st Division stationed at Rockhampton.[65] Many troops noticed a difference between the training they were undertaking in 1943 and that of the year before:

> This time the veterans of the Battalion approached jungle training much in the mood of specialists anxious to become perfectionists. To them this was no meaningless drill. To the uninitiated the use of camouflaged uniforms; the slow, noiseless infiltration through the jungle; the elaborate methods of keeping in touch and the lessons of living off the land seemed rather theatrical; but the veterans were able to appraise the value of this training, and, by their enthusiasm and leadership, inspire the newly-joined troops to apply themselves to the task in hand.[66]

Once all units had attained an acceptable standard at the sub-unit level, exercises with other corps and at battalion and brigade levels commenced. Here, too, the different challenges posed by a tropical environment were foremost in commanders' minds. In June, 18th Brigade recorded that 'improvised crossing of water obstacles to be practiced. [Engineer Platoon] to accompany Bde and give [instruction] in use of assault boats.'[67] The vast numbers of rivers and streams in New Guinea, all of which could rise rapidly after torrential rain, exacerbated the problems of movement. In jungle warfare, therefore, the importance of the engineers was greater than ever.

'A soldier first': Engineers become jungle-minded

For the engineers, just as for the infantry, operating in the jungle posed formidable challenges. Before solutions to these challenges could be found, however, there needed to be clarification of the tasks that engineers were expected to accomplish in tropical situations. Until more concrete direction was received, engineer units concentrated on improving their infantry skills in jungle conditions.[68] Soon 6th Division would record that 'RAE 7 Aust Div [was] contacted re proposed role of engineers in Jungle operations'.[69] One problem was that the reduced scales of transport—under the new 'jungle divisions' war establishment—would have a greater impact upon engineer units, which would not be able to use much mechanical equipment crucial to the construction of bridges, roads and culverts. Throughout April and May, Royal Australian Engineers (RAE) personnel of both 6th and 7th Divisions attended a series of conferences in an attempt to find solutions. In June the GSO1 of 6th Division asked HQ RAE 6th Division for information on '[engineer equipment] which would normally accompany [field companies] on jungle operations', demonstrating that there was still much confusion about exactly how the engineers would operate in the jungle.[70] In late July a letter from the commander of 6th Division RAE to the Engineer-in-Chief highlighted some of the issues: 'the engineer problem in jungle warfare is very different to the problem in open type warfare ... In jungle warfare engineer units have to rely far more on their own local resources and in [sic] their capacity to improvise and make things.'[71]

A report written after 7th Division had crossed the Markham River and established the airfield at Nadzab, near Lae, in September 1943, discussed these issues, particularly the reduced scales of vehicles and mechanical plant.[72] While the shortage of mechanical equipment was not as confounding a problem as it had been in the first Papuan campaigns, it was still not resolved to the satisfaction of the engineers. Sheer hard work by hand, often aided by natives, pioneers and infantrymen, would be the norm. Many of the issues, particularly the inadequacy of transport on the new war establishment, were not finally solved until the training period that preceded the final campaigns in late 1944 and early 1945.

Still, 1943 would see major changes in engineer training with the establishment of a centralised RAE training centre at Kapooka, in southern New South Wales. All personnel would undergo a sixteen-week training program divided into four blocks. While the engineers had always followed the maxim that 'a sapper must be a soldier first and an engineer second', the nature of jungle warfare reinforced this.[73] The first four-week segment was therefore devoted to small-arms and infantry minor tactics. Experienced field companies, which were already allotted to various units and formations, would follow the same procedure. Although the exact role of engineers in jungle conditions had not been completely resolved, all knew that in the coming operations the first necessity would be to 'produce trained sappers capable of acting as fighting troops'.[74] In May, the men of RAE 6th Division undertook a seventeen-day course to improve their ability to move, survive and fight in the jungle.[75] Only upon completing it did they move on to the more technical aspects of a sapper's role.

The 2/6th Field Company had each of its three platoons undertake a 'three-day course in Infantry jungle tactics' with one of 25th Brigade's three infantry battalions.[76] Eventually HQ RAE of each division would construct its own jungle rifle ranges and assault courses so the field companies under their command could use them as regularly as they needed. Their training instructions closely followed those of infantry units, with exercises on 'jungle living', 'movement in jungle' and 'scouting'.[77] This training period also saw infantry battalions improving their engineering skills. As part of its training syllabus,

2/27th Battalion listed that it needed to practise water crossings, the siting and digging of weapon pits, and the laying of tripwires.[78]

Meanwhile, it was realised that the School of Mechanical Engineering, instead of producing officers ready to serve in the tropics, was operating on lines almost unchanged since the First World War. When he took command of the school in May 1943, Colonel John McGowan discovered that 'drill ... digging trenches and erecting barbed wire fences as for the 1914–18 War' took up the bulk of the course, with only 'two weeks to cover bridging and all other engineering subjects'.

This was changed almost instantly, with the focus firmly upon preparing officers for the operational environment and the challenges they would soon be confronting—'booby traps and anti-personnel mines, water supply ... bridge design [and] engineers in opposed landings'.[79] These changes ultimately resulted in more highly skilled engineers, better able to solve the myriad problems that occurred regularly in the New Guinea and island campaigns. Arguably the most important lessons concerned improvisation in the field when 'companies were spread far and wide at their various activities' and had to provide immediate solutions for the infantry, artillery and armoured formations they were supporting.[80]

'Close co-operation with the infantry': Artillerymen apply the lessons of Papua

For many artillery regiments, 1943–44 was a frustrating period. As the army struggled to develop operating procedures to enable more effective use of the artillery, many units believed they would be sidelined for the remainder of the war.[81] Upon their return to Australia, the artillery regiments of 9th Division also noticed that many higher-ranking officers still believed that artillery could not be used in the jungle.[82] When the number of artillery regiments allocated to a division was reduced from three to one—in line with the 'jungle infantry division' changes—this belief only increased. It would take time, but for the final campaigns in 1944–45 these reductions were reversed, and the 6th, 7th and 9th Divisions went into battle supported by three artillery regiments each. Before then, however, the artillery, like all the combat arms, tried to determine what changes they needed to make to operate effectively in the jungle.

To assist with this process a detailed report was released on 24 February 1943 by LHQ, which summarised the recently completed campaigns and discussed solutions to the most commonly identified problems. The first point it made was that 'training for jungle warfare is additional to, and not in place of, normal artillery training'.[83] Nevertheless, it did suggest that even a skilled artilleryman would find jungle conditions extremely challenging. Covering all relevant topics, from shell and splinter ranging through observation and communications, the report made clear that one of the prerequisites for effectively operating in the jungle was to train in appropriate conditions. Regiments needed to ensure that 'guns should be manhandled over all conditions of country', that 'local protection of [observation posts] and gun areas' was done by the unit itself, and that 'shoots should be conducted in areas approximating to jungle'.[84] As a result, all artillery regiments—like the engineers—would need to practise infantry minor tactics and work more closely with infantry units than before.

The training programs instituted by the various artillery regiments to address the points in the LHQ report closely resembled those for the infantry units. Improving physical fitness with regular sessions of 'PT, route marches and obstacle courses' was first on the agenda for the 2/3rd Field Regiment. This was closely followed by overnight and multi-day exercises in which 'perimeter defence' and 'jungle craft' were incorporated.[85] The necessity for protection of gun positions, critical in jungle warfare, was reinforced by reports being received from the Wau–Salamaua campaign.[86] Once the reduction in transport and gun limbers under the new war establishment was implemented, units began practising moving their artillery cross-country by hand. A party from 2/3rd Field Regiment would take a week to drag one of their 25-pounders almost 5 kilometres, having to utilise block and tackle, cut a path through virgin scrub with axes, and build numerous small bridges to ford creeks. Although the report on this exercise claims that much valuable information was learned, the regimental history notes that 'those who took part regarded [the exercise] as sheer bastardry'.[87] But for units that had yet to see action in Papua, this training period would provide valuable insights into the difficulties they would face there.

It was in a further attempt to address the challenges of providing artillery support in mountainous and tropical terrain that the short 25-pounder was devised. The initial jungle campaigns had clearly demonstrated the need for a lighter and more portable artillery piece than the standard 25-pound gun. The director of artillery therefore suggested that 'the 25-pounder should be redesigned by shortening the barrel and recuperator and by making the trail lighter'.[88] By early 1943 the first of these was being demonstrated to artillery units. The 2/4th Field Regiment made history in September 1943 when it was parachuted into action with two short 25-pounders[89] and had one of them assembled and ready to fire in less than an hour. In time, most field regiments would include a battery of 'shorts' and two batteries of standard guns.

The majority of units who had to use them in action—especially those regiments that had used the standard Mk II 25-pounder in action in the Middle East—were unimpressed. The 2/3rd Field Regiment referred to its shorts as 'little horrors', while another regiment regarded them with 'deep loathing'.[90] The short had a range 2600 metres less than that of the standard gun, it was less accurate and more difficult to tow owing to the modified trail, and the removal of the gun shield—to save weight—was also a big drawback to the crew. Even the circumspect official history admits that the short

25-pounder 'caused a heavy blast effect on the crews, who, in consequence, sometimes suffered from severe earache and temporary deafness, as well as occasional nose-bleeding'.[91] The gun was, however, 500 kilograms lighter than the standard version, and could be broken down into transportable parts in less than two minutes, then airlifted or delivered by parachute and loaded onto a jeep. Another regimental history probably gave a more balanced appraisal of the modified gun when it stated that 'it appeared to us that the Short was an excellent jungle adjunct to the original 25-pounder, but not a substitute for it'.[92] That the gun was ready for use in action approximately a year after it was first suggested shows that in some areas at least, the army was responding rapidly to the demands of the new operational theatre.

In another sign that the artillery regiments were anticipating the problems of moving their 25-pounders through jungles and over mountains, several of them undertook training with 4.2-inch mortars. Although lacking the range of either standard Mk IIs or short 25-pounders, these British weapons outranged both the 2- and 3-inch mortars of the infantry battalions. More importantly for jungle warfare, they were portable and 'could be man-packed into difficult areas'. The 2/1st Field Regiment trained with them in 1943 and determined that 'there is a possibility that Mortar's [sic] may be able to undertake Arty roles in rugged country'.[93] When the regiment eventually saw action during the Aitape–Wewak campaign, members of one troop from the 2/1st provided support with their mortars for 17th Brigade as it moved inland through the Torricelli Mountains.[94]

While existing weapons were being modified and new weapons experimented with, the field regiments continued their training, with much time devoted to working with infantry units. To improve the level of understanding and knowledge between infantry and artillery, officers of each corps were seconded to either an infantry battalion or an artillery regiment.[95] For several training exercises, a field regiment would be tasked to support a single battalion. On other occasions, as infantry and artillery tried to adjust to the change necessitated by 'jungle division' war establishment, one battery would work with a brigade. In mid-June 1943 the fact that there was still some way to go before everyone was satisfied with the standard of doctrine was shown when an 'exercise disclosed the need for a clear conception of the tactical employment of [artillery] in the jungle'.[96] By the time the 7th and 9th Divisions embarked for Port Moresby in August and September, most of these issues would be close to resolution.

The final weeks of training in Port Moresby would allow the field regiments to hone their skills by practising tasks such as splinter and sound ranging, and to demonstrate the use of delayed action fuzes to infantry battalion commanders.[97] The lack of transport and vehicles for moving the artillery—although it had been identified in the 1943 training period—would, as predicted, cause much heartache in combat. For example, once the 2/6th Field Regiment arrived at Finschhafen, it had to 'acquire' caterpillar tractors to move its guns out of the knee-deep mud.[98] Nevertheless, the Ramu–Markham and Lae–Finschhafen campaigns saw many of the lessons of this training period come to fruition. Most notable was the much closer coordination of infantry, artillery and engineering units, which was required in jungle warfare as forward observation officers moved up with the foremost infantry companies, and engineers assisted the artillery troops in moving their guns forward.[99]

'Tanks should not operate alone': Armoured corps modifications

In the months following the Beachheads campaign, the future use of tanks in jungle conditions was still under review. The assertions made after the fighting at Milne Bay, that 'mechanized units will have little or no combat value in the jungle itself' and that they would be easily destroyed on tracks and roads, were only partially refuted by the beachheads experience.[100] Later reports agreed that, while such units were essential in overcoming Japanese resistance at

Cape Endaiadere–Giropa Point, they were completely road-bound at Sanananda and as a consequence easily picked off by Japanese anti-tank guns.[101] The one thing that all reports agreed upon was that if tanks were to be used in jungle warfare, the M3 light tank should not be chosen.[102] Its many deficiencies as an infantry tank were listed in both the main reports to appear in early 1943. Fortuitously, the most appropriate tank for jungle warfare was already available in Australia. The first Matilda Infantry Tanks (Mark II) had been acquired by the Armoured Fighting Vehicle School at Puckapunyal in October 1942 to teach infantry–armour cooperation. As Paul Handel observed, the fighting at the Gona, Buna and Sanananda beachheads had proven that 'a heavier tank, with thick armour... able to crash through jungle, was the type required for operations in the South-West Pacific'.[103] The Matilda admirably met those criteria and for the remainder of the war was the only tank used by the Australian Armoured Corps in combat.

Another change that came about in early 1943 was the realisation that it would be next to impossible to employ armour in large formations in the South West Pacific Area. As R.N.L. Hopkins noted, this '[r]esulted in the formation of the 4th Armoured Brigade [which] became in part an armoured pool from which units and even sub-units could be provided to form the armoured components of amphibious task forces'.[104] Throughout the rest of the war, various armoured regiments would be assigned to support infantry brigades or divisions as required. These units would find themselves operating in a similar manner to the artillery regiments, with squadrons and frequently three-tank troops working independently.

As it was becoming clear that the future role of the tank in the South West Pacific would involve even closer cooperation with the infantry and other corps, training along those lines expanded in mid-1943. On 13 June, 2/9th Australian Armoured Regiment received a visit from a LHQ Jungle Warfare Training Team whose members demonstrated infantry tactics.[105] Over the next month the unit used those lessons—along with the '4th Australian Armoured Brigade Training Instruction No. 3', which dealt with the use of the Matilda in the jungle—in training exercises with various infantry units.[106] It was late 1943, however, before this training resulted in the publication of appropriate training materials.

After Colonel F.D. Marshall returned with his unit, the 2/8th Armoured Regiment, from Papua, he was appointed to the Army Tactical School at Beenleigh, 'where he continued his most valuable work of setting AFV [armoured fighting vehicle] doctrine down on paper'. This work would eventually result in the publication of a manual dealing with 'the combination of tanks and infantry in tropical warfare'.[107] Throughout July, all the brigades of 7th Division undertook training exercises in infantry–armour cooperation. For 18th Brigade, initial demonstrations were attended by officers before 'one troop M3 medium tanks from C Sqn 2/9 Aust Armd Regt [was attached] to each battalion 7–11 Jul for [training] and demonstration'.[108] Ironically, 7th Division did not operate with tanks in the subsequent Lae–Ramu/Markham campaign. It was the 9th Division, in its assault on the heights of Sattelberg, that saw the 1943 training with armour put into practice.

'Tough and sweaty training': 9th Division experiences the new paradigm

Soon after the 9th Division arrived home from the Middle East, it began to concentrate on preparations for its next operational role. On 14 April, General Leslie Morshead released *2 Australian Corps Training Directive No. 1*, ordering that all formations under command—including 9th Division—should ensure that 'formations will be well fitted to undertake operations in any type of country. At the same time, all formations will be trained to fit themselves for jungle warfare.' To meet this directive, within weeks of their arrival, training cadres from 6th and 7th Divisions were being despatched to 9th Division units, with similar sized detachments from the 9th fostered in to train with the jungle-experienced units.[109] On 21 April, the commander of 9th Division held a conference of brigade commanders and commanding officers of division troops on 'reorganisation of [division] and training for jungle conditions'. Over the next two weeks, numerous training directives and instructions were issued by HQ 9th Division, the most detailed of which were based upon the 18th Brigade's Buna and Sanananda operations and the 21st Brigade's experiences on the Kokoda Track.[110] A training HQ to collate information and provide guidance across the division was established, and remained in operation until mid-July.[111]

Although the division's troops did yet not know it, they would have approximately two months to train for jungle warfare. In July, training for amphibious operations began at Trinity Beach, north of Cairns.[112] Before then, the soldiers of the 9th Division had to adjust their tactics and training to the new environment. And, like the men of the 6th and 7th Divisions before them, they came to dislike intensely the 'rotten jungle, full of leeches, big leeches, and these big— these vines with big leaves, and if they hit you they stick to you and they sting you'.[113] As training progressed, the men of the 9th quickly realised that 'combat in the jungle type of country . . . will necessitate a much higher physical condition and staying power'.[114]

Men who had been able to hide a lack of complete fitness in North Africa, where motor transport was generally available, were found out as the jungle training became more arduous. Many appeared before medical boards and had to find roles with HQ Company or outside the infantry battalions. To facilitate information exchange over the next two months, training teams from all the brigades that had fought in Papua were seconded to 9th Division, with selected personnel from 9th Division being sent to train with 7th Division units. However, the wide variety of operational experiences of the troops from the various brigades could cause confusion. As the

26th Brigade commander later recounted, 'what they were telling us differed markedly. Eventually, we made up our own minds.'[115]

Nevertheless, the men of the 9th Division were far more fortunate than those who had preceded them.[116] The 2/28th Battalion noted that the training team from 2/1st Battalion provided 'advice and suggestions [which] were to prove invaluable during the [training] period'.[117] Similarly, Alan Macfarlane recalled that the lectures and advice provided by Lieutenant Bob Thompson of the 2/14th Battalion were:

> Very helpful, because we were getting first hand knowledge of what we could expect ourselves, and it helped us in our learning experience ... Thompson would go out on a twenty-four hour stunt [with the battalion] and talk to us ... about their own experiences and what we should expect to see [in jungle combat].[118]

Critically, the men were urged to alter the methods and procedures of desert warfare, particularly those of patrolling, which necessitated a more measured approach in the jungle, and of overcoming fixed defences, which in jungle terrain were frequently very difficult to locate.[119] To improve its officers' knowledge of jungle warfare, 20th Brigade provided them with a 31-page file entitled 'Jungle Warfare Extracts'. This contained information from ten training manuals and pamphlets as well as 'Lessons Learnt' documents.[120] Throughout their jungle warfare training, the officers used this file in planning weekly syllabuses. It covered all aspects of operating in tropical conditions, from infantry minor tactics, artillery, armour and the combat support arms, to hygiene, logistics and airdropping. The manual—like the training instructions prepared for 6th and 7th Divisions—was at pains to point out, however, that 'Tactics in the Jungle are not "BLACK MAGIC". Certain special trg is needed ... but the fundamentals laid down in [*Infantry Training*] still apply.'[121]

Once the Lae–Finschhafen campaign began, most soldiers of the 9th would have been inclined to agree with Albert Palazzo that 'combat in the South West Pacific area was fundamentally different from that which the AIF had experienced in the Middle East'.[122] Although 'Jungle Warfare Extracts' does not appear to have been distributed on a formation or corps level, it serves as further evidence that the Australian Army was well on the way towards a formal jungle warfare doctrine.

Before moving on to amphibious training, the 9th Division undertook combined-operations training in June. The differences between North Africa and operations in the tropics were once again thrown into stark relief when it was realised that artillery support for a divisional exercise consisted of a single battery per brigade. Nevertheless, the 9th was far better prepared for the forthcoming operations than the 7th Division had been for Kokoda and Milne Bay. The 7th had, of course, undertaken brigade-level exercises before its deployment to Papua in 1942, but with inappropriate doctrine, its training did not adequately prepare it for the battles ahead.

After completing amphibious training in July with the US 532nd Engineer Boat and Shore Regiment, the 9th Division left for Milne Bay, Papua, in August. Only days before embarkation, the 20th Brigade received new jungle-green uniforms; the two other brigades had to fend for themselves.[123] The men of 2/24th Battalion eventually cajoled a quantity of dye and some salt from the laundry unit at Milne Bay and worked out a rudimentary process for dyeing their uniforms—as had their counterparts in the 21st Brigade a year earlier.[124] Captain Alan Macfarlane later recalled that 'everything was makeshift'; the army was 'not ready for this [jungle operations]' and they had to 'improvis[e] in a lot of things'.[125] The two and a half weeks the division spent at Milne Bay before going to Lae were of significant value, because 'the troops quickly realised that jungle [training] on the Tablelands of Qld was a pale imitation of the real thing. Only New

Guinea itself could teach them the real meaning of mud, rain, mountains and anopheles mosquitoes.'[126] Other lessons that could only be learned in the suffocating jungles of the tropics included the difficulties of observation and determining what needed to be carried and what could be discarded.[127]

Unlike the units flung desperately into battle in the dark hours of August–September 1942, when the 7th and 9th Divisions went into combat once more, they were extremely well trained and far better armed and equipped. After completing their training on the Tableland, 7th Division moved to various camps around Port Moresby where the men were able to acclimatise and undergo training tailored to the forthcoming operations. River crossings, 'intercom in semi-open country', carrying of 'two Vickers MG and [ammunition] across country' and 'cross-country practice in cable-laying and maintenance' were all practised in terrain that resembled that of the Ramu–Markham area.[128] Finally, the first brigade to be deployed— the 25th—undertook an exercise that was 'planned to simulate the Lae track from Nadzab'.[129] This training period also saw the introduction of US Army 536 handsets, generally referred to as walkie-talkies. While these hand-held radio transceivers greatly speeded communications and, it was claimed, 'saved the lives of many a runner', they did not obviate the need for telephone lines, still the most reliable means of communication in tropical conditions—so linesmen continued to toil 'tirelessly in the heat and mud' laying cable.[130]

By September 1943, great strides had been made towards developing a uniform jungle warfare doctrine. As the 9th Division returned home from the Middle East and the 6th and 7th Divisions recovered from the first Papuan campaigns, the Australian Army was still struggling to evaluate the lessons of Kokoda, Milne Bay and the beachheads. With a plethora of 'lessons learned' documents, operational reports and suggestions from all quarters on how the army should organise, train and equip itself for future operations, this was not surprising. Once the AIF divisions had re-formed and begun training on the Atherton Tableland, the experience of the first jungle campaigns was incorporated into more appropriate training programs. With the exchange of training cadres between 6th, 7th and 9th Divisions, the construction of jungle scout and assault ranges, and an increased emphasis upon acclimatisation to the jungle, the AIF was well advanced in its attempts at achieving a tactical uniformity with regard to jungle warfare that had hitherto not existed.

These changes were due in no small measure to the improvements instituted by LHQ and DMT. By June, both Canungra and Beenleigh were enjoying the benefits of increasing numbers of instructors with operational experience in the jungles of the South West Pacific Area. This in turn saw an improvement in the quality of personnel at all levels—from the rifle section up to Divisional Headquarters. With the increased numbers of experienced battalion officers being seconded to the LHQ Training Teams, the wider dissemination of jungle warfare learning across the Australian Army continued. As more streamlined and efficient systems for the collection, collation and distribution of lessons-learned material were introduced, the DMT began to produce more useful training manuals and pamphlets. The large-scale establishment and expansion of specialist schools under centralised control also improved training across the army.[131] Although not all these changes occurred in response to the new challenges posed by tropical theatres, the training provided at those establishments left soldiers much better prepared for the challenges of jungle warfare than had previously been the case.

Once the 7th and 9th Divisions returned to action in September, it quickly became apparent that there would be no repeat of the desperate defensive battles of the Kokoda Track. This can be attributed to several factors. One was identified by Lesley Cook, who in late 1943 observed that the 'high class, first class troops [of the Japanese Army] had gone, and they weren't the same soldiers at all'.[132] Moreover, many years of fighting on several fronts, and the privations imposed by the US Air Force and the US Navy's submarine fleet in particular, had taken a heavy toll on the Japanese military's capacity to fight. However, until early 1944 most of the land fighting by Allied forces in the South West Pacific Area had been done by the Australian Army.[133] If the swathe of changes and improvements across the army with respect to doctrine and training, tactics, weapons and equipment had not occurred during 1943, it is arguable that Australian casualties would still have been as heavy as in the first Papuan campaigns. There were two more years of hard fighting to come, but by September 1943 the critical elements in the development of Australian jungle warfare doctrine and training were in place. Ramu–Markham and Lae–Finschhafen would merely confirm this.

Chapter 10

'NO NEW LESSONS OF IMPORTANCE': THE FINAL CAMPAIGNS

At the port of Balikpapan, on the east coast of Borneo, on 1 July 1945, the final large-scale multinational operation of the Second World War took place.[1] As the amphibious landing vehicles carrying the assault waves of the 7th Division moved towards the shore under cover of a massive naval and air bombardment, the culmination of more than three years of learning and development unfolded. Although the overwhelming nature of the fire support available to the Australian Army—in stark contrast to their first jungle campaigns of 1942–43—appeared to render superfluous the jungle warfare skills they had developed over the years since the Kokoda and Beachheads campaigns, numerous 'quick and merciless melees' in the jungle blackness belied that view.[2] The experience gained in those bloody and expensive battles in Papua, followed by the crucial training period on the Atherton Tableland in 1943, had enabled the battle-hardened divisions of the 2nd AIF to absorb and then successfully impart their knowledge to the rest of the army and to Commonwealth forces at large.[3] While the necessity for the strategically peripheral final Australian campaigns of 1944–45 is still debated, the 'skill and professionalism' with which they were conducted would not have been possible without those initial experiences.[4] That the experience could have been obtained at lower cost does not diminish the scale of the transition that the Australian Army had undergone between 1942 and 1945.

Both the 7th Division's Ramu–Markham and the 9th Division's Lae–Finschhafen campaigns, between September 1943 and February 1944, merely served to reinforce the lessons learned in the early jungle campaigns. By the time 9th Division completed its Huon Peninsula operations in early 1944, all the AIF divisions that had served in the Middle East had jungle warfare experience. The infantry divisions of the AIF therefore spent most of 1944 training, examining the lessons of their earlier jungle campaigns and preparing to be deployed again. The *Tropical Warfare* manuals, published in December 1944 and February 1945, provide a key indicator of the state of jungle warfare training development in Australia. Although refined and expanded, the similarities between *MTP No. 23* and these manuals suggest that by late 1943 effective and appropriate doctrine and training methods were in place. The most noticeable additions covered the use of the supporting arms—especially armour—in a tropical environment. Ultimately, however, the final campaigns did not witness any major developments or revisions to the lessons that had been absorbed over the preceding three years.

Ian Kuring has correctly observed that the *Tropical Warfare* manuals 'continued to be the Australian Army's main references on the subject' until the late 1950s.[5] However, this must be qualified by the fact that they were largely ignored until 1955. Far more significant is that when the Australian Army required new jungle warfare training manuals—concurrent with both the deployment of ground forces to the Malayan Emergency and the simultaneous re-establishment of Canungra in 1955—it turned to the *Tropical Warfare* manuals of 1944–45.⁶ This confirms that the most important lessons of the jungle campaigns had already been correctly identified and translated into appropriate doctrine.

'Not as bad as we were told': 9th Division in New Guinea

Upon completion of their final training at Buna and Milne Bay, 9th Division boarded troopships and sailed for Red Beach. Their task was the capture of Lae. Neither the enemy nor the environment turned out to be as fearsome as reports had intimated. Nonetheless, it is clear that for many their first experience of jungle warfare was extremely challenging.⁷ As Joe Madeley recalled, 'fighting the Japs in the jungle was very hard on the nerves: you never knew where they were, especially snipers up trees'.⁸ While they were far better prepared than the units that had fought the Japanese in the first Papuan campaign, many of the same problems that had confronted the 6th and 7th Divisions recurred for the 9th Division. For all involved, conditions were much more unpleasant than any they had experienced before, with the constant 'mud and slush and rain' making the most simple of tasks extremely awkward.⁹ As the 2/13th Battalion's historian noted, there were 'mosquitoes, fever and disease, rain, mud and leeches, and invariably action would be fought over shocking terrain with the infantryman obliged to carry on his back everything he needed'.¹⁰

This need to carry heavy burdens over appalling terrain frequently left the troops exhausted by the time they went into combat. Since the hills were too steep for vehicles, commanders were forced to detail a sizeable percentage of their force to work as porters—as had been the case during the 17th Brigade's Wau–Salamaua campaign. This, of course, meant they had fewer troops to fight the enemy. On one occasion, 640 men from the 2/2nd Machine Gun Battalion and the 37/52nd Battalion served as carriers to keep supplies coming forward to a single infantry battalion.¹¹

For a division that had fought in the highly mechanised theatre of the Western Desert, the fact that each battalion could now call on only a dozen Jeeps for all its transport needs required a major adjustment. In a similar vein, a year later, as the 2/11th Battalion prepared for the Aitape–Wewak campaign, the men's heavy loads meant 'we were more like mechanised infantry in the Western Desert (minus transport) instead of being a Jungle Battalion'.[12] The impossibility of supply by any other means than carrier line also saw a repetition of the arguments that had occurred between Allen, Rowell, Blamey and MacArthur during the Kokoda campaign. The 2/24th Battalion recorded that higher headquarters 'were calling for more speed, and, looking at their maps and air photos, were sending constant enquiries as to why the forward coys were not gaining ground more quickly'.[13] The fact that terrain and logistics—and not the enemy—were frequently the major determinants of the pace of operations was clearly something each formation new to jungle warfare had to learn for itself.[14] Even when such lessons could be passed on to those who followed, there was no guarantee that their adaptation would be easy, let alone seamless.

Throughout the course of the Lae operation and the longer and more difficult Finschhafen–Sattelberg campaign that followed, the 9th Division—despite having the benefit of the Atherton Tableland training period—came to the realisation that first-hand experience was crucial for success in the jungle. The problems of command and control and the decentralised nature of jungle warfare were epitomised on a small scale by the 2/13th Battalion's involvement in the battle of Kakakog. The battalion history admitted that it was 'difficult to portray in detail [and that] it was, on the whole, a platoon show, though in many instances isolated sections found themselves fighting independent actions'. On a larger scale, even when a full brigade was able to undertake a coordinated assault, such as 26th Brigade's attack on the heights of Sattelberg, the commander, Brigadier David

'Torpy' Whitehead, was forced 'to attack with three battalions forward on three separate routes'.[15] Battalions would fight almost independently, unable to observe or directly assist one another, but with the outcome of the wider battle resting on each unit's succeeding at its assigned task.

As the 6th and 7th Divisions had already realised, the decentralised nature of jungle warfare, with its emphasis on self-sufficiency, demanded a higher standard of training—and not just fitness—than in the desert. When a section or platoon was allocated an independent task or cut off by enemy action from the remainder of the unit, its men had to be both skilled and self-reliant. This made it especially surprising that at least one brigade of 9th Division in action at Finschhafen received reinforcements with 'little training and no battle experience'.[16] During the rapid Japanese advances in 1941 and 1942, similarly unprepared soldiers had been thrust into combat, with unfortunate results. The division thus had to train these men and fight the Japanese at the same time. While it still achieved its strategic objectives, many of the reinforcements were killed or wounded because of their inexperience. Although this would be the last time untrained soldiers were posted to AIF units, it beggars belief that the practice continued as late as October 1943.

In the jungle every soldier required exceptional competence with all the weapons of the infantryman, and the quick thinking and reflexes to react instantly to unexpected events. The 2/32nd Battalion realised that success depended on the section leaders and platoon commanders because battalion and company commanders could no longer see their men.[17] The increased use of walkie-talkies and carrier pigeons helped with communication and control to an extent, but in these conditions a battalion or brigade commander had to rely on his subordinates to carry out his orders, with little ability to influence the course of events. This would be reflected in the *Tropical Warfare* manuals published in late 1944.

The artillery regiments and field engineers of the 9th Division also found that the jungle was more challenging than the desert, and—most importantly—that it called for much closer cooperation with the other combat arms. As the only arm to have four-wheel-drive vehicles—and Caterpillar tractors—the engineers were much in demand. The artillery, in particular, depended on them to prepare gun positions and to manoeuvre their 25-pounders. With the few tractors available in great demand, manpower, as so often in the Beachheads campaign, was generally the only possible way to move the guns.[18] And there was never sufficient manpower to accomplish all the required tasks. The 9th Division, like the 7th Division in the Ramu–Markham, soon realised that jungle warfare required more engineers and machinery than were permitted on their war establishment.[19]

When the men of the 2/6th Field Regiment arrived at Finschhafen, they were able to pass on their recently acquired knowledge to the 2/12th Field Regiment and to improve the work of the forward observation and observation post officers working with the 9th Division infantry.[20] Over the course of October and November 1943, this assistance paid dividends, with 9th Division battalion commanders saying the accuracy of fire support, especially against close targets, had been exemplary. As in the early jungle campaigns, occasional friendly casualties were unavoidable. These were a result of inaccurate maps, the difficulty pinpointing the positions of friendly troops, and the Japanese practice of 'hugging' the Australian positions in an attempt to render artillery support too dangerous.[21] Although the historian John Coates is largely correct in arguing that 'intimate air support ... was never really effective during the campaign', many of the units involved gained experience in working with artillery reconnaissance aircraft that would later prove invaluable.[22] In order to continue transmitting ideas and lessons such as these to as wide an audience as possible, more up-to-date material was included in the *Army Training Memorandum*.²³ In this manner and by the more timely distribution of comprehensive 'lessons learned' material, improvements in the dissemination of knowledge across the Australian Army continued.

'Torpy sits on Sat': Matildas prove their worth

Of great value for the conduct of jungle operations throughout the remainder of the war in the South West Pacific was the knowledge gained in the use of armour during the campaign, most notably in supporting the assault on the heights of Sattelberg. As we have seen, the usefulness of tanks in the jungle had not been categorically proven, despite their pivotal role in the beachhead battles. A brief training period at Milne Bay involving C Squadron, 1st Army Tank Battalion and 26th Brigade foreshadowed a far more important training period in late October and early November. Beginning with C Company of the 2/48th Battalion on 31 October, each rifle company, together with a platoon of engineers from the 2/13th Field Company, spent three days at Heldsbach plantation, on the road to the summit of Sattelberg, training with a troop of three Matilda tanks.²⁴

On 17 November, the assault began. As the tanks slowly advanced, they used their machine guns to spray the scrub on either side of the narrow mountain track, while a 2-pounder turret gun or 3-inch howitzer was used to destroy Japanese bunkers and gun emplacements.²⁵ Engineers, covered by the infantry, rendered mines and booby-traps safe or employed their D6 bulldozers to ensure the Matildas could continue the advance. An Armoured Corps officer— generally the troop commander—walked behind the tanks with the infantry platoon and communicated via walkie-talkie or telephone with the tanks, directing their fire and warning them of any concealed enemy positions. This method of communication was later adopted for all tank–infantry operations.²⁶ An advance of only 450 yards was made on the first day of the assault, but nine days later the summit was reached[27] and the succinct message 'Torpy sits on Sat' was relayed to General Morshead of 9th Division. The use of a combined infantry, armour and engineer force, supported by a company of the 2/2nd MG Battalion, field and heavy artillery regiments and an 'American rocket projector', was a precursor of the operational approach that would culminate at Balikpapan and Labuan Island.[28] Equally important, the lessons learned here were largely applicable during the 6th Division's coastal advance towards Wewak, and to an even greater extent to the drive by 3rd Division along Buin Road, on Bougainville.[29]

After their successful role in the seizure of Sattelberg, the Matildas continued to provide crucial support to the 9th Division, and later the 4th AMF Brigade.[30] Even before these operations were concluded, detailed reports were being compiled, initially from 4th Australian Armoured Brigade and the 26th Infantry Brigade, and soon from New Guinea Force HQ.[31] One of the first of these urged caution and suggested that although these tactics had worked effectively on Sattelberg, the Japanese would probably take countermeasures 'when they are next employed against them'.[32]

Fortunately for the Australians, throughout the remainder of the Pacific War, the Japanese military did not develop effective anti-tank weapons. The tactics developed before the assault on Sattelberg and further modified during that fight would be used with only slight alterations by Australian units in all subsequent operations in the South West Pacific. A detailed training document compiled by 9th Division's 20th Brigade before planned exercises with armoured forces in mid-October 1944 is clearly based upon these early reports released in January and February of that year.[33] Although additional suggestions derived from exercises conducted over the course of 1944 appear, the tactical formations adopted and the types of training suggested for the armour, infantry, engineers and artillery were essentially the same as those from the early 1944 reports.[34] In fact, a report written after the Oboe One landings on Tarakan in May 1945 stated that 'in all cases

Without the Papuan porters—the fuzzy-wuzzy angels—who carried ammunition and supplies forward and wounded soldiers rearward, the jungle campaigns would have ground to a halt. (AWM 013641)

Men of 2/2nd Independent Company after evacuation from Timor: although distinctly 'unmilitary', their long beards helped to camouflage their white faces, which stood out in the jungle darkness. (AWM P08424.032)

During the final assault on Giropa Point, Buna, December 1942, a mortar crew of 2/12th Battalion lays down a barrage. The close proximity of the Japanese positions can be judged from the almost vertical angle of the tube. (AWM 014004)

An Australian invention for jungle conditions, a short 25-pounder is manhandled through heavy mud during the Lae–Finschhafen campaign, November 1943. (AWM 060421)

At Milne Bay and the Beachheads, Japanese snipers extracted a deadly toll. The Australians sprayed the tops of coconut palms with machine gun fire to end this threat. (AWM 013952)

In the flat terrain of the Beachheads, observation of enemy positions was difficult. Once captured, this Japanese position was rapidly used to direct Australian artillery fire. (AWM 014023)

After the Kokoda Track and Beachheads campaigns the lessons learnt were brought home and quickly incorporated into training, as seen here in Frenchs Forest, New South Wales, in December 1943. (AWM 052504)

Private L.T. Knapp taking part in sniper training at the Jungle Warfare Training Centre (Canungra) in the Gold Coast hinterland. (AWM 060800)

The Australian-invented Owen Gun in action at Sanananda, January 1943. The transition to this new theatre can finally be seen with jungle-green full-length uniform and gaiters replacing khaki shorts and shirts. (AWM 014185)

By December 1943, more jungle warfare training ideas are being employed. Here an instructor is moving wires that make dummy Japanese soldiers spring out from various hiding places along a jungle track. (AWM 053622)

The difficulties of observation of fire in jungle warfare are clearly seen as a Vickers MG team of 2/24th Battalion fire on Japanese positions near Sattelberg, November 1943. (AWM 060570)

Men of the 2/48th Battalion advancing up Sattelberg supported by Matildas. Although obsolete in other war zones, the slow, under-gunned but heavily armoured Matilda Infantry tank was perfect for jungle warfare. (AWM 060606)

Members of 2/9th Battalion moving towards Shaggy Ridge, January 1944. The New Guinea campaigns saw units confronted by seemingly endless mountains, making supply arduous and time-consuming. (AWM 064269)

By late 1943, thousands of US Army and US Marine Corps soldiers were training in Australia. Here US Army troops are learning to cross obstacles using rope ladders. (AWM 015655)

Amphibious landing craft bringing men and supplies, July 1945, Balikpapan, Borneo. The final Australian campaign of the war was better supported than any that came before it. (AWM 110386)

Years of learning and experience coalesced at Balikpapan; Matilda tanks and infantry are seen supporting combat engineers who are using mine detectors to clear the road. (AWM 110379)

the tactics of infantry tank cooperation were those developed in the FINSCHHAFEN operations, and their soundness was confirmed'.[35]

Although the introduction of specialised bridge-laying and flame thrower–equipped tanks for the final 1945 campaigns provided more options for the infantry–armour assault, the tactics developed over the course of the advance from Finschhafen to Sio required little modification.

As with the majority of the doctrinal and training methods for jungle operations previously discussed, by January 1944 the Australian Army had effectively adapted to the tropical environment and the tactics of their Japanese opponents: 'While the jungle remained an impediment to movement, it no longer held its former terrors.'[36] Subsequent campaigns would merely refine and reinforce the lessons already learnt. This was as true of the 7th Division as it was of the 9th.

'Much better prepared': The 7th Division in the Ramu–Markham

For the men of the 7th Division, stepping from their transports at Nadzab airfield, the campaign they were about to commence, although lengthy and arduous, would be remembered more favourably than those of Kokoda and the beachheads. Having been tempered in the furnace of those campaigns and then retrained on the Atherton Tableland, they were well prepared for the battles to come. After the campaign the 18th Brigade, in an echo of 9th Division following the Lae operation, recorded that 'it is not considered that the operations brought to light any new lessons of importance, though many lessons of previous operations were again emphasised'.[37] Foremost among these were the need for high levels of fitness, close cooperation between the combat arms, and accurate, plentiful and timely fire support.

Although the small numbers of vehicles caused logistical problems, the men of 7th Division generally found this campaign less taxing than their introduction to jungle warfare in 1942. As South Australian

Raymond Baldwin later recalled, 'it was physically demanding but you couldn't compare it to the Owen Stanley Ranges, the food supply was good [and] we also we [sic] had artillery support which was very comforting'.[38] Advancing through the tall kunai grass, amid which temperatures could soar to over 50 degrees Centigrade, was enervating but did not involve sustained combat. Despite improved anti-malarial measures, the incidence of malaria as well as scrub typhus remained high,[39] but the Brigade Field Ambulance ensured faster treatment, and the seriously ill could be evacuated by Jeep to Dumpu and then by aircraft to Nadzab.[40]

Those who faced the most difficult challenges, at least until the 7th reached Dumpu, were the engineer and artillery units. As the route of the advance across the plains of the Markham and then the Ramu Valley closely followed the two rivers, there were many creeks and streams to cross. Even where infantry could wade across, the engineers had to construct bridges or fords to facilitate the passage of guns, ammunition and supplies. While supporting the 2/14th Battalion, the 2/4th Field Regiment 'got half way across this creek when the runners on the bridge gave way. The gun and everything sank down into the bed of this creek.'[41] Eventually the gunners were able to borrow enough Jeeps to drag the 25-pounder out of the creek, but in the process they destroyed the remnants of the bridge, much to the chagrin of the engineers, who then had to begin construction all over again.[42] Unlike in earlier campaigns, where the engineers appeared to have been deployed as an afterthought, on a token scale, and frequently used in rear areas, here they worked tirelessly to keep the track open. As a result, although 'husbanding of resources' was necessary, 'the men at the sharp end never felt short of food and equipment'.[43]

The importance of engineers in supporting both the forward infantry companies and logistics units was once again highlighted during this campaign. One of their most important roles in jungle warfare against the Japanese was assisting with the preparation of night defensive positions and booby-traps for the artillery regiments.[44] Although on the defensive, the Japanese frequently sent out raiding patrols that launched night attacks on infantry and artillery positions. The centrality of the engineers to a successful jungle campaign was further highlighted by Lieutenant-Colonel Arthur G. Wilson, who, visiting 7th Division as an observer, recorded that 'wherever I went the need for more engineers was stressed [and that] mechanical equipment such as bulldozers and road graders are essential'. The need for more engineers was reiterated after the campaign in a report which argued that an 'additional field company' for each division and more mechanical equipment were necessary for warfare in 'undeveloped country'.[45] By the end of the war, the Australian Army's percentage of engineers had increased dramatically, from 2 per cent in North Africa in 1941, to almost 10 per cent in 1945.[46]

For the artillery, this campaign would reinforce the lessons learned in the earlier jungle campaigns—notably 'that this type of warfare requires much training'.[47] The challenges they encountered in the tropics included the need to build 'heavy timber rafts... on which the guns floated, rather than sat', owing to the constantly waterlogged ground, and the frequent earth tremors, which knocked the guns off line. The changes in atmospheric conditions in the tropics, which altered the flight of shells once fired, and the difficulty of finding observation posts in a land of unending mountain ranges, also posed new challenges.[48]

Until the infantry began the climb up Shaggy Ridge to force the Japanese out of their positions, the advance continued in the same manner, with the infantry moving ahead fairly easily, and the artillery and engineers working hard to keep up. At the foothills of the towering Finisterre Range, the previously rapid progress of the 7th Division was halted. The nature of the fighting for Pallier's Hill, Green Sniper's Pimple and Prothero 1 and 2 would echo the battles that 17th Brigade had recently finished in the Wau–Salamaua campaign. While lessons from that campaign had been disseminated to the forces in Australia, they were not crucial to the success of the 7th Division. The experience of its first jungle campaign, combined with the training on the Atherton Tableland, would assist the 7th in eventually capturing Shaggy Ridge. The casualties it took in doing so were significantly lower than in 1942. Better prepared medical services and the greater availability of support, both artillery and air power, also contributed to this outcome.

As in previous jungle campaigns, terrain became the major determinant of tactics. Captain Fred Haupt of the 2/12th Battalion had to position his three platoons one behind the other because Shaggy Ridge was less than two metres wide in places.[49] Opposing positions were less than 100 yards apart—at times less than 30 yards. With the Japanese occupying well-constructed and sited defences, the Australians were forced to resort to tactics from a previous campaign and, at times, a previous war. The blast bomb that had been developed to destroy the Japanese bunkers at Buna was reintroduced by the 2/12th Battalion on Shaggy Ridge.[50] The short distance between the opposing forces led the Australians to construct periscopes similar to those used at Gallipoli.[51] Further improvisation would see the invention of a twin magazine for the Owen guns. As noted in Chapter 9, with unexpected contact in the jungle occurring at short ranges, the ability to provide immediate and sustained automatic fire was crucial. An extra 30 rounds could mean the difference between life and death.[52]

One of the most important lessons learned in the Beachheads campaign, in particular, was the inadvisability of attacking well-prepared Japanese positions without adequate fire support. Brigadier Frederick Chilton, commander of the 18th Brigade, therefore decided to surround the enemy and employ 'heavy artillery bombardments, mortar fire and dive-bombing' to soften them up.[53] After assaults by all three brigades of the 7th Division in turn, the 18th Brigade was finally able to capture the remaining Japanese positions on Shaggy Ridge in early February 1944. This outcome was the culmination of a 'well coordinated all-arms team effort' and a precursor to the manner in which the final campaigns would be fought, with infantry searching for Japanese positions, then pulling back to call in massive fire support, whether from artillery, tanks, or ground-attack aircraft.[54]

Although the visit occurred relatively early in the campaign, the comments by the Director of Military Training after his visit to New Guinea in October 1943 apply equally to the 7th and 9th Divisions' 1943–44 campaigns. Brigadier Ronnie Irving reported that, 'it appears that training carried out prior to the recent operations was satisfactory and no commander had any major changes in method or policy to suggest'.[55] Two months later, the observer Lieutenant-Colonel A.G. Wilson reached a similar conclusion, stating that 'Operations have proved that the training in jungle warfare received by units in AUSTRALIA was on sound lines.'[56] After the successful outcome of these campaigns in February 1944, few would have found any reason to question such conclusions. Training throughout 1944 would largely confirm them.

'Uninteresting and tedious': Training on the Atherton Tableland 1944–45

For all three AIF infantry divisions, the prospect of spending more than a year training, equipping and waiting for their next deployment was greeted with varying degrees of acceptance and resignation. As the historian of the 2/12th Field Regiment put it, they had 'entered upon the most uninteresting and tedious year of their service in the AIF'.[57] Much of the first half of 1944 was spent with units of the 7th and 9th Divisions which were recovering from their recent campaigns: 'every [company] was very much under-strength. Many men were still suffering intermittent attacks of malaria and were convalescing.'[58] As units regained full strength, with the return of men from hospitals and an influx of men who had completed the 28-day course at Canungra, training began in earnest. Elements of this would be based on the lessons of Shaggy Ridge and Finschhafen, but for the most part the content was similar to that of 1943, with increased emphasis upon cooperation with the supporting arms.[59]

Over the course of 1944, training for the infantry units progressed from individual and small-unit to battalion and brigade, culminating in divisional exercises supported by artillery, armour and aircraft. These exercises had one common denominator: unlike in the earlier jungle campaigns, fire support was expected to be available promptly and in sufficient quantity. Rather than throwing lightly armed infantry against fixed defences, overwhelming firepower would be used instead. Those units that had not had the benefit of training with tanks moved to Tank Rock for extended exercises, which 'left a feeling of great confidence that big things could be achieved with the new set-up'.[60] In their forthcoming operations, all the divisions would have the benefit of tank support. Much of this training involved exercises in 'open warfare', but it is clear from training instructions that it would 'be done with the object of teaching principles of demonstrating phases of jungle fighting. Generally it will be considered as preparatory work to training in the jungle.'[61] Later in the year, all three divisions would again practise amphibious landings.

While the 2nd AIF continued to train and waited to learn where it would next be deployed, LHQ and DMT were working on the creation of updated versions of *MTP No. 23*. Although it had proven of great value, it was clear that revisions were necessary in light of the recently completed 7th and 9th Division campaigns. In particular, expanded sections on the employment of artillery, armour and engineer units in jungle operations were crucial. A sharper delineation between the roles and responsibilities of commanders at various levels was also made. The first of the revised set of manuals to be released was

Tropical Warfare (Australia), Pamphlet No. 1, which dealt with divisional, brigade and battalion-level command.[62]

The decision to title the revised manuals *Tropical Warfare* rather than 'Jungle Warfare' also demonstrated a desire to ensure that the intended audience realised that operating in the tropics was not simply a matter for lightly armed infantry, as the 1942–43 publications tended to suggest.[63] Officers such as Porter and Vasey, of course, had argued that there had been an overreaction to the Japanese successes in the first year of the Pacific War.[64] Since the fundamental principles of war were not altered by the advent of jungle warfare, they said, many of the changes instituted during the 1942–43 period were unnecessary. The preface to *Tropical Warfare*, which stated that 'the principles of war apply equally as in any other theatre of operations' was intended to reaffirm this stance and the contents of *FSR* and *Infantry Training*, which many officers believed had fallen out of favour due to their lack of attention to operations in jungle and mountain terrain.[65]

This understanding was highlighted during the second half of 1944 in a training instruction which stated that commanders should train in open or semi-open terrain and then modify training depending on the likely theatre of operations.[66] Although the argument that jungle warfare was not 'a new art of war' was largely correct, it was indisputable that the terrain and environment of the South West Pacific Area required alteration to the standard infantry division— and the way it was employed.[67] Even Porter, at the end of his report on tactics, listed a series of problems inherent in jungle warfare operations, concluding with the statement that the 'difficulties are numerous'.[68] The campaigns of Kokoda, Wau–Salamaua, Finschhafen and Shaggy Ridge support Albert Palazzo's argument that in 'New Guinea much of the combat power of a division organised on the British standard was unemployable'.[69] The campaigns of Bougainville, New Britain and Aitape–Wewak in the final year of the war also support this interpretation.

For the 26th Brigade on Tarakan, although the greater availability and wider variety of fire support was welcome, the steep and broken terrain still demanded the heaviest sacrifice from the rifle sections.[70] Even though by early 1945 the Royal Australian Artillery had reverted to its pre-war establishment of three field regiments, this does not invalidate the argument that operations in most islands of the South West Pacific Area required altered formations, units, doctrine and training. Although it reaffirmed the pre-war doctrine of *FSR* and *Infantry Training*, much of the content of *Tropical Warfare* supported this contention. The introductory paragraphs devoted to the various arms made clear that changes to standard operating procedures were necessary to enable that arm to function successfully in the tropics.[71]

The revised 94-page *Tropical Warfare* manual collated information from the 1943 campaigns, especially Ramu–Markham and Lae–Finschhafen. It covered areas such as tactics, man management, support arms, use of native labour, administration and medical services. It was more comprehensive than *MTP No. 23* and acknowledged that 'it is necessary, therefore, that the conditions peculiar to tropical areas be studied in detail, and the limitations imposed by them thoroughly understood'. In another admission that jungle warfare did require adjustment, *Tropical Warfare* also stated that 'the terrain is not conducive to easy movement'.[72] Although deferring to the views of Vasey and Boase, the tone of the manual demonstrated that combat in tropical regions demanded alterations to 'traditional' war-fighting methods. While 'concentration of force' and 'maintenance of the objective', for example, are equally important in all theatres, implementing these principles in the tropics required markedly different measures than in North Africa and Syria. It is also clear that far more thought had gone into this publication than into its predecessors.

This more sophisticated understanding is exemplified in the section on artillery, which states that 'Observation Post Officers are therefore necessary with the forward troops [and that] registration by sound . . . will be necessary when direct observation is not possible.'[73] While the tactic had been used by the men on the front line at Buna, and later in New Guinea, this modification to doctrine formalised a change necessitated by the new challenges of jungle warfare. It also signified to readers that warfare in the tropics required close cooperation by all the combat arms. While less artillery or armour might be used than in the desert, warfare in the tropics was not solely the domain of the infantry. Where Vasey and Porter were correct was in their belief that terrain and climate should not prevent the use of the support arms. This belief had led to excessive infantry casualties in the early jungle campaigns in Papua, and *Tropical Warfare* put paid to it once and for all. Changes to the establishment of the jungle division would see the return of two field regiments in June, followed in late 1944 by a return to the original war establishment, with three field regiments for each infantry division.[74] *Tropical Warfare* was widely distributed after its publication on 30 November 1944 and remained the primary source of tropical warfare information for commanders at battalion level and above.

Published two months after *Tropical Warfare No. 1*, the second volume, *Notes for Junior Leaders*, closely resembled *MTP No. 23— Notes for Platoon & Section Leaders*.[75] The new manual was longer than *MTP No. 23* but contained several very similar chapters. As it was intended for both the company commander and his subordinates, it included expanded sections on hygiene, sanitation and the supporting arms. This manual, supplemented with 'training schemes and lectures', provided an excellent primer and reference for those who had to fight in the tropics.[76] For example, the training syllabus of the 3rd Division fighting on Bougainville drew upon *Tropical Warfare No. 1* and *No. 2*, as well as General Savige's *Tactical and Administrative Doctrine for Jungle Warfare*. This demonstrated that the manuals were at the forefront of training for the Australian Army in the latter stages of the war.[77]

These two pamphlets were distributed throughout the Australian Army in early 1945. Well before then—by June 1944, when the lessons and reports from 7th and 9th Divisions' campaigns were examined and collated—the army had completed its transformation into a battle-hardened force experienced in jungle warfare. Although both the 7th and 9th believed few new lessons had been learned during their 1943–44 campaigns, the experience of tank–infantry operations, for example, would assist in all the final campaigns. Apart from that important addition to jungle warfare learning, the transition from an army that had struggled to adapt to the terrain, climate and the enemy in 1941–42 was virtually complete by late 1943. The final campaigns of the Pacific war merely reinforced the learning that had occurred over the previous three years.

'Overwhelming fire support': The 1944–45 campaigns

When the troops of the 6th Division sailed for Aitape in October 1944, they could not have known that their longest campaign lay ahead. The order by the 17th Brigade commander that 'the maximum use will be made of air strikes, mortar and MMG fire for the support of offensive patrols' reflected the vast change in Allied fortunes—and practice—since the early battles in the South West Pacific Area.[78] Months of difficult combat lay ahead, and many more casualties would be sustained before the Japanese surrendered, but for the most part the Australian Army would be involved in 'mopping up' operations. The degree and variety of support available to the Australian Army in these campaigns exceeded any they had witnessed previously, except for that available to the 9th Division at El Alamein.

Owing to the removal of most logistical support for use in the American invasion of the Philippines, the advance by the 6th Division from Aitape to Wewak was the least well supported of the three AIF campaigns of 1945. Nonetheless, the 2/1st Battalion recorded that 'men from earlier campaigns who missed this one will no doubt have been surprised at the massive support the infantry...was receiving'.[79] Supplied by landing craft or via the oft-washed-out road back to Aitape, the 16th and 19th Brigades could call upon the guns of three field regiments, the MMGs of the 2/3rd MG Battalion, Matildas of the 2/4th Australian Armoured Regiment, naval gunfire from the RAN, and Beaufort bombers of the RAAF.[80] Despite the undoubted benefits of this increase in fire support, the nature of jungle warfare—most notably the ability of the enemy to hide from sight—for the infantry in particular had not changed. As an anonymous infantryman of the 2/3rd Battalion would ask:

> What is Jungle War? Sometimes a fierce, bloody gunspitting moment from dug-in positions, sometimes pinned down in ambush, other times foot-slogging, gut-tearing physical exertion against the toughest terrain in the world.[81]

The ever-present fear of the unknown and the unseen made jungle warfare more loathed than its counterpart in previous theatres. Men would not be lost in the same numbers as in the earlier jungle campaigns, but the need to patrol constantly in order to discover Japanese positions saw platoons and companies slowly whittled down. This occurred through death, more frequently because of injury, and constantly because of disease and sickness—despite the more regimented use of the anti-malarial Atebrin.[82] With the Japanese content to remain in their positions and force the Australians to take the initiative, 'the nature of the country...made defence much easier than attack'.[83] As Japanese numbers decreased, the trend towards a preponderance of automatic weapons for close-quarters jungle combat became more pronounced. The 2/4th Battalion would record that 'in some sections the only rifle still being carried was the "E-Y" [grenade launcher]'; everyone else carried either an Owen or a Bren gun.[84] Once shots rang out—frequently killing the lead scout—the instant reply from the Australians would be a wall of automatic-weapons fire.[85] Under cover of this barrage, men would move forward to recover their dead or wounded comrade and, if the enemy position was lightly held, assault it. If the position was more substantial they would generally retreat 50 to 100 yards so their observer could call down fire support upon the Japanese position. Depending on the number and severity of friendly casualties, the patrol would then decide to continue or retire to company or battalion headquarters and report its findings. Once it was resupplied, the scenario would begin again. For the 6th Division, it would continue in this fashion for many months.

The final two AIF campaigns of the war—the 7th and 9th Divisions' Borneo operations—involved even greater use of fire support than the Aitape–Wewak campaign. The assault on the island of Tarakan by 26th Brigade was more costly than either the 7th Division's amphibious landing at Balikpapan or the actions at Brunei Bay and Labuan Island by the 20th and 24th Brigades of 9th Division. But once again the preponderance of fire support ensured that casualties were lighter than in the Papuan campaigns.[86] In these final campaigns the nature of the terrain, combined with the type of fighting it forced upon the Australians, meant that once again the majority of the casualties were suffered by the rifle sections.[87] In particular, as *Tropical Warfare No. 2* highlighted, 'operations in the jungle demand a high standard of military knowledge and resourcefulness on the part of junior leaders'.[88] In order to fulfil those requirements in jungle warfare, section leaders were therefore forced to expose themselves to a greater level of risk than in combat in more open terrain.

Despite the Australian Army tactical doctrine for jungle warfare, the maxim that 'no attack was to be made without maximum firepower being employed beforehand' was observed in all of these campaigns.[89] At Balikpapan, Brigadier Ken Eather ordered that all his battalions were 'to move [forward] slowly making utmost use of [supporting] arms'. The 2/33rd Battalion recalled that 'the story of Balikpapan was "probe it—blast it—then occupy it"'.[90] Bridge-laying and flame-throwing tanks, air strikes by squadrons of B-24 Liberator heavy bombers, and napalm drops from P-38 Lightning fighters all helped to reduce the number of Australian casualties.

Apart from the greater availability and variety of supporting weapons, and the better organisation and coordination evident in the planning of these operations, there were few new developments in Australian jungle warfare doctrine or training. The many changes in tactics, training, weapons, equipment and medical services that had occurred between 1941 and 1943 ensured that the Australian Army of the final two years of the Second World War was arguably the most experienced, best-trained and most professional jungle warfare force in the world. With the establishment of the Jungle Warfare Training Centre at Canungra, the revised focus on combat in tropical locales at the LHQ Tactical School at Beenleigh, dissemination of doctrine via the LHQ Training Teams, and regularly updated training pamphlets and manuals, the Australian Army had become more adept at jungle warfare than any other military. From September 1943 onwards, the main requirement for more effective operations in the tropics was better cooperation between the arms and greater coordination of air and naval support. This too was achieved.

Yet that is not to suggest that the transition from 1941 to 1945 was easy or seamless. The Australian Army of 1945 was a product of bitter combat experience and hard, realistic training. The claim that the Australian soldier made 'an amazingly quick and thorough adaptation to the demands of tropical and bush warfare' is tenuous.[91] Instead, gradual learning and incremental improvement were the rule. Any criticism of the Australian Army's conduct of the early jungle campaigns is not directed at the soldiers themselves. With inadequate weapons, equipment, clothing and support, and inappropriate doctrine and training, they performed heroically against a fearsome opponent in an unfamiliar environment. By 1944 the problems evident in the early campaigns had been identified and rectified. Tough training courses had been developed in terrain similar to that of the South West Pacific islands. The lessons of those earlier campaigns, combined with the experiences of the 1943–44 campaigns and the extended training periods on the Atherton Tableland, had now been collated and disseminated across the Australian Army. No longer was it the case that 'soldiers have to be killed to learn'.[92]

CONCLUSION

The Australian Army of September 1945 was completely different from that of September 1939. Not only was it massively larger, having grown from approximately 2800 regular and 70,000 (inadequately trained) militia soldiers at the outbreak of the war to 464,000 by February 1944, it was also organised for operations in a completely different theatre.[1] Most importantly, as the historian Albert Palazzo has argued, this was the first time the Australian Army 'had developed on its own an organisation expressly for conditions in which its forces would fight'.[2] Between 1939 and 1942 the Australian Army's structure mirrored that of the British Army. While this made interoperability almost automatic and was beneficial while the army was serving alongside other empire forces in the Middle East and Mediterranean theatres, once Japan entered the war problems quickly became apparent. Changes to meet the new challenges posed by combat in the tropical jungles of the South West Pacific were initially slow and frequently resisted by higher authority. Nevertheless, before the end of the first Papuan campaign in

February 1943, LHQ and the DMT had acknowledged that major changes were essential if the Japanese were to be defeated and, more importantly, if Australian casualties were to be reduced in future operations.

The advent of the Jungle Division, the establishment of the Jungle Warfare Training Centre (Canungra), and the plethora of other changes made between November 1942 and September 1943 comprised the greatest transition the Australian Army has ever been forced to make—and occurred at a critical time in the Second World War. While the brief flirtation (between 1960 and 1964) with the US Pentropic Division system was arguably a more complex organisational change, this took place when the Australian Army had far fewer troops deployed overseas than was the case in 1942.[3] And the Pentropic system was never tested in wartime.

By the end of the Second World War, all the Australian Army infantry divisions that were deployed on operations had been re-organised into Jungle Divisions. Combat in the jungle-clad islands to Australia's north had necessitated this change—though some, then and now, claimed such adaptation was unnecessary. While the Japanese would still have been defeated if the Australian Army had not undertaken such a broad swathe of changes, it is beyond doubt that far more Australian soldiers would have died. The fact that the armies of so many Allied nations later chose to send their troops to Canungra to be trained is proof, if any were needed, that the skills of jungle warfare had to be learned—and learned in a jungle environment. It also demonstrates the Australian Army's widely acknowledged expertise in jungle warfare.

But with the end of the war and subsequent demobilisation, Australia and its society returned to peacetime concerns. In the immediate post-war years the focus of the Australian defence establishment would once again turn to great-power alliances and imperial collective defence. With the advent of the Cold War and the need to contain the Soviet Union, Australia's role, as during the Second World War, would be 'to assist the British in the defence of the Middle East'.[4] When the Chiefs of Staff examined the nation's strategic position in 1947, they concluded that the most likely theatres for future deployment of the Australian Army were Europe or the Middle East.[5] As Colonel Ted Serong—who would be put in charge of the re-establishment of Canungra—later recalled, Australian Army 'strategic concepts ... were based on fighting in or around the Suez Canal ... military training [was] based on the concept of desert warfare'.[6] Very few people, in either government or military circles, thought Australian soldiers would have to fight in the tropics again. Jungle warfare training was shelved and Canungra was closed.

In the late 1940s and early 1950s, however, the outbreak of various conflicts in South-East Asia led to a re-examination of the decisions to close Canungra and cast aside those jungle warfare skills so painstakingly acquired. The French were fighting desperately against the Viet Minh in Vietnam, and the British against the communist terrorists in Malaya; there were insurgencies in Burma, Thailand and the Philippines; and President Sukarno of Indonesia was viewed with worry by the Australian government. Some officers in the Australian Army believed that it was only a matter of time before Australian soldiers would once again be required to fight in tropical jungles. It would not be until 1955 however, that the government of Robert Menzies agreed to provide an infantry battalion to support Britain in the Malayan Emergency. The institutional knowledge and the jungle warfare skills that had lain dormant for ten years would now be required again.

Over the next twenty years, the lessons of the war against the Japanese were passed on to a new generation of soldiers, fighting now in South-East Asia. The men who searched the jungles of Malaya in the 1950s, and fought in Borneo in the early 1960s and then in Vietnam in the 1960s and '70s, were the beneficiaries of the hard-won lessons of Kokoda, Milne Bay and the beachheads. Without the accumulated knowledge of the jungle campaigns of the Second World War, Australian casualties in the Cold War conflicts in South-East Asia would have been far heavier. The jungle warriors of 1942–45 had bequeathed an invaluable heritage to those who followed them.

ACKNOWLEDGEMENTS

First and foremost I must thank those Second World War veterans who were kind enough to tell me about their war. Alan Macfarlane, Lew Manning, Gordon King, Noel Dixon, Don Hancock, Raymond James and Robert Fursdon: gentlemen all. As their numbers dwindle it is timely that we remember this generation that grew up in the aftermath of the Great War, lived through the Great Depression and then marched off to war as storm clouds once again gathered.

I must give special thanks to the eminent military historian Dr Peter Stanley. He suggested that I approach Allen & Unwin as he felt they could publish a first-rate book from my doctoral research. I hope he was correct.

Every author thanks his or her publishers, but in my case I really do have to say a heartfelt thanks to the many staff at Allen & Unwin, without whom this book would not have been published. It has been a long road since 2009 when Ian Bowring agreed with the assessment of Peter Stanley. Since then Ian has retired after four decades with A&U and Stuart Neal took over. He was followed in 2011 by Foong Ling

Kong who knocked the manuscript into shape and the final hard yards have been overseen by Angela Handley. To all of them: a big thankyou.

A book such as this obviously entails innumerable hours of research in the archives. The most important of these is at that extraordinary institution, the Australian War Memorial in Canberra. The National Archives of Australia branches in Melbourne, Sydney, Canberra and Adelaide also provided a wealth of material and unfailingly helpful staff. On my many visits to Canberra I was looked after by true friends, but Darren Marks and Paul and Felicity Dowden need special mention.

My current and former colleagues at Victoria University were always ready to provide advice and suggestions. Most important amongst these were my PhD supervisor Professor Phillip Deery, as well as Professor Robert Pascoe and Drs Richard Chauvel, Mark Stevenson and Marc Askew.

My colleague and friend at the Shrine of Remembrance in Melbourne, David Howell, ensured that I accompanied him on a trek over the Kokoda Track to the northern beachheads with his company Kokoda Historical. It was extremely valuable and very humbling to visit some of the battlefields that Australian soldiers fought and died over 70 years ago.

Finally and most importantly without the love and patience of my wife Leanne this book would not have seen the light of day. My children have kept me on my toes and my parents and brothers have been endlessly supportive. I thank them all.

As always the arguments expressed are mine, as are any mistakes or omissions.

NOTES

Introduction

1 Gavin Long, *To Benghazi: Australia in the war of 1939–1945 (Army)*, Vol. 1, Canberra: AWM, 1952, pp. 70–85.
2 E.G. Keogh, *South West Pacific 1941–45*, Melbourne: Grayflower Productions 1965, p. 474. See also Albert Palazzo, 'Organising for jungle warfare', in Peter Dennis and Jeffrey Grey (eds), *The Foundations of Victory: The Pacific War*, The Chief of Army's Military History Conference 2003, Canberra: Army History Unit, 2004, p. 89.
3 Syd Tregellis-Smith, *Britain to Borneo: A history of the 2/32 Australian Infantry Battalion*, Sydney: 2/32nd Australian Infantry Battalion Association, 1993, pp. 3–6.
4 Lieutenant-General H. Gordon Bennett, *Why Malaya Fell*, Sydney: Angus & Robertson, 1944, p. 12.
5 Frank Legg, *The Gordon Bennett Story*, Sydney: Angus & Robertson, 1965; A.B. Lodge, *The Fall of General Gordon Bennett*, Sydney: Allen & Unwin, 1988, p. 50.
6 Patrick Lindsay, *The Spirit of the Digger: Then and now*, Sydney: Macmillan, 2003, pp. 184–5.
7 Palazzo, 'Organising for jungle warfare', p. 89.
8 Peter Dornan, *The Silent Men: Syria to Kokoda and on to Gona*, Sydney: Allen & Unwin, 1999, pp. 76–8 and 92–8.
9 Deborah Avant, *Political Institutions and Military Change: Lessons from peripheral wars*, Ithaca, NY: Cornell University Press, 1994; Lloyd C. Gardner and Marilyn B. Young (eds), *Iraq and the Lessons of Vietnam or How Not to Learn from*

the Past, New York: The New Press, 2007, especially the chapters by David Elliot and Marilyn Young; Lawrence Kaplan, 'Clear and fold: Forgetting the lessons of Vietnam', *New Republic*, vol. 233, issue 25, 19 Dec 2005; John Lawrence Tone, *The Fatal Knot: The guerrilla war in Navarre and the defeat of Napoleon in Spain*, Chapel Hill: University of North Carolina Press, 1994.

Chapter 1. 'No Military Knowledge of the Region': 1914–1941

1. S.S. Mackenzie, *The Australians at Rabaul: Official history of Australia in the war of 1914–1918*, vol. X, Sydney: Angus & Robertson, 1938, pp. 50, 31.
2. Ibid., p. 5. A similar request was made to New Zealand with regard to the seizure of Samoa.
3. Michael Piggott, 'Stonewalling in German New Guinea', *The Journal of the Australian War Memorial*, no. 12, Apr 1988, p. 3.
4. Mackenzie, *The Australians at Rabaul*, p. 29.
5. Six men were killed in action, four wounded.
6. Mackenzie, *The Australians at Rabaul*, p. 31.
7. Piggott, 'Stonewalling in German New Guinea', p. 8.
8. Tony Sweeney, *Malaria Frontline: Australian Army research during World War II*, Melbourne: Melbourne University Press, 2003, p. 10.
9. C.E.W. Bean, *Anzac to Amiens*, Canberra: AWM, 1946, p. 502.
10. Sweeney, *Malaria Frontline*, pp. 11–13; Mackenzie, *The Australians at Rabaul*, p. 364.
11. Jeffrey Grey, *The Australian Army, Vol. I, The Australian Centenary History of Defence*, South Melbourne: Oxford University Press, 2001, p. 72.
12. Long, *To Benghazi*, p. 10.
13. Peter Cochrane, *Australians at War*, Sydney: ABC Books, 2001, p. 89.
14. David Horner, *High Command: Australia and Allied strategy 1939–1945*, Sydney: George Allen & Unwin, 1982, p. 1.
15. See John Robertson, 'The distant war: Australia and Imperial defence, 1919–41', pp. 223–44, in M. McKernan and M. Browne (eds), *Australia: Two centuries of war and peace*, Sydney: Allen & Unwin, 1988.
16. AWM 1, item 20/7, 'Report on the Military Defence of Australia by a Conference of Senior Officers of the Australian Military Forces 1920', p. 4.
17. Horner, *High Command*, p. 2.
18. Grey, *The Australian Army*, p. 82.
19. Margot Simington, 'The southwest Pacific islands in Australian interwar defence planning', *Australian Journal of Politics and History*, vol. xxiii, no. 2, Aug 1977, pp. 173–5.
20. David Horner, 'Lieutenant-General Sir Vernon Sturdee: The chief of the general staff as commander', in David Horner (ed.), *The Commanders: Australian military leadership in the twentieth century*, Sydney: Allen & Unwin, 1984, pp. 146–7. (The quote was taken from a lecture Sturdee gave regarding the 'Plan of Concentration' [for the defence of Australia].)

21 Quoted in Jeffrey Grey, *A Military History of Australia*, Cambridge: Cambridge University Press, 1999, p. 124.
22 Grey, *The Australian Army*, p. 80.
23 Albert Palazzo, *The Australian Army: A history of its organisation 1901–2001*, Melbourne: Oxford University Press, 2001, p. 104.
24 Neil Gow, 'Australian Army strategic planning 1919–39', *Australian Journal of Politics and History*, vol. xxiii, no. 2, Aug 1977, pp. 169–71.
25 Palazzo, *The Australian Army*, p. 95.
26 AWM, 3DRL 6850, Papers of General Mackay, item 59, 'Notes on Training of Officers', n.d. (probably 1941), p. 5.
27 Ian Kuring, *Redcoats to Cams: A history of Australian infantry, 1788–2001*, Loftus, NSW: Australian Military History Publications, 2004, p. 210.
28 Lionel Wigmore, *The Japanese Thrust: Australia in the war of 1939–45 (Army)*, Vol. IV, Canberra: AWM, 1957, p. 10.
29 NAA, MP729/6, item 40/401/86, 'Notes on the Japanese Army'.
30 Simington, 'The southwest Pacific islands in Australian interwar defence planning', p. 173.
31 Dudley McCarthy, *South-West Pacific Area: First year—Kokoda to Wau, Australia in the war of 1939–1945 (Army)*, Vol. V, Canberra, AWM, 1959, p. 41.
32 Wigmore, *The Japanese Thrust*, p. 10.
33 Ibid.
34 Captain D.M. Kennedy, 'The Japanese Army as a fighting force', *The Army Quarterly*, vol. xxx, no. 2, Jul 1935, pp. 238–9. See also, Brevet Major B.R. Mullaly, 'The evolution of the Japanese Army', *The Army Quarterly*, vol. XVI, no. 1, Apr 1928, pp. 52–64.
35 Both these manuals were British War Office publications, reprinted for the Australian Army.
36 John Moremon, 'No "black magic": Doctrine and training for jungle warfare', in Dennis and Grey (eds), *The Foundations of Victory*, p. 78; John Sholl, 'Points Noted and Lessons Learnt: The nature and determinants of Australian Army tactical changes, 1941–1943', BA (Hons), ADFA, 1991, p. 34.
37 Moremon, 'No "black magic"', p. 77; Chris Coulthard-Clark, *A Heritage of Spirit: A biography of Major-General Sir William Throsby Bridges*, Melbourne: Melbourne University Press, 1979, pp. 85–6.
38 Tim Moreman, 'Jungle, Japanese and the Australian Army: Learning the lessons of New Guinea', paper presented to the *Remembering the War in New Guinea* Symposium, Australian National University, 19–21 Oct 2000, on the Australia–Japan Research Project/AWM website (no pagination).
39 *Field Service Regulations, Vol. II, Operations—General, 1935*, London: War Office, 1935 (reprinted 1939), p. 184.
40 Ibid.
41 Moreman, 'Jungle, Japanese and the Australian Army', p. 2.
42 *Voorschrift Voor De Uitoefening Van De Politiek-Politioneele Taak Van Het Leger (VPTL)* [Guidelines for the implementation of the Army's Counter-Insurgency Tactics (Police Actions)], Batavia-Centrum, 1937.

43 Simington, 'The southwest Pacific islands in Australian interwar defence planning', p. 177.
44 *Small Wars Manual*, United States Marine Corps, 1940 (revised version of 1935 edition). The 1940 version is 492 pages in length.
45 Major-General R.R. McNicoll, *Ubique: The Royal Australian Engineers 1919–1945—Teeth and tail*, Canberra, ACT: Corps Committee of the Royal Australian Engineers, 1982, p. 18.
46 Long, *To Benghazi*, p. 3. (Long was discussing the comments by a member of Parliament in the 1920s who had used that argument to support large cutbacks in military spending.)
47 AWM 52, 1/5/12, 6 Australian Division General Staff Branch (6 Aust Div GS Branch), Oct–Dec 1939, Appx A, p. 2.
48 Palazzo, *The Australian Army*, p. 141.
49 AWM 52, 1/5/12, Oct–Dec 1939, Appx A, p. 6.
50 DVA, AAWFA, William Booth, 2/3rd Battalion, Archive No. 1420, transcript, time: 6.13.00.00.
51 W.P. Bolger and J.G. Littlewood, *The Fiery Phoenix: The story of the 2/7 Australian Infantry Battalion 1939–1946*, Parkdale, Vic: 2/7 Battalion Association, 1983, p. 10.
52 F.W. Speed (ed.), *Esprit de Corps: The history of the Victorian Scottish Regiment and the 5th Infantry Battalion*, Sydney: Allen & Unwin, 1988, p. 161.
53 DVA, AAWFA, Raymond Baldwin, 2/27th Bn, Archive No. 1214, transcript, time: 2.17.30.00.
54 Reginald Davidson, *With Courage High: The history of the 2/8th Field Company Royal Australian Engineers, 1940–1946*, Melbourne: 2/8th Field Company, RAE Association, 1964, p. 5.
55 E.C. Givney (ed.), *The First at War: The story of the 2/1st Australian Infantry Battalion 1939–45, The City of Sydney Regiment*, Sydney: The Association of First Infantry Battalions, Editorial Committee, 1987, p. 39.
56 E.V. Haywood, *Six Years in Support: Official History of 2/1st Australian Field Regiment*, Sydney: Angus & Robertson, 1959, p. 15.
57 Mark Johnston, *At the Front Line: Experiences of Australian soldiers in World War II*, Cambridge: Cambridge University Press, 1996, p. 110.
58 Long, *To Benghazi*, p. 99.
59 See, for example, Stan Wick, *Purple Over Green: The history of the 2/2 Australian Infantry Battalion 1939–1945*, Sydney: 2/2 Australian Infantry Battalion Association, 1978, p. 43.
60 Mark Johnston, *The Silent 7th: An illustrated history of the 7th Australian Division 1940–46*, Sydney: Allen & Unwin, 2005, p. 2; Long, *To Benghazi*, p. 100, on composition of 6th Division.
61 For more information see Johnston, *The Silent 7th* and the same author's *That Magnificent 9th: An illustrated history of the 9th Australian Division 1940–46*, Sydney: Allen & Unwin, 2002; Long, *To Benghazi*, pp. 82–3; the various battalion histories.
62 Wick, *Purple Over Green*, p. 47.

63 Long, *To Benghazi*, p. 123. See also Grey, *A Military History of Australia*, p. 154.
64 Gordon Dickens, *Never Late: The 2/9th Australian Infantry Battalion 1939–1945*, Loftus, NSW: Australian Military History Publications, 2005, p. 53.
65 Johnston, *At the Front Line*, p. 108.
66 AWM 54, 937/1/2, pp. 3–4.
67 W. Cremor (ed.), *Action Front: The history of the 2/2nd Australian Field Regiment Royal Australian Artillery AIF*, Melbourne: 2/2nd Field Regiment Association, 1961, p. 31.
68 David Hay, *Nothing Over Us: The story of the 2/6th Australian Infantry Battalion*, Canberra: AWM, 1984, p. 78.
69 Gavin Keating, *The Right Man for the Right Job: Lieutenant-General Sir Stanley Savige as a military commander*, South Melbourne, Vic: Oxford University Press, 2006, p. 40.
70 Johnston, *At the Front Line*, p. 110.
71 Phillip Masel, *The Second 28th: The story of a famous battalion of the Ninth Australian Division*, Perth: 2/28th Battalion and 24th Anti-Tank Company Association, 1961, p. 24.
72 John Coates, *Bravery Above Blunder: The 9th Australian Division at Finschhafen, Sattelberg and Sio*, Melbourne: Oxford University Press, 1999, p. 33.
73 *FSR*, p. 186.
74 Sholl, 'Points Noted and Lessons Learnt'; see especially pp. 42–5.
75 AWM, KMSA, Owen Curtis, 2/12th Bn, Archive No. S541, transcript, p. 67.
76 Sholl, 'Points Noted and Lessons Learnt', p. 42.
77 Ibid., p. 43.
78 *Infantry Minor Tactics, Australia, 1941*, Melbourne: HMSO, 1941, pp. 84–5.
79 Sholl, 'Points Noted and Lessons Learnt', pp. 45–6.
80 Ibid., p. 34.
81 W.B. Russell, *The Second Fourteenth Battalion: A history of an Australian Infantry Battalion in the Second World War*, Sydney: Angus & Robertson, 1948, pp. 54 and 68.
82 John Burns, *The Brown and Blue Diamond at War: The story of the 2/27th Battalion AIF*, Adelaide: 2/27th Battalion Ex-Servicemen's Association, 1960, p. 55; Allan W. Draydon, *Men of Courage: A history of the 2/25 Australian Infantry Battalion 1940–1945*, Chermside, Qld: 2/25 Australian Infantry Battalion Association, 2000, p. 92.
83 Grey, *A Military History of Australia*, p. 159.

Chapter 2. 'Everything was so Different': The 8th Division in Malaya

1 Hank Nelson, 'Travelling in memories: Australian prisoners of the Japanese, forty years after the fall of Singapore', *Journal of the Australian War Memorial*, no. 3, Oct 1983, p. 16.
2 AWM 52, 1/5/17, 8 Australian Division General Staff Branch, Nov 1940—Jan 1941, 'GOC's Circular Letter No. 3', 16 Dec 1940.

3. AWM 52, 1/5/17, 'Copies of Indoor Tactical Exercise—Western Desert', 11 Nov 1940.
4. James Burfitt, *Against All Odds: The history of the 2/18th Battalion AIF*, Sydney: 2/18th Battalion Association, 1991, p. 24. See also DVA, AAWFA, Frederick Power, 2/19th Bn, Archive No. 1142, transcript, time: 04.07.30.00.
5. Peter Henning, *The Doomed Battalion: The Australian 2/40th Battalion 1940-45—Mateship and leadership in war and captivity*, Sydney: Allen & Unwin, 1995, p. 121.
6. DVA, AAWFA, Donald Wall, 2/20th Bn, Archive No. 0429, transcript, time: 3.24.00.19.
7. AWM, KMSA, Erwin Heckendorf, 2/30th Bn, Archive No. S763 transcript, p. 18.
8. DVA, AAWFA, Colin Finkmeyer, 4th Anti-Tank Regiment, Archive No. 0093, transcript, time: 01.21.00.00 (This was true); Peter Henning, *Doomed Battalion: The Australian 2/40 Battalion 1940-45—Mateship and leadership in war and captivity*, Sydney: Allen & Unwin, 1995, p. 17.
9. Wigmore, *The Japanese Thrust*, p. 44 (It should be possible); Horner, *High Command*, p. 53 (One outcome of).
10. AWM 52, 1/5/17, 31 Jan 1941. 'Elbow Force' was the codename for the 8th Division's deployment to Malaya.
11. AWM, 3DRL 1892, Diary of Brigadier H.B. Taylor, 11 Feb 1941.
12. Brigadier Ian Stewart, *History of the Argyll and Sutherland Highlanders 2nd Battalion (The Thin Red Line) Malayan Campaign 1941-42*, London: Thomas Nelson, 1947, p. 1.
13. Angus Rose, *Who Dies Fighting*, London: Jonathon Cape, 1944, p. 9 (We received very little); Peter Elphick, *The Pregnable Fortress: A study in deception, discord and desertion*, London: Hodder & Stoughton, 1996, p. 189 (No jungle-training school).
14. Stewart, *The Argyll and Sutherland Highlanders*, pp. 3-5.
15. Wigmore, *The Japanese Thrust*, p. 68.
16. Wigmore, *The Japanese Thrust*, p. 68. See also, AWM 67, 3/9, Part 1 'Personal Records of Lt-Col. CGW Anderson, VC, MC', letter 16 Nov 1948, p. 3.
17. See, for example, NAA, MP729/7, 33/421/96, 'Prevention of Disease Among Troops in Tropics', 29 Jan 1941.
18. AWM 52, 8/2/22, 22 Bde GP, 'Tng of Officers' (Further Syllabus of Lectures), 12-14 Feb 1941.
19. R. Newton (ed.), *The Grim Glory of the 2/19 Battalion AIF*, Sydney: 2/19 Battalion Association, 1975, p. 69.
20. Moreman, 'Jungle, Japanese and the Australian Army'.
21. Wigmore, *The Japanese Thrust*, p. 67.
22. John Moremon, 'Most Deadly Jungle Fighters?': The Australian infantry in Malaya and Papua, 1941-43, Honours thesis, University of New England, 1992, p. 13. See also Moreman, 'Jungle, Japanese and the Australian Army', p. 3.
23. Moreman, 'Jungle, Japanese and the Australian Army', p. 3.
24. AWM 52, 1/5/17, 'Training' Circular G13, 27 Mar 1941, p. 1.
25. Moremon, 'Most Deadly Jungle Fighters?', p. 13.
26. AWM 52, 8/2/22, HQ 22 Inf Bde, 'Tng Instruction No. 1', 20 Feb 1941.

27 Newton (ed.), *The Grim Glory of the 2/19*, p. 74.
28 Bennett, *Why Malaya Fell*, p. 12.
29 AWM 52, 8/2/22, 24/29 Feb 1941.
30 Frank Colenso, quoted in Burfitt, *Against All Odds*, p. 26.
31 'Jacky Roo', quoted in Newton (ed.), *The Grim Glory of the 2/19*, pp. 85–6.
32 AWM 52, 8/2/22, 'Tng Instruction No. 1', HQ 22nd Inf Bde, 20 Feb 1941.
33 AWM 52, 8/3/18, 'Training Instruction No. 1', HQ AIF Malaya, 28 Feb 1941.
34 Ron Magarry, *The Battalion Story: 2/26th Infantry Battalion, 8th Division AIF*, Jindalee, Qld: Ron Magarry, 1995, p. 43.
35 See, for example, Bob Goodwin, *Mates and Memories: Recollections of the 2/10th Field Regiment RAA*, Rochedale Qld, Boolarong Press, 1995, p. 19.
36 Ron Jackson, *The Broken Eighth: A history of the 2/14th Australian Field Regiment*, Melbourne: Clipper Press, 1997, p. 162.
37 Cliff Whitelocke, *Gunners in the Jungle: A story of the 2/15 Field Regiment Royal Australian Artillery, 8 Division, Australian Imperial Force*, Sydney: 2/15 Field Regiment Association, 1983, p. 63.
38 AWM 52, 8/3/20, 'Syllabus of Training: Week Ending 1 Mar '41', attached to War Diary, 19–24 Feb 1941.
39 AWM 52, 8/3/18, 'Syllabus', 28 Feb 1941.
40 AWM 52, 8/3/19, 'Syllabus as from 25 Feb 41', 25 Feb 1941.
41 AWM, 3DRL 1892. See entries for 20, 24 and 28 Feb 1941, for example.
42 Alan Loxton, quoted in Burfitt, *Against All Odds*, p. 26.
43 DVA, AAWA, Colin Finkmeyer, 4th Anti-Tank Regiment, Archive No. 0093, transcript, time: 01.31.30.00.
44 Stewart, *The Argyll and Sutherland Highlanders*, p. 2.
45 Whitelocke, *Gunners in the Jungle*, p. 83.
46 DVA, AAWA, Keith Pope, 8th Division Signals, 6th Line Section, Archive No. 0701, transcript, time: 04.09.00.00.
47 Whitelocke, *Gunners in the Jungle*, p. 108 ('As in all theatres', 'The burden upon' and 'once battle was joined'). See also R.L. Henry, *The Story of the 2/4th Field Regiment: A history of a Royal Australian Artillery Regiment during the Second World War*, Melbourne: Merrion Press, 1950, p. 142.
48 DVA, AAWA, Allan McNevin, 2/10th Field Artillery Regiment, Archive No. 1295, transcript, time: 1.17.00.00. For Borneo, see Henry, *The Story of the 2/4th Field Regiment*, p. 388.
49 DVA, AAWA, James Ling, 8th Division Signals Unit, Despatch rider, Archive No. 0015, transcript, time: 03.30.30.04.
50 AWM 52, 8/3/18, 31 Dec 1941. See also *Signals: Story of the Australian Corps of Signals*, Various, Canberra: AWM, 1945, pp. 177–81; Stan and Les Briggs (eds), *Ike's Marines: The 36th Australian Infantry Battalion 1939–1945*, Loftus, NSW: Australian Military History Publications, 2003, p. 180.
51 *Infantry Minor Tactics*, Chapter XX, 'The passage of water obstacles', pp. 154–5.
52 AWM 52, 8/2/22, 4–14 Apr 1941.
53 AWM 52, 8/3/20, 'Outline Syllabus—Week Ending 12 April '41, FSPB Pam. 4 Pages 55–56' was the suggested reading.

54 Wigmore, *The Japanese Thrust*, p. 71; Burfitt, *Against All Odds*, p. 27; Janet Uhr, *Against the Sun: The AIF in Malaya, 1941–42*, Sydney: Allen & Unwin; 1998, p. 16.
55 Newton (ed.), *The Grim Glory of the 2/19*, p. 73.
56 Johnston, *At the Frontline*, p. 7.
57 A.J. Marshall (ed.), *Nulli Secundus Log*, Sydney: 2/2nd Australian Infantry Battalion AIF, 1946, p. 82.
58 AWM 52, 8/3/18, 31 Jul 1941.
59 HQ AIF Malaya Memorandum: 'Jungle Fighting', 15 Mar 1941 in AWM 54, item 553/6/3 (italics in original).
60 DVA, Howard, 2/19th Bn, transcript, time: 03.05.00.00.
61 AWM 52, 8/3/20, 9 Jul 1941.
62 Don Wall, *Singapore and Beyond: The story of the men of the 2/20th Battalion— Told by the survivors*, East Hills, NSW: 2/20 Bn Ass, 1985, p. 14.
63 With regard to discarding helmets see G.E. Lambert (ed.), *Commando: From tidal river to Tarakan—The story of No. 4 Australian Independent Company AIF*, Melbourne: 2nd/4th Commando Association, 1994, p. 263. For the value of automatic weapons, see Ian Morrison, *Malayan Postscript*, Kuala Lumpur, Malaysia: S. Abdul Majeed & Co, 1993, pp. 72–3.
64 See, for example, Hay, *Nothing Over Us*, p. 131. For the initial issue of the TSMG in Malaya see AWM 52, 8/3/18, 'Syllabus 14/19 April 41'.
65 AWM 52, 8/3/18, 28 Mar 1941.
66 See, for example, AWM 52, 8/3/18, 'Syllabus 27 Oct–1 Nov 41', TEWT [Tactical Exercise Without Troops]. For exchanges of officers see AWM 52, 8/3/19, 1 Dec 1941.
67 See, for example, AWM 52, 8/3/18, 'Tactical Exercise—22 Aust Inf Bde and Att Tps', 17 Apr 1942. Also, Newton (ed.), *The Grim Glory of the 2/19*, p. 104.
68 The 27th Brigade consisted of the 2/26th Battalion (Qld), the 2/29th (Vic) and the 2/30th (NSW). After the departure of the 22nd Brigade, the units of the 27th Brigade were able to concentrate at the recently vacated Bathurst and Ingleburn training camps.
69 AWM 52, 8/2/27, 'Training Instruction No. 8', May 1941.
70 AWM 52, 8/3/29, '2/29 Bn Exercise—Wattle Flat Area', 30 Jun 1941.
71 AWM 52, 8/2/23, 'Training' Circular G13, from HQ 8 Aust Div, 27 Mar 1941.
72 See, for example, AWM 52, 8/3/21, entries for September, October and November. The 2/40th Battalion fared no better, see AWM 52, 8/3/34, 'Training Report D Coy 2/40 Bn AIF Week ending 31 Aug 41: Factors Affecting Training': 'As training is impossible, factors affecting road construction will be dealt with.'
73 AWM 52, 8/3/21, 'General Comments' for June, July and August 1941.
74 See Joan Beaumont, *Gull Force: Survival and leadership in captivity 1941–1945*, Sydney: Allen & Unwin, 1988, pp. 23–40; Henning, *Doomed Battalion*, pp. 28–48; and Horner, *High Command*, pp. 130–7, for discussion of strategic reasons for the deployments.
75 Henning, *Doomed Battalion*, p. 47.
76 AWM 52, 8/3/21, 'Tng Instruction No. G. 3', 22 May 1941.

77 AWM 52, 8/3/21, 'Secret', 9 Aug 1941, attached as an appendix to the August War Diary.
78 AWM 52, 8/3/21, '2/21 Bn. Tng Exercise No. 14 Two Sided Coy Exercise', 7 Nov 1941.
79 AWM 52, 8/3/21, '2/21 Bn Training Cadre', 24/28 Nov 1941, and the attached appendix 'Bayonet Assault Course'.
80 AWM 52, 8/2/23, 6 Nov 1941, 'Extracts from 27 Aust Inf Bde Tng Instruction No. 15'.
81 Beaumont, *Gull Force*, p. 23.
82 DVA, AAWFA, Benjamin Amor, 2/21st Bn, Archive No. 0566, transcript, time: 2.26.30.00.
83 AWM 52, 8/3/21, 'Gull G & I Matters', 24 Dec 1941.
84 Beaumont, *Gull Force*, p. 57.
85 All material in this paragraph is taken from the 2/21st Bn War Diary, entries for May to September 1941. For example, AWM 52, 8/3/34, 'First Aid Cadre—Week 15–19 Sep', Appx XIII.
86 All material in this paragraph is taken from Henning, *Doomed Battalion*, p. 55.
87 David Horner, *Blamey: The commander in chief*, Sydney: Allen & Unwin, 1998, p. 324.
88 R.P. Serle (ed.), *The Second Twenty-Fourth Australian Infantry Battalion of the 9th Division*, Brisbane, Qld: Jacaranda Press, 1963, p. 250.
89 AWM 52, 8/3/22, 'Voyage Report of Advance Party "L" Force on M/V Neptuna', 24/3/41.
90 AWM 52, 8/3/22, (this suggests that) and (foremost among these).
91 AWM, KMSA, Bill Harry, 2/22nd Bn, Archive No. S908, transcript, p. 21 (As a consequence); AWM, KMSA, Fred Kollmorgen, 2/22nd Bn, Archive No. S911, transcript, p. 24.
92 AWM 52, 8/3/22, 'Tactical Training Information No. 1', 25 Jun 1941, Appendices. (All material in this paragraph comes from the training bulletin in the unit war diary.)
93 AWM 52, 8/3/22, 4–8 Sept 1941. (All material in this paragraph comes from the unit war diary.)
94 AWM 52, 8/3/22, 'Comments and Conclusions Two-Sided Exercise Conducted by "A" and "D" Companies', 1000hrs Mon 8 Sep 1941 to 0600hrs Wed 10 Sep 1941. (All material in this paragraph comes from the unit war diary.)
95 Lt-Gen. S.F. Rowell, 'Report on Operations New Guinea Force, 11 Aug to 28 Sep 42', Nov 1942, AWM 54 519/6/60. Similarly *Notes on Forest Warfare* stated that 'Training in forest warfare can only be carried out in forest country', p. 8.
96 AWM 52, 8/2/23, 'Extracts from 27 Aust Inf Bde Tng Instruction No. 15'.
97 AWM 52, 8/2/27, 'Tng Instn No. 14', 20 Aug 1941. Appx 20 to August War Diary.
98 Ibid., p. 2.
99 *Tactical Notes for Malaya 1940*, Reprinted for General Staff, AHQ, Melbourne, 1940, Chapter II, p. 8.
100 AWM, KMSA, Erwin Heckendorf, 2/30th Battalion, Archive No. S763, transcript, p. 26.

101 W.C. Bayliss, K.E. Crispin and A.W. Penfold, *Galleghan's Greyhounds: The story of the 2/30th Australian Infantry Battalion*, Sydney: 2/30th Bn AIF Association, 1979, p. 35.
102 Wall, *Singapore and Beyond*, p. 31.
103 Bayliss et al., *Galleghan's Greyhounds*, p. 73.
104 AWM 54, 4/4/4, entries for 19/20 through to 30 July.
105 Whitelocke, *Gunners in the Jungle*, pp. 58–9.
106 R.W. Christie (ed.), *A History of the 2/29 Battalion, 8th Australian Division AIF*, Stratford, Vic: High Country Publishing, 1991, p. 28.
107 As was discussed in Chapter 1, *Infantry Training* was the 'bible' of the junior infantry officer, and contained within its 250 pages details of every topic thought relevant to an infantry officer. *Infantry Training (Training and War) 1937* and *Infantry Training: Supplement: Tactical Notes for Platoon Commanders, 1937*, London: HM Stationery Office, 1938, were published by the British Army and subsequently re-issued for the Australian Army. For reference to them see AWM 52, 8/3/30, 'Syllabus of Training', Period 8–13 Sept 1941.
108 AWM 67, Gavin Long papers 2/109 and 3/140. Also AWM, 3DRL 1892, Private Papers of Brigadier Taylor and AWM PR 85/42, Taylor; Lodge, *The Fall of General Gordon Bennett*, p. 50.
109 Magarry, *The Battalion Story*, p. 43. See also Bayliss et al., *Galleghan's Greyhounds*, pp. 45, 51–2, 58; Lodge, *The Fall of General Gordon Bennett*, p. 50.
110 Burfitt, *Against All Odds*, p. 35; Newton (ed.), *The Grim Glory of the 2/19*, p. 199.
111 AWM 52, 8/3/18, 14 Nov 1941.
112 Lodge, *The Fall of General Gordon Bennett*, p. 50; AWM 52, 8/3/20, 21 Jan 1942. See also AWM 54, 553/5/25.
113 AWM 52, 8/2/27, 'Tng Instn No. 18' Tng Policy for Period Ending 1 Nov 1941. A brigade-level conference attended by COs and regimental medical officers in late October had been called to discuss the issue.
114 Bayliss et al., *Galleghan's Greyhounds*, p. 58; AWM 54, 923/2/7 (Japanese troops have little); AWM 54, 56/4/2, 'Japanese Army Minor Tactics', AHQ Melbourne, 6 Jun 1941, pp. 3–4.
115 Burfitt, *Against All Odds*, p. 38; Australian Army, *The Jap was Thrashed: An official story of the Australian soldier*, Melbourne: AHQ, 1944, p. 4. See also Wigmore, *The Japanese Thrust*, p. 114; Elphick, *The Pregnable Fortress*, p. 189.
116 Bryan Perrett, *Canopy of War: Jungle warfare, from the earliest days of forest fighting to the battlefields of Vietnam*, Wellingborough: Patrick Stephens Limited, 1990, p. 30. See also Keogh, *South West Pacific, 1941–45*, p. 71.
117 Masanobu Tsuji, *Singapore: The Japanese version*, Sydney: Ure Smith, 1960, pp. 3–6.
118 *Tactical Notes for Malaya*, pp. 3–4.
119 Elphick, *The Pregnable Fortress*, p. 189.
120 Burfitt, *Against All Odds*, p. 26. See also Magarry, *The Battalion Story*, p. 56; DVA, AAWFA, John Varley, 2/19th Bn, Archive No. 1220, transcript, time: 05.05.30.04.
121 AWM 52, 8/3/30, 'Diary Record for Month of December 1941', 2 Jan 1942. See also Whitelocke, *Gunners in the Jungle*, p. 59.
122 Bayliss et al., *Galleghan's Greyhounds*, p. 76.

123 AWM 52, 8/3/30, 'Intelligence Summary No. 9', 15 Dec 1941. Of the Japanese rifle it was stated that 'SAA [Small Arms Ammunition] is approx .25 ... and inflicts very slight wounds. Very small duck egg grenades were used at the initial landings. Anti-personnel aircraft bombs have lead cases, and shrapnel content is not very effective ... small mortars, but shell has no blast.'
124 Newton (ed.), *The Grim Glory of the 2/19*, p. 156.
125 Sturdee to Bennett, 19 Jan 1942, in AWM 54, item 553/6/3, Part 10.
126 AWM 52, 8/3/29, 'Main Features of Enemy Tactics', 21 Dec 1941.
127 AWM 52, 8/2/22, 'Message', 20 Dec 1941, p. 2.
128 Newton (ed.), *The Grim Glory of the 2/19*, p. 156.
129 AWM 52, 8/3/19, Appx 2, 'Message', December Messages, 25 Dec 1941.
130 Wigmore, *The Japanese Thrust*, p. 155.
131 Tsuji, *Singapore*, p. 13.
132 See Bayliss et al., *Galleghan's Greyhounds*, pp. 84–118; AWM, KMSA, Erwin Heckendorf, 2/30th Bn, Archive No. S763, transcript, p. 37.
133 Whitelocke, *Gunners in the Jungle*, pp. 64–5; also Bayliss et al., *Galleghan's Greyhounds*, pp. 87–9.
134 Garth Pratten, *Australian Battalion Commanders in the Second World War*, Melbourne, Vic: Cambridge University Press, 2009, p. 155.
135 AWM 52, 8/2/27, Thursday 15 Jan 1942 (Maxwell carried the report); Magarry, *The Battalion Story*, pp. 71–3 (Within days Maxwell).
136 Pratten, *Australian Battalion Commanders in the Second World War*, p. 156; Christie (ed.), *A History of the 2/29 Battalion*, pp. 43–60; Newton (ed.), *The Grim Glory of the 2/19*, pp. 198–220.
137 Newton (ed.), *The Grim Glory of the 2/19*, p. 227.
138 Ibid., p. 252.
139 Kuring, *Redcoats to Cams*, pp. 175–6.
140 Lodge, *The Fall of General Gordon Bennett*, pp. 193–5.
141 Bennett to Sturdee, AWM 54, 553/6/3, 16 Dec 1941. See also Bennett, *Why Malaya Fell*, p. 75.
142 Moremon, 'Most Deadly Jungle Fighters?', p. 26; Bennett, *Why Malaya Fell*, p. 225.
143 Stewart, *The Argyll and Sutherland Highlanders*, pp. 25–6; Bennett, *Why Malaya Fell*, pp. 75–6.
144 Burfitt, *Against All Odds*, p. 67; Newton (ed.), *The Grim Glory of the 2/19*, p. 227.
145 Mark Johnston, *Fighting the Enemy: Australian soldiers and their adversaries in World War II*, Cambridge: Cambridge University Press, 2000, p. 86. See also *The Jap Was Thrashed*, p. 33.
146 Horner, *High Command*, p. 173; Burfitt, *Against All Odds*, p. 59; Wall, *Singapore and Beyond*, p. 54; Newton (ed.), *The Grim Glory of the 2/19*, p. 256; Christie (ed.), *A History of the 2/29 Battalion*, pp. 97–9. See also DVA, AAWFA, William Nankervis, 2/29th Bn, Archive No. 0236, transcript, time: 03.07.30.00.
147 Christie (ed.), *A History of the 2/29 Battalion*, p. 100.
148 Peter Brune, *Those Ragged Bloody Heroes*, Sydney: Allen & Unwin, 1991, p. 12; Paul Ham, *Kokoda*, Sydney: HarperCollins, 2004, p. 486. Several militia units would be thrown into battle virtually untrained.

Chapter 3. 'Completely Devoid of Ideas': The 6th Division on Ceylon

1. NAA, A816, 52/302/142, 'Strategical situation in the Far East and Pacific following the fall of Singapore: Future employment of AIF', Cablegram from PM Curtin to PM Churchill, 2 Mar 1942.
2. AWM 52, 1/5/12 (6 Aust Div GS Branch), 'Notes of Conference Held at GOC's Mess, Baalbek, 1630hrs, 13 Dec 41', November–December 1941.
3. AWM 52, 1/5/12, 'Minutes of Meeting Held to Discuss Relief of Portion of 6 Aust Div for tng by 5000 AIF Reinforcements', November–December 1941.
4. John Armstrong, cited in Ken Clift, *War Dance: The 2/3rd Australian Infantry Battalion*, Sydney: P.M. Fowler and 2/3rd Battalion Association, 1980, p. 248.
5. AWM 52, 8/2/17, 'Training Instruction No. 3', 10 Dec 1941. For use of mules see also Bolger and Littlewood, *The Fiery Phoenix*, pp. 231–2.
6. Ibid., p. 179.
7. AWM 52, 8/3/6, 10 Mar 1942.
8. Moremon, 'No "black magic"', pp. 76–85.
9. Ibid., p. 79.
10. AWM 52, 8/2/16, 26 Mar 1942. See also the comments by McCarthy, *South-West Pacific Area First Year*, p. 79.
11. AWM 52, 8/3/2, Apr 1942.
12. AWM 52, 8/2/16, 13 Apr 1942.
13. AWM 52, 8/2/17, 3 Apr 1942.
14. AWM 52, 8/3/7, '2/7 Weekly Report, week ending 11 Apr 42', [Handwritten], Mar–Apr 1942.
15. Lew Manning, 2/43rd and 2/10th Bns, interview, Adelaide, 7 Mar 2006.
16. *Infantry Minor Tactics*, pp. 17 and 123.
17. Rose, *Who Dies Fighting*, p. 12.
18. AWM 52, 8/2/16, 'Notes on COs Conference 28 Mar 42', Appx H, 28 Mar 1942.
19. AWM 52, 8/3/2, 'Training Week Commencing 30 Mar 42', 29 Mar 1942.
20. AWM 52, 8/2/17, '17 Aust Inf Bde GP Tactical School', 30 Apr 1942.
21. AWM 52, 8/3/2, 'Training Week Commencing 30 Mar 42'.
22. AWM 52, 8/3/7, 1 Apr 1942.
23. Hay, *Nothing Over Us*, p. 232.
24. AWM 52, 8/3/2, 'Notes on Conference Bn HQ—28 Apr. Ref Notes on Fighting in Malaya', 29 Apr 1942.
25. NAA, MP 729/6, 50/401/256, 'Tactics to Combat Japanese Military Methods', 26 Mar 1942, in 'Training in Jungle Warfare'.
26. *Military Training Pamphlet No. 9 (India), Extensive Warfare—Notes on Forest Warfare*, Simla (India), 1940.
27. Louis Morton, *Strategy and Command: The first two years*, Washington, DC: Center of Military History, US Army, 1965 (2000 reprint), p. 156.
28. 'Tactical Methods', Army Headquarters Melbourne, 2 Mar 1942.
29. Ibid., p. 2.
30. Ibid.
31. AWM 52, 8/2/16, 'Notes on COs Conference 28 Mar 42', Appx H, 28 Mar 1942.

32 AWM 52, 8/3/7, 2 Apr 1942.
33 AWM 52, 8/3/7, 2 Apr 1942.
34 AWM 52, 8/3/1, 11 Apr 1942.
35 AWM 52, 8/3/2, 16 Apr 1942.
36 AWM 52, 8/2/16, 'Carrying 3-in Mortar on Bicycle. Result of Test—22 May 42', Appx B, 25 May; AWM 52 8/3/7, 5 Jun 1942. The entry for this day includes discussion on the experiments carried out by the Pioneer Platoon with a modified bicycle fitted with a stretcher to transport casualties more rapidly from the frontline. Mention is not made of who won the dubious honour of playing the casualty.
37 AWM 52, 8/2/16, 'Information for Australia', 30 Apr 1942, Appendices, Apr–May 1942.
38 Givney (ed.), *The First at War*, p. 232.
39 AWM 52, 8/2/17, 5 May 1942.
40 AWM 52, 8/3/1, 29 Apr 1942.
41 AWM 52, 8/3/17, 4 May 1942.
42 Cam Bennett, *Rough Infantry: Tales of World War II*, Melbourne: Warrnambool Institute Press, 1985, pp. 136 and 149.
43 AWM 52, 8/3/1, 'Report on Unit G (R) Training Period 7 May 42–6 June 42', 5 Jun 1942. This report makes it starkly clear that well-trained infantry could, at very little cost to themselves, render unaccompanied carriers—and in fact most mechanised vehicles—worthless in jungle warfare.
44 AWM 52, 8/2/16, 24 Apr 1942.
45 AWM 52, 8/3/2, 8 Apr 1942.
46 Bolger and Littlewood, *The Fiery Phoenix*, p. 187.
47 AWM 52, 8/2/16, 25 May 1942, 'Notes on Rafts—3-in Mortar Platoon', Appx A.
48 *ATM No. 11* (June 1942), 'Operations in Malaya, Dec. '41–Feb. 42', Appx A, p. 38. 'The importance of patrol training cannot be over emphasised. It is the side which wins the patrol actions which wins the jungle war. It must be remembered that as units and tps [troops] train so they fight, this was proved in Libya and Syria . . . In 1914–18 our Australian patrols dominated the Germans and paved the way to victory in the ensuing battles.'
49 AWM 52, 8/2/16, 31 May 1942.
50 AWM 52, 8/2/16, 'Information for Australia', Appx C, 21 May 1942.
51 See, for example, Margaret Barter, *Far Above Battle: The experience and memory of Australian soldiers in war 1939–1945*, Sydney: Allen & Unwin, 1994, p. 226. She also states that 'at Aitape-Wewak, small group patrolling dominated everything'.
52 AWM 52, 8/2/16, 'Information for Australia', Appx B, 30 Apr 1942.
53 Givney (ed.), *The First at War*, p. 248.
54 AWM 52, 8/3/7, 15 May. These can rightly be seen as the precursor to the jungle assault, stalker and scout courses constructed by every unit training on the Atherton Tableland in 1943. They will be dealt with in detail in Chapter 6.
55 Givney (ed.), *The First at War*, p. 235.
56 AWM 52, 8/3/2, 2 May 1942.
57 See, for example, Stan and Les Briggs (eds), *Ike's Marines*, p. 180.

58 AWM 52, 8/2/16, 'General Resume of Work Done by 2/1 Aust Fd Amb in Ceylon', 14 Nov 1942, Jun 1942 Appendices.
59 See, for example, AWM 52, 5/5/10, HQ RAE 6 Aust Div War Diary, Mar to Jul 1942.
60 AWM 52, 8/2/16, 'Artillery Training' in 'Glossary of Events', Appx E [undated].
61 Moremon, 'Most Deadly Jungle Fighters?', p. 46.
62 AWM 52, 8/2/17, 29 Apr 1942. (All the quotes in this paragraph (except for Moremon above) come from this document.)
63 AWM 52, 8/2/17, 'Précis of Bde Comd's Conference', 1 May 1942, Apr 1942, Appx 6. (All the quotes in this paragraph come from this document.)
64 AWM 52, 8/2/17, '17 Aust Inf Bde Gp Training Instruction No. 8 INF Training For Two Weeks Ending 31 May 1942', 14 May 1942. The training instruction stated that 'training will commence with simple section exercises based upon lessons learnt at 17 Aust Bde Junior Tactical School'.
65 AWM 52, 8/3/7, 30 May 1942.
66 AWM 52, 8/3/5, 26 May 1942. See also the comments in the 17 Bde War Diary, 26 May 1942.
67 Bennett, *Rough Infantry*, p. 139.
68 AWM 52, 8/2/17, 11–13 Jun 1942.
69 AWM 52, 8/2/17, 13 Jun 1942.
70 See, for example, AWM 52, 8/3/1, 'Report on G (R) Training 7 June—6 July 42', 11 Jul 1942, June/July Appendices.
71 George Tarlington, *Shifting Sands and Savage Jungle*, Loftus, NSW: Australian Military History Publications, 1994, p. 56.
72 AWM 54, 577/7/29, Pt 15, 'Report on Operations in New Guinea, 16 Aust Inf Bde', 28 Dec 1942.

Chapter 4. 'Physical Fitness is Vital': Training in Australia, 1942

1 AWM 52, 8/2/18, 15 Feb 1942: 'Owing to the limited space tng has been restricted but particular attention is being paid to the hardening of tps by organised games and physical tng'.
2 AWM 52, 8/2/18, 18 Feb 1942, 'Comds Discussion: Decentralisation of Arty and Jungle Warfare', 'Problems of Treatment and Evacuation of Casualties'.
3 AWM 52, 8/2/18, 'Decentralisation of Arty and Jungle Warfare', p. 1.
4 AWM 52, 8/2/21, 30 Jan 1942.
5 AWM 52, 8/2/21, 26 Feb 1942.
6 Frank Allchin, *Purple and Blue: The history of the 2/10th Battalion AIF (The Adelaide Rifles) 1939–1945*, Adelaide: Griffin Press, 1958, p. 231.
7 AWM 52, 1/5/14, 'Warfare in Thick Country', 7 Australian Division General Staff Branch (hereafter 7 Aust Div GS Branch), 2 Mar 1942, Appx T.1, p. 1.
8 AWM 52, 8/2/18, 'Tng Instn No. 23', Appx A, March War Diary; AWM 52, 8/2/21, 'Training Instruction No. 28', 26 Mar 1942, p. 1 (capitalisation in original).
9 Russell, *The Second Fourteenth Battalion*, 1948, p. 107. See also AWM 52, 8/3/14, 'Syllabus of Tng—Rifle Coys—Week Ending 2 May 42'.

10 Alex Graeme-Evans, *Of Storms and Rainbows: The story of the men of the 2/12th Battalion AIF, Volume Two*, Hobart: 12th Battalion Association, 1991, p. 7.
11 See, for example, AWM 52, 8/3/25, 'Report on Tactical Exercise with Carriers', Apr 1942; AWM 52, 8/2/18, 'Notes on Defence Against Tank Attack', 29 Mar 1942.
12 AWM 52, 8/2/18, 'Intelligence Summary No. 118', 27 Apr 1942, and 'Intelligence Summary No. 119', 4 May 1942.
13 M.C.J. Welburn, *The Development of Australian Army Doctrine 1945–64*, Canberra: Australian National University (Research School of Pacific and Asian Studies), 1994, p. 7.
14 Ibid.
15 AWM 52, 8/3/14, 'Company Tactical Exercise: The Deliberate Attack', April War Diary.
16 AWM 52, 8/3/16, '2/16 Aust Inf Bn Tng Instn No. 1', 29 Mar 1942.
17 AWM 52, 8/3/12, War Diary entries for 19 and 20 May 1942.
18 Bill Spencer, *In the Footsteps of Ghosts: With the 2/9th Battalion in the African desert and the jungles of the Pacific*, Sydney: Allen & Unwin, 1999, p. 88.
19 AWM 52, 8/3/27, 'Report on Bn Exercise—Glen Innes—5 May 1942'.
20 Graeme-Evans, *Of Storms and Rainbows*, p. 32.
21 AWM 52, 8/2/18, 18 Jun 1942.
22 See, for example, Russell, *The Second Fourteenth Battalion*, p. 110; AWM 52, 8/3/16, 'Summary' for Jul 1942; AWM 52, 8/3/27, Jul 1942.
23 Burns, *The Brown and Blue Diamond at War*, p. 105.
24 AWM 52, 8/3/14, 'Outline Plan—Coast Watching', 29 May 1942.
25 For more information on the intelligence triumph of the Allied forces see, for example, Stephen Budiansky, *Battle of Wits: The complete story of codebreaking in World War II*, New York: Free Press, 2002; John Prados, *Combined Fleet Decoded: The secret history of American Intelligence and the Japanese Navy in World War II*, New York: Random House, 1995; Michael Smith, *The Emperor's Codes: Bletchley Park and the breaking of Japan's secret ciphers*, London: Random House, 2000.
26 McCarthy, *South West Pacific Area*, p. 80.
27 John B. Lundstrom, *The First Team: Pacific Naval Air Combat from Pearl Harbor to Midway*, Annapolis, Maryland, USA: Naval Institute Press, 1984, pp. 283–4.
28 AWM 54, 937/3/18, 'First Army Trg Instn Nos 1 & 3: Jungle Warfare 1942'.
29 AWM 52, 8/2/25, 'Tactical Exercise with Troops No. 5', Appx H, 29 Jun 1942.
30 Russell, *The Second Fourteenth Battalion*, p. 112.
31 Burns, *The Brown and Blue Diamond at War*, p. 105.
32 AWM 52, 8/3/9, 1 Jun, Appx B, '2/9 Aust Inf Bn Exercise'; AWM 52, 1/5/14, 'Murgon TEWT', 13 Jun 1942, and '7 Aust Div TEWT', 6 Jul 1942.
33 Sydney Rowell, *Full Circle*, Melbourne: Melbourne University Press, 1974, p. 110.
34 AWM 52, 8/3/27, 18 May 1942; AWM 52, 8/3/14, 4 May 1942.
35 See, for example, AWM 52, 8/3/10, 'Tactical Exercise with Tps to be Held on Friday, 15 May, 42'; AWM 52, 8/2/18, Appx H, 'Tactical Exercise with Troops No. 5', 29 Jun 1942.

36 AWM 52, 1/5/14, 'The Will to Win', 13 May 1942; AWM 52, 1/5/14, 'Warfare in Thick Country', 2 Mar 1942.
37 AWM 52, 1/5/14, 'Appx B1', 28 May 1942.
38 AWM 52, 8/2/25, 'Experiments in Jungle Warfare', 21 Jun 1942.
39 AWM 52, 8/3/25, 22 Jun 1942.
40 AWM 52, 8/3/14, 'Report on five day march 19–24 May Lt Pearce'.
41 AWM 52, 8/2/21, 'Report on Patrol Endurance Report', Appx A, 5/21 May 1942.
42 AWM 52, 8/2/25, 'Q Notes by Capt E.S. Owens—SQ 25 Aust Inf Bde' from 25 Aug to 26 Sept 1942, p. 2.
43 Allchin, *Purple and Blue*, p. 238. See also Burns, *The Brown and Blue Diamond at War*, p. 105; Malcolm Uren, *A Thousand Men At War: The story of the 2/16th Battalion AIF*, Melbourne: William Heinemann Ltd, 1959, p. 114.
44 DVA, AAWFA, Lindsay Mason, 2/14th Bn, transcript, tape 3.11.00.00. See also AWM, KMSA, Charles Sims, 2/27th Bn, Archive No. S789, tape 2, side A, 5–10 minutes; DVA, AAWFA, John Kirkmoe, 2/10th Bn, Archive No. 1814, time: 1.06.30.00.
45 Spencer, *In the Footsteps of Ghosts*, pp. 88–9.
46 Steve Edgar, *Warrior of Kokoda: A biography of Brigadier Arnold Potts*, Sydney: Allen & Unwin, 1999, p. 117.
47 AWM 52, 8/2/21, 'Appx 5' and 'Preliminary Report by Director—21 Aust Inf Bde Test Exercise 24–30 Jun 42'.
48 AWM 52, 8/2/21, 'Preliminary Report by Director'.
49 Ibid., p. 1.
50 J.C. McAllester, *Men of the 2/14th Battalion*, Melbourne: 2/14th Battalion Association, 1990, p. 52: See also William Crooks, *The Footsoldiers: The story of the 2/33rd Australian Infantry Battalion AIF in the war of 1939–45*, Sydney: Printcraft Press, 1971, p. 78; John Warby, *The 25 Pounders . . . From Egypt to Borneo: Campaigns in Syria, Kumusi River, Salamaua, Lae, Finschhafen and Balikpapan—The story of the 2/6th Australian Field Regiment, RAA, AIF, 1940–1946*, Sydney: 2/6th Fd Regt Association, 1995, p. 115.
51 McAllester, *Men of the 2/14th Battalion*, p. 57.
52 AWM 52, 8/2/21, 'Preliminary Report by Director', p. 4.
53 Ibid.
54 Sholl, 'Points Noted and Lessons Learnt', pp. 82–3.
55 AWM 52, 8/2/25, 'Tng Instn No. 19', 5 Jul 1942.
56 Sholl, 'Points Noted and Lessons Learnt', p. 82–3.
57 AWM 52, 8/2/25, 'Tng Instn No. 16: Notes on Lessons from Tactical Exercise with Troops No. 4', 22 Jun 1942. See, also AWM 54, 943/1/14, 'Jungle Warfare as carried out by the 25th Aust Inf Bde 1942'.
58 Stewart, *The Argyll and Sutherland Highlanders*, p. 2.
59 AWM 52, 8/2/21, 'Bde Test Exercise No. 1, General Notes', Appx 4, p. 2.
60 AWM 52, 8/2/21, Appx 5, p. 1.
61 See, for example, the discussion in Cremor (ed.), *Action Front*, pp. 172–83; R.L. Henry, *The Story of the 2/4th Field Regiment: A history of a Royal Australian Artillery Regiment during the Second World War*, Melbourne: Merrion Press, 1950, pp. 194–8.

62 AWM 52, 4/2/4, 25–27 Jun 1942.
63 See AWM 52, 4/2/2 and 4/2/3, and the unit histories, Les Bishop, *The Thunder of the Guns! A history of 2/3 Australian Field Regiment*, Sydney: 2/3 Australian Field Regiment Association, 1998, and Cremor (ed.), *Action Front*, in particular, for further information.
64 For defence work in southern Queensland see John W. O'Brien, *Guns and Gunners: The story of the 2/5th Australian Field Regiment in World War II*, Sydney: Angus & Robertson, 1950, p. 145. For artillery unit jungle warfare training prior to departure for Papua see DVA, AAWFA, Peter Gibson, 2/5th Field Regiment, Archive No. 0012, time: 5.01.00.05.
65 DVA, AAWFA, Eustace Marsden, 2/4th Field Regiment, Archive No. 0455, transcript, time: 5.10.30.00.
66 DVA, AAWFA, Raymond Widdows, 2/12th Field Regiment, Archive No. 1786, time: 7.08.30.00.
67 AWM 52, 8/2/21, 'Preliminary Report by Director', p. 2.
68 AWM 52, 8/2/25, 'Tng Instn No. 15: Notes on Lessons from Tactical Exercise with Troops No. 4', 22 Jun 1942.
69 AWM 52, 8/3/31, 'CO's Report' in Jul 1942 War Diary: 'Exercises carried out, showed that carriers were not suitable in jungle country in their recce role. They proved far too vulnerable.'
70 Bennett, *Rough Infantry*, pp. 136, 149.
71 AWM 52, 8/2/21, Appx 5, p. 1.
72 DVA, AAWFA, William Abbott, 2/4th Field Company RAE, Archive No. 1023, transcript, time: 1.22.30.00.
73 AWM 52, 5/13/6, see War Diary entries for May, June and July 1942.
74 AWM 52, 5/13/6, 23 May 1942, 'Engineers News Item No. 2—First Aust Army—Notes on the Employment of Engineers in Certain Theatres in the Middle East', p. 3.
75 AWM 54, 553/5/16 Pt 2, 'Report by Major General Gordon Bennett on Malayan Campaign 7th Dec to 15th Feb 1942'.
76 AWM 52, 5/13/4, War Diary entries for May to Aug 1942.
77 AWM 52, 8/2/18, 'Notes on Comd's Discussions Pt III, Training of Employment and Pioneer Pl', Jul 1942.
78 Horner, *High Command*, p. 196.
79 General John R. Galvin, 'Uncomfortable wars: Towards a new paradigm', pp. 9–18, in Max G. Manwaring (ed.), *Uncomfortable Wars: Towards a new paradigm of low intensity conflict*, Boulder, CO: Westview Press, 1991.
80 AWM 52, 8/3/14, 14 Jul, '7 Offrs and 50 ORs attached to our Unit for three weeks training—from 24 Bn AMF'.
81 AWM 52, 8/3/25, 8 Jun 1942; John Hetherington, *Blamey: The biography of Field-Marshal Sir Thomas Blamey*, Melbourne: F.W. Cheshire, 1954, p. 142.
82 Steve Eather, *Desert Sands, Jungle Lands: A biography of Major-General Ken Eather*, Sydney: Allen & Unwin, 2003, p. 53.
83 Moremon, 'Most Deadly Jungle Fighters?', p. 44.
84 AWM 54, 553/6/3, Lt-Col. J.R. Wolfenden, 'Lessons from Operations against the Japanese: Resume of activities of LHQ Instructional Staff to Nov 43', tabled

as evidence to Army Court of Inquiry into Bennett escape, 26–30 Oct 1954, in Bennett papers.
85 AWM 52, 4/2/6, 27 Sept 1942.
86 AWM 52, 8/2/25, 'Report by Lt-Col J. R. Wolfenden. Demonstrations—30 August 1942'.
87 Ibid., p. 2.
88 Eather, *Desert Sands, Jungle Lands*, pp. 55–6.
89 AWM 52, 8/2/17, 24 Sept 1942.
90 AWM 52, 8/3/27, 'Fd Firing Exercise', 21 Jul 1942.
91 See, for example AWM 52, 8/3/14, 'Training Instruction No. 29', 31 Mar 1942; AWM 52, 8/3/9, 'Monthly Syllabus', 8 Jun 1942; AWM 52, 8/3/25, 'Syllabus of Training', 13–19 Jul 1942; AWM 52, 8/3/14, 'Tng Syllabus for Week Ending 8 Aug 42'.
92 DVA, AAWFA, George Connor, 2/33rd Battalion, Archive No. 1175, time: 6.33.30.00.
93 AWM 52, 8/3/10, 'Quartermaster's Report', Jul 1942.
94 AWM 52, 8/2/18, 'Routine Orders Part 1, No. 85 Gaiters SD', 11 Jun 1942.
95 Ibid., War Diary, 18 Jun 1942.
96 Ibid.
97 Graeme-Evans, *Of Storms and Rainbows*, p. 32.
98 AWM 52, 8/2/16, 16 Aug 1942. See also Burns, *The Brown and Blue Diamond at War*, p. 110.
99 AWM 52, 1/5/14, 'Experiments in Jungle Warfare Final Report', Appx A, 7 Aug 1942.
100 NAA (Sydney), SP 300/4, Item: 321, 'Observations on the New Guinea Campaign August 26th—September 26th 1942', p. 4.
101 Allan W. Draydon, *Men of Courage: A history of the 2/25 Australian Infantry Battalion 1940–1945*, Chermside Queensland: 2/25 Australian Infantry Battalion Association, 2000, p. 108.
102 AWM 52, 8/3/2, 14 Sept, 'On being ordered to move every effort was made to bring the Bn up to establishment in amn and eqpt. There was an issue of 42 extra TSMGs.'
103 AWM 52, 8/3/14, 'Tng Syllabus for Week Ending 8 Aug 42'.
104 *ATM No. 11*, 'Appx A (Parts 1 and 2)', pp. 35–49.
105 Uren, *A Thousand Men at War*, p. 114.
106 McAllester, *Men of the 2/14th Battalion*, p. 334.

Chapter 5. 'Jesus Christ! I Can't See Anything': Milne Bay and Kokoda

1 William W. Rogal, *Guadalcanal, Tarawa and Beyond: A mud marine's memoir of the Pacific Island War*, Jefferson, NC: McFarland, 2010, p. 55.
2 See AWM 52, battalion war diaries of 18th and 21st Bde, for information.
3 Burns, *The Brown and Blue Diamond at War*, p. 105, and DVA, AAWFA, Ronald Hansen, 2/9th Bn, Archive No. 0878, time: 6.15.00.00. See also DVA, AAWFA, Robert Thompson, 2/14th Bn, Archive No. 1594, time: 6.25.00.00; Clive Baker and

Greg Knight, *Milne Bay 1942: The story of 'Milne-Force' and Japan's first military defeat on land*, Loftus, NSW: Baker-Knight Publications, 1992, p. 89.
4   Sholl, 'Points Noted and Lessons Learnt', p. 38.
5   The 49th Bn arrived in Port Moresby in October 1940, 3rd Bn arrived on 27 May 1942, and 39th and 55/53rd Bns arrived in January 1942. See Victor Austin, *To Kokoda and Beyond: The story of the 39th Battalion 1941–43*, Melbourne: Melbourne University Press, 1988, pp. 26–29; F. M. Budden, *That Mob! The story of the 55th/53rd Australian Infantry Battalion, AIF*, Sydney: Wild & Wooley, 1973, pp. 10–12; F. Cranston, *Always Faithful: The history of the 49th Battalion*, Brisbane: Boolarong Press, 1983, pp. 128–130; Brune, *Those Ragged Bloody Heroes*, pp. 10–16; Ham, *Kokoda*, pp. 22–5; Osmar White, *Green Armour*, Ringwood Vic: Penguin, 1992, pp. 47–8.
6   See, for example, NAA, MP729/6, 39/401/293, 'Overland Routes Port Moresby to Buna', 25 Jun 1942.
7   Hank Nelson, 'Kokoda: The track from history to politics', *Journal of Pacific History*, vol. 38, no. 1, 2003, p. 115. See also Colin Kennedy, *Port Moresby to Gona Beach: 3rd Australian Infantry Battalion*, Canberra: The Practical Group, 1991, Appx One, NGF Intelligence Report No. 34 'Recce Report Sogeri-Kokoda Track, 27th June—4th July 1942'.
8   H.D. Steward, *Recollections of a Regimental Medical Officer*, Melbourne: Melbourne University Press, 1983, p. 77 (issued with quinine tablets) and 87 (The space they occupied).
9   Russell, *The Second Fourteenth Battalion*, p. 121 (urgent preparation) and AWM 52, 8/3/14, 14 Aug 1942 (each company was asked).
10 Russell, *The Second Fourteenth Battalion*, p. 122 (Eventually the entire 21st); Uren, *A Thousand Men at War*, p. 134 (Two of the first items).
11 Brune, *Those Ragged Bloody Heroes*, p. 47.
12 DVA, AAWFA, Robert Iskov, 2/14th Bn, Archive No. 1999, transcript, time: 5.10.30.00.
13 AWM 52, 8/3/78, 29 Jul 1942.
14 A.T. Ross, *Armed and Ready: The industrial development and defence of Australia 1900–1945*, Sydney: Turton & Armstrong, 1995, p. 414.
15 McCarthy, *South-West Pacific Area First Year*, pp. 124–5.
16 See *Infantry Minor Tactics*, p. 51 for a description of how MMGs should be employed.
17 Sholl, 'Points Noted and Lessons Learnt', p. 23.
18 Australian Military Forces, *Tropical Warfare (Australia), Pamphlet No. 1—General Principles*, LHQ, Australian Army, Melbourne, 1944, p. 21.
19 Sholl, 'Points Noted and Lessons Learnt', p. 32.
20 See, for example AWM 54, 577/7/29, Pt. 16, 'Notes on New Guinea Fighting', by Lt-Col. Cameron, 3rd Battalion; AWM 54, 937/3/33, 'Vasey to Adv LHQ (DMT)', 13 Mar 1943.
21 AWM, KMSA, Charles Sims, 2/27th Bn, S789, tape 2, side A, 5–10 minutes.
22 For the controversies between Blamey, MacArthur, Allen etc. see, for example, Stuart Braga, *Kokoda Commander: A life of Major-General 'Tubby' Allen*, South

Melbourne, Vic.: Oxford University Press, 2004; Brune, *Those Ragged Bloody Heroes*; David Horner, *Crisis of Command: Australian generalship and the Japanese threat, 1941–1943*, Canberra: ANU Press, 1978; McCarthy, *South-West Pacific First Year*; Rowell, *Full Circle*.

23 DVA, AAWFA, Lindsay Mason, 2/14th Bn, Archive No. 1197, transcript, time: 6.11.00.00.
24 AWM 52, 8/3/16, 16 Aug, and 8/3/27, 23–24 Aug 1942, '415 prs of gaiters (American type) received and issued to tps'.
25 Russell, *The Second Fourteenth Battalion*, p. 122.
26 DVA, AAWFA, Robert Thompson, 2/14th Bn, Archive No. 1594, time: 3.36.30.00.
27 AWM 54, 581/7/19, 'Notes on and Lessons from Recent Operations in Gona Sanananda Areas', by Lt-Col. R. Honner, Commander, 39 Australian Infantry Battalion, p. 2.
28 Lawrence Fitzgerald, *Lebanon to Labuan: A story of mapping by the Australian Survey Corps World War II (1939–1945)*, Melbourne: J.G. Holmes, 1980, p. 68.
29 AWM 52, 1/5/14, 19 Aug 1942 (owing to acute shortage); AWM 52, 8/2/21, 16 Aug 1942 (otherwise our knowledge).
30 AWM 52, 8/3/27, 18–19 Aug 1942; Russell, *The Second Fourteenth Battalion*, p. 121; Uren, *A Thousand Men at War*, p. 117; John Laffin, *Forever Forward: The history of the 2/31st Australian Infantry Battalion, 2nd AIF 1940–45*, Newport, NSW: 2/31st Australian Infantry Battalion Association, 1994, p. 88.
31 AWM 52, 8/3/14, 'Extract from Daily Telegraph Sep 14 1942' (All the chaps feel); White, *Green Armour*, p. 181 (that their packs weighed). See also General Rowell's ADC Lt Darling in Neil McDonald, *Damien Parer's War*, South Melbourne: Lothian Books, 2004, p. 206.
32 McDonald, *Damien Parer's War*, p. 214 (observed Kanga Force); AWM 54, 905/1/3, Kanga Force Headquarters: 'Recommendations re equipment used in jungle warfare', Jul 1942 (is too easily seen), p. 1.
33 Russell, *The Second Fourteenth Battalion*, pp. 122–3, and DVA, AAWFA, Raymond Baldwin, 2/27th Bn, Archive No. 1214, time: 5.35.00.30.
34 Baker and Knight, *Milne Bay 1942*, p. 70.
35 AWM 52, 8/3/14, 24 Aug 1942.
36 AWM, KMSA, Harry Katekar, 2/27th Bn, Archive No. S903, tape 2, 5–10 minutes; DVA, AAWFA, Frank Patterson, 7th Division Signals, Archive No. 0193, transcript, time: 4.04.30.00.
37 DVA, AAWFA, Angus Suthers, 2/12th Bn, Archive No. 0399, time: 5.34.30.00 (knew absolutely nothing) and 6.05.00.20 (nor were the 18th).
38 McCarthy, *South-West Pacific Area*, p. 121. See also Spencer, *In the Footsteps of Ghosts*, p. 95.
39 DGM Rickards, 'Eighty two years of Life's Recollections', unpublished memoirs, 2001, Battalion Military Archive, Brisbane, Qld; quoted in Dickens, *Never Late*, p. 158.
40 AWM 52, 8/2/10, 17 Aug 1942; Dickens, *Never Late*, p. 161.
41 AWM, KMSA, Paul Hope, 2/12th Bn, Archive No. S529, p. 67.
42 Baker and Knight, *Milne Bay 1942*, p. 89.

43 AWM, KMSA, Owen Curtis, 2/12th Bn, Archive No. S541, p. 67. See also Wick, *Purple Over Green*, pp. 224–5.
44 DVA, AAWFA, Neil Russell, 2/12th Bn, Archive No. 0692, transcript, time: 6.14.30.00.
45 Dickens, *Never Late*, p. 168.
46 Peter Brune, *A Bastard of a Place: The Australians in Papua*, Sydney: Allen & Unwin, 2003, p. 380.
47 DVA, AAWFA, Harvey Wockner, 2/9th Bn, Archive No. 1028, transcript, time: 5.32.00.20.
48 Baker and Knight, *Milne Bay 1942*, p. 220. See also Peter Brune, *200 Shots: Damien Parer and George Silk with the Australians at war in New Guinea*, Sydney: Allen & Unwin, 2004, pp. 128–9.
49 AWM, KMSA, Geoffrey Holmes, 2/12th Bn, Archive No. S540, p. 54 (we were given); Dickens, *Never Late*, p. 165 (repugnant to the men).
50 See, for example, Brune, *The Spell Broken*, pp. 115–16; Graeme-Evans, *Of Storms and Rainbows*, p. 116; McCarthy, *South-West Pacific Area*, p. 178; Spencer, *In the Footsteps of Ghosts*, pp. 107–8; AWM, KMSA, Paul Hope, 2/12th Bn, Archive No. S529, p. 74.
51 Brune, *The Spell Broken*, pp. 115–16, and Graeme-Evans, *Of Storms and Rainbows*, p. 155.
52 DVA, AAWFA, Charles Howell, 2/12th Bn, Archive No. 1606, transcript, time: 7.28.30.00.
53 AWM 52, 8/2/18, 'Points Noted and Lessons Learnt in Recent Ops', 16 Sept 1942, p. 3.
54 Baker and Knight, *Milne Bay 1942*, p. 256.
55 AWM, KMSA, Owen Curtis, 2/12th Bn, Archive No. S541, p. 67.
56 AWM, KMSA, Paul Hope, 2/12th Bn, Archive No. S529, p. 72.
57 Baker and Knight, *Milne Bay 1942*, p. 38.
58 Allan S. Walker, *The Island Campaigns, Australia in the War of 1939–1945, Series Five: Medical, Vol. III*, Canberra: AWM, 1957, p. 56.
59 Graeme-Evans, *Of Storms and Rainbows*, p. 172 (The 2/12th Bn); McCarthy, *South-West Pacific Area*, p. 306 (Similarly, the 16th Brigade).
60 Crooks, *The Footsoldiers*, p. 124.
61 AWM 54, 'Report on 10th Australian Field Ambulance—Buna Campaign—December 1942—February 1943'.
62 DVA, AAWFA, Frederick Williams, 2/2nd Bn, Archive No. 0780, time: 7.25.30.00 (In combat it proved); AWM 52, 1/5/14, Appx in Jan 1943 War Diary, 'Medical Service 7 Aust Div During Papuan Campaign' (the campaign presented).
63 See, for example, AWM 54, 'Field Ambulance Notes, Jungle Warfare, by Col. G.B.G. Maitland', May 1943.
64 AWM 52, 8/3/12, CO's Report and Comment on Month, 31 Aug 1942.
65 See Dickens, *Never Late*, p. 198; Graeme-Evans, *Of Storms and Rainbows*, p. 213 (the lessons of Milne Bay); Spencer, *In the Footsteps of Ghosts*, p. 111 (Replacements for those men).
66 AWM 52, 8/3/12, Appx G, 'Report on Operations Goodenough Island, 22nd to 26th October 42'.

67 DVA, AAWFA, Edmond Jones, 2/9th Bn, Archive No. 1138, time: 4.13.30.00.
68 Baker and Knight, *Milne Bay 1942*, p. 243.
69 AWM 52, 4/2/3, 1 Aug 1942; Bishop, *The Thunder of the Guns!*, pp. 500 and 530.
70 O'Brien, *Guns and Gunners*, pp. 147 and 152.
71 McCarthy, *South-West Pacific Area First Year*, p. 241.
72 O'Brien, *Guns and Gunners*, p. 152.
73 Ibid. See also Walker, *The Island Campaigns*, pp. 47–9 and 108–19; Sweeney, *Malaria Frontline*, p. 29.
74 McCarthy, *South-West Pacific Area First Year*, p. 169.
75 O'Brien, *Guns and Gunners*, p. 163 (the new techniques); AWM 52, 8/2/18, 'Report on Artillery Operations at Gili Gili Aug/Sep 42', p. 1 (These were then radioed).
76 AWM 52, 8/2/18, p. 1. See also Baker and Knight, *Milne Bay 1942*, pp. 244–5; David Horner, *The Gunners: A history of Australian artillery*, Sydney: Allen & Unwin, 1995, p. 339.
77 AWM 52, 8/2/18, p. 1.
78 O'Brien, *Guns and Gunners*, p. 164.
79 See, for example, David Goodhart, *The History of the 2/7 Australian Field Regiment*, Adelaide: Rigby Ltd, 1952, p. 316; W.T. Lewis (ed.), *Observation Post: Six years of war with the 2/11th Australian Army Field Regiment*, W. Essendon: 2/11th Field Regiment Association, 1989, pp. 156–9.
80 Cremor (ed.), *Action Front*, p. 193 (Each unit appears). For reports on artillery use, see AWM 54, 581/6/9, 'Artillery Operations in Buna—Gona Area', by Brigadier L.E.S. Barker, 31 Jan 1943, pp. 9–11, especially the paragraphs on 'Engagement of Targets' and 'Proximity Shooting'; AWM 54, 75/4/18, 'Artillery in Jungle Warfare—Notes compiled from reports, from Pacific War Zone, 1943', pp. 2 'Observation', 3 'Ranging' and 7 'Summary'; AWM 54, 937/3/7, 'Notes on New Guinea Campaign', p. 2. This very detailed 30-page report, compiled by two company commanders of the 2/2nd Battalion, would by Feb 1943 be widely circulated by LHQ.
81 AWM 52, 8/2/18, 'Points Noted and Lessons Learnt in Recent Ops', HQ 18 Aust Inf Bde, p. 4.
82 Warby, *The 25 Pounders*, p. 169. See also DVA, AAWFA, Roy Dockery, 14th Field Regiment, Archive No. 2023, time: 4.26.00.00; Horner, *The Gunners*, p. 341.
83 AWM 54, 577/7/22 [Owen Stanley: Reports]. See also AWM 52, 8/6/1, 4 Oct 1942.
84 Ibid., 'Report of Movement of 25 pounder to Ubiri [Uberi] Valley' by Maj CC Thomas BC of the Battery.
85 Ibid. See the attached Appx H written by the Brigade Major, Royal Artillery, NGF 6 Nov 1942 discussing these experiments. See also AWM 52, 4/2/1, 25 Sept 1942; AWM 54, 577/7/35, 'Notes on 7th Division Operations Kokoda to Soputa', by Major Parbury, Jan 1943, p. 11.
86 AWM 52, 4/2/1, 1 Oct and 4/2/6, 12 Oct 1942 respectively.
87 See, for example, Ian Downs, *The New Guinea Volunteer Rifles 1939–1943: A history*, Broadbeach Waters, Qld: Pacific Press, 1999, p. 146; AWM 54, 578/6/1,

'Appendices 1 to 19 to first narrative of Kanga Force Operations 1st May 1942 to 15th January 1943', Appx 8, Report by War Correspondent Osmar White (Jul 1942), p. 5.

88 Haywood, *Six Years in Support*, p. 142 (They continued to experiment); AWM 52, 4/2/1, 1 Nov 1942 (On 1 November).

Chapter 6. 'Deep in Unmapped Jungles': 21st Brigade on the Kokoda Track

1 AWM 54, 313/4/28, 'Report on Engineer Works During New Guinea Campaigns 1942'.
2 AWM, 3DRL, 6643, Private Papers of Field Marshal Sir Thomas Albert Blamey, Series 2, Wallet 138 of 1141; see the letters from Vasey to Rowell, 28 Aug 1942, Blamey to Rowell, 1 Sept 1942, and Rowell to Blamey, 3 Sept 1942.
3 McNicoll, *Ubique*, p. 154. See also AWM 52, 5/13/6, Aug–Sept 1942.
4 T. Fairhall, *Brisbane Courier Mail* and reprinted in the Moresby Army News Sheet, 12 Oct 1942, in Gordon Osborn, Steve Clarke, Bill Jollie and Max Law (eds), *The Pioneers: Unit history of the 2nd/1st Australian Pioneer Battalion Second AIF*, Sydney: MD Herron, 1988, p. 105.
5 AWM 52, 5/13/6.
6 AWM 54, 313/4/28, p. 4.
7 DVA, AAWFA, Robert Thompson, 2/14th Bn, Archive No. 1594, time: 6.30.30.00.
8 Uren, *A Thousand Men at War*, p. 119.
9 AWM 52, 8/2/21, 19 Aug 1942.
10 AWM 52, 8/3/14, 29 Aug 1942.
11 Frank Sublet, *Kokoda to the Sea: A history of the 1942 campaign in Papua*, McCrae, Vic.: Slouch Hat Publications, 2000, p. 56.
12 Sholl, 'Points Noted and Lessons Learnt', p. 43.
13 Johnston, *The Silent 7th*, p. 35.
14 Geoffrey Hamlyn-Harris, *Through Mud and Blood to Victory*, Sydney: 2/31 Australian Infantry Battalion Association (NSW), 1994, p. x. This quote is by Major Bruce Robertson, at the time a junior officer with the 2/31st Bn.
15 AWM, KMSA, Robert Johns, 2/27th Bn, Archive No. S799, tape 1, side B, 20–25 minutes. See also, DVA, AAWFA, Gilbert Simmons, 2/25th Bn, Archive No. 1186, time: 5.36.30.00.
16 AWM, KMSA, Curtis, 2/12th Bn, transcript, p. 67.
17 CAL, LWDC, [Unnumbered box] *Infantry Minor Tactics*, p. 86.
18 Sholl, 'Points Noted and Lessons Learnt', p. 45.
19 *Infantry Minor Tactics*, p. 81 (italics in original).
20 Sholl, 'Points Noted and Lessons Learnt', pp. 81–3.
21 Hamlyn-Harris, *Through Mud and Blood to Victory*, p. x. This quote is from the introduction by Major Robertson of the 2/31st Bn.
22 Sublet, *Kokoda to the Sea*, p. 25.
23 Hamlyn-Harris, *Through Mud and Blood to Victory*, pp. 22–3.

24 AWM 52, 8/3/14, 'Reports on Operations in New Guinea', 28 Sept 1942.
25 White, *Green Armour*, pp. 195–6.
26 NAA, SP300/4, 321, 'New Guinea Report 1942 Most Confidential'. This file contains two reports, the first of which is Wilmot's six-page, 'Observations on the New Guinea Campaign August 26th—September 26th, 1942', which was written for Maj-Gen. Allen upon Wilmot's return to Port Moresby. The above quote is taken from that report, p. 4.
27 DVA, AAWFA, Eric Williams, 2/16th Bn, Archive No. 1117, time: 8.21.30.10.
28 AWM 52, 8/3/14, 22 Aug 1942.
29 Lex McAulay, *Blood and Iron: The battle for Kokoda 1942*, Sydney: Arrow Books, 1991, p. 126.
30 DVA, AAWFA, Robert Thompson, 2/14th Bn, Archive No. 1504, time: 6.17.30.00.
31 Moremon, 'Most Deadly Jungle Fighters?', p. 66.
32 McAulay, *Blood and Iron*, p. 139.
33 Austin, *To Kokoda and Beyond*, p. 134.
34 White, *Green Armour*, p. 197. See also DVA, AAWFA, Eric Williams, 2/16th Bn, Archive No. 1117, time: 8.20.30.00; Lt-Col. Phil Rhoden, in Patrick Lindsay, *The Spirit of Kokoda: Then and now*, South Yarra, Vic: Hardie Grant Books, 2002, p. 59.
35 Budden, *That Mob!*, p. 35. See also AWM, KMSA, Harry Katekar, 2/27th Bn, Archive No. S903, tape 2, side A, 5–10 mins.
36 DVA, AAWFA, Lindsay Mason, 2/14th Bn, Archive No. 1197, time: 6.05.00.00.
37 NAA, S459/1, 546/1/8498, 'Training Notes—Tropical and Jungle Warfare No. 1', p. 1.
38 NAA, SP1008/1, 538/1/311, 'Jungle Warfare—Construction of Rifle Ranges', 30 Dec 1942, p. 1.
39 Sublet, *Kokoda to the Sea*, p. 63.
40 McAulay, *Blood and Iron*, p. 145.
41 Burns, *The Brown and Blue Diamond at War*, p. 117.
42 Laffin, *Forever Forward*, p. 86. Dunbar was the CO of the 2/31st Bn.
43 Peter Charlton, *The Thirty-Niners*, Melbourne: Macmillan, 1981, p. 229. See also AWM 54, 579/6/5, 'Operation Milne Bay 24/8/42 to 8/9/42, Lessons from Operations No. 2', 28 Oct 1942, p. 2.
44 AWM 54, 937/3/7, p. 1. See also AWM 254, 169, 'Suggestions for the Training of Infantry Companies in Jungle Warfare Gained from Experiences by Major I.B. Ferguson in the Advance from Templeton's Crossing to Buna. Sep–Dec 1942'.
45 See, for example, Australian Military Forces, *Tropical Warfare (Australia), Pamphlet No. 2—Notes for Junior Leaders*, LHQ Australian Army, Melbourne, 1945, p. 23.
46 AWM 54, 937/3/7, 'Notes on the New Guinea Campaign, Aspects of the Campaign', 8 Feb 1943.
47 AWM 54, 923/2/25, 'Notes on Japanese Tactics', by Lieutenant R.W.T. Cowan IO 21 Aust Inf Brigade', Aug 26–13 Sept, p. 2.
48 Ibid., p. 3.
49 Sublet, *Kokoda to the Sea*, p. 81.

50 AWM 52, 8/3/14, 8 Sept 1942 (the enemy was); Uren, *A Thousand Men at War*, p. 139 (heavy casualties were inflicted).
51 Kerry L. Lane, *Guadalcanal Marine*, Jackson, MI: University Press of Mississippi, 2004, pp. 134–7.
52 Lane, *Guadalcanal Marine*, p. 138.
53 AWM 52, 8/3/16, 8 Sept 1942.
54 Russell, *The Second Fourteenth Battalion*, p. 133.
55 Rowell, *Full Circle*, p. 126. See also McDonald, *Damien Parer's War*, p. 207.
56 AWM 52, 1/5/14, 'Warfare in Thick Country' 7 Aust Div Tng Instn No. 4, Appx F, 5 Sept 1942.
57 NAA, SP 300/4, 'Chester Wilmot Files'. Transcripts of broadcasts which discuss the problems of the Kokoda Track include: SP 300/4, file 175, 'Japanese Tactics In New Guinea', dated 12 Aug 1942; file 178, 'Japanese Mastery of Movement', 6 Sept 1942, and file 182, 'Japs Are Not Supermen but They Went to School', 21 Sept 1942. See especially Horner, *Crisis of Command*, for further information on the leadership problems.
58 AWM 54, 923/2/29, 'Broadcast by Chester Wilmot, ABC, on Japanese tactics in New Guinea', Sept 1942.
59 AWM, 3DRL 4142, file 7 of 9, item no. 38–39, letter from General Allen to Raymond Paull, Tuesday 11 Nov 1947 (The 7th Division Commander); AWM 67, 1/9 Gavin Long Diary No. 9, 4 Oct 1942 (ordered they all be returned).
60 NAA, SP 300/4, 321, 'New Guinea Report 1942 Most Confidential', 'Observations on the New Guinea Campaign Aug 26th—September 26th 1942', Chester Wilmot.
61 NAA, S459/1, 546/1/8498, 'Training Notes—Tropical and Jungle Warfare No. 1', 23 Sept 1942 (At the same time); NAA, 3549/1, 546/1/8510, 'Training Notes—Tropical and Jungle Warfare No. 2', 6 Oct 1942 (It did nevertheless).
62 AWM 52, 8/3/14, 28 Sept 1942; AWM 52, 8/3/16, 26 and 28 Sept 1942.
63 Givney (ed.), *The First at War*, p. 254.
64 AWM 52, 8/3/25, 11 Sept (They were nevertheless) and (Both Brigades were).
65 Crooks, *The Footsoldiers*, p. 144.
66 AWM 52, 1/5/14, 'Notes on Ops 25 Aust Inf Bde', Appx H, 8–28 Sept 1942 (Even though General Blamey); AWM 52, 8/2/16, 28 Sept 1942 (The 16th Brigade would).
67 DVA, AAWFA, William Booth, 2/3rd Battalion, Archive No. 1420, transcript, time: 2.32.00.00.
68 Crooks, *The Footsoldiers*, p. 145 (Other changes were in); Givney (ed.), *The First at War*, p. 254 (When the 16th Brigade). See also AWM 52, 8/3/1, 2 Oct.
69 AWM 52, 8/3/14, 'Reports on Operations in New Guinea', 28 Sept 1942, p. 5.
70 AWM 52, 8/2/16, 5 Oct 1942.
71 Sublet, *Kokoda to the Sea*, p. 83.
72 Edgar, *Warrior of Kokoda*, p. 183.
73 Brune, *Those Ragged Bloody Heroes*, p. 207 (21st Brigade polished) and (This instance suggests).
74 Ross, *Armed and Ready*, pp. 420–1.
75 DVA, AAWFA, Gilbert Simmons, 2/25th Bn, Archive No. 1186, transcript, time: 8.12.00.00.

76 Givney (ed.), *The First at War*, p. 262.
77 McCarthy, *South-West Pacific Area*, p. 306.
78 Laffin, *Forever Forward*, p. 97.
79 DVA, AAWFA, Colin McRostie, 2/6th Field Ambulance and later 2/16th Bn, Archive No. 1237, time: 5.19.30.00 (Some of these lessons) and: 5.25.00.00 (The need for shorter length). See also DVA, AAWFA, Ian King, 2/33rd Bn, Archive No. 0132, transcript, time: 1.23.00.00.
80 AWM 54, 581/7/31, Part 2 of 2, 'Report on Operations, 18th Infantry Brigade', Jan 1943, War Establishment—Stretcher Bearers, p. 1 (A report written); AWM 54, 49/1/3, 'Tests of Equipment ... Lightened Rifle (Aust) No 1 Mark III in Jungle Warfare', Jul 1945 (It would, however).
81 DVA, AAWFA, Colin McRostie, 2/6th Field Ambulance and later 2/16th Bn, Archive No. 1237, time: 5.19.30.00.
82 DVA, AAWFA, Frederick Williams, 2/2nd Bn, Archive No. 0780, time: 6.31.00.00 (Other troops would find); AWM, 3DRL 6599, 'Aust Trg Centre (Jungle Warfare)—Canungra, Trg Syllabus Precis & Instructions', Serial No 62 'Jungle Fighting', p. 2 (Eventually the lessons).
83 AWM 52, 8/3/33, 'General Notes', Sept 1942 War Diary.

Chapter 7. 'The Worst Experience of the War': Kokoda to the Beachheads

1 Peter Thompson, *Pacific Fury: How Australia and her allies defeated the Japanese scourge*, North Sydney: William Heinemann, 2008, p. 356.
2 Charles R. Anderson, *Papua: The US Army campaigns of World War II*, Vol. 7, US Army Center of Military History, 1990, p. 7.
3 Max Dimmack, *Signals of the Silent Seventh: A short history of signals 7th Australian Division, 2nd AIF, 1940–1945*, Sassafras, Victoria: Benchmark Publications, 2001, p. 58.
4 Russell, *The Second Fourteenth Battalion*, p. 81. See also Crooks, *The Footsoldiers*, p. 78.
5 Clift, *War Dance*, p. 126. See also DVA, AAWFA, Frank Patterson, 7 Div Sigs, Archive No. 0193, time: 4.26.00.00.
6 DVA, AAWFA, Neville Lewis, 2/33rd signalman, Archive No. 1636, time: 2.28.00.00.
7 Dimmack, *Signals of the Silent Seventh*, p. 70.
8 AWM 54, 577/7/29 Part 18, 'New Guinea Force Report Signal Communication Buna—Kokoda—Sanananda', 21 Jul 1942—22 Jan 1943, p. 7.
9 Stan and Lee Briggs (eds), *Ike's Marines*, p. 180.
10 Theo Barker, *Signals: A history of the Royal Australian Corps of Signals 1788–1947*, Canberra: Royal Australian Corps of Signals Committee, 1987, pp. 262–3.
11 AWM 52, 8/6/1, 2/1st Australian Pioneer Battalion, 11 Sept 1942.
12 Austin, *To Kokoda and Beyond*, p. 106.
13 See also DVA, AAWFA, Lindsay Mason, 2/14th Bn, Archive No. 1197, time: 5.27.00.00; DVA, AAWFA, William Booth, 2/3rd Bn, Archive No. 1420, time: 10.20.00.00.

14 Stewart, *The Argyll and Sutherland Highlanders*, p. 2.
15 Barker, *Signals*, pp. 170–1 (Eventually organisations). See NAA, D5172, Item 107, 'Preservative treatment of fabrics'; NAA, D5172, Item 103A, 'Tropic Proofing'.
16 Sholl, 'Points Noted and Lessons Learnt', pp. 58–9 (Did increase the tempo); AWM 54, 589/7/26 Part 3, '9 Aust Div Report on Operations', p. 30.
17 See, for example, *ATM No. 20*, Feb 1943, pp. 15–16; *ATM No. 28*, 20 Dec 1943, pp. 29–31.
18 NAA, MP 729/6, 50/401/348, 'Signal Officer-in-Chief's Training Memoranda No. 11, Notes on Signals in Jungle Warfare', 27 Nov 1942, p. 1 (obtained from a report). NAA, MP 729/6, 50/401/361, 'Signal Officer-in-Chief's Training Memorandum No. 12, Training of Signal Personnel for Jungle Warfare', 17 Dec 1942, p. 1.
19 Various, *Signals*, p. 126.
20 AWM 54, 577/7/35, 'Notes on 7th Division Operations Kokoda to Soputa', Major Parbury, Jan 1943, pp. 6–7 (all material in this paragraph taken from this file).
21 AWM 54, 937/3/27, 'Aspects of Jungle Warfare from the Point of View of a Company Comd Divisional Signals', p. 1.
22 AWM 54, 581/7/19, 'Notes on and Lessons from Recent Operations in Gona Sanananda Areas', Part 5: Supply Problems.
23 *Soldiering in the Tropics (S.W. Pacific Area)*, LHQ, Melbourne, 1942.
24 AWM 54, 937/3/4, 'Soldiering in the Tropics'.
25 AWM 54, 805/5/1.
26 AWM, 3DRL 4142, 'Notes on a talk to Officers NT Force', [No Date]. On p. 2 Allen has written 'Soldiering in the Tropics—Read it—Its good'.
27 AWM 54, 805/5/1, 29 Dec 1942.
28 AWM 54, 937/2/9, 'Japanese Tactics' (In early September); AWM 54, 937/3/35, 'Information Bulletin No. 123, Subject: Jungle Warfare', 24 Nov 1942 (Two months later). See for example, NAA, MP729/6, item: 50/401/338, 'Operations Solomon Islands—7–29 Aug 42 Lessons From Operations—No. 3' (Gradually a detailed).
29 AWM 54, 577/7/29, Pt 22, 'New Guinea Force Reports—Notes on Operations 7 Aust Division Kokoda—Soputa—2 November 42—3 December 42', p. 8.
30 AWM 52, 8/2/21, '21 Aust Inf Bde Report on Operations Owen Stanley Range 16 Aug—20 Sep', Appx J, p. 62.
31 McCarthy, *South-West Pacific Area*, p. 243 (It is essential that); AWM 54, 519/6/60, 'Report on Operations New Guinea Force 11 Aug to 28 Sep 42', Nov 1942, p. 12 (the only way to train).
32 Rod Hamilton, 'A History of Canungra' [Unpublished manuscript], 2002 [Copy forwarded from Australian Army Training Team Association, Queensland Branch], p. 6.
33 AWM 54, 937/1/2, 'Directorate of Military Training. Account of Activities, 1939 to 1946', pp. 3–4.
34 AWM 60, 290A, 'Reinforcement Training Depot—Independent Coys'.
35 NAA, S459/1, 546/1/8555, 'Establishment for Jungle Warfare Training Depot', 17 Sept 1942.
36 AWM 54, 937/1/2, p. 12.

37 NAA, S459/1, 546/1/8555, 'Jungle Warfare Tng Depot', 16 Oct 1942 (Jungle Warfare Tng Depot); NAA, S459/1, 546/1/8555, 'Establishment for Jungle Warfare Training Depot', 23 Nov 1942 (By late November).
38 Hamilton, 'A History of Canungra', p. 6.
39 McCarthy, *South-West Pacific Area*, p. 85.
40 Hamilton, 'A History of Canungra', p. 7.
41 NAA, MP742/1, 323/1/135, 'Instructions for LHQ Training Centre (Jungle Warfare)' and 'Formation of LHQ Trg Centre (Jungle Warfare)', 3 Nov 1942.
42 Hamilton, 'A History of Canungra', p. 7.
43 AWM 54, 937/1/2, 'Report on Aust Trg Centre (Jungle Warfare) Canungra', Annexure C to 'Directorate of Military Training Account of Activities, 1939 to 1946', p. 2.
44 AWM 52, 35/5/65, 'Brief Report on Drafts Received Canungra Month of December 1942'.
45 AWM 52, 35/5/65, 'Formation of LHQ Trg Centre (Jungle Warfare)', p. 1.
46 Hamilton, 'A History of Canungra', pp. 9–10 (unless otherwise stated all material in this paragraph is taken from this source); Moremon, 'Most Deadly Jungle Fighters?' pp. 70–1.
47 AWM 54, 937/1/2, p. 2.
48 Ibid., Annexure C, Report on Aust Trg Centre (Jungle Warfare) Canungra, p. 2.
49 AWM, 3DRL 6643, 2/65, Blamey to Lt-Gen. Morshead, 23 May 1943.
50 AWM 54, 937/1/2, p. 6 (an AIF Reinforcement Depot) and p. 12 (listed for movement to New Guinea).
51 AWM, 3DRL 6643, 2/65, Berryman to Blamey, 26 Sept 1942; NAA, MP508/1, 323/701/862, 'Training in Jungle Warfare: First Australian Army', 16 Oct 1942, pp. 1–2 (Lt-Gen. Boase).
52 AWM 52, 1/2/1, 'Adv LHQ GS Instn No 17', 21 Oct 1942.
53 AWM 54, 937/1/2, p. 12.
54 See AWM 54, 937/3/9, 'Experiments in Jungle Warfare' and 'Precis on Jungle Fighting Part I', 14 Dec 1942.
55 See, for example, *ATM No. 21*, Mar 1943, p. 16, section 10: Conduct of Training Exercises in Jungle Warfare.
56 See for example, AWM 52, 8/3/14, 19 Oct 1942.
57 AWM 54, 937/1/2, Annexure C, 'Report on Aust Trg Centre (Jungle Warfare) Canungra', p. 6.
58 AWM 54, 579/6/5, Operation Milne Bay 24/8/42 to 8/9/42, Lessons from operations, No. 2, p. 15.
59 Samuel Eliot Morison, *The Struggle for Guadalcanal, August 1942–February 1943*, Vol. 5 of *History of United States Naval Operations in World War II*, Boston: Little, Brown and Company, 1958, pp. 207–18.
60 Richard Frank, *Guadalcanal: The definitive account of the landmark battle*, New York: Random House, 1990, pp. 497–9.
61 AWM 52, 8/3/5, 17 Oct 1942.
62 AWM 52, 8/2/17, '17 Aust Inf Bde Gp Demonstration–28 Sep 42 Mobile Defence'.
63 AWM 52, 8/2/17, 10 Dec 1942.

64 Tregellis-Smith, S., *All the King's Enemies: A history of the 2/5th Australian Infantry Battalion*, Ringwood East, Vic.: 2/5th Battalion Association, 1988, p. 188.
65 Hay, *Nothing Over Us*, pp. 246–7 (As the 2/6th Battalion); AWM 52, 8/2/17, 2 Sept (information exchange).
66 AWM 52, 8/3/5, 9 Oct 1942.
67 Bolger and Littlewood, *The Fiery Phoenix*, p. 198.
68 AWM 52, 8/2/17, 22 Oct 1942.
69 AWM 52, 8/2/17, 28 Nov 1942.
70 Bolger and Littlewood, *The Fiery Phoenix*, pp. 231–2.
71 AWM 52, 8/2/17, 4 Nov 1942, Operations Diary.
72 Tregellis-Smith, *All the King's Enemies*, pp. 191–3.
73 Brune, *Those Ragged Bloody Heroes*, p. 264. Lt-Col. Cooper was the CO of the 2/27th Battalion.
74 AWM, KMSA, Harry Katekar, 2/27th Bn, Archive No. S903, tape 2, side A, 20–30 minutes.
75 AWM, KMSA, Robert Johns, 2/27th Bn, Archive No. S799, tape 2, side A, 10–15 minutes. See also, AWM, KMSA, Charles Sims, 2/27th Bn, Archive No. S789, tape 2, side A, 15–20 minutes.
76 AWM 52, 1/5/14, 3 Dec 1942.
77 AWM 54, 85/3/8, 'Air Support During Recent Operations in New Guinea—Papers on Close Air Support Doctrine—September 1942—January 1943', p. 1.
78 Russell, *The Second Fourteenth Battalion*, p. 192.
79 Lex McAulay, *To the Bitter End: The Japanese defeat at Buna and Gona, 1942–43*, Sydney: Arrow Books, 1993, pp. 31–2.
80 Ibid., p. 115.
81 For information on these issues see works such as Peter Brune, *Gona's Gone! The Battle of the Beachhead, 1942*, Sydney: Allen & Unwin, 1994; Brune, *A Bastard of a Place*; Eather, *Desert Sands, Jungle Lands*; Horner, *Crisis of Command* and McAulay, *To the Bitter End*.
82 Moremon, 'Most Deadly Jungle Fighters?', p. 72.
83 Graeme-Evans, *Of Storms and Rainbows*, p. 260.
84 AWM 52, 8/2/18, 'Dying of Web Equipment', 16 Apr 1943.
85 Dickens, *Never Late*, p. 198.
86 DVA, AAWFA, Oscar Isaachsen, 36th Bn (AMF), Archive No. 1687, time: 7.05.30.00.
87 AWM 54, 581/7/13, 'Report on Operations in Sanananda Area', by Lt-Col. Kessels, 30th Australian Infantry Brigade, Dec 1942 to Jan 1943, p. 1 (emphasis in original).
88 AWM 52, 8/2/17, 18 Dec 1942.
89 Johnston, *The Silent 7th*, p. 141.
90 See Brune, *The Spell Broken*, pp. 151–4, for various intelligence figures.
91 Keogh, *South West Pacific 1941–45*, p. 279.
92 Paul Handel, *Dust, Sand and Jungle: A history of Australian armour during training and operations 1927–1948*, Hopkins Barracks, Puckapunyal, Vic: RAAC Memorial and Army Tank Museum, 2003, p. 69.

93 Hopkins, R.N.L., *Australian Armour: A history of the Royal Australian Armoured Corps 1927–1972*, Canberra: AWM, 1978, p. 104.
94 Brune, *The Spell Broken*, p. 160.
95 AWM 54, 581/7/31, Part 2 of 2, 'Report on Operations, 18th Infantry Brigade', Giropa Point and Sanananda Area 14 Dec 42—22 Jan 43', Appx A, 'Notes on Tank and Inf Cooperation', p. 1. See also Handel, *Dust, Sand and Jungle*, p. 70.
96 AWM 54, 577/7/29, Part 1 'Report on Operations in New Guinea, Owen Stanleys—Buna Area: Operations using M3 Light Tanks in New Guinea', pp. 13 and 4.
97 Brune, *The Spell Broken*, p. 169.
98 Spencer, *In the Footsteps of Ghosts*, p. 126.
99 DVA, AAWFA, Bryan Wells, 2/9th Bn, Archive No. 0696, transcript, time: 1.35.00.00.
100 AWM 54, 577/7/29, Part 1, p. 5.
101 AWM 52, 8/2/18, 'Constructional Details of Enemy Emplacements', 21 Dec 1942.
102 Allchin, *Purple and Blue*, pp. 286–92.
103 AWM 54, 577/7/29, Part 1, pp. 6–7.
104 Graeme-Evans, *Of Storms and Rainbows*, pp. 256–7.
105 AWM 54, 581/7/31, Appx E to Report on Operations 18 Aust Inf Bde Gp, 'Japanese Strong Points—Expedients in Assisting Attack', 4 Jan 1943.
106 AWM, KMSA, Geoffrey Holmes, 2/12th Bn, Archive No. S540, p. 65.
107 AWM 52, 8/2/18, 4 Jan 1943, 'Blast Bombs'.
108 Frank Hartley, *Sanananda Interlude: The 7th Australian Division Cavalry Regiment*, Melbourne: Book Depot, 1949, p. 11. Hartley was the chaplain to the regiment.
109 Graeme-Evans, *Of Storms and Rainbows*, p. 325.
110 McCarthy, *South-West Pacific Area*, pp. 516–17.
111 Brune, *The Spell Broken*, p. 243.
112 McAulay, *Blood and Iron*, p. 413.
113 Sholl, 'Points Noted and Lessons Learnt', p. 29.
114 McCarthy, *South-West Pacific Area*, p. 591.
115 Horner, *High Command*, p. 217.
116 McCarthy, *South-West Pacific Area*, p. 112.

Chapter 8. 'Rain, Mud, Rottenness, Gloom': 17th Brigade's Wau–Salamaua Campaign

1 Coates, *Bravery Above Blunder*, pp. 52–3.
2 Centre for Army Lessons (CAL), Allied Land Forces in the South-West Pacific Area, *Operations—Supplement to Military Training Pamphlet (Australia) No. 23 XX Jungle Warfare (Provisional) Notes for Platoon & Section Leaders* would be printed in May 1943.
3 Coates, *Bravery Above Blunder*, p. 52.
4 Serle (ed.), *The Second Twenty-Fourth Australian Infantry*, p. 6.
5 AWM 52, 1/5/20, 9 Australian Division General Staff Branch (hereafter 9 Aust Div GS Branch), 24 Feb 1942, Appx A to 9 Aust Div Intelligence Summary

No. 207, 'Japanese Tactics'; 2 Mar 1942, Appx B to 9 Aust Div Intel Summary No. 208, 'Japanese Combined Operations—Detail of Landings at Kota Bharu' and 20 Mar 1942, Appx A to 9 Aust Div Intel Summary No. 219, 'The Japanese Army in Malaya'.
6 Coates, *Bravery Above Blunder*, p. 47.
7 AWM, 3DRL 6643, Private Papers of Field Marshal Sir Thomas Albert Blamey, Series 2 of 2, Wallet 138 of 141, 2 Dec 1942.
8 AWM, 3DRL6643, 'From NGF. Personal for General Morshead from General Blamey'.
9 Serle (ed.), *The Second Twenty-Fourth Australian Infantry Battalion*, p. 235. See also AWM 52, 1/5/20, '9 Aust Div Trg Instn No. 30', 6 Jan 1943.
10 AWM 52, 1/5/20, '9 Aust Div Trg Instn No. 29: Liddington', 3 Jan 1943.
11 AWM 52, 8/3/13, 14 Jan 1943.
12 Pat Share (ed.), *Mud and Blood 'Albury's Own': Second Twenty-Third Australian Infantry Battalion*, Frankston, Victoria: Heritage Book Publications, 1978, p. 238.
13 AWM 52, 8/2/24, 7 Jan 1943.
14 AWM 52, 8/2/24, 1 Jan 1943. See also AWM 52, 8/3/32, 1–7 Jan 1943; Serle (ed.), *The Second Twenty-Fourth Australian Infantry Battalion*, p. 235.
15 AWM 52, 8/2/20, 2 Feb 1943.
16 AWM 52, 8/3/13, 15 Feb 1943.
17 AWM 52, 8/3/28, 27 Mar 1943.
18 AWM 54, 923/4/1, 'Tactical Doctrine for Jungle Warfare Applicable to All Formations under Command 2 Aust Corps', prepared by Lt-Gen. Savige.
19 Speed (ed.), *Esprit de Corps*, p. 216.
20 Hay, *Nothing Over Us*, p. 255.
21 AWM 52, 8/3/7, 4 Jan 1943, Movement Order No. 1.
22 AWM 52, 8/2/17, 29 Jan 1943.
23 AWM 52, 8/3/7, 29 Jan 1943.
24 AWM 52, 8/2/17, 1 Feb 1943.
25 AWM 52, 8/3/7, 30 Jan 1943.
26 DVA, AAWFA, Francis Hall, 2/7 Bn, Archive No. 2053, transcript, time: 5.05.30.00.
27 Speed (ed.), *Esprit de Corps*, p. 299.
28 Tregellis-Smith, *All the King's Enemies*, p. 192.
29 'Report on Operations 3 Aust Div in Salamaua Area 23 April to 25 August 1943', cited in David Dexter, *The New Guinea Offensives: Australia in the war of 1939–1945 (Army)*, Vol. VI, Canberra: AWM, 1961, p. 21.
30 DVA, AAWFA, Wallace Cameron, 2/6th Bn, Archive No. 1133, transcript, time: 7.08.00.00.
31 Keating, *The Right Man for the Right Job*, p. 99.
32 Eric Bergerud, *Touched with Fire: The land war in the South Pacific*, New York: Penguin Books, 1996, p. 279.
33 Ibid.
34 AWM 52, 8/3/5, 29 Mar 1943.
35 Hay, *Nothing Over Us*, p. 258.
36 Tregellis-Smith, *All the King's Enemies*, p. 212.

37 Bolger and Littlewood, *The Fiery Phoenix*, p. 246.
38 AWM 52, 8/2/17, May War Diary Appendices, 'Report on Operations Period 1 Mar to 31 Mar 43', p. 3.
39 Keating, *The Right Man for the Right Job*, p. 132.
40 AWM 52, 8/3/7, 21 Feb 1943.
41 McNicoll, *Ubique*, p. 177.
42 Davidson, *With Courage High*, pp. 113–14.
43 AWM 52, 8/3/7, 14 Feb 1943.
44 Grey, *The Australian Army*, p. 149.
45 AWM 52, 8/2/17, Kanga Force 'Report on Operations 1 Apr to 23 Apr 43', p. 1.
46 Ibid., 22 Mar 1943.
47 Alan Powell, *The Third Force: ANGAU's New Guinea war, 1942–46*, Melbourne: Oxford University Press, 2003, p. 37.
48 Bolger and Littlewood, *The Fiery Phoenix*, pp. 231–2.
49 Ibid., p. 231.
50 AWM 52, 8/2/17, 30 Apr 1943.
51 Ibid., 15 Apr 1943.
52 George Raudzens, 'Testing the air power expectations of the Kokoda Campaign: July to September 1942', *Journal of the Australian War Memorial*, no. 21, Oct 1992, pp. 20–9.
53 AWM 54, 85/3/8, 'Air Support During Recent Operations in New Guinea—Papers on Close Air Support Doctrine—Sep 42–Jan 43'. See also Nicola Baker, *More Than Little Heroes: Australian Army Air Liaison Officers in the Second World War*, Canberra: Strategic and Defence Studies Centre, ANU, 1994, especially pp. 70–7.
54 NAA, MP742/1, item 240/1/504, 'Army/Air Co-Operation Policy'.
55 See Captain H. Phillip Braddock, 'A story of army air co-operation in the Second World War', *Journal of the Royal United Services Institute of Australia*, vol. 17, Nov 1996, pp. 61–71.
56 George Odgers, *Air War Against Japan 1943–1945: Australia in the war of 1939–1945 (Air), Vol. II*, Canberra: AWM, 1957, p. 25.
57 Bolger and Littlewood, *The Fiery Phoenix*, p. 246.
58 AWM 52, 8/2/17, 27 Mar 1943.
59 Keating, *The Right Man for the Right Job*, p. 124.
60 Dexter, *The New Guinea Offensives*, p. 31.
61 AWM 54, 75/4/24, 'Artillery Operations in New Guinea January 1943 to Mid-February 1944', RAA New Guinea Force, p. 11.
62 Heather McRae, *Soldier Surveyors: A history of the 3 Australian Field Survey Company (AIF), 1940–1945*, Victoria: 3 Australian Field Survey Company, 1996, p. 78.
63 Ibid.
64 Both the above report—AWM 54, 75/4/24—and AWM 54, 587/6/6, 'Notes on Artillery Operations Salamaua 1943 by HQ RAA 1 Aust Corps', suggest that a proper topographical survey was necessary prior to the despatch of RAA Survey Teams.

65 Haywood, *Six Years in Support*, p. 163. See also Capt A.R. Ross (ed.), *The Magazine of 17 Australian Infantry Brigade 1939–1944*, Melbourne: 1944, p. 52; Norrie Jones, 'Eyewitness: 1st Battery, 2/1st Field Regiment', *Wartime: Official Magazine of the Australian War Memorial*, issue 40, Nov 2007, pp. 40–2.
66 AWM 52, 4/2/1, 15 Feb 1943. Appx II contains the full procedure.
67 Jack Allan and Chris Cutts (eds), *As It Seemed to Us: The 1st Australian Mountain Battery RAA AIF*, Brisbane: Aebis Publishing, 1994, p. 84.
68 AWM 52, 8/2/17, Kanga Force 'Report on Operations 1 Apr to 23 Apr 43', p. 7. This was a distance of approximately 20 miles.
69 Ibid., Appx C, 'Report by OC 1 Aust Mtn Bty on Operations to 23 Apr 43', p. 1.
70 Ibid.
71 Ibid.
72 AWM 52, 8/3/7, 21 Apr 1943.
73 Allan and Cutts, *As It Seemed to Us*, p. 92.
74 AWM 52, 8/3/7, 25 Feb 1943.
75 AWM 52, 8/2/17, 30 Nov 1943, 'Report on the Operations of the 17 Aust Inf Bde Group in the Mubo-Salamaua Area from 23 April to 24 Aug 1943'.
76 See, for example, AWM 54, 578/7/3, 'Kanga Force: Report on Wau–Mubo Ops Period 11 Jan 43—1 Mar 43'; AWM 52, 8/2/17, 'Kanga Force: Report on Operations 1 Apr to 23 Apr 43'.
77 AWM 52, 8/3/7, 9 Aug 1943: 'A party of officers from 47 Bn under Major Leech attached to unit for experience.' See also DVA, AAWFA, Keith Ross, 2/6th Bn, Archive No. 0373, transcript, time: 4.33.30.00.
78 AWM 52, 8/2/17, 2/7 Aust Inf Bn: 'Report on Ops—Bobdubi Area 29 Jul—6 Aug 43', p. 1.
79 Richard Overy, *Why the Allies Won*, London: Pimlico, 2006, p. 7.
80 AWM 254, 168 Pts 1 and 2, '15 Aust Inf Bde—Staff School Course 1. 29 Nov–12 Dec 43'.
81 Keating, *The Right Man for the Right Job*, p. 154.
82 AWM 52, 8/2/17, Appx 14, 'Own Tactics: Patrolling', p. 4.
83 Hamilton, 'A History of Canungra', p. 11.
84 *ATM No. 21*, Mar 1943, 'Training the reinforcement for jungle warfare', pp. 12–16.
85 AWM 54, 937/1/2, 'Directorate of Military Training. Account of Activities, 1939–1945', p. 12.
86 Ibid.
87 Hay, *Nothing Over Us*, p. 326.
88 AWM 52, 8/2/17, 15 Mar 1943.
89 AWM 52, 35/5/65, 'Report on Observer Tour of New Guinea', 23 Apr 1943.
90 Ibid., 'Report on Observer Trip by Capt A.T. Irwin—Aust Trg Centre (JW) Canungra'.
91 Burns, *The Brown and Blue Diamond at War*, p. 163.
92 AWM 52, 1/2/1, Advanced Land Headquarters G Branch (Adv LHQ G Branch), Appx B, 'Resume of Training Activities', p. 1.
93 Ibid., p. 1. For Lt-Col. Wolfenden visit to Canungra see AWM 52, 35/5/65, 1 Feb 1943.

94 AWM 52, 8/2/19, Feb War Diary and Appx 4.
95 AWM 52, 8/2/17, 14–16 Jun 1943.
96 AWM 52, 35/5/65, 'Formation of LHQ Trg Centre (Jungle Warfare)', 3 Nov 1942, p. 2.
97 AWM 52, 937/1/2, p. 11.
98 Ibid.
99 AWM 52, 8/3/9, 'Table F Seconded Officers: Capt Hoad—Instructor LHQ Tactical School', 26 Jun 1943.
100 AWM 52, 35/5/65, 'Notes for the Commander in Chief', May 1943, p. 3.

Chapter 9. 'The Ideal Training Ground': Atherton Tableland 1943

1 AWM 52, 8/3/14, 1 Apr 1943. See also Johnston, *The Silent 7th*, p. 163.
2 AWM 52, 8/3/16, Appx to December 1942 War Diary, 'Reinforcement Training Syllabus—Period 25 Jan 43—22 March 43'.
3 AWM 52, 8/2/16, 21 Feb 1943, '16 Aust Inf Bde Training Instruction No.1', p. 1.
4 NAA, MP729/6, item: 26/401/748, 'Sub Machine Guns New Guinea'.
5 AWM 52, 8/3/10, 24 Jan 1943.
6 For more information on the Owen Gun saga see Ross, *Armed and Ready*, pp. 371–81; Kevin Smith, *The Owen Gun Files: An Australian wartime controversy*, Sydney: Turton & Armstrong, 1994.
7 AWM 52, 8/3/16, Appx to December 1942 War Diary, 'Reinforcement Training Syllabus—Period 25 Jan 43–22 Mar 43'.
8 AWM 54, 721/2/11, 'Organization Jungle Divisions', Part 2 of 5. The above quote is taken from the file entitled 'Re-Organization of Infantry Formations in the AMF', p. 1.
9 Ibid., p. 1. 3rd AMF Division would also change to a jungle division.
10 AWM 54, 721/2/11, pp. 2 and 4.
11 Russell, *The Second Fourteenth Battalion*, p. 215.
12 AWM 52, 17 Dec 1942.
13 Ross, *Armed and Ready*, p. 423.
14 Ross, *Armed and Ready*, p. 423. See also Kuring, *Recoats to Cams*, p. 212.
15 Major Horie Masao, quoted in Peter D. Williams and Naoko Nakagawa, 'The Japanese 18th Army in New Guinea', in *Wartime: Official Magazine of the Australian War Memorial*, issue no. 36, Sept 2006, p. 60.
16 Bishop, *The Thunder of the Guns!*, p. 530.
17 Palazzo, *The Australian Army*, p. 184.
18 See AWM 54, 923/1/6, 'Notes on Recently Expressed Concepts of Tactics', HQ 30 Aust Inf Bde, 11 Oct 1942, p. 2; AWM 54, 721/2/11, 'Re-organization of Inf Formations for Jungle Warfare', 15 Mar 1943.
19 AWM 52, 905/20/2, 'Equipment for Jungle Warfare: Entrenching tool, light utility cart', p. 1 (Carts Hand Jungle Special); AWM 54, 577/7/35, 'Notes on 7th Division Operations Kokoda to Soputa by Major Parbury', p. 11 (These two-wheeled).
20 Ibid., p. 11.

NOTES

21 AWM 54, 589/7/11, 'Report by Lt-Col. A.G. Wilson on Tour as Observer in New Guinea from 26 Nov to 16 Dec 1943', p. 19.
22 AWM 52, 8/2/21, 17 Feb 1943 (discussed the agenda) and AWM 52, 1/5/20, 19 Feb 1943.
23 Ibid., 22 Feb 1943, 'Direct Air Support—Jungle Warfare', Appx D.
24 Ibid., 24 Feb 1943 (The final day) and 'Notes on Div Conference 0900 Hrs 19 Feb 43', p. 2 (the conference decided).
25 AWM 52, 1/2/1, Apr 1943, p. 1.
26 AWM, 3DRL 6643 (Papers of General Sir Thomas Blamey), Series 3, Wallet 19 of 160 Box 28, 1 of 2 'Jungle Warfare Training Pamphlet March 1943'.
27 AWM 54, 937/3/33, 'Military Training Pamphlet No. 23 Jungle Warfare', comments on Draft by Maj-Gen. Vasey.
28 Ibid., 'Jungle Warfare Pamphlet' comments by General Vasey GOC 7 Aust Div, 13 Mar 1943; 'Subject: Military Training Pamphlet (Australia) No. 23 Jungle Warfare', comments by Lt-Gen. Boase, Commander, First Aust Army, 19 Mar 1943.
29 AWM, Allied Land Forces in the South-West Pacific Area, *Operations: Military Training Pamphlet (Australia) No. 23 XX—Jungle Warfare (Provisional)*, p. 3.
30 AWM 54, 937/3/33, 'Jungle Warfare Pamphlet', comments by General Vasey, p. 1.
31 *ATM No. 21*, Mar 1943, Part II Training: 'Military Training Pamphlet (Australia) No. 23 XX—Jungle Warfare'.
32 *Operations: Military Training Pamphlet (Australia) No. 23 XX Jungle Warfare (Provisional)*, Melbourne, 1943, p. 5.
33 AWM 52, 8/2/25, 24 Feb 1943. See also AWM 52, 8/2/16, 19–24 Feb 1943.
34 AWM 52, 8/2/25, 'Tactical Exercise with Troops—Company Ambush', p. 1.
35 The full title is as follows: *Operations—Supplement to Military Training Pamphlet (Australia) No. 23 XX—Jungle Warfare (Provisional) Notes for Platoon and Section Leaders*, Allied Land Forces in the South-West Pacific.
36 *MTP No. 23—Jungle Warfare*, p. 6.
37 AWM 54, 937/3/33, 'Jungle Warfare Pamphlet', comments by General Vasey, p. 1. LHQ comments appear in the introduction to *MTP No. 23—Jungle Warfare*, p. 6.
38 *MTP No. 23—Jungle Warfare*, p. 6 (points and considerations) and p. 5 (Japanese characteristics).
39 AWM 52, 1/2/1, 'Resume of Training Activities', p. 1. *Friendly Fruits and Vegetables*, LHQ, 31 May 1943.
40 See *MTP No. 23—Notes for Platoon and Section Leaders,* Appx C, p. 32.
41 Laffin, *Forever Forward*, pp. 116–17.
42 AWM 52, 8/2/25, 1 Jul 1943, 'Bn Exercise with Troops No. 2', p. 1.
43 *Tropical Warfare No. 2—Notes for Junior Leaders*, p. 28.
44 Kuring, *Red Coats to Cams*, pp. 170–1.
45 Moreman, 'Jungle, Japanese and the Australian Army', p. 10.
46 Moremon, 'No "black magic"', clearly supports this stance. Palazzo, 'Organising for jungle warfare', appears to disagree.
47 AWM 52, 8/2/16, 17 Apr 1943.

48 AWM, PR84/370, Private Papers of Lt-Gen. Sir F.H. Berryman, Series 3, Item 41, *1 Aust Corps Training Instructions* (To this end 6th) and 27 Mar 1943, '6 Aust Div Training Instruction No. 1—Jungle Warfare', p. 1 (Training for jungle warfare) (Emphasis in original.)
49 Ibid., 14 Apr 1943, '6 Aust Div Training Instruction No. 2—Jungle Warfare Training', p. 1.
50 AWM, 355.423 J95.
51 AWM 54, 937/3/7. See pp. 2–3 and appendices A, B, C and D.
52 6 Aust Div Training Instruction No. 11 Jungle Warfare, p. 1.
53 Ibid., p. 1.
54 AWM 52, 8/2/21, 'Conference Notes—Conference of COs on 11 Mar 43', Appx B, 11 Mar 1943.
55 AWM 52, 8/2/16, 'Training Conference', 26 Mar 1943, p. 1.
56 Barter, *Far Above Battle*, p. 212.
57 F. Kingsley Norris, *No Memory for Pain: An autobiography*, Melbourne: William Heinemann, 1970, p. 185. For discussion of the lack of understanding of the threat posed by malaria see Walker, *The Island Campaigns*, pp. 114–16; Sweeney, *Malaria Frontline*, pp. 29–31.
58 *ATM No. 21*, Mar 1943, pp. 12–16, 'Training the Reinforcement for Jungle Warfare', p. 13.
59 AWM 52, 8/3/2, 30 Apr 1943. See also Wick, *Purple Over Green*, p. 248.
60 Serle (ed.), *The Second Twenty-Fourth Australian Infantry Battalion*, p. 244.
61 AWM 52, 8/3/31, Appx F to Apr War Diary, 'Sketch of Proposed Assault Course No. 1 with Proposed Aiming Points'.
62 AWM 52, 8/3/27, '2/27 Aust Inf Bn Scout Course', 13 May 1943.
63 AWM 52, 8/3/16 'Musketry Training', 30 Apr 1943. See also, AWM 52, 8/2/25, 22 Feb, Appx A 'Trg Instn No. 21', p. 2 'Field Firing'.
64 AWM 52, 8/2/21, 17 Apr 1943, '[A party of officers] moved to HQ 25 Aust Inf Bde and inspected "individual battle practice course" of the 2/33 Aust Inf Bn'.
65 NAA, SP1008/1, item: 538/1/311 'Jungle Warfare—Construction of Rifle Range'.
66 Uren, *A Thousand Men at War*, p. 187.
67 AWM 52, 8/2/18, 2–5 Jun 1943.
68 AWM 54, 937/3/20, 'RAE First Aust Army—CRE Lecture No. 21—Jungle Fighting' [nd].
69 AWM 52, 5/5/10, HQ RAE, 6th Division, 16 Apr 1943.
70 AWM 52, 5/5/11, HQ RAE 7th Division, 2 Jun 1943 (One problem was that) and 28 Apr 1943 (engr eqpt which would).
71 AWM 52, 5/5/10, 'Matters for representation to the E in C', 28 Jul 1943.
72 AWM 52, 5/5/11, Appx C5, 'RAE Appendix E to 7 Aust Div Report on Operations July–September 1943'.
73 McNicoll, *Ubique*, p. 145 (Notwithstanding these problems) and p. 146 (a sapper must be).
74 AWM 52, 5/5/10, 'Training Instructions to RAE Units 6 Aust Div RAE', 1 Jun 1943, p. 1.
75 Ibid., 5/5/10, 14 May 1943, 'Outline Training Programme to HQ RAE 6 Aust Div for period 15/5/43 to 31/5/43'.
76 AWM 52, 5/13/6, 2/6 Fd Coy RAE, 31 May 1943.

77 AWM 52, 5/5/10, 'Training Instructions to RAE Units 6 Aust Div RAE', 1 Jun 1943, pp. 1–2.
78 AWM 52, 8/3/27, Appendices, A Coy, 'Training Syllabus', 3–8 May.
79 McNicoll, *Ubique*, p. 146 (drill ... digging trenches) and (booby-traps and anti-personnel mines).
80 J.A. Anderson and G. Jackett, *Mud and Sand: 2/3 Pioneer Bn at war*, Sydney: 2/3 Pioneer Battalion Association, 1994, p. 132.
81 See, for example, Henry, *The Story of the 2/4th Field Regiment*, p. 196.
82 Goodhart, *The History of the 2/7 Australian Field Regiment*, p. 260.
83 AWM 54, 75/4/18, 'Artillery in Jungle Warfare—Notes Compiled from Reports, from Pacific War Zone—1943', p. 1.
84 Ibid., p. 7.
85 AWM 52, 4/2/3, 23 Jun 1943, Appx G, 'Training Instruction No. 2', p. 1 (Improving physical fitness) and (this was closely followed by).
86 AWM 52, 75/4/24, Appx B, 'Local Protection Gun Positions', p. 32.
87 AWM 52, 4/2/3, 3 Apr 1943, 'Jungle Training' (A party from); Bishop, *The Thunder of the Guns!*, p. 523 (those who took part).
88 D.P. Mellor, *The Role of Science and Industry: Australia in the war of 1939–1945 (Civil)*, Vol. V, Canberra: AWM, 1958, p. 238.
89 AWM 52, 4/2/4, 4 Sept 1943.
90 Bishop, *The Thunder of the Guns!*, p. 545; Warby, *The 25 Pounders*, p. 302.
91 Mellor, *The Role of Science and Industry*, p. 239.
92 Ross, *Armed and Ready*, p. 399 (It was, however); Goodhart, *The History of the 2/7 Australian Field Regiment*, p. 260 (it appeared to us).
93 Horner, *The Gunners*, p. 397 (could be man-packed); AWM 52, 4/2/1, 3 Aug 1943, 'Report on Mortar—Arty Course' (there is a possibility).
94 Haywood, *Six Years in Support*, pp. 187–90. See also AWM 52, 4/2/1, War Diary for Jan, Feb and Mar 1945.
95 AWM 52, 8/3/14, 20 Jun 1943.
96 AWM 52, 4/2/4, 15 Jun 1943. The 2/4th Fd Regt had been working with 25 Bde.
97 AWM 52, 4/2/4, 22–24 Aug 1943.
98 Warby, *The 25 Pounders*, p. 338.
99 AWM 52, 4/2/4, Sept and Oct 1943, War Diary entries. See also Henry, *The Story of the 2/4th Field Regiment*, pp. 217–23; Horner, *The Gunners*, p. 371.
100 AWM 54, 579/6/5, 'Operation Milne Bay 24/8/42 to 8/9/42—Lessons from Operations', p. 15.
101 See AWM 54, 581/7/31 Part 2 of 2, 'Report on Operations, 18th Infantry Brigade', Appx A, 'Notes on Tank and Inf Cooperation in Cape Endaiadere–Giropa Point and Sanananda Area Ops', pp. 11–12; AWM 54, 577/7/29, Part 1, 'Report on Operations in New Guinea—Notes on Operations Owen Stanleys—Buna Area, Serial I Operations using M3 Light Tanks in New Guinea', pp. 3–5.
102 To this end an order for 142 more of them was cancelled in Sept 1943. See NAA, 729/6, item: 51/403/350, 'Review of Tank Situation', Sept 1943.
103 Handel, *Dust, Sand and Jungle*, p. 63 (The first Matilda Infantry) and pp. 63–4 (a heavier tank).
104 Hopkins, *Australian Armour*, pp. 125–6.
105 AWM 52, 3/1/15, 2/9 Aust Armd Regt War Diary, 12 Jun 1943.

106 AWM 52, 3/1/15, 'Training Instruction No. 3', 5 Jun 1943.
107 Hopkins, *Australian Armour*, p. 128 (where he continued) and (the combination of).
108 AWM 52, 8/2/18, 1–11 Jul 1943. See also AWM 52, 8/3/33, 1 Jul 1943.
109 AWM 52, 1/5/20, 9 Australian Division General Staff Branch (9 Aust Div GS Branch), 18 Apr 1943, '2 Aust Corps Training Directive No. 1', p. 1 (At the same time) and 20 Apr 1943 (To meet this directive).
110 AWM 52, 1/5/20, 21 Apr 1943 (On 21 April) and 29 Apr 1943, '9 Aust Div Training Instruction No. 4—Lessons from Operations in New Guinea' and 1 May, 'Owen Stanley—Buna Operations Information Gained on the Enemy'.
111 AWM 52, 1/5/20, 17 Jul 1943, 'Decided that Trg HQ will be disbanded early in the week'.
112 AWM 52, 8/3/28, 30 Apr 1943 (Although they did not); AWM 52, 8/2/20, 1 Jul 1943 (In July, training).
113 DVA, AAWFA, Ronald Burridge, 2/13th Bn, Archive No. 2142, transcript, time: 7:38:00:00.
114 AWM 52, 8/3/24, 26–30 Apr 1943.
115 AWM 52, 8/3/32, 20 Apr 1943, 4, 13 and 17 May 1943 (To facilitate information). Coates, *Bravery Above Blunder*, p. 53. The quote is taken from the 26th Brigade Commander, Brigadier Whitehead.
116 AWM 54, 589/2/26, Part 3, '9 Aust Div Report on Operations and Capture of Lae and Finschhafen 4 Sep–2 Oct 43', p. 1 'These attachments [6 and 7 Div trg teams] proved of greatest benefit'.
117 AWM 52, 8/3/28, 25 Apr 1943. See also, John Broadbent, Phil Pike, Ray Rudkin and Bruce Trebeck (eds), *'What We Have . . . We Hold': A History of the 2/17th Australian Infantry Battalion 1940–45*, Sydney: 2/17th Battalion History Association, 1990, p. 195.
118 Interview, Major Alan Macfarlane (Retd), 2/24th Bn, 26/5/06, tape 1, side B.
119 G.H. Fearnside (ed.), *Bayonets Abroad: A history of the 2/13th Battalion AIF in the Second World War*, Swanbourne WA: John Burridge Military Antiques, 1993, p. 326.
120 AWM 54, 923/1/5, 'Jungle Warfare Extracts 1943'. Included in the source materials for this document were the 'Notes on Operations' from Malaya, Milne Bay, Kokoda and the Beachheads, the 'Soldiering in the Tropics' pamphlet and the draft version of *MTP No. 23—Jungle Warfare*.
121 Ibid., Part 2: 'Our Tactics in the Jungle', p. 3.
122 Palazzo, 'Organising for jungle warfare', p. 89.
123 W.G. Loh and J.D. Yeats (eds), *Red Platypus: A record of the achievements of the 24th Australian Infantry Brigade Ninth Australian Division 1940–45*, Perth WA: Imperial Printing Company Ltd, 1945, p. 44.
124 Serle (ed.), *The Second Twenty-Fourth Australian Infantry Battalion*, pp. 250–1.
125 Interview, Alan Macfarlane, 2/24th Bn, 26/5/06, tape 1, side B.
126 Masel, *The Second 28th*, p. 130.
127 For observation problems see AWM 52, 8/3/15, 15 Aug 1943. The mortar platoon held a practice shoot and realised it was 'impossible to observe the [fall of] shot'. For anti-malarial and weight issues see John G. Glenn, *Tobruk to Tarakan: The story of a fighting unit*, Adelaide: Rigby Ltd, 1960, p. 195.
128 AWM 52, 3/3/31, 'Tng Syllabus—Week ending 8 Aug 43', p. 1.

129 Crooks, *The Footsoldiers*, p. 264.
130 Crooks, *The Footsoldiers*, p. 276; Dimmack, *Signals of the Silent Seventh*, p. 90.
131 AWM 54, 937/1/2, Appxs F and H.
132 DVA, AAWFA, L. Cook, 21 Brigade Sigs, Archive No. 0804, transcript, time: 09.01.00.00.
133 Coates, *Bravery Above Blunder*, p. 256; Gavin Long, *The Six Years War: A concise history of Australia in the 1939–1945 war*, Canberra: AWM, 1973 p. 323; Gavin Long, *The Final Campaigns: Australia in the war of 1939–1945 (Army), Vol. VII*, Canberra: AWM, 1963, p. 40.

Chapter 10. 'No New Lessons of Importance': The Final Campaigns

1 Long, *The Final Campaigns*, p. 502.
2 Crooks, *The Footsoldiers*, p. 392.
3 NAA, MP729/6, item 17/401/581, 'Lethbridge Mission'. See also Moreman, 'Jungle, Japanese and the Australian Army', pp. 8–11.
4 Peter Stanley, *Tarakan: An Australian tragedy*, Sydney: Allen & Unwin, 1997, p. 203. (Although Stanley was referring to Oboe One—the Tarakan operation—it is appropriate for all the final campaigns.) For other works that discuss the controversial 1945 campaigns see, for example, Charlton, *The Unnecessary War*; Grey, *The Australian Army*, p. 157, and *A Military History of Australia*, pp. 184–8; Keogh, *South West Pacific 1941–45*, p. 406; Long, *The Final Campaigns*, p. 547; Karl James, *The Hard Slog: Australians in the Bougainville Campaign, 1944–45*, Melbourne: Cambridge University Press, 2012; John Robertson, *Australia at War 1939–1945*, Melbourne: Heinemann, 1981, p. 179.
5 Kuring, *Redcoats to Cams*, p. 175.
6 AMF, *Infantry Training Vol. IV (Australia), Tactics (Tropical Warfare) Part I*, 'Infantry Section Leading', 1956 and *Infantry Training Vol. IV (Australia), Tactics (Tropical Warfare) Part II*, 'Platoon and Company in Battle', 1957.
7 See Dexter, *The New Guinea Offensives*, p. 650.
8 Joe Madeley, 2/13th Bn, quoted in Janet Hawley, 'Once Were Soldiers', *The Age*, Good Weekend supplement, 25–27 Apr 2008, p. 26.
9 DVA, AAWFA, Joseph Backhouse, 2/28th Bn, Archive No. 0735, transcript, time: 7.20.30.00.
10 Fearnside (ed.), *Bayonets Abroad*, p. 355.
11 Serle (ed.), *The Second Twenty-Fourth Australian Infantry Battalion*, p. 265.
12 H.M. Bink (ed.), *The 2/11th (City of Perth) Australian Infantry Battalion 1939–45*, Perth: 2/11th Battalion Association, 1984, p. 132.
13 Serle (ed.), *The Second Twenty-Fourth Australian Infantry Battalion*, p. 281.
14 Ronald J. Austin, *Let Enemies Beware: 'Caveant Hostes': The History of the 2/15th Battalion, 1940–45*, McCrae, Vic: 2/15th Battalion AIF, 1995, p. 216.
15 Fearnside (ed.), *Bayonets Abroad*, p. 343 (difficult to portray); Palazzo, 'Organising for jungle warfare', p. 89; Coates, *Bravery Above Blunder*, p. 209 (to attack with).
16 Broadbent et al. (eds), *'What We Have ... We Hold!'*, p. 275; Fearnside (ed.), *Bayonets Abroad*, p. 350.

17 Tregellis-Smith, *Britain to Borneo*, p. 201.
18 Max Parsons, *Gunfire! A history of the 2/12 Australian Field Regiment 1940–1946*, Cheltenham, Vic.: 2/12 Australian Field Regiment Association, 1991, p. 159.
19 AWM 54, 589/7/9, 'Operation Postern: Lessons and Comments ex Royal Australian Engineers, 9th Aust Division reports—1943', p. 35.
20 AWM 52, 4/2/6, 9 Nov and 9 Dec 1943.
21 Tregellis-Smith, *Britain to Borneo*, p. 202.
22 Coates, *Bravery Above Blunder*, p. 252. See also AWM 52, 4/2/6, 9 Dec 1943; Warby, *The 25 Pounders*, p. 359.
23 See, for example, *ATM No. 29*, 17 Jan 1944, Part II, Training—Artillery and Infantry Co-operation, p. 13.
24 Hopkins, *Australian Armour*, p. 132 (A brief training period); Handel, *Dust, Sand and Jungle*, p. 76; Coates, *Bravery Above Blunder*, p. 210. See also AWM 52, 8/3/36, Nov to Dec 1943.
25 AWM 54, 925/7/29, 'Report of Employment of Tanks in Operations North of Finschhafen', pp. 1–3, '1 Aust Tk Bn AIF Narrative for November 1943'.
26 Handel, *Dust, Sand and Jungle*, p. 65 (An Armoured Corps officer); AWM 54, 617/7/3, 'C Squadron 2/9 Aust Armd Regt. Ops Reports Tank–Inf Fighting Vehicles and activity reports Oboe One Tarakan—July 1945', p. 3.
27 Dexter, *The New Guinea Offensives*, p. 652.
28 Coates, *Bravery Above Blunder*, p. 210.
29 See DVA, AAWFA, Colin Salmon, 2/4th Aust Armd Regt, 'A' Sqn, Archive No. 0388, transcript, time: 4.20.30.00.
30 Coates, *Bravery Above Blunder*, p. 243.
31 See AWM 54, 591/7/25, 'Employment of Tanks in Jungle Warfare 4th Armoured Brigade Nov/Dec 43—Finschhafen–Sattelberg–Wareo' (This file contains three reports, including sections of AWM 54, 925/7/29); AWM 54, 593/7/3, 'Main Lessons from Recent Operations Sattelberg–Wareo The Employment of Army Tanks in Jungle Warfare—Jan 44', HQ 26 Aust Inf Bde; AWM 54, 925/7/21 'Tank Operations—New Guinea', 19 Feb 1944, HQ NGF.
32 AWM 54, 925/2/2, 'Tank Tactics—Employment of Tanks in New Guinea 1944', HQ 1 Aust Tank Bn (AIF) 23 Feb 1944, p. 1.
33 AWM 54, 589/7/11 (The tactics developed); AWM 54, 925/7/27, 'Training with Tanks—Notes on a Discussion Held 10.10.44, Before Commencement of Training, 20th Aust Inf Bde' (A highly detailed).
34 See, for example, AWM 54, 423/8/41, Pt 2, 'Employment of Matilda Tanks in Jungle—Extracts from 4 Aust Armd Brigade Training Instructions', Jan 1944.
35 AWM 54, 617/7/47, 'Report on Operations "Oboe One" The Landing at Tarakan Island Borneo', p. 24. See also AWM 54, 925/7/25, 'AFV User Report Op—Oboe One', 2/9 Aust Armd Regt, May 1945, p. 1.
36 Keogh, *South West Pacific 1941–45*, pp. 342–3.
37 AWM 254, item 214, 'The New Guinea Campaign: Report on Operations of 18 Australian Infantry Brigade, Ramu Valley—Shaggy Ridge 1 January to 6 February 1944', Lessons, p. 9.
38 DVA, AAWFA, Raymond Baldwin, 2/27th Bn, Archive No. 1214, transcript, time: 9.03.30.02–9.06.00.00.
39 Dickens, *Never Late*, p. 29; Draydon, *Men of Courage*, p. 186.

40 Draydon, *Men of Courage*, p. 186.
41 DVA, AAWFA, Eustace Marsden, 2/4th Fd Regt, Archive No. 0455, transcript, time: 6.15.00.00.
42 Ibid., time: 6.15.30.00. See also, Henry, *The Story of the 2/4th Field Regiment*, p. 230.
43 Johnston, *The Silent 7th*, p. 206.
44 AWM 52, 4/2/4, 14 Dec 1943.
45 AWM 54, 589/7/11, p. 14 (wherever I went); AWM 54, 589/7/2, Part 5, '7 Australian Division Report on Operation "Outlook" Appendix A to G. S Ops, 29/1/44', p. 1 (additional field company).
46 McNicoll, *Ubique*, pp. 327–8.
47 AWM 52, 4/2/4, 29 Dec 1943.
48 See Henry, *The Story of the 2/4th Field Regiment*, p. 266 for timber rafts, p. 272 for earth tremors, p. 291 for atmospheric problems and p. 252 for OP issues.
49 Dexter, *The New Guinea Offensives*, p. 739.
50 Graeme-Evans, *Of Storms and Rainbows*, p. 371.
51 Spencer, *In the Footsteps of Ghosts*, p. 178.
52 AWM 54, 589/7/11, p. 15.
53 Dexter, *The New Guinea Offensives*, p. 754.
54 See Graeme-Evans, *Of Storms and Rainbows*, p. 385, for 'all-arms effort'; Givney (ed.), *The First at War*, p. 389 for 'massive' fire support.
55 MP742/1, 240/1/1325, 'LHQ Tactical School—3(a) Policy'. This large file contains over 80 documents, one of which is entitled 'Notes of visit DMT to New Guinea 28 Sep to 6 Oct', 11 Oct 1943.
56 AWM 54, 589/7/11, p. 13.
57 Parsons, *Gunfire!*, p. 209. See also, Johnston, *The Silent 7th*, p. 207; Barter, *Far Above Battle*, p. 215.
58 Serle (ed.), *The Second Twenty-Fourth Australian Infantry Battalion*, p. 298.
59 Dickens, *Never Late*, p. 293.
60 Clift, *War Dance*, p. 409 (This meant that); Burns, *The Brown and Blue Diamond at War*, p. 204.
61 AWM 52, 925/7/27, 'Training with Tanks—Notes on a Discussion Held 10/10/1944, Before Commencement of Training, 20th Aust Inf Bde'. The above quote is from '9 Aust Div Training Instruction No. 5 General, 20 May 44', p. 2, Training in Open Country and Jungle.
62 *Tropical Warfare No. 1*, p. 3.
63 Moreman, 'Jungle, Japanese and the Australian Army'.
64 AWM 54, 923/1/6, 'Notes on Recently Expressed Concepts of Tactics', 11 Oct 1942, Brigadier SHWC Porter, 30th Bde, especially pp. 1–2.
65 *Tropical Warfare No. 1*, p. 9.
66 AWM 54, 925/7/27, '9 Aust Div Training Instruction No. 18, 6 Sep 44', Training in Open and Close Country and Nature of Training.
67 Moreman, 'Jungle, Japanese and the Australian Army'.
68 AWM 54, 923/1/6, p. 8.
69 Palazzo, 'Organising for jungle warfare', p. 90.

70 Serle (ed.), *The Second Twenty-Fourth Australian Infantry Battalion*, pp. 352–3.
71 *Tropical Warfare No. 1*, pp. 9, 17–20.
72 Ibid., p. 9 (It is necessary therefore) and p. 12 (the terrain is not).
73 Ibid., p. 19.
74 Horner, *The Gunners*, pp. 377 and 397.
75 *Tropical Warfare No. 2*.
76 *Tropical Warfare No. 1*, p. 3.
77 AWM 54, 945/5/1, 'Training Syllabus—3 Australian Division', Jul 1945, pp. 1–2.
78 Hay, *Nothing Over Us*, p. 423.
79 Givney (ed.), *The First at War*, p. 389.
80 Ibid.
81 Clift, *War Dance*, p. 384.
82 Barter, *Far Above Battle*, pp. 235–6.
83 Hay, *Nothing Over Us*, p. 446.
84 The Unit History Editorial Committee, *White Over Green: The 2/4th Infantry Battalion*, Sydney: Angus & Robertson, 1963, p. 272.
85 Wick, *Purple Over Green*, p. 274. See also, Joe Madeley, 2/13th Bn, in Hawley, 'Once Were Soldiers', p. 26.
86 For casualty figures see Stanley, *Tarakan*, p. 1. For the Balikpapan operation, see Johnston, *The Silent 7th*, p. 239. For Brunei Bay and Labuan see Johnston, *That Magnificent 9th*, p. 238.
87 Serle (ed.), *The Second Twenty-Fourth Australian Infantry Battalion*, pp. 352–3.
88 *Tropical Warfare No. 2*, p. 23.
89 Serle (ed.), *The Second Twenty-Fourth Australian Infantry Battalion*, p. 334.
90 AWM 52, 8/2/25, 4 Jul 1945: 'Conference with Bn COs and COs of supporting arms, 1330 hrs' (to move fwd slowly); Crooks, *The Footsoldiers*, p. 392 (probe it—blast it).
91 McCarthy, *South-West Pacific Area First Year*, p. 591.
92 Lt-Gen. Sir Henry Wells, CGS 1957, in Grey, *The Australian Army*, p. 192.

Conclusion

1 Palazzo, *The Australian Army*, p. 184.
2 Ibid.
3 Grey, *A Military History of Australia*, pp. 227–8.
4 Palazzo, *The Australian Army*, p. 195.
5 NAA, A816/1, item 14/301/321, 'An Appreciation by the Chiefs of Staff on the Strategical Position of Australia', p. 35.
6 Hamilton, 'A History of Canungra', p. 17.

BIBLIOGRAPHY

1. Government and other official publications
2. Archival sources
   (a) Australian War Memorial
   (b) National Archives of Australia
   (c) Department of Veterans' Affairs
3. Interviews
4. Newspapers
5. Secondary sources
   (a) Unit histories
   (b) Books and book chapters
   (c) Journal articles
6. Unpublished manuscripts and theses

1. GOVERNMENT AND OTHER OFFICIAL PUBLICATIONS

Field Service Regulations, Vol. II, Operations—General, 1935, London: War Office, 1935

Field Service Regulations, Vol. III, Operations—Higher Formations, 1935, London: War Office, 1935

Infantry Training (Training and War) 1937, (War Office), Reprinted by Australian Government Publishing Service

Voorschrift Voor De Uitoefening Van De Politiek-Politioneele Taak Van Het Leger (VPTL), Batavia-Centrum, 1937

Field Drill for Rifle Battalions (Deployment), Extracts from Military Training Pamphlet No. 1, 1938, London: HMSO

Tactical Notes for Malaya 1940, Reprinted for General Staff, AHQ, Melbourne, 1940
Small Wars Manual, United States Marine Corps, 1940 (revised version of 1935 edition)
Military Training Pamphlet No. 9 (India), Extensive Warfare—Notes on Forest Warfare (1940), Simla, India (Reproduced by Victorian Railways Print for the Australian Army, November 1940)
Infantry Minor Tactics, Australia, 1941, Melbourne, HMSO, December 1941
Tactical Methods A. Characteristics—Japanese Tactics—Equipment and Armament. B. Tactics and Equipment for Operations against Japanese Forces, South West Pacific Zone 1942, Army Headquarters, Melbourne, March 1942
Soldiering in the Tropics (S.W. Pacific Area), LHQ, Melbourne, August 1942
Jungle Fighting, Part II, *Tactics of the Squad*, US Army, 1942
Military Training Pamphlet No. 9 (India), Jungle Warfare, Simla, India, August 1942
Military Training Pamphlet Operations (Australia) No. 23 XX Jungle Warfare, LHQ, Melbourne, 1943
Supplement to Military Training Pamphlet (Australia) No. 23 XX Jungle Warfare—Notes for Platoon & Section Leaders, LHQ, Melbourne, May 1943
Friendly Fruits and Vegetables, Prepared by the General Staff, LHQ Australian Army, 31 May 1943
6 Aust Div Training Instruction No. 11 Jungle Warfare, LHQ, Australian Army, 30 June 1943
Military Training Pamphlet No. 9 (India), The Jungle Book, Simla, India, September 1943
Australian Military Forces, *Tropical Warfare (Australia), Pamphlet No. 1—General Principles*, LHQ, Australian Army, Melbourne, November 1944
Australian Military Forces, *Tropical Warfare (Australia), Pamphlet No. 2—Notes for Junior Leaders*, LHQ, Australian Army, Melbourne, February 1945
Tactical and Administrative Doctrine for Jungle Warfare, General Savige, 2nd Aust Army Corps, Bougainville, 1945
Army Training Memoranda (ATM)
    ATM No. 7, February 1942
    ATM No. 8, March 1942
    ATM No. 9, April 1942
    ATM No. 10, May 1942, 'Notes on Japanese Tactics in Malaya and Elsewhere and Tactics to Counter-attack and Destroy the Enemy' (General Bennett's Manual)
    ATM No. 11, June 1942
    ATM No. 12, June 1942
    ATM No. 13, July 1942
    ATM No. 16, October 1942
    ATM No. 17, November 1942
    ATM No. 20, February 1943
    ATM No. 21, March 1943
    ATM No. 28, 20 December 1943
    ATM No. 29, 17 January 1944
AMF, *Infantry Training Vol. IV (Australia), Tactics (Tropical Warfare) Part 1, 'Infantry Section Leading'*, 1956 draft

AMF, *Infantry Training Vol. IV (Australia), Tactics (Tropical Warfare) Part 2, 'Platoon and Company in Battle'*, 1957 draft

2. ARCHIVAL SOURCES

(a) Australian War Memorial, Canberra

AWM 52, AIF unit war diaries (1939–45)
AWM 54, Written records (1939–45 war)
AWM 60, Northern Command Registry Files
AWM 61, Eastern Command Registry Files
AWM 67, Gavin Long, papers of the Official Historian
AWM 172, Official History, 1939–45 War, Series 1 (Army), vol. 6: Records of David Dexter
AWM 254, Written records, 1939–45 War, second series

Private records

3DRL 1892 Diary of Brigadier H.B. Taylor
3DRL 2529 Papers of Lieutenant-General Sir Stanley Savige
3DRL 4142 Papers of Major-General A.S. Allen
3DRL 6643 Papers of Field Marshal Sir Thomas Albert Blamey
3DRL 6599 Papers of Lieutenant-Colonel Starr
3DRL 6850 Papers of Lieutenant-General I.G. Mackay
PR 84/370 Papers of Lieutenant-General Sir F.H. Berryman

Keith Murdoch Sound Archive

Curtis, Owen, 2/12th Battalion, Archive No. S541
Harry, Bill, 2/22nd Battalion, Archive No. S908
Heckendorf, Erwin, 2/30th Battalion, Archive No. S763
Holmes, Geoffrey, 2/12th Battalion, Archive No. S540
Hope, Paul, 2/12th Battalion, Archive No. S529
Innes, Bob, 2/27th Battalion, Archive No. S902
Johns, Robert, 2/27th Battalion, Archive No. S799
Katekar, Harry, 2/27th Battalion, Archive No. S903
Kollmorgen, Fred, 2/22nd Battalion, Archive No. S911
Reddin, Jack, 2/27th Battalion, Archive No. S790
Sims, Charles, 2/27th Battalion, Archive No. S789

(b) National Archives of Australia

Adelaide

D5172 Miscellaneous records of the Design Division Detachment, single number series

Melbourne

B5505 Miscellaneous publications collected by the Australian Women's Army Service
MP508/1 General correspondence files, multiple number series, Jan 1939–Dec 1942
MP729/6 Secret correspondence files, multiple number series with '401' infix, Jan 1936–Dec 1945
MP729/7 Secret correspondence files, multiple number series with '421' infix, Jan 1939–Dec 1945
MP729/8 Secret correspondence files, multiple number series, Jan 1945–Dec 1955
MP742/1 General and civil staff correspondence files and Army personnel files, multiple number series

Sydney

SP300/3 War correspondents' talk scripts, general wartime scripts and related correspondence, Jan 1940–Dec 1947
SP300/4 Chester Wilmot series (includes scripts, reports and personal files), Aug 1936–Feb 1955
SP459/1 Correspondence relating to the administration, function and policy of Eastern Command, Jan 1912–Dec 1964
SP1008/1 General correspondence files, multiple number series, relating to the administration, function and policy of Eastern Command, Jan 1871–Dec 1965

(c) Department of Veterans' Affairs

Australians at War Film Archive

Abbott, William, 2/4th Field Company RAE, Archive No. 1023
Allaway, Archie, 2/12th Battalion, Archive No. 0545
Allen, Walter, 2/11th Battalion, Archive No. 1524
Amor, Benjamin, 2/21st Battalion, Archive No. 0566
Baldwin, Raymond, 2/27th Battalion, Archive No. 1214
Backhouse, Joseph, 2/28th and 2/14th Battalions, Archive No. 0735
Bedggood, Kenneth, 2/5th Field Company RAE, Archive No. 1873
Bisset, Stan, 2/14th Battalion, Archive No. 1223
Booth, William, 2/3rd Battalion, Archive No. 1420
Burridge, Ronald, 2/13th Battalion, Archive No. 2142
Cameron, Wallace, 2/6th Battalion, Archive No. 1133
Catterns, Basil, 2/1st Battalion, Archive No. 1505
Clarke, Ian, 2/5th Battalion, Archive No. 0630
Cody, Donald, 2/3rd Field Company RAE, Archive No. 1772
Cook, Lesley, 6th & 7th Division Signals, 2/14th Battalion, Archive No. 0804
Coombes, Raymond, 2/2nd Battalion, Archive No. 1224
Connor, George, 2/33rd Battalion, Archive No. 1175
Crowhurst, John, 2/4th Armoured Regiment, Archive No. 0423
Dockery, Roy, 14th Field Regiment, Archive No. 2023
Edwards, Clive, 2/27th Battalion, Archive No. 1657

Finkmeyer, Colin, 4th Anti-Tank Regiment, Archive No. 0093
Peter Gibson, 2/5th Field Regiment, Archive No. 0012
Halden, Kenneth, 2/43rd Battalion, Archive No. 1475
Hall, Francis, 2/7th Battalion, Archive No. 2053
Hansen, Ronald, 2/9th Battalion, Archive No. 0878
Hewit, Edward, 2/1st Field Regiment, Archive No. 0116
Howell, Charles, 2/12th Battalion, Archive No. 1606
Hudson, Colin, 2/7th Field Regiment, Archive No. 1484
Isaachsen, Oscar, 2/27th Battalion & 36th Battalion (AMF), Archive No. 1687
Iskov, Robert, 2/14th Battalion, Archive No. 1999
Johns, Robert, 2/27th Battalion, Archive No. 1195
Jones, Edmond, 2/9th Battalion, Archive No. 1138
Jorgenson, Kenneth, 2/1st Field Regiment, Archive No. 0893
King, Ian, 2/33rd Battalion, Archive No. 0132
King, Kelvin, 3rd & 2/4th Battalion, Archive No. 0228
Kirkmoe, John, 2/10th Battalion, Archive No. 1814
Kuschert, Bernard, 2/3rd Battalion, Archive No. 0115
Lardelli, Michael, 2/1st Field Regiment, Archive No. 0016
Lewis, Neville, 2/33rd Battalion, Archive No. 1636
Lilley, Alfred, 2/9th Battalion, Archive No. 1794
Ling, James, 8th Division Signals Unit, Archive No. 0015
Lupp, John, 2/1st Battalion, Archive No. 0125
McNevin, Allan, 2/10th Field Artillery Regiment, Archive No. 1295
McRostie, Colin, 2/6th Field Ambulance & 2/16th Battalion, Archive No. 1237
Marsden, Eustace, 2/4th Field Regiment, Archive No. 0455
Mason, Lindsay, 2/14th Battalion, Archive No. 1197
Moore, Bernard, 2/2nd Battalion, Archive No. 0028
Nankervis, William, 2/29th Battalion, Archive No. 0236
Palmer, Graham, 2/6th Battalion, Archive No. 2111
Patterson, Frank, 7th Division Signals, Archive No. 0193
Pearce, Oswald, 2/1st Field Regiment, Archive No. 0876
Phelan, Kenneth, 39th Battalion & 2/2nd Battalion, Archive No. 0509
Pope, Keith, 8th Division Signals, Archive No. 0701
Powers, Frederick, 2/19th Battalion, Archive No. 1142
Robey, Herbert, 2/6th Field Regiment, Archive No. 0585
Ross, Keith, 2/6th Battalion, Archive No. 0373
Ryan, Maurice, 2/3rd Pioneer Battalion, Archive No. 0149
Russell, Jack, 2/12th Battalion, Archive No. 0497
Russell, Neil, 2/12th Battalion, Archive No. 0692
Salmon, Colin, 2/4th Aust Armoured Regiment, Archive No. 0388
Sambell, Eric, 2/27th Battalion, Archive No. 2231
Simmons, Gilbert, 2/25th Battalion, Archive No. 1186
Snowdon, James, 9th Division Signals, Archive No. 0485
Suthers, Angus, 2/12th Battalion, Archive No. 0399
Thompson, Robert, 2/14th Battalion, Archive No. 1594

Varley, John, 2/19th Battalion, Archive No. 1220
Wall, Donald, 2/20th Battalion, Archive No. 0429
Wallace, Walter, 2/15th Battalion, Archive No. 1920
Wells, Bryan, 2/9th Battalion, Archive No. 0696
Widdows, Raymond, 2/12th Field Artillery Regiment, Archive No. 1786
Williams, Eric, 2/16th Battalion, Archive No. 1117
Williams, Frederick, 2/2nd Battalion, Archive No. 0780
Wilson, Donald, 2/3rd Battalion, Archive No. 0252
Wockner, Harvey, 2/9th Battalion, Archive No. 1028

3. INTERVIEWS

King, Gordon, 2/6th Independent Company, Sydney, 24/10/06
Macfarlane, Alan, 2/24th Australian Infantry Battalion, Melbourne, 26/5/06 & 13/6/06
Manning, Lew, 2/43rd and 2/10th Australian Infantry Battalions, Adelaide, 7/3/06

4. NEWSPAPERS

Hawley, Janet, 'Once Were Soldiers', *The Age*, Good Weekend supplement, 25–27 April 2008, pp. 24–33
McKernan, Michael, Book review of *A Bastard of a Place*, *The Age*, Saturday, 17 January 2004
Thompson, E.P., 'History from Below', *Times Literary Supplement*, 7 April 1966, pp. 279–80

5. SECONDARY SOURCES

(a) Official histories

First World War

Bean, C.E.W., *Anzac to Amiens*, Canberra: AWM, 1946
Mackenzie, S.S., *The Australians at Rabaul: Official history of Australia in the war of 1914–1918*, vol. X, Sydney: Angus & Robertson, 1938

Second World War

Dexter, David, *The New Guinea Offensives: Australia in the war of 1939–1945 (Army)*, Vol. VI, Canberra: AWM, 1961
Gillson, Douglas, *Royal Australian Air Force 1939–1942: Australia in the war of 1939–1945 (Air)*, Vol. I, Canberra: AWM, 1962
Long, Gavin, *The Final Campaigns: Australia in the war of 1939–1945 (Army)*, Vol. VII, Canberra: AWM, 1963
——*The Six Year War: A concise history of Australia in the 1939–1945 war*, Canberra: AWM, 1973

——— *To Benghazi: Australia in the war of 1939–1945 (Army)*, Vol. I, Canberra: AWM, 1952
McCarthy, Dudley, *South-West Pacific Area—First Year: Australia in the war of 1939–1945 (Army)*, Vol. V, Canberra, AWM, 1959
Mellor, D.P., *The Role of Science and Industry: Australia in the war of 1939–1945 (Civil)*, Vol. V, Canberra: AWM, 1958
Odgers, George, *Air War Against Japan 1943–1945: Australia in the war of 1939–1945 (Air)*, Vol. II, Canberra: AWM, 1957
Walker, Allan S., *The Island Campaigns: Australia in the war of 1939–1945 (Medical)*, Vol. III, Canberra: AWM, 1957
Wigmore, Lionel, *The Japanese Thrust: Australia in the war of 1939–45 (Army)*, Vol. IV, Canberra: AWM, 1957

(b) Unit histories

Allan, Jack and Cutts, Chris (eds), *As It Seemed to Us: The 1st Australian Mountain Battery RAA AIF*, Brisbane: Aebis Publishing, 1994
Allchin, Frank (Lt-Col.), *Purple and Blue: The history of the 2/10th Battalion, AIF (The Adelaide Rifles) 1939–1945*, Adelaide: Griffin Press, 1958
Anderson, J.A. and Jackett, G., *Mud and Sand: 2/3 Pioneer Battalion at war*, Sutherland, NSW: 2/3 Pioneer Battalion Association, 1994
Austin, Ronald J., *Let Enemies Beware: 'Caveant Hostes': The history of the 2/15th Battalion, 1940–45*, McCrae, Vic: 2/15th Battalion AIF Association, 1995
Austin, Victor (ed.), *To Kokoda and Beyond: The story of the 39th Battalion 1941–43*, Melbourne: Melbourne University Press, 1988
Barker, Theo, *Signals: A history of the Royal Australian Corps of Signals 1788–1947*, Canberra: Royal Australian Corps of Signals Committee, 1987
Barter, Margaret, *Far Above Battle: The experience and memory of Australian soldiers in war 1939–1945*, Sydney: Allen & Unwin, 1994
Bayliss, W.C., Crispin, K.E. and Penfold, A.W., *Galleghan's Greyhounds: The story of 2/30th Australian Infantry Battalion*, Sydney: 2/30th Battalion AIF Association, 1979
Bellair, John, *From Snow to Jungle: A history of the 2/3rd Australian Machine Gun Battalion*, Sydney: Allen & Unwin, 1987
Bentley, Arthur, *The Second Eighth: A history of the 2/8th Australian Infantry Battalion*, Melbourne: 2/8th Battalion Association, 1984
Bink, H.M. (ed.), *The 2/11th (City of Perth) Australian Infantry Battalion 1939–45*, Perth, 2/11th Battalion Association, 1984
Bishop, Les, *The Thunder of the Guns! A history of 2/3 Australian Field Regiment*, Sydney: 2/3 Australian Field Regiment Association, 1998
Blair, Ron, *A Young Man's War: A history of the 37th/52nd Australian Infantry Battalion in World War Two*, Melbourne: 37/52 Australian Infantry Battalion Association, 1992
Bolger, W.P. and Littlewood, J.G., *The Fiery Phoenix: The story of the 2/7 Australian Infantry Battalion 1939–1946*, Parkdale, Vic.: 2/7 Battalion Association, 1983

Brigg, Stan and Les, *Ike's Marines: The 36th Australian Infantry Battalion 1939–1945*, Loftus, NSW: Australian Military History Publications, 2003

Broadbent, John, Pike, Phil, Rudkin, Ray and Trebeck, Bruce (eds), *'What We Have... We Hold': A history of the 2/17th Australian Infantry Battalion, 1940–45*, Sydney: 2/17th Battalion History Association, 1990

Budden, F.M., *That Mob! The story of the 55th/53rd Australian Infantry Battalion, AIF*, Sydney: Wild & Woolley, 1973

Burfitt, James, *Against All Odds: The history of the 2/18th Battalion AIF*, Frenchs Forest, NSW: 2/18th Battalion Association, 1991

Burns, John, *The Brown and Blue Diamond at War: The story of the 2/27th Battalion AIF*, Adelaide: 2/27th Battalion Ex-Servicemen's Association, 1960

Charlott, Rupert (ed.), *The Unofficial History of the 29/46th Australian Infantry Battalion AIF, September 1939–September 1945*, Melbourne: Halstead Press, 1952

Christensen, George (ed.), *That's the Way It Was: The history of the 24th Australian Infantry Battalion (AIF) 1939–1945*, Hawthorn, Vic: 24th Battalion AIF Association, 1982

Christie, R.W. (ed.), *A History of the 2/29 Battalion—8th Australian Division AIF*, Stratford, Vic.: High Country Publishing, 1991

Clift, Ken, *War Dance: The 2/3rd Australian Infantry Battalion*, Kingsgrove, NSW: P.M. Fowler and 2/3rd Battalion Association, 1980

Cody, Les, *Ghosts in Khaki: The history of the 2/4th Machine Gun Battalion, 8th Australian Division*, AIF, Carlisle, WA: Hesperian Press, 1997

Combe, G., Ligertwood, F. and Gilchrist, T., *The Second Forty-Third Australian Infantry Battalion, 1940–1946*, Adelaide: Second 43rd Battalion AIF Club, 1972

The Corps of Royal Australian Engineers in the Second World War 1939–45, Melbourne: Specialty Press, 1947

Cranston, F., *Always Faithful: The history of the 49th Battalion*, Brisbane: Boolarong Press, 1983

Cremor, W. (ed.), *Action Front: The history of the 2/2nd Australian Field Regiment Royal Australian Artillery AIF*, Melbourne: 2/2nd Field Regiment Association, 1961

Crooks, William, *The Footsoldiers: The story of the 2/33rd Australian Infantry Battalion AIF in the War of 1939–45*, Sydney: Printcraft Press, 1971

Davidson, Reginald, *With Courage High: The history of the 2/8th Field Company Royal Australian Engineers, 1940–1946*, Melbourne: 2/8th Field Company, RAE Association, 1964

Devine, W., *The Story of a Battalion (48th Battalion)*, Melbourne, 1919

Dickens, Gordon, *Never Late: The 2/9th Australian Infantry Battalion 1939–1945*, Loftus, NSW: Australian Military History Publications, 2005

Dimmack, Max, *Signals of the Silent Seventh: A short history of Signals 7th Australian Division, 2nd AIF, 1940–1945*, Sassafras, Vic.: Benchmark Publications, 2001

Draydon, Allan W., *Men of Courage: A history of the 2/25 Australian Infantry Battalion 1940–1945*, Brisbane: 2/25 Australian Infantry Battalion Association, 2000

Donovan, Peter, *Waltzing Matildas: The men and machines of the 2/9th Australian Armoured Regimental Group in Australia and Borneo 1941–1946*, Blackwood, SA: 2/9 Australian Armoured Regimental Group Association, 1988

Downs, Ian, *The New Guinea Volunteer Rifles: 1939–1945—A history*, Broadbeach Waters, Qld: Pacific Press, 1999

Fearnside, G.H. (ed.), *Bayonets Abroad: A history of the 2/13th Battalion AIF in the Second World War*, Swanbourne, WA: John Burridge Military Antiques, 1993

Gillan, Hugh (ed.), *We Had Some Bother: Tales from the infantry*, Sydney: Hale & Iremonger, 1985

Givney, E.C. (ed.), *The First at War: The story of the 2/1st Australian Infantry Battalion 1939–45 The City of Sydney Regiment*, Earlwood, NSW: The Association of First Infantry Battalions, 1987

Glenn, John G., *Tobruk to Tarakan: The story of a fighting unit*, Adelaide: Rigby, 1960

Glover, E.W., *Official Souvenir History of 2/9 Australian Field Regiment RAA, AIF*, Sydney: R. Bale, 1945

Goodhart, David, *The History of the 2/7 Australian Field Regiment*, Adelaide: Rigby, 1952

Goodwin, Bob, *Mates and Memories: Recollections of the 2/10th Field Regiment RAA*, Rochedale Qld: Boolarong Press, 1995

Gorman, E., *With the Twenty-Second*, Melbourne: E. Gorman and H.H. Champion, Australasian Author's Agency, 1919

Graeme-Evans, Alex, *Of Storms and Rainbows: The story of the men of the 2/12th Battalion AIF, Volume Two*, Hobart: 12th Battalion Association, 1991

Hay, David, *Nothing Over Us: The story of the 2/6th Australian Infantry Battalion*, Canberra: AWM, 1984

Haywood, E.V., *Six Years in Support: Official History of 2/1st Australian Field Regiment*, Sydney: Angus & Robertson, 1959

Henning, Peter, *Doomed Battalion: The Australian 2/40 Battalion 1940–45—Mateship and leadership in war and captivity*, Sydney: Allen & Unwin, 1995

Henry, R.L. *The Story of the 2/4th Field Regiment: A history of a Royal Australian Artillery Regiment during the Second World War*, Melbourne: Merrion Press, 1950

Jackson, Ron, *The Broken Eighth: A history of the 2/14th Australian Field Regiment*, Melbourne: Clipper Press, 1997

Kennedy, J.J., *The Whale Oil Guards* (53rd Battalion), Dublin, 1919

Kennedy, Colin, *Port Moresby to Gona Beach: 3rd Australian Infantry Battalion 1942*, Canberra: The Practical Group, 1991

Lack, John and Hosford, Peter (eds), *No Lost Battalion: An oral history of the 2/29th Battalion AIF*, Rosebud, Vic.: Slouch Hat Publications, 2005

Laffin, John, *Forever Forward: The history of the 2/31st Australian Infantry Battalion, 2nd AIF 1940–45*, Newport, NSW: 2/31st Australian Infantry Battalion Association, 1994

Lambert, G.E. (ed.), *Commando: From Tidal River to Tarakan: The story of No. 4 Australian Independent Company, AIF*, Sydney: Australian Military History Publishers, 1996

Lewis, W.T. (ed.), *Observation Post: Six years of war with the 2/11th Australian Army Field Regiment*, West Essendon, Vic.: 2/11th Australian Field Regiment Association, 1989

Loh, W.G. and Yeates, J.D., *Red Platypus: A record of the achievements of the 24th Australian Infantry Brigade Ninth Australian Division 1940–45*, Perth: Imperial Printing, September 1945

McAllester, J.C., *Men of the 2/14th Battalion*, Melbourne: 2/14th Battalion Association, 1990

McRae, Heather, *Soldier Surveyors: A history of the 3 Australian Field Survey Company (AIF), 1940–1945*, Vic.: 3rd Australian Field Survey Company, 1996

Newton, R. (ed.), *The Grim Glory of the 2/19 Battalion AIF*, Sydney: 2/19th Battalion AIF Association, 1975

Magarry, Ron (Lt-Col.), *The Battalion Story: 2/26th Infantry Battalion, 8th Division AIF*, Jindalee, Qld: Ron Magarry, 1995

Marshall, A.J. (ed.), *Nulli Secundus Log*, Sydney: 2/2nd Australian Infantry Battalion AIF, 1946

Masel, Phillip, *The Second 28th: The story of a famous battalion of the Ninth Australian Division*, Perth: 2/28th Battalion & 24th Anti-Tank Company Association, 1961

Mathews, Russell, *Militia Battalion at War: The history of the 58/59th Australian Infantry Battalion in the Second World War*, Sydney: 58/59th Battalion Association, 1961

Oakes, Bill, *Muzzle Blast: Six years of war with the 2/2 Australian Machine Gun Battalion, AIF*, Sydney: 2/2nd Machine Gun Battalion History Committee, 1980

O'Brien, John W., *Guns and Gunners: The story of the 2/5th Australian Field Regiment in World War II*, Sydney: Angus & Robertson, 1950

O'Leary, Shawn, *To the Green Fields Beyond: The story of the 6th Division Cavalry Commandos*, Sydney: 6th Division Cavalry Unit, History Committee, 1975

Osborn, Gordon, Clarke, Steve, Jollie, Bill and Law, Max (eds), *The Pioneers: Unit history of the 2nd/1st Australian Pioneer Battalion Second AIF*, Sydney: MD Herron, 1988

Parsons, Max (ed.), *We Were the 2/12th: 1940–1946*, Carnegie, Vic.: McKellor Renown Press, 1985

——*Gunfire! A history of the 2/12 Australian Field Regiment 1940–1946*, Cheltenham, Vic.: 2/12 Australian Field Regiment Association, 1991

——*Take Post: A pictorial history of 2/12 Australian Field Regiment 1940–1946*, Cheltenham, Vic.: 2/12 Australian Field Regiment Association, 1993

Pura, Colin, *Black Berets: The history and battles of the 9th Division Cavalry Regiment*, Melbourne: 9th Australian Division Regiment Association, 1983

Ross, A.R. (Capt.) (ed.), *The Magazine of 17 Australian Infantry Brigade, 1939–1944*, Melbourne, 1944

Russell, W.B., *The Second Fourteenth Battalion: A history of an Australian Infantry Battalion in the Second World War*, Sydney: Angus & Robertson, 1948

Serle, R.P. (ed.), *The Second Twenty-Fourth Australian Infantry Battalion of the 9th Australian Division*, Brisbane: Jacaranda Press, 1963

Share, Pat (ed.), *Mud and Blood 'Albury's Own': Second Twenty-Third Australian Infantry Battalion, Ninth Australian Division*, Frankston, Vic.: Heritage Book Publications, 1978

Smith, Neil, *TID-APA: The history of the 4th Anti Tank Regiment 1940–1945*, Melbourne: Mostly Unsung Military History Research and Publications, 1992

Speed, F.W. (ed.), *Esprit De Corps: The history of the Victorian Scottish Regiment and the 5th Infantry Battalion*, Sydney: Allen & Unwin, 1988

Spencer, Bill, *In the Footsteps of Ghosts: With the 2/9th Battalion in the African desert and the jungles of the Pacific*, Sydney: Allen & Unwin, 1999

Stewart, I.M. (Brig.), *History of the Argyll and Sutherland Highlanders 2nd Battalion (The Thin Red Line) Malayan Campaign 1941–42*, London: Thomas Nelson, 1947

Tregellis-Smith, S., *All the King's Enemies: A history of the 2/5th Australian Infantry Battalion*, Ringwood East, Vic.: 2/5th Battalion Association, 1988

Tregellis-Smith, Syd, *Britain to Borneo: A history of 2/32 Australian Infantry Battalion*, Sydney: 2/32 Australian Infantry Battalion Association, 1993

Turrell, A.N., *Never Unprepared: A history of the 26th Australian Infantry Battalion (AIF) 1939–1946*, Wynnum, Qld: 26th Battalion Reunion Association, 1992

The Unit History Editorial Committee, *White over Green: The 2/4th Infantry Battalion*, Sydney: Angus & Robertson, 1963

Uren, Malcolm, *A Thousand Men at War: The story of the 2/16th Battalion, AIF*, Melbourne: William Heinemann, 1959

Wall, Don, *Singapore and Beyond: The story of the men of the 2/20th Battalion—Told by the survivors*, East Hills, NSW: 2/20 Bn Ass, 1985

Warby, John, *The 25 Pounders . . . from Egypt to Borneo: Campaigns in Syria, Kumusi River, Salamaua, Lae, Finschhafen and Balikpapan—The story of the 2/6th Australian Field Regiment, RAA, AIF, 1940–1946*, Pymble, NSW: 2/6th Field Regiment Association, 1995

Ward-Harvey, Ken, *The Sappers' War: With the 9th Australian Division Engineers 1939–1945*, NSW: Sakoga/9 Div RAE Association, 1992

Whitelocke, Cliff, *Gunners in the Jungle: A story of the 2/15 Field Regiment Royal Australian Artillery, 8 Division, Australian Imperial Force*, Eastwood, NSW: 2/15th Field Regiment Association, 1983

Wick, Stan, *Purple Over Green: The history of the 2/2 Australian Infantry Battalion 1939–1945*, Guildford, NSW: 2/2nd Australian Infantry Battalion Association, 1978

(c) Books and book chapters

Adam-Smith, Patsy, *The Anzacs*, Melbourne: Nelson, 1978

Adkin, Mark, *The Last Eleven?*, London, Leo Cooper, 1991

Aplin, Douglas, *Rabaul 1942*, Melbourne: 2/22nd Battalion AIF Lark Force Association, 1980

Arneil, Stan, *One Man's War*, Sydney: Alternative Publishing Co-Operative, 1981

——*Black Jack: The life and times of Brigadier Sir Frederick Galleghan*, Melbourne: Macmillan, 1983

Australian Army, *The Australian Army at War*, Nos 1–4, Department of Information: Sydney, 1944

——*The Jap was Thrashed: An official story of the Australian soldier*, Melbourne: AHQ, 1944

Avant, Deborah, *Political Institutions and Military Change: Lessons from peripheral wars*, Ithaca, NY: Cornell University Press, 1994

Baker, Clive and Knight, Greg, *Milne Bay 1942: The story of 'Milne-Force' and Japan's first military defeat on land*, Loftus, NSW: Baker-Knight Publications, 1992

Baker, Nicola, *More Than Little Heroes: Australian Army Air Liaison Officers in the Second World War*, Canberra: Strategic and Defence Studies Centre, Australian National University, 1994

Barker, Anthony J., *Fleeting Attraction: A social history of American servicemen in Western Australia during the Second World War*, Nedlands, WA: University of Western Australia Press, 1996

John Barrett, *We Were There: Australian soldiers of World War II tell their stories*, Ringwood, Vic.: Penguin Books, 1988

Beaumont, Joan, *Gull Force: Survival and leadership in captivity 1941–1945*, Sydney: Allen & Unwin, 1988

Bennett, H. Gordon (Lt-Gen.), *Why Malaya Fell*, Sydney: Angus & Robertson, 1944

Bennett, Cam, *Rough Infantry: Tales of World War II*, Melbourne: Warrnambool Institute Press, 1985

Bergerud, Eric, *Touched with Fire: The land war in the South Pacific*, New York: Penguin Books, 1996

Bradley, Phillip, *On Shaggy Ridge: The Australian Seventh Division in the Ramu Valley Campaign: From Kaiapit to the Finisterre Ranges*, Melbourne, Vic.: Oxford University Press, 2004

Braga, Stuart, *Kokoda Commander: A life of Major-General 'Tubby' Allen*, South Melbourne, Vic.: Oxford University Press, 2004

Brune, Peter, *Those Ragged, Bloody Heroes: From the Kokoda Track to Gona Beach, 1942*, Sydney: Allen & Unwin, 1991

——*Gona's Gone! The battle for the beachhead 1942*, Sydney: Allen & Unwin, 1994

——*The Spell Broken: Exploding the myth of Japanese invincibility*, Sydney: Allen & Unwin, 1997

——*We Band of Brothers: A biography of Ralph Honner, soldier and statesman*, Sydney: Allen & Unwin, 2000

——*A Bastard of a Place: The Australians in Papua*, Sydney: Allen & Unwin, 2003

Bushby, R.N., *'Educating an Army': Australian Army doctrinal development and the operational experience in South Vietnam, 1965–72*, Strategic and Defence Studies Centre, Australian National University, 1998

Carlyon, Les, *Gallipoli*, Sydney: Macmillan, 2001

Catell, Tim, *Gallipoli and All That: Illustrated blackline masters*, Wollongong, NSW: Dabill Publications, 2003

Chan, Gabrielle (ed.), *War on Our Doorstep: Diaries of Australians at the frontline in 1942*, South Yarra, Vic.: Hardie Grant, 2003

Chapman, Ivan, *Iven G. Mackay: Citizen and soldier*, Melbourne: Melway Publishing, 1975

Charlton, Peter, *The Thirty-Niners*, Melbourne: Macmillan, 1981

——*The Unnecessary War: Island campaigns of the South-West Pacific 1944–45*, Melbourne: Macmillan, 1983

Clisby, Mark, *Guilty or Innocent?: The Gordon Bennett Case*, Sydney: Allen & Unwin, 1992

Coates, John, *Bravery Above Blunder: The 9th Australian Division at Finschhafen, Sattelberg and Sio*, Melbourne: Oxford University Press, 1999

—— *An Atlas of Australia's Wars, vol. VII, The Australian Centenary History of Defence*, Melbourne: Oxford University Press, 2001
Cochrane, Peter, *Australians at War*, Sydney: ABC Books, 2001
Coombes, David, *Morshead: Hero of Tobruk and El Alamein*, Melbourne: Oxford University Press, 2001
Coulthard-Clark, Chris, *A Heritage of Spirit: A biography of Major-General Sir William Throsby Bridges*, Melbourne: Melbourne University Press, 1979
—— *Australia's Military Map-makers: The Royal Australian Survey Corps 1915–96*, Melbourne: Oxford University Press, 2000
Damousi, Joy and Lake, Marilyn (eds), *Gender and War: Australians at war in the twentieth century*, Cambridge, UK: Cambridge University Press, 1995
Damousi, Joy, *Living with the Aftermath: Trauma, nostalgia and grief in post-war Australia*, Cambridge: Cambridge University Press, 2001
Dandy, Philip, *The Kookaburra's Cutthroats, Volume One*, Highton, Vic.: Philip Dandy, 1995
Dawes, Allan, *'Soldier Superb': The Australian fights in New Guinea*, Sydney: F.H. Johnston, 1943
Day, David, *Menzies and Churchill at War*, Melbourne: Oxford University Press, 1993
—— *Reluctant Nation: The politics of war*, Sydney: HarperCollins, 2003
Dornan, Peter, *The Silent Men: Syria to Kokoda and on to Gona*, Sydney: Allen & Unwin, 1999
Dunn, J. B. 'Lofty', *Eagles Alighting: A history of the Australian Parachute Battalion*, East Malvern, Vic.: 1 Australian Parachute Battalion Association, 1999
Eather, Steve, *Desert Sands, Jungle Lands: A biography of Major-General Ken Eather*, Sydney: Allen & Unwin, 2003
—— *Warrior of Kokoda: A biography of Brigadier Arnold Potts*, Sydney: Allen & Unwin, 1999
Edwards, John K., *Curtin's Gift: Re-interpreting Australia's greatest prime minister*, Sydney: Allen & Unwin, 2005
Elphick, Peter, *The Pregnable Fortress: A study in deception, discord and desertion*, London: Hodder & Stoughton, 1996
Evans, Michael, *'Forward from the Past': The development of Australian Army doctrine, 1972–present*, Duntroon, ACT: Land Warfare Studies Centre, 1999
Farquhar, Murray, *Derrick, VC*, Adelaide: Rigby, 1982
Farrell, Brian, *The Defence and Fall of Singapore, 1940–1942*, Stroud, Gloucestershire: Tempus, 2005
Fearnside, G.H. and Clift, K., *Dougherty: A great man among men*, Sydney: Alpha Books, 1979
Finkmeyer, Colin E., *It Happened to Us: The unique experiences of 20 members of the 4th Anti-Tank Regiment*, Cheltenham, Vic: Self-published, 1994
Firkins, Peter, *The Australians in Nine Wars: Waikato to Long Tan*, London: Pan Books Ltd, 1973
Fitzgerald, Lawrence, *Lebanon to Labuan: A story of mapping by the Australian Survey Corps World War II (1939–1945)*, Melbourne: J.G. Holmes, 1980
FitzSimons, Peter, *Kokoda*, Sydney: Hodder, 2004

Forbes, Cameron, *Hellfire: The story of Australia, Japan and the prisoners of war*, Sydney: Macmillan, 2005
Frank, Richard, *Guadalcanal: The definitive account of the landmark battle*, New York: Random House, 1990
Galvin, John R. (General), 'Uncomfortable wars: Towards a new paradigm', in Max G. Manwaring (ed.), *Uncomfortable Wars: Towards a new paradigm of low intensity conflict*, Boulder, CO: Westview Press, 1991, pp. 9–18
Gamble, Bruce, *Darkest Hour: The true story of Lark Force at Rabaul—Australia's worst military disaster of World War II*, St Paul, MN: Zenith Press, 2006
Gammage, Bill, *The Broken Years*, Melbourne: Penguin, 1974
Gandhi, Leela, *Postcolonial Theory: A critical introduction*, Sydney: Allen & Unwin, 1998
Gardner, Lloyd C. and Young, Marilyn B. (eds), *Iraq and the Lessons of Vietnam or How Not to Learn from the Past*, New York: The New Press, 2007
Geddes, Margaret, *Blood, Sweat and Tears: Australia's WWII remembered by the men and women who lived it*, Camberwell, Vic.: Penguin, 2004
Geraghty, Tony, *Who Dares Wins: The story of the SAS, 1950–1980*, London: Fontana/Collins, 1981
Grant, Ian, *Jacka, VC: Australia's finest fighting soldier*, South Melbourne: Macmillan Australia, 1989
Grey, Jeffrey, *A Military History of Australia*, Cambridge: Cambridge University Press, 1999
——*The Australian Army, Vol. I, The Australian Centenary History of Defence*, Melbourne: Oxford University Press, 2001
Gullet, Henry 'Jo', *Not as a Duty Only: An infantryman's war*, Melbourne: Melbourne University Press, 1976
Hall, Robert A., *The Black Diggers: Aborigines and Torres Strait Islanders in the Second World War*, Sydney: Allen & Unwin, 1989
Ham, Paul, *Kokoda*, Sydney: HarperCollins, 2004
Hamilton, Nigel, *Monty: The making of a general 1887–1942*, London: Hamish Hamilton, 1981
Hamlyn-Harris, Geoffrey, *Through Mud and Blood to Victory*, Stanthorpe, Qld: self-published, 1993
Handel, Paul, *Dust, Sand and Jungle: A history of Australian armour during training and operations 1927–1948*, Hopkins Barracks, Puckapunyal, Vic.: RAAC Memorial and Army Tank Museum, 2003
Harrison, Courtney T., *Ambon: Island of mist—2/21st Battalion AIF (Gull Force) prisoners of war 1941–45*, North Geelong, Vic.: T.W. & C. T. Harrison, 1988
Hartley, Frank, *Sanananda Interlude*, Melbourne: Book Depot, 1949
Hetherington, John, *Blamey: The biography of Field-Marshal Sir Thomas Blamey*, Melbourne: F.W. Cheshire, 1954
Hillman, Robert, *The Kokoda Trail*, Carlton, Vic: Echidna Books, 2003
Holledge, James, *For Valour*, Melbourne: Horowitz, 1965
Hopkins, R.N.L., *Australian Armour: A history of the Royal Australian Armoured Corps 1927–1972*, Canberra: AWM, 1978

Horne, Donald, *Billy Hughes*, Melbourne: Bookman Press, 2000
Horner, David, *Crisis of Command: Australian generalship and the Japanese threat, 1941–1943*, Canberra: Australian National University Press, 1978
——*High Command: Australia and Allied strategy 1939–1945*, Sydney: Allen & Unwin, 1982
——(ed.), *The Commanders: Australian military leadership in the twentieth century*, Sydney: Allen & Unwin, 1984
——'Lieutenant-General Sir Vernon Sturdee: The chief of the general staff as commander', in David Horner (ed.), *The Commanders: Australian military leadership in the twentieth century*, Sydney: Allen & Unwin, 1984, pp. 143–58
——*SAS: Phantoms of the jungle*, Sydney: Allen & Unwin, 1989
——*General Vasey's War*, Melbourne: Melbourne University Press, 1992
——*The Gunners: A history of Australian artillery*, Sydney: Allen & Unwin, 1995
——*Blamey: Commander-in-chief*, Sydney: Allen & Unwin, 1998
——*Defence Supremo: Sir Frederick Shedden and the making of Australian defence policy*, Sydney: Allen & Unwin, 2000
James, Robert Rhodes, *Gallipoli*, London: Pimlico, 1999
Jenkin, Owen (ed.) *Little Hell: The story of the 2/22nd Battalion and Lark Force*, Blackburn, Vic.: History House, 2004
Johnson, William Bruce, *The Pacific Campaign in World War II: From Pearl Harbor to Guadalcanal*, London: Routledge 2006
Johnston, Mark, *At The Front Line: Experiences of Australian soldiers in World War II*, Cambridge: Cambridge University Press, 1996
——*Fighting the Enemy: Australian soldiers and their adversaries in World War II*, Cambridge: Cambridge University Press, 2000
——and Stanley, Peter, *Alamein: The Australian story*, Melbourne: Oxford University Press, 2002
——*That Magnificent 9th: An illustrated history of the 9th Australian Division 1940–46*, Sydney: Allen & Unwin, 2002
——*The Silent 7th: An illustrated history of the 7th Australian Division 1940–46*, Sydney: Allen & Unwin, 2005
Keating, Gavin, *The Right Man for the Right Job: Lieutenant-General Sir Stanley Savige as a military commander*, South Melbourne, Vic.: Oxford University Press, 2006
Keogh, E.G. (Col.), *The South West Pacific 1941–45*, Melbourne: Grayflower Productions, 1965
Kidd, Reg and Neal, Ray, *The 'Letter' Batteries: The history of the 'letter' batteries in World War II*, Castlecrag, NSW: Neal & Kidd, 1998
Kier, Elizabeth, *Imagining War: French and British military doctrine between the wars*, Princeton, NJ: Princeton University Press, 1997
King, Jonathon, *Gallipoli Diaries: The Anzacs' own stories day by day*, East Roseville, NSW: Kangaroo Press, 2002
Kingsford-Smith, Rollo, *I Wouldn't Have Missed It for Quids*, self-published, 1999
Kuring, Ian, *Redcoats to Cams: A history of Australian infantry, 1788–2001*, Loftus, NSW: Australian Military History Publications, 2004
Laffin, John, *Anzacs at War*, London: Horowitz, 1965

Lambert, Eric, *The Twenty Thousand Thieves*, Melbourne: Newmont, 1951

Lee, Norman E., *John Curtin: Saviour of Australia*, Melbourne: Longman Cheshire, 1983

Legg, Frank, *War Correspondent*, Adelaide: Rigby, 1964

——*The Gordon Bennett Story*, Sydney: Angus & Robertson, 1965

Lindsay, Patrick, *The Spirit of Kokoda: Then and now*, Melbourne: Hardie Grant Books, 2002

——*The Spirit of the Digger: Then and now*, Sydney: Macmillan, 2003

——*The Essence of Kokoda*, Melbourne: Hardie Grant Books, 2005

Lodge, A.B., *The Fall of General Gordon Bennett*, Sydney: Allen & Unwin, 1988

McAulay, Lex, *Blood and Iron: The battle for Kokoda 1942*, Sydney: Arrow Books, 1991

——*To the Bitter End: The Japanese defeat at Buna and Gona 1942–43*, Sydney: Arrow Books, 1992

McCullagh, C.B., *The Truth of History*, London: Routledge, 1998

McDonald, Neil, *Damien Parer's War*, South Melbourne: Lothian Books, 2004

——and Brune, Peter, *200 Shots: Damien Parer and George Silk with the Australians at War in New Guinea*, Sydney: Allen & Unwin, 2004

Macdougall, Anthony, *Gallipoli and the Middle East, 1915–18*, Port Melbourne, Vic: Moondrake, 2004

McKernan, Michael, *All In: Australia during the Second World War*, Melbourne: Thomas Nelson, 1983

Macklin, Robert, *Jacka VC: Australian hero*, Sydney: Allen & Unwin, 2006

McNeill, Ian, *The Team: Australian Army advisers in Vietnam, 1962–72*, St Lucia, QLD: University of Queensland Press/AWM, 1984

McNicoll, R.R. (Maj-Gen.), *Ubique: The Royal Australian Engineers 1919 to 1945—Teeth and tail*, Canberra: Corps Committee of the Royal Australian Engineers, 1982

Mallett, Ross, 'Logistics in the South-West Pacific 1943–1944', in Peter Dennis and Jeffrey Grey (eds), *The Foundations of Victory: The Pacific War*, The Chief of Army's Military History Conference 2003, Canberra: Army History Unit, 2003, pp. 102–17

Moremon, John, 'No "black magic": Doctrine and training for jungle warfare', in Peter Dennis and Jeffrey Grey (eds), *The Foundations of Victory: The Pacific War*, The Chief of Army's Military History Conference 2003, Canberra: Army History Unit, 2004, pp. 76–85

Malone, J.M. (ed.), *SAS: A pictorial history of the Australian Special Air Service 1957–97*, Northbridge, WA: Access Press, 1997

Marcus, Alex, *'DEMS? What's DEMS?' The story of the men of the Royal Australian Navy who manned defensively equipped merchant ships during World War II*, Brisbane: Boolarong Publications, 1986

Morrison, Ian, *Malayan Postscript*, Kuala Lumpur: S. Abdul Majeed, 1993

Morton, Louis, *Strategy and Command: The first two years*, Washington, DC: Center of Military History, US Army, 1965 (2000 reprint)

Norris, F. Kingsley, *No Memory for Pain: An autobiography*, Melbourne: William Heinemann, 1970

O'Brien, Michael, *Australian Army Instructional Tactical Books & Pamphlets: A bibliography*, Loftus, NSW: Australian Military History Publications, 2002

Overy, Richard, *Why the Allies Won*, London: Pimlico, 2006
Palazzo, Albert, *The Australian Army: A history of its organisation 1901–2001*, Melbourne: Oxford University Press, 2001
——*Defenders of Australia: The Third Australian Division, 1916–1991*, Loftus, NSW: Australian Military History Publications, 2002
——'Organising for jungle warfare', in Peter Dennis and Jeffrey Grey (eds), *The Foundations of Victory: The Pacific War*, The Chief of Army's Military History Conference 2003, Canberra: Army History Unit, 2003, pp. 86–101
Pedersen, Peter, 'The AIF on the Western Front: The role of training and command', in M. McKernan and M. Browne (eds), *Australia: Two centuries of war and peace*, Sydney: Allen & Unwin, 1988, pp. 167–93
Perry, Roland, *Monash: The outsider who won a war—A biography of Australia's greatest military commander*, Sydney: Random House, 2004
Perrett, Bryan, *Canopy of War: Jungle warfare, from the earliest days of forest fighting to the battlefields of Vietnam*, Wellingborough: Patrick Stephens, 1990
Perversi, Frank G., *From Tobruk to Borneo: Memoirs of an Italian Aussie volunteer*, Kenthurst, NSW: Rosenberg Publications, 2002
Pitt, Barrie, *The Crucible of War: Western Desert 1941*, London: Futura, 1980
Poole, P., *Of Love and War: The letters and war diaries of Captain Adrian Curlewis and his family, 1939–1945*, Sydney: Lansdowne Press, 1982
Powell, Alan, *The Third Force: ANGAU's New Guinea war, 1942–46*, Melbourne: Oxford University Press, 2003
Pratten, Garth, *Australian Battalion Commanders in the Second World War*, Melbourne: Cambridge University Press, 2009
Raggett, Sidney George, *All About Sid: The story of a gunner in World War II*, Mornington, Vic.: self-published, 1991
Robertson, John, 'The distant war: Australia and Imperial Defence, 1919–41', in M. McKernan and M. Browne (eds), *Australia: Two centuries of war and peace*, Sydney: Allen & Unwin, 1988, pp. 223–44
Rogal, William W., *Guadalcanal, Tarawa and Beyond: A mud marine's memoir of the Pacific Island War*, Jefferson, NC: McFarland, 2010
Rolleston, Frank, *Not a Conquering Hero: The siege of Tobruk, the battles of Milne Bay, Buna, Shaggy Ridge*, Mackay, Qld: F. Rolleston, 1995
Rolley, Ailsa, *Survival on Ambon*, Qld: Ailsa Rolley, 1994
Rose, Angus, *Who Dies Fighting*, London: Jonathan Cape, 1944
Ross, A.R. (Capt) (ed.), *The Magazine of 17 Australian Infantry Brigade 1939–1944*, Melbourne: 17th Australian Infantry Brigade, 1944
Ross, A.T., *Armed and Ready: The industrial development and defence of Australia 1900–1945*, Sydney: Turton & Armstrong, 1995
Rothenberg, Gunther E., *The Napoleonic Wars*, London: Cassell, 1999
Rowell, Sydney, *Full Circle*, Melbourne: Melbourne University Press, 1974
Rowley, C.D., *The Australians in German New Guinea, 1914–1921*, Melbourne: Melbourne University Press, 1958
Ryan, Peter, *Fear Drive My Feet*, Sydney: Angus & Robertson, 1959
Serle, Geoffrey, *John Monash: A biography*, Melbourne: Melbourne University Press, 1982

Shadbolt, Maurice, *Voices of Gallipoli*, Sydney: Ling Publishing, 2001
Sharpe, Jim, 'History from below', in P. Burke (ed.), *New Perspectives on Historical Writing*, University Park, PA: Pennsylvania State University Press, 1991, pp. 25–42
Smith, Adele Shelton (ed.), *The Boys Write Home*, Sydney: Australian Women's Weekly, 1944
Smith, Kevin, *The Owen Gun Files: An Australian wartime controversy*, Sydney: Turton & Armstrong, 1994
Spector, Ronald H., *Eagle Against the Sun: The American war against Japan*, London: Cassell, 2000
Stanley, Peter, *Tarakan: An Australian tragedy*, Sydney: Allen & Unwin, 1997
——'The green hole reconsidered', in Peter Dennis and Jeffrey Grey (eds), *The Foundations of Victory: The Pacific War, 1943–44*, The Chief of Army's Military History Conference 2003, Canberra: Army History Unit, 2003, pp. 202–11
Starr, Alison, *Neville Howse VC: Biography of an authentic Australian hero*, Sydney: Les Baddock & Sons, 1991
Steel, Nigel, *Battleground Europe: Gallipoli*, London: Leo Cooper, 1999
Steward, H.D., *Recollections of a Regimental Medical Officer*, Melbourne: Melbourne University Press, 1983
Sublet, Frank, *Kokoda to the Sea: A history of the 1942 campaign in Papua*, McCrae, Vic.: Slouch Hat Publications, 2000
Sweeney, Tony, *Malaria Frontline: Australian Army research during World War II*, Melbourne: Melbourne University Press, 2003
Taafe, Stephen, *MacArthur's Jungle War: The 1944 New Guinea campaigns*, Lawrence: University Press of Kansas, 1998
Tarlington, George, *Shifting Sands and Savage Jungle*, Loftus, NSW: Australian Military History Publications, 1994
Taylor, C.R., *I Sustain the Wings: A history of No. II Repair and Servicing Unit, RAAF, 1942–45*, Burwood, Vic.: self-published, 1992
Tone, John Lawrence, *The Fatal Knot: The guerrilla war in Navarre and the defeat of Napoleon in Spain*, Chapel Hill: North Carolina Press, 1994
Tsuji, Masanobu, *Singapore: The Japanese version*, Sydney: Ure Smith, 1960
Tyquin, Michael B., *Neville Howse: Australia's first Victoria Cross winner*, Melbourne, Oxford University Press, 1999
Uhr, Janet, *Against the Sun: The AIF in Malaya, 1941–42*, Sydney: Allen & Unwin, 1998
Various, *Signals: Story of the Australian Corps of Signals*, Canberra: AWM, 1945
Vincent, John, *An Intelligent Person's Guide to History*, London: Duckworth, 1996
Warner, Phillip, *The Special Air Service*, London: Sphere Books, 1982
Warren, Alan, *Singapore 1942: Britain's greatest defeat*, South Yarra, Vic.: Hardie Grant Books, 2002
Welburn, M.C.J., 'The development of Australian Army Doctrine, 1945–1964', Strategic and Defence Studies Centre: Australian National University, 1994
Wells, H.D., *'B' Company Second Seventeenth Infantry*, Toowoon Bay, NSW: H.D. Wells, 1984
White, Osmar, *Green Armour*, Sydney: Angus & Robertson, 1945

Whitney, Courtney, *MacArthur: His rendezvous with history*, New York: Knopf, 1955
Wigmore, Lionel and Harding, Bruce (eds), *They Dared Mightily*, Canberra: AWM, 1963
Winton, Harold and Mets, David (eds), *The Challenge of Change: Military institutions and new realities, 1918–1941*, Lincoln, Nebraska: University of Nebraska Press, 2000

(d) Journal articles

Body, O.G. (Capt), 'Bush and forest fighting against modern weapons', *The Army Quarterly*, vol. viii, no. 2, July 1924, pp. 314–24

Braddock, H. Phillip (Capt), 'A story of Army Air Co-Operation in the Second World War', *Journal of the Royal United Services Institute of Australia*, vol. 17, Nov 1996, pp. 61–71

Dean, Peter, 'The forgotten man: Lieut-General Sir Frank Berryman', *Journal of the Australian War Memorial*, no. 37, October 2002 [no pagination.]

Dening, Major B.C., 'Modern problems of guerrilla warfare', *The Army Quarterly*, vol. xiii, no. 2, Jan 1927, pp. 347–53

Editorial Staff, 'Sherlock of the Sixth', *The Australian Army Journal*, no. 49, June 1953, pp. 5–10

Editorial Staff, 'The Battle of Milne Bay', *The Australian Army Journal*, no. 50, July 1953, pp. 22–38

Gow, Neil, 'Australian Army Strategic Planning 1919–39', *Australian Journal of Politics and History*, vol. xxiii, no. 2, Aug 1977, pp. 169–72

Henning, Peter, 'Tasmanians in Timor 1941–42: "A magnificent display of very bad strategy"', *The Journal of the Australian War Memorial*, no. 5, October 1984, pp. 15–25

Norrie Jones, 'Eyewitness: 1st Battery, 2/1st Field Regiment', *Wartime: Official Magazine of the Australian War Memorial*, issue 40, Nov 2007 pp. 40–2

Kaplan, Lawrence, 'Clear and fold: Forgetting the lessons of Vietnam', *New Republic*, vol. 233, issue 25, 19 December 2005, pp. 12–15

Kennedy, D.M. (Capt), 'The Japanese Army as a fighting force', *The Army Quarterly*, vol. XXX, no. 2, July 1935, pp. 231–40

Lavarack, J.D. (Col.), 'The defence of the British Empire, with special reference to the Far East and Australia', *The Army Quarterly*, vol. xxv, no. 2, January 1933, pp. 207–17

Mullaly, B.R. (Brevet Major), 'The evolution of the Japanese Army', *The Army Quarterly*, vol. xvi, no. 1, April 1928, pp. 52–64

Nelson, Hank, 'Travelling in memories: Australian prisoners of the Japanese, forty years after the fall of Singapore', *Journal of the Australian War Memorial*, no. 3, Oct 1983, pp. 13–24

——'Kokoda: The Track from history to politics', *Journal of Pacific History*, vol. 38, no. 1, 2003, pp. 109–27

Piggott, Michael, 'Stonewalling in German New Guinea', *Journal of the Australian War Memorial*, no. 12, April 1988, pp. 3–15

Raudzens, George, 'Testing the air power expectations of the Kokoda Campaign, July to September 1942', *Journal of the Australian War Memorial*, no. 21, October 1992, pp. 20–9

Reinhold, W.J. (Lt-Col.), 'The Bulldog–Wau Road: An epic of military engineering', *Australian Army Journal*, no. 4, Dec 1948–Jan 1949, pp. 16–21

Robertson, H.C.H. (Maj.), 'The defence of Australia', *The Army Quarterly*, vol. xxx, no. 1, April 1935, pp. 15–33

Robinson, R.E.R. (Maj.), 'Reflections of a company commander in Malaya', *The Army Quarterly*, vol. lxi, October 1950, pp. 80–87

Shindo, Hiroyuki, 'Japanese air operations over New Guinea during the Second World War', *Journal of the Australian War Memorial*, no. 34, June 2001 [no pagination.]

Simington, Margot, 'The southwest Pacific islands in Australian interwar defence planning', *Australian Journal of Politics and History*, vol. xxiii, no. 2, August 1977, pp. 173–7

Stevens, David, 'The naval campaigns for New Guinea', *Journal of the Australian War Memorial*, no. 34, June 2001 [no pagination]

Vickery, C.E. (Lt-Col.), 'Small wars', *The Army Quarterly*, vol. vi, no. 2, July 1923, pp. 307–17

Von Schmidt, Eric, 'The Alamo remembered—From a painter's point of view', *Smithsonian*, March 1986, vol. 16, pp. 54–67

Williams, Peter D. and Nakagawa, Naoko, 'The Japanese 18th Army in New Guinea', *Wartime: Official Magazine of the Australian War Memorial*, no. 36, September 2006, pp. 58–63

6. UNPUBLISHED MANUSCRIPTS AND THESES

Blair, Dale, '"An Army of Warriors, These Anzacs": Legend and illusion in the First AIF', PhD thesis, Victoria University of Technology, 1997

Hamilton, Rod, 'A History of Canungra', [unpublished manuscript] 2002 [copy forwarded from Australian Army Training Team Association, Queensland Branch]

Lithgow, Shirley, 'Special Operations: The organisation of Special Operations Executive in Australia and their operations against the Japanese during WWII', PhD thesis, ADFA, 1992

Lovejoy, Valerie, 'Mapmakers of Fortune: A history of the Army Survey Regiment', MA thesis, La Trobe University, 2000

Moremon, John, '"Most Deadly Jungle Fighters?": The Australian infantry in Malaya and Papua, 1941–43', Honours thesis, University of New England, 1992

Moremon, John, '"A Triumph of Improvisation": Australian Army operational logistics and the campaign in Papua, July 1942 to January 1943', PhD thesis, UNSW, 2000

Moreman, Tim, 'Jungle, Japanese and the Australian Army: Learning the lessons of New Guinea', paper presented to the *Remembering the War in New Guinea* symposium, Australian National University, 19–21 October 2000, on the Australia–Japan Research Project/AWM website [no pagination]

Rickards, D.G.M., 'Eighty-two Years of Life's Recollections', [unpublished memoir] 2001, Battalion Military Archive, Brisbane, Qld, quoted in Gordon Dickens, *Never Late: The 2/9th Australian Infantry Battalion 1939–1945*, Loftus, NSW: Australian Military History Publications, 2005

Parkin, Russell, 'Learning While Fighting: The evolution of Australian Close Air Support doctrine 1939–1945,' PhD thesis, UNSW, 1999

Sholl, John George, 'Points Noted and Lessons Learnt: The nature and determinants of Australian Army tactical changes 1941–1943', Honours thesis, ADFA, 1991

Tonna, David, 'Wantok Warriors: An analysis of the activities of the Pacific Islands Regiment in Papua New Guinea during the Second World War', Honours thesis, ADFA, 1993

Zwillenberg, Hans, 'The Logistics Infrastructure of the Australian Army 1939–1945', MA Thesis, ADFA, 1993

INDEX

ABDACOM 56, 64
Advanced Dressing Station 110
Afrika Korps 19, 57
aircraft
  B-24 Liberator 229
  DC-3 172
  P-38 Lightning 229
  P-40 Kittyhawk 111
  Wirraway 172
  Zero fighter 60
Aitape–Wewak campaign 199, 212, 223, 228
Akuressa *see* 17th Brigade Tactical School, Ceylon
Allan, Maj. Herbert 161–2
Allen, Maj-Gen. Arthur 'Tubby' 121, 127, 130, 139, 161, 212
Alola 183
Ambon 13, 39–40, 41–2
Amor, Pte Benjamin 40
Anderson, Maj. Charles 27–9, 52–3
Armoured Fighting Vehicle School 201
Armstrong, Pte John 58
Army Headquarters 28, 39, 42, 45, 59, 94
Army Training Memoranda 68, 80, 83, 91–2, 94, 137, 176, 185–7, 192
Arnold, Col Arthur 111
Atherton Tableland 157, 159, 180, 207–9, 230

6th Division and 190
7th Division and 217, 220–1
9th Division and 162, 212
Austen sub-machine gun 181
Australian Army 1, 3, 14
Australian Army Land HQ Medical Research Unit 6
Australian Army Training Centre (Jungle Warfare) *see* Jungle Warfare Training Centre (Canungra)
Australian Army units and formations
  2nd AIF 14, 17, 37, 57, 85, 103, 209, 222
  I Corps 76, 81, 90, 150, 167
  II Corps 163, 174, 181, 191
  III Corps 91
  3rd Division 163, 174, 216, 225
  5th Division 181
  6th Division 14–18, 21, 24–5, 37, 46, 123, 161
    Ceylon 55–61
    training in Australia 1942 81, 86, 88, 94
    Atherton Tableland 180, 190–1, 194–5
    Aitape–Wewak 216, 226, 228
  7th Division 6, 16, 21, 42, 57, 159, 161–5, 169–70, 173
    training in Australia 1942 75–8, 80, 84, 86, 90–5

Australian Army units and formations *continued*
  Kokoda campaign 97, 102, 104, 114, 117–18, 120–9, 132
  Beachheads campaign 150, 156
  Atherton Tableland 176, 181, 183–6, 190–2, 194, 202–6
  Ramu–Markham campaign 209–11, 213–14
  final campaigns 217–20, 228
8th Division 2, 13, 22, 61, 63–4, 81, 85, 123, 161, 163
  Malayan campaign 23–9, 31–7, 45, 50–2, 54, 58
9th Division 16, 21
  training in Middle East 157, 159–62
  training on Atherton Tableland 1943 169, 181, 184, 187, 196–7, 200
  Lae–Finschhafen campaign 202–7, 210–14, 216–17
  training on Atherton Tableland 1944 221–2, 226
  Borneo campaign 228
11th Division 181
4th Australian Armoured Brigade 202, 216
7th Brigade 99, 106
14th Brigade 156
16th Brigade 35
  Ceylon 59–60, 62, 66, 68–70, 73
  Kokoda Track 94, 109, 123, 125, 128–30
  Atherton Tableland 180, 192
17th Brigade 15, 18, 35, 91, 199, 211, 219, 226
  training on Ceylon 55, 57–9, 61–2, 66–7, 71–3, 78, 147–8, 152
  Wau–Salamaua campaign 158, 162–5, 168–9, 172–5, 177
18th Brigade
  training in Australia 1942 84, 89, 93
  Milne Bay 105–10, 112–14, 122, 124

Beachheads 145–7, 151, 155, 157 161
training on Atherton Tableland 1943 193, 202–3
Ramu–Markham campaign 217, 220
19th Brigade 59, 177, 227
20th Brigade 161–2, 204–5, 216
21st Brigade 42, 138, 140
  training in Australia 1942 75, 82–3, 86–8, 91, 93–5
  Port Moresby 98–106, 115
  Kokoda campaign 117–18, 120–1, 123, 125–6, 128–30, 133
  training on Atherton Tableland 1943 180, 184, 203, 205
22nd Brigade 22, 24–5, 28–9, 33, 35
23rd Brigade 28
24th Brigade 161, 228
25th Brigade
  training in Australia 1942 82, 84–5, 88, 91, 93
  Kokoda Track 120, 128–9, 131–2
  Beachheads 146–7
  training on Atherton Tableland 1943 187–8, 195
26th Brigade 204, 212, 215, 224, 228
27th Brigade 22, 28
30th Brigade 98–9, 121, 132, 156
2/4th Armoured Regiment 227
2/5th Armoured Regiment 152
2/6th Armoured Regiment 152
2/8th Armoured Regiment 202
2/9th Armoured Regiment 201
13th Field Artillery Regiment 112
14th Field Artillery Regiment 112
2/1st Field Regiment 16
2/2nd Field Regiment 16, 18
2/3rd Field Regiment 197–8
2/4th Field Regiment 87, 198, 218
2/5th Field Regiment 111–12, 114
2/6th Field Regiment 91, 115, 200, 214
2/10th Field Regiment 34
2/12th Field Regiment 214, 221

INDEX

2/15th Field Regiment 32
4th Anti-Tank Regiment 33
1st Mountain Battery 170, 173
2/6th Field Company RAE 89, 195
2/8th Field Company RAE 15, 168
2/13th Field Company RAE 215
2/1st Independent Company 79
2/5th Independent Company 105
2/1st Battalion 15, 67, 69, 129–30, 204, 226
2/2nd Battalion 35, 62, 65, 67, 70, 124–5, 130–1, 191–2
2/3rd Battalion 15, 58, 227
2/4th Battalion 227
2/5th Battalion 67, 72, 165, 167
2/6th Battalion 63, 163, 176, 178
2/7th Battalion 61–9, 163–8
2/9th Battalion 97, 107, 111, 147, 152
2/10th Battalion 75, 82, 92, 153, 180
2/11th Battalion 212
2/12th Battalion 20, 77, 109–10, 154, 220
2/13th Battalion 161, 211–12
2/14th Battalion 80, 90, 94
   Kokoda campaign 100, 104–5, 115, 117, 121–2, 125
   Gona 150
   training on Atherton Tableland 180, 182
   training teams 204
   Ramu–Markham campaign 218
2/16th Battalion 77, 94, 98–9, 120, 131, 180–1, 193
2/18th Battalion 24, 30, 32, 34
2/19th Battalion 23, 27, 29–30, 32
2/20th Battalion 32, 34
2/21st Battalion 38–40, 42
2/22nd Battalion 38, 42–5, 60
2/24th Battalion 205, 212
2/25th Battalion 94
2/27th Battalion 77–8, 81, 97, 103, 115, 149, 196
2/28th Battalion 19, 162, 204
2/29th Battalion 38, 51
2/30th Battalion 24, 46, 51–2

2/31st Battalion 119–20
2/32nd Battalion 213
2/33rd Battalion 92, 129, 132, 229
2/40th Battalion 24, 38–40, 42, 93
2/48th Battalion 215
2/2nd Machine Gun Battalion 211
2/3rd Machine Gun Battalion 227
24th Battalion 90
25th Battalion 109
36th Battalion 151
37/52nd Battalion 211
39th Battalion 42, 100, 118, 121–2, 135, 150
53rd Battalion 123
2/1st Field Ambulance 70
7th Division Field Companies 117
17th Brigade Pack Transport Unit 169
Australian Infantry Training Battalions 142
Australian Instructional Corps 14
Australian Naval & Military Expeditionary Force 5–6, 11
Australian Navy 8
Australian New Guinea Administrative Unit (ANGAU) 98, 103–4, 121
Australian Recruit Training Centre, Cowra 18
Australian Training Centre (Jungle Warfare) Canungra see Jungle Warfare Training Centre (Canungra)
Australian War Memorial 3

baboons 34
Bakri 52
Baldwin, Pte Raymond 218
Balikpapan 209, 216, 228–9
Ballams 164
Bardia 17–18
Bataan 56
Beachheads campaign 181, 184–5, 193, 200, 209, 214, 220
Bean, Charles 6
Beaumont, Joan 40
Beenleigh 142, 175–6, 178, 202, 207, 229

Bennett, Capt Cam 67
Bennett, Maj.-Gen. Gordon 3, 130, 187
  Malaya 24–5, 30–1, 33, 50–5, 63
  return to Australia 80, 83, 89
  training manual 91, 94–5
Berryman, Lt-Gen. Frank 144, 161
Bidstrup, Capt M.L. 100, 135
Black Cat Track 148, 169
Blackall Ranges 78
Blackburn, Cpl Andy 171
Blackburn, Col Arthur 75
Blamey, Gen. Thomas 16, 37, 91, 144, 150, 160–1, 212
  and Kokoda campaign 93, 117, 121, 127, 129–30
blitzkrieg 53
Boase, Lt-Gen. Allan 185, 189–90, 224
Boer War 12
Booth, Pte William 15
Borneo 2, 34
Bougainville 2
Boys anti-tank rifle 15, 66
Bren light machine gun 15, 17, 46, 70, 81–2, 129, 188, 192, 227
Bren-gun carrier *see* Universal Carrier
Brigade Hill 121, 126, 138
Brink, Lt-Col Francis G. 63–4, 80, 95, 187
Brisbane LHQ 140, 147, 185
British Army 12, 15, 28, 64, 131, 231
British Army units 26, 29, 48, 61, 75, 81
British War Office 10
Brune, Peter 130, 155
Brunei Bay 228
Buin Road 216
Buna 2, 67, 77, 88
  armour at 201–3
  Battle of 110, 133–4, 146, 149, 151–5, 173
  Japanese bunkers at 220
  sound ranging 225
  9th Division trains at 211
Buttrose, Lt-Col Alfred 132

Canberra 57
Canungra *see* Jungle Warfare Training Centre (Canungra)

Cape Endaiadere–Giropa Point 154, 201
Caroline Islands 5
Catalina flying boat 79
CBI 57
Central Training Depot 9, 14
Ceylon 35, 78, 81–2, 85–8, 94, 123, 147–8, 187
  6th Division training on 55–73, 152, 161, 168
Charlton, Peter 124
Chilton, Brig. Fred 220
China 11–12
Churchill, Winston 25, 56–7
Citizen Military Forces (Militia) 6, 9, 14
Coates, Lt-Gen. John 159, 189, 214
Cochrane, Peter 7
Colenso, Pte Frank 30
Colombo 57, 59–60
Connor, Pte George 92
Cook, Pte Lesley 207
Cooper, Lt-Col Geoff 149
Coral Sea, Battle of 74, 79
Cremor, Lt-Col William 72
Crete 2, 37, 175
Crystal Creek 148, 169
Curtin, John 56–7
Curtis, Cpl Owen 20, 107, 109

Darwin 38–40, 56, 59–60, 79
Dawkins, Maj. Clarence 25–6, 30, 50
Director of Military Training 63, 140, 221
Directorate of Military Training 50, 143
Dumpu 218
Duropa Plantation 151–2
Dutch East Indies 13, 56, 139

Eather, Brig. Ken 90, 129, 188, 228
Echunga 77, 162
Egypt 2, 15, 24, 68, 162
Eichelberger, Gen. Robert 150

INDEX

El Alamein 160, 226
Enterprise, USS 146
Eora Creek 121, 131, 189
Europe 8, 10–11, 25–7, 30, 36, 49, 83, 233

Fairbrother, Capt Donald 191
Far East 9–10, 57, 64
Ferguson, Capt Ian 191
Field Ambulance 66, 70, 110, 218
Field Drill for Rifle Battalions (1938) 20
Field Service Regulations (1935) 12, 19, 143, 186
First World War 2, 5–8, 11, 15–16, 26–7, 53, 149, 196
Fleay, Maj. Norman 105
Formosa 48
forward observation officer 112–13, 170–1, 173, 200

Galleghan, Lt-Col Frederick 'Black Jack' 52
Gallipoli 53, 220
Galvin, Gen. John 90
Gemas 51
Gili Gili 106
Golden Staircase 105
Gona 2, 134, 146, 149–50, 152–5, 189, 201
Goodenough Island 11
Grant M3 medium tank 152–3, 202
Greece 2, 58, 175
Greek campaign 37, 134
Green Sniper's Pimple 219
Grey, Jeffrey 21
Guadalcanal 79, 96–7, 126, 133–4, 139, 145–6
Guerrilla Warfare School 142
Guinn, Lt-Col Henry 59
Gull Force 40–1

Handel, Paul 201
Hansen, Pte Ronald 97
Hartley, Padre Frank 154

Haupt, Capt Fred 220
Heldsbach plantation 215
Henderson Field 145
Henning, Peter 24
Herbertshohe 5
Hermes, HMS 60
Herring, Lt-Gen. Edmund 150, 167
Hopkins, Brig. Ronald N.L. 201
Horii, Gen. Tomitaro 133, 146
Hornet, USS 146
Howell, Pte Charles 108
HQ Buna Force 153
HQ RAE 194–5
Huggins Road Block 151, 154
Huon Peninsula 157, 210

Ichiki, Col Kiyonao 126
Imamura, Gen Hitoshi 146
Imita Ridge 98, 117, 123, 125, 133–4
Imperial Conference 8–9
Imperial Japanese Army *see* Japanese Army
Imperial Japanese Navy *see* Japanese Navy
Infantry Minor Tactics 1941 Australia 20, 61, 119–20, 143, 186–8
Infantry Training (Training and War) 1937 12–13, 19, 38, 43, 47, 81, 186, 204, 223–4
Ingleburn, NSW 15, 30
Inoue, Admiral Shigeyoshi 80
Irving, Brig. Ronnie 140, 221
Isaachsen, Lt-Col Oscar 151
Isurava 117–18, 121–2, 125
Itiki 99, 104, 117

Japan 8, 10–12
Japanese Army 1, 8, 10, 21–4, 28, 111, 135, 139–40, 231–3
  Malayan Campaign 34, 39–42, 45–9, 51–5
  Ceylon 57–60, 62–5, 71–3
  training in Australia to repel 74–81, 89, 91–2

Japanese Army *continued*
  Papuan campaign 96–110
  Milne Bay 108–14
  Kokoda 115–35
  Guadalcanal 145–6
  Beachheads 146–9, 150–9
  9th Division training to meet 160–2
  17th Brigade opposed to at Wau 164–74
  training at Atherton Tableland to meet 182–91
  armoured training for 200–1, 207–8
  Lae–Finschhafen 211–19
  Shaggy Ridge 219–21
  final campaigns 223–8
Japanese Navy 79, 146
Java 75
Jeeps 135, 169, 184, 199, 212, 218
Jimna Ranges 77
Jones, Pte Edmond 111
Juki medium machine gun 101
Jungle Division 53, 183, 194, 200, 225, 232
Jungle Warfare Training Centre (Canunga) 18, 55, 76, 98, 123, 132
  establishment 140–8, 157–8, 175–9
  operation of 207, 210, 222, 229, 232–3
Just, Capt Mal 109

Kakakog 212
Kanga Force 58, 73, 105, 167, 170, 172
Kapooka 195
Kappe, Maj. Charles 25
Katukurunda 60
Keatinge, Brig. Maurice 141
Kienzle, Capt Bert 121
Kilcoy 78, 82
Killerton Track 154
Kingsley-Norris, Col Frank 192
Koitaki 117, 128
Kollmorgen, Cpl Fred 43
Kuring, Ian 10, 189, 210

Labuan Island 216, 228
Lae 42, 194
Lae–Finschhafen campaign 169, 200–2, 205–6, 208–12, 224
Laffin, John 188
Leggatt, Maj. Bill 44
Lewis light machine gun 15
Lexington, USS 80
LHQ Tactical School (Beenleigh) 142, 176, 178, 229
LHQ Training Centre (Jungle Warfare) *see* Jungle Warfare Training Centre (Jungle Warfare) Canungra
LHQ Training Teams 145–6, 157, 177, 179, 207, 229
Libya 17
Lind, Brig. Edmund 39
Lodge, A.B. 53
Lowanna 141
Lunn, Maj. T.T. 177

MacArthur, Gen. Douglas 56, 90, 117, 150, 212
McAulay, Lex 155
McCarthy, Dudley 11, 131
MacDonald, Lt-Col A.B. 'Bandy' 143
Macfarlane, Capt Alan 204–5
McGowan, Col John 196
Mackay, Lt-Gen. Iven 10
McLellan, Pte Arch 17
McNevin, Bdr Allen 34
McRostie, Pte Colin 131
Madeley, Pte Joe 211
malaria 6, 83, 96, 99, 166, 180, 221
  anti-malarial treatment 192, 218, 227
  Malaya 21, 26–7
  Milne Bay 106–7, 110, 112, 143, 148, 151, 163
Malaya 2, 18, 22
Malayan Emergency 210, 233
Manning, Lt Lew 61
Marshall, Col Frank 202
Mason, Lt Lindsay 82, 123
Matilda Infantry tanks 201–2, 215–16, 227

INDEX

Maxwell, Brig. Duncan 47, 52
Mediterranean Theatre 1, 37, 81, 119, 165, 171, 231
Menzies, Robert 233
Middle East 1, 3, 11, 14, 16, 18, 21
Midway, Battle of 74, 80, 90, 146
Military Training Pamphlet No. 9 (India) Extensive Warfare—Notes on Forest Warfare 28, 64
Military Training Pamphlet Operations (Australia) No. 23 XX Jungle Warfare 143
Milne Bay 2, 42, 55, 76–7, 146, 150, 173, 205–6, 234
    artillery at 84–5
    18th Brigade at 97–9, 105–6, 109–15, 122
    17th Brigade training at 147–9, 163–4, 168
    lessons of 128, 132–4, 139–43, 155, 158, 161, 168, 189, 200
    9th Division trains at 211, 215
Moreman, Tim 189
Moremon, John 59
Morris, Maj.-Gen. Basil 100, 104, 126
Morshead, Lt-Gen. Leslie 160, 202, 216
Moten, Brig. Murray 71, 148, 167, 177
Muar–Bakri, Battle of 52
Mubo 176
Myola 117, 121, 126

Nadzab 194, 206, 217–18
Nauru 5
Nazi Germany 11
Nelson, Hank 98
Neosho, USS 80
New Britain 5–6
    2/22nd Battalion on 38, 42–3, 45
    Japanese base 80, 97
    militia campaign 135, 223
New Caledonia 97
New Guinea 2, 11, 21
New Guinea Force Headquarters 95, 100
New Guinea Volunteer Rifles 105

New South Wales 2, 7
Nimitz, Admiral Chester 79
North African Theatre 1, 20–1
Northcott, Gen. John 182

Oboe One 216
observation post officers 214, 224
Observations on the New Guinea Campaign 127
Old Strip 151, 154
Owen Gun 179–80, 220
Owen Stanley Ranges 41, 77, 82, 155, 218
Owens, Capt Ernest 82
Owers' Corner 114, 117

Pacific Area 7, 11–12, 21
Palazzo, Albert 3, 183, 205, 223, 231
Palestine 2, 6, 15–16
Pallier's Hill 219
Palm Island 5
Papua 2, 11, 19, 21
Parer, Damien 105, 126
Parit Sulong 52
Pearce, George 8
Perrett, Bryan 48
Perth, HMAS 56
Philippines 56, 66, 95, 100, 116, 138, 186, 226, 233
Pope, Pte Keith 33
Port Moresby 6, 79, 95, 115, 146, 163, 200, 206
    21st Brigade at 97–100, 103–6
    artillery units and 112–14
    base for Kokoda campaign 126–33
Porter, Brig. Selwyn 223, 225
Potts, Brig. Arnold 99–100, 129–30, 140, 174
Prothero 1 and 2 219
Puckapunyal Army Base (Vic.) 15, 68, 201

Queen Mary 23–4

Rabaul 5
Ramu–Markham campaigns 214, 217–18, 224
Regimental Aid Post 110
Report on Operations—21 Aust Inf Bde Owen Stanley Campaign 129
Rhoden, Lt-Col Phil 3
Rickards, Pte Desmond 107
Roach, Lt-Col Leonard 39
Rommel, Gen. Erwin 19
Roosevelt, Franklin 57
Rose, Maj. Angus 26, 61
Rouna 117
Rowell, Lt-Gen. Sydney 44, 81, 121, 126–7, 130, 140, 212
Royal Australian Air Force
  Army cooperation 170
  Direct Air Support 170, 185
  11 RAAF Squadron 79
  22 RAAF Squadron 170
  75 RAAF Squadron 111
  76 RAAF Squadron 111
Russo-Japanese War 8

Sanananda 2, 77, 134, 146–7, 155, 201–3
Santa Cruz Islands, Battle of 145
Sattelberg 202, 212, 215–16
Savige, Maj.-Gen. Stanley 18, 163, 166, 174, 191, 225
School of Mechanical Engineering 196
Segamat 51
Serong, Col Ted 233
Seven Mile Drome 103
17th Brigade Tactical School 62, 71
Shaggy Ridge 170, 219–23
Shoho 79
Shokaku 79
'short' 25-pounder 183, 198–9
Sims, Charles 102
Sims, USS 80
Singapore 8, 26
Singapore Conference 25
Singapore Strategy 7–9, 14
6 Aust Div Training Instruction No. 11 Jungle Warfare 125, 190

Skindewai 164, 167
Small Arms Training manuals 47
Small Wars Manual (USMC) 13
Soldiering in the Tropics 139
Solomon Islands 97, 146
Somerville, Admiral James 60
South East Asia 48, 233–4
South West Pacific Area vi, 1, 3, 13, 46, 186
Spencer, Pte Bill 77, 83, 153
Stepsister convoy 59
Stevenson, Capt 121
Steward, Capt Henry 99
Stewart, Lt-Col Ian 29, 32
Stuart M3 light tank 201, 202
Sturdee, Lt-Gen. Vernon 8, 18
Sublet, Capt Frank 182
Suez Canal 233
Sunda Strait, Battle of 56
Sydney, HMAS 5
Sydney Harbour 5, 23
Syria 2, 6, 16

Tactical Doctrine for Jungle Warfare 163
Tactical Methods 62–3, 80, 187
Tactical Notes for Malaya 28–9, 43
Tarakan 216, 224, 228
Tarlington, Pte George 73
Taylor, Brig. Harold B. 25–6, 33
Tenaru, Battle of 126
Thompson, Capt Robert 103, 117, 204
Thompson sub-machine gun 36, 46, 69, 81, 94, 180
Timor 13, 24, 39–42, 93, 106
Tobruk 17, 19
Tokyo 79
Tommy guns *see* Thompson sub-machine gun
Torricelli Mountains 199
Trincomalee Harbour 60
Trinity Beach 203
Tropical Warfare manuals 189, 191, 210, 213, 223–8

Tulagi and Florida Islands 97
25-pounder 46, 111, 113–15, 170, 172, 179, 198–9, 214, 218; *see also* 'short' 25-pounder

Uberi 117–18
United States Marine Corps 13
US 1st Marine Division 96
US 1st Marine Regiment 126
US 41st Division 193
US 5th Air Force 170
US 532nd Engineer Boat and Shore Regiment 205
Universal Carrier 53, 67, 77, 88, 151–2

Vampire, HMAS 60
Vasey, Maj.-Gen. George 155, 184–5, 187, 189–90, 223–5
Vichy French 115
Vickers medium machine gun 99, 101, 129, 151, 182, 206
Victoria 2, 7
Viet Minh 233
Vietnam War 4

Walker, Allan 109
walkie-talkie (536 handset) 84, 136, 138, 206, 213, 215
Wall, Pte Donald 24
Washington, DC 57
Wau 173–6
Western Australia 91, 115, 120, 162, 193
White, Osmar 104–5, 120–2, 126
Whitehead, Brig. David 213
Wigmore, Lionel 10–11, 27
Wilmot, Chester 121, 126
Wilson, Lt-Col Arthur G. 219, 221
Wilson, Tpr John 153
Wolfenden, Lt-Col Reginald 91, 139, 147, 177–8
Woodpecker medium machine gun 101
Wootten, Maj.-Gen. George 93
Wright, Col John 32

Yorktown, USS 79–80
Youl, Lt-Col Geoffrey 41–2, 45, 93